Developing Solutions with Office 2000 Components and VBA

ISBN 0-13-026305-2

90000

9 780130 263056

PRENTICE HALL PTR MICROSOFT® TECHNOLOGIES SERIES

Peter G. Aitken

Developing Solutions with Office 2000 Components and VBA

PH
PTR

Prentice Hall PTR, Upper Saddle River, NJ 07458
www.phptr.com

Library of Congress Cataloging-in-Publication Data
Aitken, Peter G.
  Developing solutions with Office 2000 components and VBA / Peter G. Aitken.
    p. cm. -- (Prentice Hall PTR Microsoft technologies series)
  ISBN 0-13-026305-2
  I. Title. II. Series
QA76.76.D47 A29 2000
005.369--dc21   00-027557

Editorial/Production Supervision: *Vanessa Moore*
Acquisitions Editor: *Tim Moore*
Marketing Manager: *Bryan Gambrel*
Buyer: *Maura Goldstaub*
Cover Design: *Anthony Gemmellaro*
Cover Design Direction: *Jerry Votta*
Series Design: *Gail Cocker-Bogusz*
Project Coordinator: *Anne Trowbridge*

© 2000 Prentice Hall PTR
Prentice-Hall, Inc.
Upper Saddle River, NJ 07458

ISBN 0-13-026305-2

Prentice-Hall International (UK) Limited, *London*
Prentice-Hall of Australia Pty. Limited, *Sydney*
Prentice-Hall Canada Inc., *Toronto*
Prentice-Hall Hispanoamericana, S.A., *Mexico*
Prentice-Hall of India Private Limited, *New Delhi*
Prentice-Hall of Japan, Inc., *Tokyo*
Pearson Education Asia Pte. Ltd.
Editora Prentice-Hall do Brasil, Ltda., *Rio de Janeiro*

CONTENTS

SEVEN

Using Data Access Components   141

EIGHT

Using PowerPoint Components   169

FIFTEEN
Working with Strings   285

PART FOUR **Other Office Development Tools** *371*

PART FIVE   Putting It All To Work   *439*

TWENTY-SIX

Custom Report Generation   473

APPENDIX

KeyCode Constants and Values   483

INDEX   489

When most people think of Microsoft Office, they think of a powerful set of office applications—Word for word processing, Excel for spreadsheets, Access for databases, and so on. There is, however, much more to Office than that. Hidden behind the application's programs is a powerful set of development tools that can be used to create sophisticated custom solutions to address specific needs. The foundation of these development capabilities is the Office object model, a rich set of programmable objects, sometimes referred to as software components. These components provide the functionality of the individual applications that make up Office, and are also available for customized programming. When combined with the powerful Visual Basic for Applications (VBA) programming language, also part of Office, the result is a powerful and flexible development tool that is often your best choice when faced with a Windows development project.

Is Office a replacement for traditional programming languages such as Visual Basic, C++, and Java? In a word, *no*. From the developer's perspective, Office is specialized for creating custom applications that perform the same general sorts of tasks that the Office applications themselves do—manipulate text, work with numbers, display graphs, send and receive e-mail, and so on. Since it is exactly this type of functionality that is often needed, there are many situations in which Office will be your best choice of development tools. Outside this area, however, Office is not a good choice. For example, an astronomer writing a program to analyze crater patterns on Mars would not turn to Office. There are so many situations in which Office is the best choice that any Windows developer really should have some familiarity with its capabilities. Office may be your only development tool, or it may be one of half a dozen that you use, but it cannot be ignored.

This book is aimed at individuals who are at the beginner and intermediate level and who want to use Office to develop custom solutions. No previous programming experience is required, although if you do have such experience, particularly with Visual Basic, you'll be able to work through some sections of the book more quickly, Part Three in particular. My approach is a combination of reference material and demonstrations. I am a strong believer in learning by doing, and I feel that the best approach to learning how to use a development tool is a mixture of presenting the raw information you need, and showing you how it is used in a real-world situation.

I make no pretense of covering all the details of Office development. There is no way a single book can include all the related information, and even if such a book were possible, no one would want to read it. My goal is to cover to most important fundamentals of Office—those tools and techniques that you will need most often. Once you understand these fundamentals, it is an easy matter to turn to the online reference materials for the details that could not be included in the book.

Peter G. Aitken
Chapel Hill, North Carolina
January 2000

Acknowledgments

While this book has only a single author, it was in many ways a team effort. My thanks go to the following people who were instrumental in bringing the book from idea to reality: Tim Moore, acquisitions editor, Vanessa Moore, production editor, Stephanie English, copy editor, and Miriam O'Neal, technical proofreader.

Introduction to Office Development

Microsoft Office 2000 provides one of the most powerful tools for developing Windows solutions, a fact that some people find surprising. After all, Office is a suite of productivity tools and applications programs, isn't it? That is certainly true, but the programmers at Microsoft have designed Office so that the capabilities of its various applications—word processing, e-mail, numeric calculation, and so on—are available as building blocks that can be used to create custom solutions. And that's exactly what Office development is all about—creating customized applications that are specifically tailored for your clients' needs. The better that you, the developer, know your tools, the better the end product will be and the less work it will take to create it. The four chapters in the first section of this book get you started on your journey.

Chapter 1, "Why Develop with Office and VBA?", provides an introduction to the fundamentals of Office development and the features that Office 2000 makes available to developers, with an emphasis on goodies that are new with this version of Office. You'll also learn about some of the advantages of using Office 2000 as your development tool as compared with more traditional programming tools.

Chapter 2, "The Basics of Office Development," gets a bit further into the details of Office development. You'll see how Office development has two main parts: the software components that are exposed, or made available, by the Office applications, and the Visual Basic for Applications (VBA) programming language that is used to stitch these components together to create a custom solution. You'll create a working, albeit simple, custom Office application to give you a taste of how simple the process can be. You'll also learn the importance of planning, visual interface design, data access, and security.

Chapter 3, "Visual Basic for Applications—the Fundamentals," introduces you to VBA, the powerful programming language that is embedded in Office. A programming language is nothing more than a way for you to tell the computer what you want it to do. VBA is not only a very powerful and flexible language, it is also relatively easy to learn. You'll get started with VBA in this chapter, and also learn to use the Visual Basic editor.

Chapter 4, "Working With Office Objects," delves into the software components that Office provides. These components are called *objects* and each Office application exposes a number of interrelated objects, known collectively as the *object model*. A good understanding of Office's object model is essential for any Office developer, and with more than 600 objects to choose from there is much to learn! This chapter gets you started, with more details to come in later chapters.

Why Develop with Office and VBA

To some people, the idea of using Microsoft Office as a solutions devel-opment tool may sound a bit strange. On the one hand, Office is a set of business productivity applications, each designed to perform a spe-cific task—Word processes text, Excel manipulates numbers, Outlook manages e-mail, and so on. On the other hand, solutions development means the creation of custom programs to fulfill specialized needs. The two seem incompatible—how can you use fixed, defined purpose programs to create custom solutions?

Not too long ago, the answer to this question would have been "You can't." Application programs did their specialized job and that was that. You might at best be able to do some minor customization using the program's built-in macro language, but that was about all. For sophisticated custom solutions you had to turn to a true program-ming language, such as C++ or Visual Basic.

Over the past few years things have changed—changed for the bet-ter, I might add. While Microsoft Office continues to provide a powerful set of dedicated-purpose applications programs, it now also gives you a flexible and robust platform for the development of custom business solutions. And that, in a nutshell, is the subject of this book.

In this chapter we will take a look at some of the advantages of Office development, then we will investigate how Office development works. Finally, we'll examine some of the features that are new with the latest version, Office 2000.

Advantages of Office Development

Any programmer who is faced with a Windows development project has quite a range of development tools available. The first step in the development process, and a very important one, is selecting the tool you will use. Make an inappropriate choice here, and a likely outcome is greater work and expense in developing the project, and a final product that is not as good as it might be. Office is not the best choice in all situations, but by understanding its many advantages you will know when it is the best choice of development tools.

Office Is a Familiar Environment

One of the main advantages of Office is that it is so widely used. Millions of people around the world are already using the Office applications in their day-to-day work. In computer lingo this is known as an *installed base*, and it means that you have millions of potential customers who have already decided they like Office and will therefore be more receptive to custom solutions that have been developed with Office and which therefore do not require the introduction of new technology. Also, since your end users are already familiar with the Office applications, at least to some extent, any custom solutions you create will run in a familiar environment. As a result, the training curve will be more shallow, training time and costs will be minimized, and need for support is also likely to be minimized.

Office Development Decreases Development Time and Expense

In any custom solution, much of the functionality you need is not really new—tasks such as finding files, displaying charts, performing financial calculations, and searching databases are already performed by the Office applications. By using Office as your development platform, all of this functionality is available to you in the form of Office components. The enormous amount of code writing, testing, and debugging that these components represent has already been done for you. Combining these components to create the finished application takes a small fraction of the time that would be required to do it from scratch. Furthermore, VBA code that you write can be saved and reused in other projects, providing additional efficiency. In today's competitive development environment, with ever more demanding clients, these advantages can make a big difference to your success as a developer.

Office Provides an Integrated Solution

All of the components that are available in Office were designed to work together, as they do within the individual Office applications programs. This means that a custom solution created using Office components will also have the resulting advantages of this tight integration. User interfaces will share a familiar look and feel, menu commands will have a similar structure, the familiar common dialog boxes will be used, and so on. Also, error handling—an important part of any Office application—will be consistent. In many cases, a custom Office solution does not appear to the user to be "custom"—it simply appears as a built-in extension of one of the Office applications programs.

Office Development Is Extensible

The components that are exposed by Office are not limited to use within Office, but are available for use with any development tool that supports the Windows COM (Component Object Model) specification. This includes such heavyweight stand-alone development tools as Visual Basic and Visual C++. What this means to you, the developer, is that in the unlikely event that your project's needs cannot be met within the Office development environment, you can go to a more flexible tool, such as Visual C++, to program the functionality you need while still retaining the advantages of using the Office components. This extensibility means that you need not avoid adopting Office as a development tool because of fears that someday it won't quite do what you need.

Not Always Your Best Choice

Despite Office's many advantages as a development tool, it is not always the tool of choice. If your client does not use the Windows platform, then obviously you cannot use Office. Even if your client does run Windows, he or she may have standardized on a different suite of applications programs, and trying to introduce Office is likely to be an unwelcome or at least tiresome approach. Also, remember that Office is designed for the sorts of tasks that are found in a typical business office environment. If your project's needs fall outside of this area—image processing, for example—then Office is not a good choice.

Software Components

Software developers are like anyone else in that they do not like to do unnecessary work. One way to avoid unnecessary work is to try not to do anything twice. For a programmer, this means that once you create the code or visual interface to perform a specific task, you should not have to program that same task again because you should be able to use the original code or visual interface over and over. With this idea the concept of *software components* was born.

In their earliest form, software components consisted simply of sections of source code that were packaged in a way to make them easily reusable. If, for example, you wrote some code that calculates loan payments, you could put that code in a function library where it would be available to use in any other programs that need to calculate loan payments. This approach was called *structured programming* and for many years it was the most important paradigm used by software developers.

With the introduction of graphical user interfaces such as Windows, the old structured programming paradigm was found wanting. Now it was not enough to simply reuse code, developers also wanted to reuse the visual elements that are such an important part of most Windows applications. Once you had put in the effort to create a visual screen element, such as a box for the display and editing of text, you would of course want to be able to reuse that element in other programs. The first successful attempt at reusable visual elements was Microsoft's Visual Basic, which provided its own set of ready-to-use visual elements, called *controls*, as well as permitting programmers to create their own reusable visual elements. Visual Basic was a true revolution in programming, and the use of prepackaged visual components is a central part of all Windows development.

With the increased complexity of programming for a graphic user interface, however, a new paradigm was needed to extend the old structured programming approach. It is called *object-oriented programming* and it is at the heart of Office development.

Objects and Components

As programs became larger and more complex, the problem of program bugs and errors became increasingly difficult to deal with. Many of these problems are the result of unintended and unexpected interactions between different parts of a program, so by decreasing or eliminating these interactions you would go a long way toward preventing errors and bugs. This was accomplished by encapsulating a program's various functions into a number of independent modules, then combining the modules to create the final program. As you may have guessed, these modules are the objects in object-oriented programming.

One of the basic ideas behind objects is that what goes on inside the object is completely hidden from the rest of the program. This means that unintended interactions, with the resulting errors and bugs, are much less likely to happen. Of course an object must interact with the rest of the program in some way or it would not be of any use, but with object-oriented programming the ways an object can interact are closely defined and controlled. The means by which the program can interact with an object is called the object's *interface* (not to be confused with visual interface, something different altogether).

We saw earlier how programmers want to package functionality into self-contained, reusable components in order to increase efficiency in the development process. Now we see that programmers also want to divide program functionality into independent objects in order to improve program reliability and to reduce errors and bugs. It turns out that these two goals are mutually supportive, and the object-oriented programming paradigm fulfills both the need for reusable software components and the need for programs constructed of independent modules.

Objects in Office

Given the powerful advantages of the object-oriented paradigm, it is not surprising that Microsoft would use this approach in creating the Office programs. When you are working in Word, Excel, or one of the other Office applications, just about everything you see or do involves objects. On the screen, each toolbar is an object, and each button on the toolbar is also an object. The document you are working on is an object, and each paragraph in that document is an object. The list goes on and on—there are literally hundreds of objects involved in Office—but you get the idea. One important thing to note from this description is that objects can contain other objects, as in a `Document` object containing one or more `Paragraph` objects. This sort of hierarchical arrangement is an important part of the Office object model.

Another important aspect of objects in Office is that as a developer you can create your own. That's right, you are not limited to the objects that are already part of Office but you can design custom objects to meet your development needs, with all the accompanying benefits of reusability and modularity. You may not need to create custom objects all that often, given the wide array of objects provided by Office, but it is a very powerful technique when you do need it.

Now that you understand the fundamentals of objects, we need to look at the three elements that make up an object's interface: properties, methods, and events.

Classes and Instances

You'll sometimes hear the terms *class* and *instance* used in relation to object-oriented programming—what exactly do they mean? A class can be thought of as the blueprint, or plan, for an object, while an instance is a single example of the object created from the class. As an analogy, suppose you have drawn up plans to build a table—those plans are the class. If you build a table from those plans, the table (or object) is an instance of the class. If you then build a second table, that is another instance of the class. There is only one plan (class) but you can create as many objects (tables) as you like.

Office works the same way. There is, for example, a single `Document` class. For each actual document being used, an instance of the class is created—this is a `Document` object. Likewise, there is a `Toolbar` class, with one instance created for each toolbar that is needed. Sometimes the term *object* is used when *class* would be technically correct, but as long as you understand the difference between the plan for an object (the class) and the object itself (an instance) you will not get confused.

Properties

Properties are the way in which objects store information. Sometimes a property represents user data, while other times it determines some characteristic of the object. For example, each cell in an Excel worksheet is represented by a `Range` object. The `Range` object's `Value` property specifies the text or number that is displayed in the cell, while the `FormatNumber` property controls the way the cell displays its data. Some properties are read/write, meaning that you can both determine and change the property. Other properties are read-only, in which case you can determine it but not change it. Some object properties refer to other objects, which is how Office's object hierarchy is constructed.

Methods

A method performs an action on an object. For example, the `Shape` object (which displays a geometric shape on-screen) has a `Flip` method that lets you flip the object either vertically or horizontally. Likewise, the `Document` object, representing a Word document, has the `PrintOut` method that prints the document. If properties are an object's nouns, then methods are its verbs.

Events

Many objects respond to events. Most events correspond to actions performed by the user, such as pressing a key, clicking with the mouse, opening a file, or changing data. Events can also be triggered by VBA code or by the computer operating system. You can write code that responds to events as needed, making your custom application responsive to the user's input. For example, a `Form` object has an `Open` event that is triggered when the form is first displayed on the screen. You can write code to be executed whenever the `Open` event occurs to ensure that the form always displays centered on the screen regardless of the user's specific screen size.

The Office 2000 Suite

Before starting to develop custom solutions with office, it is a good idea to have some familiarity with the Office applications programs. There are two good reasons for this.

First, working with the Office applications can give you a good idea of what capabilities are available to you, the developer, in the various components that Office makes available. For example, knowing that Excel can calculate the average of a column of numbers, you can assume that this same capability is exposed in an Excel component and will be available to you for use in your custom projects. The same is true for Outlook being able to send an e-mail message, Word being able to underline text, and PowerPoint being able to display a bar chart. These may be trivial examples, but they make the point that you must thoroughly know your tools' capabilities before you can apply them effectively.

Second, a familiarity with the Office applications' built-in capabilities may save you some time and effort. The Office suite is very powerful, and the individual applications have some surprisingly sophisticated facilities. Some tasks may not require a custom project but rather can be accomplished by an application's native functionality. It is somewhat frustrating (not to mention embarrassing) to work at creating a custom solution only to learn that the same thing can be accomplished with a couple of menu commands!

Office 2000 Developer Edition

Office 2000 is sold in several editions, and you can use any edition for development purposes with the limitation that you'll have available only the components exposed by the installed applications. If your edition lacks Access, for example, you will not have its components available.

For serious Office development, however, I recommend Office 2000 Developer. This includes all the applications in Office 2000 Premium (the most complete edition) as well as some special tools for developers. This includes extra add-ins for the VBA editor, Visual Source Safe for source code management, and the Data Environment Designer. You also get the Microsoft Developer Network library, which contains complete reference information for Office development.

Here we'll take a quick look at the Office applications and the components they expose. Much of the remainder of the book will be devoted to exploring these components in detail.

Word

Word is designed for creating documents that will be printed or displayed as a Web page. As such it is organized around the concept of a *document*, which can be anything from a two-line memo to a 500-page multichapter report. Word's basic capabilities include entering and editing text, formatting the appearance of text and its arrangement on the page, and arranging text in columns and tables. Specialized elements, such as headers and footers, page numbers, indexes, and tables of contents are also supported. Word also provides a dictionary for checking spelling, a thesaurus for finding alternate word forms, and a grammar checker. If your custom application needs to work with text, you should look at the Word object framework first. The Word object model is covered in Chapter 5.

Excel

Excel is a spreadsheet program, intended for numerical manipulation and display. It is designed around the *worksheet*, which can be thought of as a sheet of digital paper ruled into rows and columns. At the intersection of each row and column is a *cell* where you can place text, a number, or a formula referring to other cells and/or perform calculations. Worksheets are organized into multipage workbooks. Excel includes a large number of predefined formulas that let you perform a variety of calculations, including many commonly needed statistical, financial, and scientific calculations. You can also write your own formulas as required. Excel also provides sophisticated charting capabilities that permit you to create a variety of chart types that automatically update when the worksheet data changes. For numerical analysis in your custom application, Excel is the place to look. The Excel object model is covered in Chapter 6.

Access

Access is a database management program. Of course, all the Office programs manage data in one form or another, but in the world of computers the term *database* refers specifically to data organized in a record and field format. An address book is a common example of a database, with each person representing a record and each piece of information (first name, last name, address, etc.) representing a field. Access provides tools for creating databases, adding and editing data, searching for specific information, and creating reports based on database data. Look to the Access object model for your custom application's database manipulation needs. Note, however, that many database capabilities are also provided by the shared data access tools (see "Data Access" on page 12) which are not specifically part of Access but rather are a shared component of Office or Windows. You'll learn about the Access object model in Chapter 7.

PowerPoint

PowerPoint is a presentation program. Its primary purpose is to create "slide shows" for presentation at meetings, on the Web, and so on. Each page or "slide" in a presentation can combine text, charts, and graphical elements, including movies. Sounds can be associated with slides as well. The emphasis in PowerPoint is the creation of presentations that show data in a clear, easy to understand, and pleasant manner. As such, it has excellent tools for text formatting, drawing, page layout, and color control. Look in PowerPoint's object model when your custom application requires these capabilities. I'll cover the PowerPoint object model in Chapter 8.

Outlook

Rather than having a single focus like the other Office applications, Outlook is more of a personal assistant that takes care of a variety of tasks: e-mail, address book, calendar, to-do list, and the like. Its object model reflects this diversity, and you'll be turning to Outlook when your application requires sending or receiving e-mail, calendar functions, and so on. The Outlook object model is covered in Chapter 10.

FrontPage

FrontPage is specialized for creating and publishing Web content—in other words, pages that will be viewed on the World Wide Web. While other Office applications are Web-enabled, their capabilities are rather basic when compared to a specialized tool such as FrontPage. You will use FrontPage objects when your custom application needs to work with Web sites, which can be located either locally on an intranet or remotely on the Web. I'll deal with FrontPage objects in Chapter 9.

Shared Components

Office includes a significant number of components that do not belong to any specific application but are shared by two or more of them. Called shared components, these objects are also available to the developer of custom solutions. They provide, among other things, the ability to search for files, to manipulate Command Bars, to provide animated end-user help, to work with document properties, and to program scripts. Shared components are covered in Chapter 11.

Data Access

Strictly speaking, the data access components are shared because they do not belong to a specific single Office application. They are usually discussed separately from the other shared components, however, because of the great importance that data access has in most custom Office solutions. For the most part, data access in Office uses a strategy called Universal Data Access. There are two parts to this: OLE DB, which provides the low-level data access components, and ActiveX Data Objects, or ADO, which provides a high-level COM-compliant programming interface. These components are covered in Chapter 7.

Web Technologies

Including Internet Explorer version 5, Microsoft's latest Web browser, Office provides the developer with a number of Web-related components. These include:

- Web components, a set of ActiveX controls that let you publish fully interactive documents (spreadsheets, reports, databases, etc.) on the World Wide Web.
- Office Server Extensions can be used to create online threaded discussions.
- Script editor for programmatically working with the scripts and objects that make up an HTML page.
- Data access pages permit users to work interactively with a database on a Web page.

Web-related components are scattered throughout the Office model and are covered as needed throughout the book, in addition to having an entire chapter, Chapter 23, devoted to them.

What's New in Office 2000

Microsoft Office has always offered some degree of programmability, and the number of features available to developers has increased with each subsequent release. The latest incarnation, Office 2000, offers significant enhancements over earlier versions in areas that will be of interest to developers. If you have worked with Office 97, the previous version of Office, this section should be of interest to you. Space limitations preclude covering all of these new features in detail.

Web Integration

In recognition of the increasing importance of the Internet and the World Wide Web, Office now fully integrates its applications programs with the Web. You can publish information to the Web as easily as saving it to disk, which means that you can concentrate on the content of your documents without worrying about their format. HTML, the language of the Web, is now fully supported as an Office file format. These new Web-related technologies are available to Office developers as well as to users of the applications programs.

Virus Protection

Most everyone has heard of the new breed of computer viruses that are spread inside Office documents, commonly known as macro viruses. The recent Melissa virus was only one example. Given the widespread use of Office, and the fact that an Office document can contain executable VBA code, it seems an obvious target for virus creators. In previous versions, macro virus protection was limited to identifying Office documents that contained VBA code and giving the user the option of enabling the code or preventing it from executing. Now, Office documents can be scanned by third-party virus protection software to identify actual viruses. In addition, Microsoft's Authenticode technology permits the digital signing of software components. A user can then identify the source of a component, and open documents only if the contained components have been signed by trusted sources.

Add-In Architecture

An *add-in* is a supplemental program that adds additional capabilities to an Office application. For example, Excel comes with several add-ins that add sophisticated statistical analysis functions to your worksheets. From the user's perspective, the advantage of add-ins is that you can load only the functionality you need, and you can obtain highly specialized capabilities from third-party vendors in addition to those provided as part of Office. For the developer, the add-in architecture is one way to provide a custom solution, one that is tightly integrated with the host application.

Previous versions of Office supported add-ins, but only *application-specific* add-ins that could run in only a particular Office application, such as Word or Excel. The new add-in architecture also supports add-ins based on the Component Object Model, or COM, specification. This specification permits a single add-in to run in any Office application, which provides you with significant flexibility.

More Comprehensive Event Model

Events are a central part of Office development, and the new event model adds more than 20 new events, mostly associated with the Document and Windows objects in Word and PowerPoint. There are also several new events related to Command Bar objects that can be used in all Office applications. And, while previous versions of VBA let you create your own object, you can now define custom events and interfaces associated with those objects.

More Objects

I'll mention only two of the new objects in Office 2000. The `Dictionary` object opens up many possibilities. It is similar to a `Collection` object except that it can hold objects of different data types. File access and management is made easier with the `FileSystemObject`, which provides object-oriented access to the drives, folders, and files on your system.

New VBA Language Elements

VBA includes several new functions that provide additional power for parsing and manipulating strings and for formatting data. For example, the functions `FormatCurrency`, `FormatNumber`, `FormatDateTime`, and `FormatPercent` do just what their names imply. The `Split` function parses a string into substrings based on rules you provide, and the `Filter` and `Join` functions provide other welcome string handling abilities. The new VBA also permits functions to return arrays, and the direct assignment of one array to another.

Improved Data Access

Access to data is an important part of most custom Office solutions. Office supports Universal Data Access (which was described briefly earlier in the chapter) to permit an Office application to access data in essentially any format or location. You are no longer limited to accessing data that is located in recognized relational database file formats. OLE DB, the low-level part of Universal Data Access, is an open specification designed to access data in essentially any format, whether it be a legacy mainframe database, a list of e-mail messages, a graphical format, or what have you. The other part of Universal Data Access is ActiveX Data Objects (ADO), which provide a high-level programmable interface to OLE DB. If you are accustomed to using the older data access technologies, such as Open Database Connectivity (ODBC), Data Access Objects (DAO), or Remote Data Objects (RDO), I think you will be delighted at the power and ease of use of the new tools.

Custom Help Files

A complete Office application includes online help information for the end users. Windows Help has changed recently, and now uses an HTML-based system in place of the older Windows help file format. You can see this in the help files that are provided with the Office applications, but more to the point you can now create your own help files to distribute as part of your custom solution. Custom Help files are covered in Chapter 21.

Summing Up

After reading this chapter I think you'll agree that Office is indeed a powerful tool for developing custom Windows solutions. It is not the best choice in every situation, but I have found that it is a surprisingly versatile development tool that is applicable to a wide range of needs. What's even better, it is relatively easy to learn and to use.

The remaining three chapters in this section cover the fundamentals of Office development. We'll start with an essential topic: how to plan your Office project and how to approach visual interface design. Then we'll get right to work, creating a useful Office application which, while simple, is a great way to get your feet wet. You'll learn how to work with objects and their properties, methods, and events. You'll also get started with VBA and learn how to use the VBA editor, which is an essential part of Office development.

The Basics of Office Development

When learning about Office development, I think it is useful to start off with an overview of the entire process. Then when you start to learn the details—and there are plenty of details—you'll be able to see where the individual parts fit into the big picture. That's the purpose of this chapter. You'll start by looking at the technologies that Office uses to provide for custom development. Then, you will get a feel for the steps that are involved in bringing a custom Office application from concept to completion. Finally, you'll get a feel for the nuts and bolts of Office development by creating and testing a custom application.

Objects and Automation

The "bricks" that you use to construct your Office applications are the various components, or objects, that are exposed by the Office applications. Collectively, these are referred to as the *Office object model*. In order to efficiently develop effective solutions you need to understand this model both in its details and in the overall picture. The details consist of the multitude of properties, methods, and events that comprise each object's interface, and to be honest with you, I don't think there's anyone who knows *all* of the details! With more than 600 objects exposed, and each object having multiple properties, methods, and events, it is clearly an enormous mass of information. Just to give you some idea, Microsoft's official reference to Office 2000 development consists of six volumes running to many thousands of pages!

Please don't think I am trying to discourage you. Learning all the details may be an impossible task, but fortunately it is not necessary. You can always look up the details you don't know, using the excellent online reference material provided by Microsoft. Before you can look up the details, however, you need to have some idea of what you are looking for. You need to know the broad outline of the Office object model, the capabilities of the individual applications, and how all the parts fit together to create an integrated whole.

The Component Object Model

At the heart of the Office applications and Office programmability is the Component Object Model, or COM. To be more specific, it is a COM technology known as *Automation* (called *OLE Automation* in the past) that is at work here. It is Automation that permits Visual Basic for Applications (VBA) code to create and control instances of Office components. Automation permits you to program an individual Office application—for example, a VBA procedure that performs calculations and displays charts in an Excel workbook. Automation is also what makes it possible for two or more Office applications to interact and exchange data. You can, for example, extract data from an Access database, send it to Excel for numerical processing, then use Outlook to send the results to a colleague.

Whenever you create an Office project, no matter how simple or complex, you are using Automation. In a way, therefore, understanding Automation is the key to understanding Office development. But since Automation is so intimately linked to the components exposed by Office applications (its object model), we come full circle and see that the foundation for building your skills as an Office developer is the Office object model. From a developer's perspective, Automation is simply a fancy term for the way that Office components can interact with each other and be controlled by VBA.

How Automation Works

The COM components that Automation works with exist as files on your hard disk that contain compiled code that defines classes. Remember from the previous chapter that a class is a plan, or blueprint, for an object. There are two ways a component can be used:

- An *Automation client* makes use of objects exposed by other components.
- An *Automation server* makes its objects available (exposes) for use by other components.

A COM component that supports Automation can serve either one or both of these roles. Not all COM components support Automation, but it's only those that do that are of interest to the Office developer.

What does "supporting Automation" really mean? In the previous chapter I introduced the idea of an object's interface, the sum of all its properties, methods, and events by which other objects and VBA can control and interact with the object. All objects have properties, methods, and/or events, but only if they are exposed—made available to VBA and other components—does the object support Automation. There are two ways an object can expose its interface (some objects make both methods available).

The first is called the IDispatch interface. A potential Automation client can use IDispatch to query an object about the details of its interface. This occurs at runtime, which means that the information about an object's custom interface is not available at design time. This information may of course be available in documentation, but it is not available programmatically to the Object Browser or the VBA development editor. This method of exposing an interface permits *late binding*.

The second way an object can expose its interface is by means of a *virtual function table*, or vtable, which provides access at design time to information about the object's interface. Objects that use vtable also provide a *type library* (sometimes called an *object library*) with additional information about the object's interface. This method of exposing an interface permits *early binding*.

Early binding is by far the preferred method, as it makes a developer's task a lot easier, and fortunately it is supported by all the Office components. While you are working in the VBA editor, you can add a reference to the type library that corresponds to the objects you want to use in your project. This permits the compiler to perform certain types of error checking, catching errors such as passing the wrong type or number of arguments to an object's methods, rather than letting these errors slip through only to be caught when the project is executing.

Another advantage of early binding is that you can use the Object Browser to view information about an object's interface while you are working on the project. Finally, early binding is required to use some of the VBA editor's convenience features, such as automatic listing of properties and methods in the editing window. You'll learn more about these things in Chapter 3 when I cover the use of the VBA editor.

The Office Object Model

If you are familiar with any of the Office applications, then you already have a head start in understanding the Office object model. This is because object models in general, and the Office object model in particular, are designed so that the various objects correspond as much as possible to the actual things, or elements, that you work with in the application.

Let's take Word for an example, because word processing is probably the task that most readers have some familiarity with. The most obvious "thing" that you work with in Word is a document, or file. Whether it's a long report with lots of fancy formatting, or a half-page memo, all documents have a lot of things in common: each one exists in a separate disk file, has a beginning and end, can be printed, and so on. It's not surprising, therefore, to find out that that the `Document` object is near the top of the Word object model.

Within a document, what do you work with? Paragraphs are important, as are styles (which control the formatting of paragraphs). In the object model, these are represented by the `Paragraph` and `Style` objects. If we keep drilling down we finally arrive at perhaps the most basic piece of data that Word works with, a single character. And yes indeed, there is a `Character` object in the object model too!

Other Office applications use a similar design for their object models. Excel, for example, has a `Workbook` object that is analogous to Word's `Document` object—it corresponds to a single open file. Likewise, PowerPoint has the `Presentation` object.

For each Office application, the top-level object is called `Application`, which represents a running instance of the program. All other elements in the object model are subsidiary to the `Application` object. The entire Office object model is built in this way, with a hierarchy of objects starting at the top with the `Application` object and working down through several layers to the simplest, most basic objects. Except for the top-level `Application` object, all objects in the hierarchy are dependent on the existence of higher-level objects. You cannot, for example, have a Word `Document` object without first having a Word `Application` object. Likewise, you cannot have a `Paragraph` object without having a `Document` object. The terms *parent* and *child* are used to describe this relationship; the `Application` object is the parent of the `Document` object, and the `Document` object is the child of the `Application` object. Child objects can have their own children, such as the `Paragraph` object being the child of the `Document` object. Many objects, therefore, are both child and parent.

You will frequently find that multiple copies of some objects are required. Word can work with multiple files at once, which will require one `Document` object for each open file. Also, a single document can contain multiple paragraphs. Office deals with multiple objects by means of a special object called a *collection*.

Collections

A `Collection` is a special kind of object whose function is to keep track of multiple copies of other objects. A given `Collection` object will keep track of a single type, or class, of object. Standard syntax is to name a `Collection` object as the plural of the object type it contains. Thus, the `Collection` object that keeps track of multiple `Document` objects is named `Documents`.

`Collection` objects are, therefore, an important part of the Office object model. You will often see the object model represented graphically, and it is usually the case that collections are represented by rectangles while other objects are represented by ovals. You can see this in Figure 2–1, which shows a graphical representation of a small part of the Word object model. You can see from this figure that:

- The `Application` object contains a `Documents` collection.
- Each `Document` object in the `Documents` collection contains a `Paragraphs` collection.
- Each `Paragraph` object in the `Paragraphs` collection contains a `Style` object.

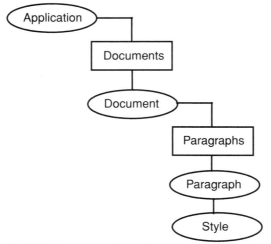

Figure 2–1   *The Office object model includes collections (rectangles) as well as other objects (ovals).*

Collections are a very powerful tool in Office development. They permit you to access all the objects in the collection, to work with a specific single object, and to add and remove objects. For example, the following code looks through the `Documents` collection to see if the document named "SalesReport.doc" is already open. If so, the document is activated for editing; if not, it is opened.

```
DocumentFound = False
For Each doc In Documents
    If doc.Name = "SalesReport.doc" Then DocumentFound = True
Next doc

If DocumentFound Then
    Documents("SalesReport.doc").Activate
Else
    Documents.Open Filename := _
        "c:\mydocuments\SalesReport.doc"
End If
```

You may not understand the details of this code, but that's OK for now. You'll learn more about collections in Chapter 4.

Designing Your Custom Application

When creating a custom Office solution, a lot of the work happens before you write a single line of code. Identifying *what* your application needs to do, and *how* it should be done, are crucial steps in any Office project. An extremely talented engineer might build the world's best refrigerator, but if the customer needed a microwave oven then the project is a failure.

It should go without saying that the customer's wants and needs are the developer's top priority, but all too often this essential part of the design process is given short shrift. You may *think* you know what the customer is asking for, but do you really? It has happened to me, and more than once, that I incorrectly interpreted a customer's description of what he wanted.

A Simple Office Application

You can learn only so much by listening or reading, then you have to try it for yourself. While you are just starting to learn the details of Office development, it will still be valuable for you to create a small, simple project if for no other reason than to give you an idea of what's involved and how simple it can be.

Since the purpose of this application is to send a Word document to a list of e-mail recipients, Word will be the "parent" application. To start the project, open Word and press Alt+F11 to open the VBA editor. In the top left corner, the editor's Project Explorer window lists the current VBA projects and their components. There is always a project called Normal, one project for each open document, and possible additional projects depending on your Office setup. For now, click the + sign next to the Normal project to expand its sublistings, then click the + next to the Modules entry to display the project's modules. Your Project Explorer window will look like Figure 2–2.

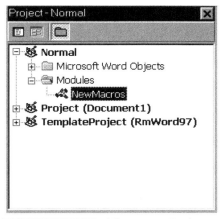

Figure 2–2	*The Project Explorer window displays current projects and their contents.*

You should have a single module named NewMacros, as shown in the figure. Click the module name, then click the View Code button just under the Project Explorer window's title bar. The editor's code editing window will display the code that is currently in the module—which, unless someone has added some macros to this project, should be none.

The next step is to add a VBA procedure to the module. This procedure will contain the code (yet to be written) that performs the desired actions. Here are the steps to add a VBA procedure:

1. Select Insert, Procedure to display the Add procedure dialog box (see Figure 2–3).
2. Type the procedure name in the Name box. You should use a name that describes the procedure's purpose; in this case, use `SendDocTo-EmailList`.

3. Be sure that the dialog box's Sub and Public options are selected, and that the All Local Variables as Statics option is not selected.
4. Click OK.

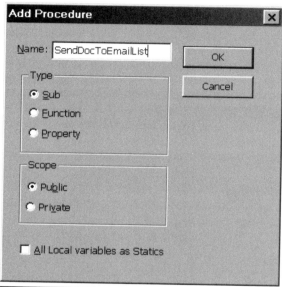

| Figure 2–3 | *Using the Add Procedure dialog box to create a new VBA procedure.* |

The VBA editor inserts the first and last lines of the procedure into the code editing window; it looks like this:

```
Public Sub SendDocToEmailList()

End Sub
```

Once these two lines of code are in place, it's time to write the code that performs the actual task of sending the document to all of your contacts. Let's walk through the code a section at a time. You can enter this code into your project, in the order shown. Do not worry if you don't understand the details of this code—indeed I would be surprised if you did! My goal at this point is to illustrate the creation of a simple Office project. We will spend plenty of time on the details later.

The first step required is to declare, or create, a number of variables that the procedure will use to hold information while it is running. The following code, which should be entered immediately after the `Public Sub` line above, performs this task:

```
Dim OlApp
Dim myNameSpace
Dim myContactList
Dim myContactsEntries
Dim MessageSubject
Dim NewMessage
Dim i As Integer
```

Since we will be using Outlook to send the messages, we next need to create an instance of the Outlook application:

```
Set OlApp = CreateObject("Outlook.Application")
```

Once the instance of the Outlook application is created, we use it to obtain a reference to your address book. This code assumes that your Outlook address book is called "Contacts" and you will have to modify the code if you have used a different name:

```
Set myNameSpace = OlApp.GetNameSpace("MAPI")
Set myContactsList = myNameSpace.AddressLists("Contacts")
Set myContactsEntries = myContactsList.AddressEntries
```

The following line displays a small dialog box prompting the user to enter a subject for the message and offering the option of canceling by entering a blank:

```
MessageSubject = InputBox("Message subject (blank to cancel)?")
```

The next line of code terminates execution without sending anything if the user does in fact enter a blank subject:

```
If MessageSubject = "" Then Exit Sub
```

We want to send one message to each entry in your contacts list. The most efficient way to do this is set up a *loop* that executes one time for each address:

```
For i = 1 To myContactsEntries.Count
```

Within the loop, we start by creating a new e-mail message:

```
Set NewMessage = OlApp.CreateItem(olMailItem)
```

Then we set the new message's subject to the text entered by the user, its body to the contents of the current Word document, and its "To" address to the current address in the contacts list:

```
NewMessage.Subject = MessageSubject
NewMessage.Body = ActiveDocument.Content.Text
NewMessage.To = myContactsEntries(i).Address
```

Now that the message is ready, we use the Send method to send it (which places the message in Outlook's outbox, to be sent according to the mail options you have set in Outlook):

```
NewMessage.Send
```

As the last step in the loop, we should destroy the message in preparation for looping back and creating the next one. Note that this does not affect the copy of the message that has been placed in the outbox, but destroys only the copy being used by the procedure:

```
Set NewMessage = Nothing
```

The following line marks the end of the loop:

```
Next i
```

Once the loop has completed executing, we display a message to the user indicating that the messages have been sent:

```
MsgBox "Your messages have been sent."
```

Finally, we perform "clean up" by destroying the various objects that were created by the code in the procedure:

```
Set OlApp = Nothing
Set myNameSpace = Nothing
Set myContactsList = Nothing
Set myContactsEntries = Nothing
```

The entire procedure is shown in Listing 2–1. Once you have completed entering the code, you should save it by selecting File, Save Normal or by clicking the Save button on the toolbar.

Listing 2–1 *Complete code for the SendDocToEmailList procedure.*

```
Public Sub SendDocToEmailList()

Dim OlApp
Dim myNameSpace
Dim myContactList
Dim myContactsEntries
Dim MessageSubject
Dim NewMessage
Dim i As Integer

Set OlApp = CreateObject("Outlook.Application")
Set myNameSpace = OlApp.GetNameSpace("MAPI")
Set myContactsList = myNameSpace.AddressLists("Contacts")
Set myContactsEntries = myContactsList.AddressEntries

MessageSubject = InputBox("Message subject (blank to cancel)?")
If MessageSubject = "" Then Exit Sub

For i = 1 To myContactsEntries.Count
    Set NewMessage = OlApp.CreateItem(olMailItem)
    NewMessage.Subject = MessageSubject
    NewMessage.Body = ActiveDocument.Content.Text
    NewMessage.To = myContactsEntries(i).Address
    NewMessage.Send
    Set NewMessage = Nothing
Next i

MsgBox "Your messages have been sent."

Set OlApp = Nothing
Set myNameSpace = Nothing
Set myContactsList = Nothing
Set myContactsEntries = Nothing

End Sub
```

Now, of course, you will want to try it out. You can run this procedure in two ways. One way is to keep the VBA editor open and press F5. The other is to close the VBA editor and return to Word by pressing Alt+Q. Then in Word press Alt+F8 to display the Macros dialog box (Figure 2–4). The procedure you just created will be listed there, along with any other defined macros. Simply click the macro name to highlight it, then click the Run button. Be careful, however—this macro really will send a message to everyone in your address book!

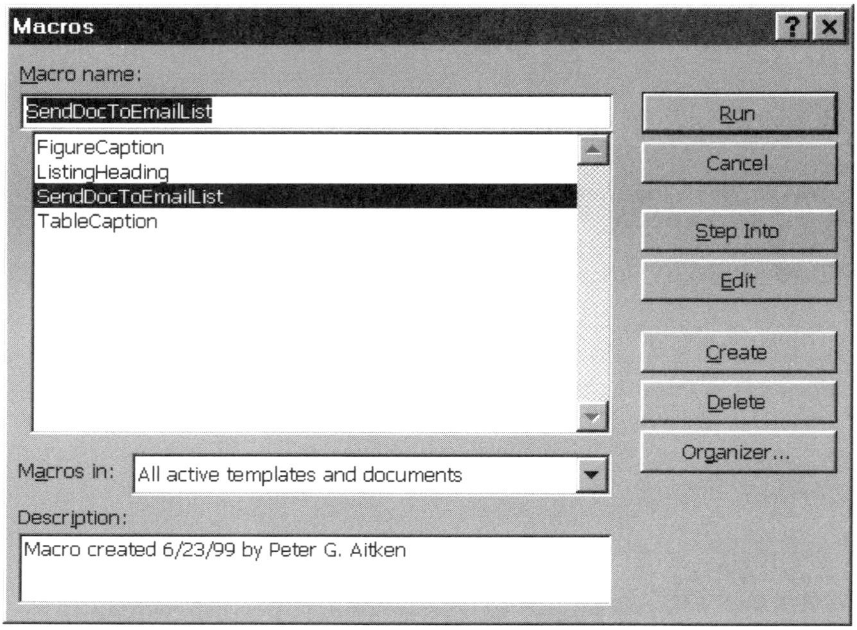

Figure 2–4 *Selecting a macro to run in Word's Macros dialog box.*

Summing Up

The Office development tools are powerful and unavoidably complex, but it is a lot easier to understand them once you know the overall picture. Office provides, in its object model, a wide range of objects, or classes, that are designed to perform specific tasks. Automation lets you use VBA code to string these objects together to perform the specific task or tasks that your custom application requires. You can think of the Office objects as the tools, and VBA code as the instructions. Ninety-five percent of creating an Office application consists of selecting the proper tools and creating the required instructions. You'll learn how in subsequent chapters.

Visual Basic for Applications — the Fundamentals

When you develop custom Office applications, most of your work will be done using the VBA editor, which is an integral part of Office. Before you can get started learning the details of the VBA language, you need to know your way around the editor. Despite its name, the VBA editor is much more than a simple text editor, and provides many features and tools to make your job as a developer all the easier. In this chapter I'll show you how to use the editor and most of its tools. Some of its features, such as debugging tools, will be covered in later chapters.

In this chapter—and indeed throughout the rest of the book—I will assume that you know the fundamentals of working with Windows programs. I am not going to explain basics, such as moving and resizing screen windows, selecting menu commands, working in dialog boxes, or using the mouse.

Parts of the VBA Editor

The VBA editor is shown in Figure 3–1. Since the VBA editor can be customized, it will not always look just like this, but this is the general appearance it will have when you first start using it. At the top, of course, are the menu bar and the toolbar from which you select the various editor commands. Of interest to us are the four windows displayed below the toolbar. They are:

- **Editing window.** Displays VBA code for editing and User Forms for design.
- **Project Explorer window.** Displays the loaded VBA projects and the components of each project.
- **Properties window.** Used to view and edit the properties of the current object.
- **Immediate window.** Displays the output of debugging statements in your code.

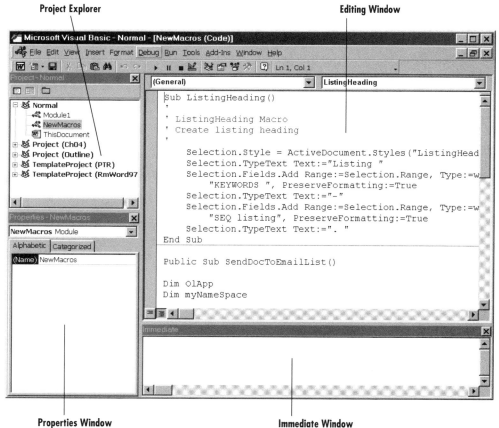

Figure 3–1   *The main components of the VBA editor.*

You can control the relative sizes of the various VBA windows by pointing at the border between them and dragging. You can close windows you are not using by clicking the X in the title bar. To redisplay the Project Explorer, Properties window, or Immediate window, select the corresponding command from the View menu.

The Immediate window is mostly used as an aid when developing a program. You can include the `Debug.print` statement in your code to display information in this window. For example, the line

```
Debug.print x, y
```

displays the value of the variables x and y in the Immediate window. This can be a very useful tool during program development. When your program is compiled and distributed, the `Debug.print` statement has no effect.

Editing Window

The editing window can actually display two or more "subwindows" or panes at the same time, each with a different element for editing. You can also expand a single subwindow to fill the entire editing window. Use the commands of the VBA editor's Window menu to control the display of subwindows.

There are two types of editing done in the editing window. One is the design of UserForms, which are custom windows displayed by an Office application. I will cover UserForms in detail in Chapter 19, and will not deal with them in depth at this time.

The second type of editing is source code editing, entering and modifying the VBA code that makes up the various parts of your project. Editing text in the VBA editor is very much like editing in any word processor, but of course there is no formatting involved, just plain text. Basic editing tasks, such as moving the insertion point, deleting text, selecting text, and so on are the same as in Word. One major difference, aside from the lack of formatting, is that you must press Enter to start a new line—there is no automatic word wrap.

There are several special aspects to editing VBA source code. One is the use of *comments*, which do not have any effect on how the program runs but are used by the programmer to document the source code. In VBA, you mark the start of a comment with an apostrophe ('). Any text between the apostrophe and the end of the line is a comment. A comment can be alone on a line, like this:

```
' This is a comment.
```

It can also be at the end of a line following a VBA statement, like this:

```
x = 100 ' This is a comment too.
```

The only time an apostrophe does not signal the start of a comment is when it is part of a literal string (text within quotation marks).

VBA source code is written one statement per line. Sometimes a single line of code can get quite long, and is inconvenient to work within the editor. In this situation you can use the line continuation character to break a VBA statement over two or more lines. To continue a line, type a space followed by an underscore at the end of the line, then continue on the next line. The following code, therefore, is treated exactly as if it were all typed on a single line:

```
Selection.Fields.Add Range:=Selection.Range, _
    Type:=wdFieldEmpty, Text:= _
    "KEYWORDS ", PreserveFormatting:=True
```

You'll note that I have indented the second and third lines, which is not necessary but helps to make it clear that they are continuations of the first line and not separate lines of code. You cannot use a line continuation character within a literal string (text in quotation marks).

Multi-Statement Lines in VBA

I stated that VBA source code is written one statement per line, but strictly speaking this is not always true. VBA allows you to put more than one statement on a single line, separating them by colons. Thus:

```
x = 100: y = 200: z = 300
```

is exactly the equivalent of this:

```
x = 100
y = 200
z = 300
```

I never use this style, because I see no advantage to it and it can make your source code difficult to read.

The VBA editor has a lot of convenience features that can make your life easier—or can drive you batty if you do not like them. You can work with them for a while and decide which ones you like, then you can turn individual features on or off by selecting Tools, Options to display the VBA Options dialog box (Figure 3–2). The "convenience" options are listed in the Code Settings part of the dialog box:

- **Auto Syntax Check.** When you complete a line of code, VBA checks it for proper syntax and displays an error message if there is a syntax problem.
- **Require Variable Declaration.** Automatically inserts an option Explicit statement into each code module, which means that all variables must be declared before being used (explained later in this chapter).
- **Auto List Members.** When you are entering a statement, displays a list of items that could logically complete the statement at that point. You can select from the list rather that typing it in yourself.
- **Auto Quick Info.** After you type a function name, displays information about the function's parameters to help you complete the statement.
- **Auto Data Tips.** Displays the current value of the variable over which the cursor is placed. Used in break mode during debugging (see Chapter 21).
- **Auto Indent.** Each new line of code is automatically indented the same as the previous line.

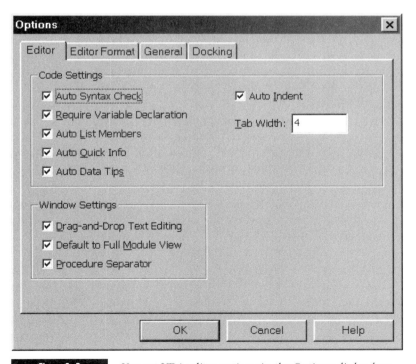

Figure 3–2   *You set VBA editor options in the Options dialog box.*

The VBA editor has the ability to color-code different parts of your code based on content. The default settings display regular text in black, comments in green, VBA keywords in blue, and so on. You can change these settings to suit your preferences, and you can also change the default font (typeface and size) used to display code. To do so, display the Options dialog box (select Tools, Options) and click the Editor Format tab.

At the top of each individual code editing window you will see two drop-down lists. The left side lists the categories of procedures that are available in the module whose code is being edited, while the right side lists the individual procedures for the category selected. Using these two lists greatly simplifies the task of navigating among the various parts of your code.

Project Explorer

The Project Explorer lists the available projects. In Office, projects are associated with documents and templates so the projects you see listed in the Project Explorer depend on the specific Office application from which you started the VBA editor, as well as the documents you have open at the time. If you start the editor from Word, for example, the Project explorer will contain a project for the Normal template, one project for each open document, and one project for each template (other then Normal) that is in use. If you switch from the editor to the application and open or close files, the list of projects will adjust automatically.

A project contains one or more *modules*. It is these modules that contain the VBA code and other elements that make up an Office project. There are three types of modules:

- **Standard module.** (Previously called a *code module*). Contains VBA procedures and data declarations.
- **Class module.** Contains the VBA code that defines a class.
- **UserForm module.** Contains the definition of a window or dialog box and associated VBA code.

A project may also contain one or more *references*. A reference provides a link between one project and the contents of another project or a library of COM objects. References are discussed in more detail later in this chapter.

The Project Explorer is organized as a collapsible outline. Each project name has a + sign next to it. Click this + sign to expand the project and view its modules. When a project is expanded it has a – sign next to it, which you can click to collapse the project and hide its modules.

At the top of the Project Explorer are three buttons. From left to right they are:

- **View code.** Click to view and edit the selected module's code.
- **View object.** Click to edit the selected object's visual interface.
- **Toggle folders.** Click to toggle the Project Explorer between regular view and folders view.

Each of the two View buttons is available only when appropriate for the selected module.

Properties Window

The Properties window is used to view and edit the properties of the currently selected object or module. At the top of the Properties window is a drop-down list that displays the name of the currently selected object. If the object contains other objects, then this list drops down to display their names and can be used to select one.

The bottom part of the Properties window displays the names and values of all the object's properties. There are two tabs that display exactly the same properties but one is organized alphabetically and the other by category. In the list, the left column displays the property name and the right column displays the current value.

To edit a property value, select it by clicking its name. The way you edit a value depends on the specific property:

- If the property is one you select from a list of predefined values, a down arrow will display. Click the arrow then select the new property value from a list.
- If the property is one you select using a dialog box, a button with an ellipses (...) will display. Click the button to display the dialog box.
- Otherwise, click in the property value column and edit the property value using the keyboard.

Use Your Right Mouse Button!

Like many Microsoft applications, the VBA editor makes extensive use of pop-up menus (sometimes called context menus). If you right-click on just about any screen element, VBA will pop up a menu containing commands that are relevant to the item you clicked. Often this is faster than using the regular menus. For example, if you select some code in the editing window then right-click, the pop-up menu offers Cut, Copy, and Paste options (among others). I won't mention the pop-up menu shortcuts for the various commands I am discussing, simply because it would take up a lot of space, but you should explore them on your own.

Working with Code

Most of your time as an Office developer will be spent working with code. By learning the ins and outs of VBA code, and picking up some "tips and tricks" from an experienced programmer (that's me!) you can hopefully maximize your productivity and minimize your frustration.

Using Modules

All VBA code is in modules. Certain guidelines for writing code apply regardless of the type of module you are dealing with, and I'll get to those soon. In any case you need to know how to work with the various types of modules. You learned about the three types of modules—standard, class, and User-Form—earlier in this chapter.

To add a module to a project, make sure the project is active in the Project Explorer then pull down the Tools menu and select the desired type of module. When a new module is added it is assigned a default name of the form Class*n* (for class modules), Module*n* (for standard modules) or User-Form*n* (for UserForm modules) in which *n* is a sequential number starting at 1 and increasing as you add more modules of a given type. Class and User Form modules are covered in Chapters 18 and 19.

The first thing you should do after adding a new module is change its name to something a bit more meaningful than the default name. You do this in the Properties window, changing the module's Name property. You should assign a name that is descriptive of the contents of the module. If, for example, you are creating a UserForm for the entry of a person's name and address, you might call it EnterAddress. Likewise, a standard module that will contain procedures for statistical analysis might be assigned the name Statistical. You can always change the name again later, but why not start out with a proper name?

Where Should You Put Code?

Some people who are just getting started with VBA programming are confused about where they should put VBA code—should it go in a standard module, a UserForm module, or a class module? If you're not sure, then put it in a standard module. Here's why: you use a UserForm module to define a dialog box or window, and it should contain only that code, such as event handlers, that is directly related to the functioning of the dialog box or window. Likewise, a class module defines a class and should contain only the code that is part of the class, defining its properties and methods. By default, any code not related to a UserForm or a class will therefore go in a standard module.

IMPORTING AND EXPORTING MODULES

Modules are not stored as separate files, but rather as a part of the project they are in. If you want a copy of a module to use in another project, or to give to a colleague, you must export the module to create a separate file containing the module's code. To export a module, be sure it is active (selected in the Project Explorer). Then select Export File from the File menu. VBA will display the Export File dialog box where you specify the location for the file and, if desired, change the default filename (which is the same as the module's Name property). You should not change the default file extension, which is .BAS for standard modules, .FRM for UserForm modules, and .CLS for class modules.

To import a module, select the desired project in the Project Explorer then select Import File from the File menu. A dialog box will be displayed where you can locate and select the .FRM, .BAS, or .CLS file to import.

Two Code-Viewing Modes

The VBA editor offers you two ways to view code in the editing window. You select the desired mode using the two buttons at the lower left corner of each editing window, just to the left of the horizontal scroll bar. In Procedure View the window displays only a single VBA procedure at a time, and you display other procedures either by selecting from the drop-down lists at the top of the window or by pressing PgUp and PgDn. In Full Module View the window displays all of the module's procedures with a horizontal line between them. Which mode you use has no effect on your code, just on the way it is displayed.

Writing Good Code

It might be tempting to say "good code is code that works," and it is certainly true that the ultimate test of any code you write is whether it performs the desired tasks. However, there is more to good code, and any experienced programmer will tell you that code that works fine can still be "bad code." How can this be?

Code is not a static thing that you write and then forget about forever. During the course of a project you'll be testing and modifying code multiple times, so you'll be returning to code that you wrote a couple of days ago, last week, or even last month. Also, you may be using code written by others, just as other developers may be using your code. These are all excellent reasons for writing code that not only works but is clear and easy to understand. And clarity aside, there are certain "good code" practices that can actually reduce the occurrence of errors and bugs.

USE CODE COMMENTS LIBERALLY

In VBA anything following an apostrophe is a comment, and is ignored by the compiler and therefore has no effect on program execution. You can and should use comments to document your code, explaining what the code does and exactly how it works. This is particularly important for more complex code that even a skilled programmer might not be able to figure out just by reading it. In effect, code comments provide a plain English description of what the code is doing.

Here's an example, some code from the demo Office project that was presented in Chapter 2. Here's the code without comments; can you easily figure out what's happening?

```
For i = 1 To myContactsEntries.Count
    Set NewMessage = OlApp.CreateItem(olMailItem)
    NewMessage.Subject = MessageSubject
    NewMessage.Body = ActiveDocument.Content.Text
    NewMessage.To = myContactsEntries(i).Address
    NewMessage.Send
    Debug.Print "Sent to " & NewMessage.To
    Set NewMessage = Nothing
Next i
```

Now, here's the same code with comments:

```
' Loop once for each address book entry.
For i = 1 To myContactsEntries.Count
    ' Create a new email message object.
    Set NewMessage = OlApp.CreateItem(olMailItem)
    ' Assign the subject to the new message.
    NewMessage.Subject = MessageSubject
    ' Add the current document contents as the message body.
    NewMessage.Body = ActiveDocument.Content.Text
    ' Assign the current address as the message's "to"
    ' address.
    NewMessage.To = myContactsEntries(i).Address
    ' Send the message.
    NewMessage.Send
    ' Destroy the email object in preparation for next loop.
    Set NewMessage = Nothing
Next I
```

I don't think there is any doubt as to which is clearer! Now it might be said that I went a little overboard with these comments, but they do get the point across. Another essential reason to include comments is to document procedures. Because any procedure you write is at least potentially reusable, it's wise to fully explain the way the procedure works in comments. Traditionally, these comments are placed at the start of the procedure. Here's an example:

```
Function ConcatenateFiles(strFile1 As String, strFile2 As _
String) As Boolean

' Appends the contents of strFile2 onto the end of strFile1.
' strFile2 is not modified in any way. Returns True on
' success.
' Returns False if either strFile1 or strFile2 does not
' exist or if there is any file access error.
```

```
...
...
End Function
```

Comments can also be used at the start of a module to describe the purpose of the module, give credit to the author(s), provide a history of revision dates, and so on. Some developers, in fact, write the comments first! This may sound strange, but by writing comments describing what you plan to do, you create a useful outline for the code that you have yet to write.

REQUIRE VARIABLE DECLARATION

A *variable* is a named location where you can store data or object references during program execution. Before a VBA program can use a variable, the compiler must set aside some space in memory for the data to be stored, and also must associate a name with that location. VBA has two approaches to creating variables.

One approach, the default, is automatic. You, the programmer, need do nothing special other than use the variable name in code. Whenever the VBA compiler comes across a name it does not know, it assumes it is a new variable and allocates memory space for it. If you decide your code needs a variable named `MyTotal`, just use the name:

```
MyTotal = X + Y
```

The other approach requires that the program include an explicit statement to *declare* each variable before it can be used. If the compiler comes across a name it does not know about, it displays an error message. To use a variable named `MyTotal` you would have to declare it like this before using it:

```
Dim MyTotal
...
MyTotal = X + Y
```

You will learn the details of declaring and using variables in Chapter 12. For now it is enough for you to know that good code practice includes requiring variable declaration. Why is this? Doesn't it seem that the automatic declaration is easier?

There are two reasons to prefer the former approach. If you are using automatic variable declaration then a misspelled variable name will not be caught by the compiler; VBA will simply treat it as a new variable, which will be initialized to either 0 or a blank string depending on the type. This can cause pesky program bugs that are difficult to track down. If you are requiring variable declaration then a misspelled variable name will cause an error, and you can correct it.

The second reason has to do with VBA's variable types. You'll learn in Chapter 12 about the various types of variables that VBA provides, designed to hold specific types of data. When you declare variables, you can specify the data type, meaning that you can tailor your variable types to best suit the data they will hold. With automatic variable declaration, variables are always VBA's default data type, which is not always the most efficient method of storage.

To require the declaration of variables, put the `Option Explicit` statement at the start of the code in each module. You can have the VBA editor do this automatically by setting an option: select Tools, Options to display the Options dialog box. Then on the Editor tab turn the Require variable Declaration option on.

USE DESCRIPTIVE VARIABLE AND PROCEDURE NAMES

VBA gives you a great deal of flexibility when it comes to naming variables and procedures. In a nutshell the rules are:

- The first character must be a letter.
- You cannot use a space or any of these characters: . ! @ & $ or #
- The maximum length is 255 characters.
- You cannot use any VBA keywords or the names of built-in functions.

As long as you follow these rules, VBA does not care one whit what you name your variables and procedures. However, you (and anyone else who uses your code) will be really glad if you use descriptive names—in other words, names that describe the data that the variable is holding or the purpose of the procedure. A variable that holds interest rate data can be called `X45` or `JoeSmith` but don't you think the code would be a lot more readable if you called it `InterestRate`? The same thing holds for procedures—a function that returns the largest value in an array of numbers could be named `Largest` but might better be named `LargestValueInArray`.

One step beyond the simple use of descriptive names is the use of naming conventions. A naming convention assigns prefixes to variable names so that the data type of the variable is indicated. This can hold for both simple variables (which hold data) and for object references. For example, using the `str` prefix for string (text) variables you would name a string variable that holds a person's first name `strFirstName`. Then, if you used a `Text Box` object for the entry of a person's first name, you could call it `txtFirstName`. By combining descriptive names with naming conventions, you ensure that anyone reading your code (and this includes you) will know what data the variable or object holds and the type of the data or object. Note that naming convention prefixes are used for variable and object reference names but not for procedures.

In my experience the use of descriptive variable names is very important, but the use of naming conventions is less so, at least for variables (I do use it for the names of controls on a UserForm). One reason is that the VBA editor makes it so easy to find out the type of a variable; simply right click a variable name and select Definition from the pop-up menu. My advice is to definitely use descriptive variable and procedure names, but use naming conventions only if it suits your style.

Microsoft Naming Conventions

You can find information on the VBA naming conventions suggested by Microsoft at: http://support.microsoft.com/support/kb/articles/Q110/2/64.asp.

FORMAT YOUR CODE FOR CLARITY

Formatting refers to the use of line breaks and indentation to arrange your code on the page. I will start this section by telling you that the VBA compiler does not care in the least how your code is formatted. However, by following some fairly simple formatting conventions you can make your code a lot easier to read.

Your main tool for formatting the source code is the use of indentation. To indent a line press Tab one or more times at the start of the line. The width (number of spaces) of each tab is set in the Options dialog box (Select Tools, Options). The default value of 4 seems like the best compromise between a larger indent, which is easy to see but wastes space, and a smaller indent, which conserves space but is not so obvious visually. To remove indentation, place the cursor at the start of the text on the line and press Backspace one or more times.

The primary use of indentation is to mark sections of code as being logically subsidiary to other code. This occurs primarily in VBA's loops and conditional structures, where the execution of a group of one or more statements is controlled by two other statements, one at the start and the other at the end of the group of statements. By convention the inner statements are indented with respect to the first and last statements. You'll see this formatting style used throughout the book.

Another use for indentation is when you use the line continuation character to break a long line of code over two or more lines. You'll remember from earlier in this chapter that you break a line by typing a space followed by an underscore and then pressing Enter. The second and subsequent continued lines should be indented with respect to the first line.

Most programmers feel that all the lines inside a procedure should be indented with respect to the first and last lines:

```
Function CubeRoot(X As Double) As Double

    ' Returns the cube root of the value passed.
    CubeRoot = X^(1/3)

End Function
```

I do not like this approach because, since 95 percent of your code is inside procedures you are wasting a lot of space and will find that you need to use the line continuation character more frequently. If you want to set off the start and end of procedures visually, you can do so with a comment like this:

```
'******************************************
Function CubeRoot(X As Double) As Double

' Returns the cube root of the value passed.
CubeRoot = X^(1/3)

End Function
'******************************************
```

While the code formatting guidelines presented here are a good place to start, the formatting you end up using should suit your personal preferences. Don't use anything too weird, however, as you never know when someone else will need to read your code.

Adding References

When you are working on a VBA project you will often want to add to the project a reference to the various objects, or components, you are using. What is the purpose of adding these references to your project? First, some background information.

Classes and Type Libraries

The various components that you use in Office development can be thought of as having two parts. One part is the definitions of all the objects—in other words, the classes—that are used when Office or a custom application is running. These class definitions are for the most part contained in dynamic link library files (*.DLL) that are part of the Office installation. The other part consists of information about the classes (distinct from the classes themselves), such as what a class's properties and methods are, what arguments and return values the methods have, etc. This information is contained in the type libraries (also called object libraries) that were mentioned in Chapter 2. Type libraries are contained in *.OLB or *.TLB files that are also part of the Office installation. Occasionally, class information is combined with the actual class definition in a .DLL file.

To create and use objects you do not need the type libraries, but they can make programming a lot easier. To make use of the information in a type library you must reference it from within the VBA editor. This is done using the References dialog box, displayed by selecting References from the Tools menu. This dialog box is shown in Figure 3–3.

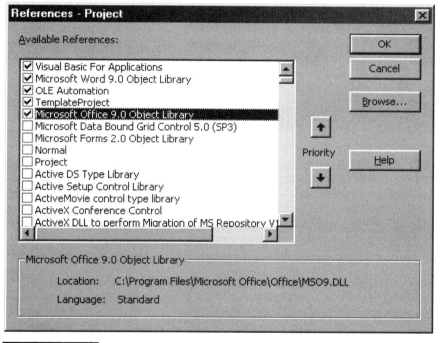

Figure 3–3   *Selecting type library references.*

The dialog box lists all of the type libraries that are registered on the system. Those that are available in the VBA project are marked with a ✔. If you select a library by clicking it, details about that library are displayed at the bottom of the dialog box. To make a specific library available in your VBA project, click to put a ✔ in the adjacent box. Having unnecessary libraries selected can slow things down, so you may want to remove the ✔ adjacent to those libraries you will not be using. If a library is in use, you will not be allowed to remove it.

What References Are Available?

Your References dialog box will list all references that exist on your system, not just those that are part of Office. Each reference, you will remember, corresponds to an object model exposed by an application. If, for example, you have the Adobe Photoshop graphics program installed on your system then its type library will be included in the references list. You can use objects exposed by other applications in your VBA projects, but you must be aware of licensing and distribution issues. Just because you have a program installed on your system does not mean that the end users of your Office application will also have it. You would have to distribute some of the program's DLL files along with your Office application for things to work properly, and you cannot do so legally without permission. This does not apply to the various Office components, which can be distributed freely with your application.

Table 3.1 lists the entries in the References list that are related to the Office object model.

Table 3.1   References to parts of the Office object model.

Reference Name	Type Information About	File
Microsoft Word 9.0 Object Library	Word object model	MSWORD9.OLB
Microsoft Access 9.0 Object Library	Access object model	MSACC9.OLB
Visual Basic for Applications	VBA objects	VBE6EXT.OLB
Microsoft Office 9.0 Object Library	Shared components	MSO9.DLL
Microsoft Excel 9.0 Object Library	Excel object model	EXCEL9.OLB
Microsoft FrontPage 4.0 Page Object Reference Library	FrontPage Object Model	FPEDITAX.DLL
Microsoft Outlook 9.0 Object Library	Outlook object model	MSOUTL9.OLB
Microsoft PowerPoint 9.0 Object Library	PowerPoint object model	MSPPT9.OLB
Microsoft Graph 9.0 Object Library	Graph object model	GRAPH9.OLB
Microsoft ActiveX Data Objects 2.1 Library	ActiveX data objects (ADO)	MSADO15.DLL
Microsoft ADO Ext 2.1 for DDL and Security	ADO data definition language and security objects	MSADOX.DLL
Microsoft ActiveX Data Objects (Multidimensional) 1.0 Library	Multidimensional ADO objects	MSADOMD.DLL
Microsoft Scripting Runtime	File access objects	SCRRUN.DLL
Microsoft Office Web Components 9.0	Various web-related objects	MSOWC.DLL

When VBA comes across a reference to a specific class name in your code, it looks through the loaded type libraries in the order they are listed in the References box. It then uses the first matching class. This is relevant of course only when the same class name is used by more than one type library, but this is not all that rare. To change the search order of the type libraries, select one in the References list and click the Up or Down Priority button to change the reference's position in the list.

While changes in type library priority can be useful, it is much preferred to use fully qualified class names. A fully qualified class name includes not only the name of the class but the programmatic identifier, or ProgID, of the object library that is exposing it. This has the following form:

```
ProgID.ClassName
```

When you use a fully qualified class name there is no ambiguity and the priority of entries in the References list makes no difference. One good example is the `Application` class, which is present in all Office object models. If you use the class name `Application` by itself you will always get an instance of the host application that the code is running in. To get an instance of a different `Application` object you must use the fully qualified class name:

```
Dim MyWordApp As Word.Application
Dim MyExcelApp As Excel.Application
```

Similarly, there are two classes named `RecordSet`, one part of the Data Access Objects object model and the other part of the ActiveX Data Objects (ADO) model. To be sure you get the one you want, use the fully qualified class name:

```
Dim MyDAORecordSet As DAO.RecordSet
Dim MyADORecordSet As ADODB.RecordSet
```

There are two advantages to referencing a type library in your VBA project. One is that you can use the Object Browser while you are programming to obtain information about classes and their methods and properties. (You'll learn about the Object Browser in Chapter 4). The second advantage is that you can use *early binding* in your VBA code. Because these two topics are closely related to working with objects, I will postpone explaining them until Chapter 4, which deals with objects in detail.

Securing Your Code

There are two aspects to the general topic of code security. One involves protecting your code from unauthorized access and tampering. The other has to do with virus protection.

Preventing Unauthorized Access

Wherever your Office solution is installed, anyone who knows how to use the VBA editor can view and modify your code. This presents two potential problems. First, you may not want anyone "borrowing" the code you sweated over for so long to use, free of charge, in their own projects. Second, there is the possibility that someone will modify your code, causing it to work improperly or not at all or, in the worst scenario, introducing a virus or some other harmful code. To prevent such unauthorized access to your code, you can *lock* each of your VBA projects. A locked project is assigned a password, and no one can view or modify the code without this password. To lock a project:

1. In the VBA editor, select the project you want to lock in the Project Explorer.
2. Select Tools, Project Properties to display the Project Properties dialog box.
3. On the Protection tab, turn on the Lock Project for Viewing option.
4. Enter the password in the Password and Confirm Password boxes.
5. Click OK.

To remove the password from a project, open the project and follow the above steps again, this time turning off the Lock Project for Viewing options and deleting the password (which will display as asterisks) from the boxes. Note that VBA passwords are case-sensitive. Be sure to keep a physical copy of the password in a safe place. If you forget the password, there is no way that I know of to "break" the security and access the project code.

You can lock a VBA project in any Office application: Word, Excel, PowerPoint, Access, Outlook, and FrontPage. Additional security considerations apply to Access databases, and will be covered in Chapter 7.

Summing Up

Most of your time spent developing Office applications will be spent in the VBA editor. It's a carefully designed editing tool that makes many repetitive tasks as easy as possible. Writing good code, and following programming guidelines such as commenting your code and using proper formatting, should become second nature after a while—but only if you follow these guidelines faithfully! Code security is not always a concern, but when it is you'll be glad to know that Office provides the required tools.

Working with Office Objects

Much of the power of Office development comes from the many components, or objects, that you can easily plug into your projects. Despite their power these objects still need to be told what to do, and that is one of your main jobs as a VBA developer. In this chapter you will learn the fundamentals of creating and working with Office objects.

Objects and References

When an Office object is created, it exists in your computer's memory. Fortunately, you do not have to deal with the details of memory addresses and the like, but rather you manipulate objects by means of *references*. A reference is nothing more than an expression or variable that has been initialized to "point" at the object in memory. While it is possible to have more than one reference to a single object, it is important to remember that only a single copy of that object exists (although there may of course be multiple copies, or instances, of the same *type* of object).

There are two parts to using object references. You must create a variable to hold the reference, then you must create an instance of the object, obtain the reference to the instance, and store the reference in the variable. Let's look at these tasks in turn.

Object Variables

A variable that will hold an object reference must be of an appropriate type. Assuming that you are requiring variable declaration (which was explained and highly recommended in Chapter 3), you must declare the variable before, or in some situations at the same time as, you assign the reference. The most general type of variable is VBA's default type, which is called `Variant`. Because this is the default data type you do not have to specify it in the `Dim` statement, although you can; both forms are shown here:

```
Dim MyObjectVariable1
Dim MyObjectVariable2 As Variant
```

After these declarations you have two variables that can hold object references. Because they are the `Variant` type they can also hold other data, such as numbers or text.

Not quite as general is to specify the `Object` data type:

```
Dim MyObjectVariable As Object
```

This creates a variable that can hold a reference to any type of object, but cannot be used for other types of data, such as numbers or text. It is preferable to use the `Object` type rather than the generic `Variant` type when the variable will be used only to hold object references.

The most specific way to declare an object variable is to specify the exact class of object it will refer to:

```
Dim MyObjectVariable As ClassName
```

In this syntax, *ClassName* is the specific name of a class, as in these examples:

```
Dim MyDocument As Word.Document
Dim MyRecordset As ADODB.RecordSet
```

This type of declaration creates an object variable that can be used only to hold a reference to the specific type of object. To use this form you must add a reference to the object's type library to your project, as explained in Chapter 3. This method of declaring object variables is called *early binding*, while using the `Object` or `Variant` data types is called *late binding*. I'll have more to say about early and late binding later in this chapter.

Creating New Objects

In some situations the object you need does not yet exist—you must create it and, in the process, obtain a reference to it. An example is adding a new `Document` object to a Word application. There are several ways to create a new object and obtain a reference to it.

USING New

Most often you will use the `New` keyword to create top-level objects as shown here:

```
Set ObjectVariable = New ClassName
```

in which *ObjectVariable* is a variable declared as an appropriate type for the object being created, and *ClassName* is the name of the class. For example, to create an instance of the Word application:

```
Set MyWordApp = New Word.Application
```

Note that assigning object references is always done with the `Set` keyword in conjunction with the assignment operator (=). You can also use the `New` keyword as part of the object variable's declaration statement:

```
Dim MyWordApp As New Word.Application
```

This is called *implicit* object creation. The object is not actually created by the `Dim` statement, but it is created the first time the object variable is referenced. There is no need to use the `Set` statement in this case. For example, suppose you create a new `Document` object as follows:

```
Set MyWordDocument = MyWordApp.Documents.Add()
```

If this were the first reference to `MyWordApp` to be encountered in the code during execution, the actual instance of the Word application would be created at this time. I suggest that you avoid implicit object creation, as there are no advantages to it and one possible disadvantage in that you may not know exactly when a given object is actually created.

Note that `New` can be used only to create instances of top-level objects (typically `Application` objects). Child objects cannot be created in this way. As I have mentioned previously, child objects are dependent on the existence of their parent object, and the parent will have a method to create new child objects. In fact, the last example showed how to use the `Add` method of the `Word.Application` object's `Documents` collection to create a new Document object. You'll learn about collections later in this chapter, and the details of creating specific child objects will be covered in subsequent chapters.

USING `CreateObject`

An alternative to using `New` is to use the `CreateObject` function. You use this function in situations where `New` does not provide the needed features. `CreateObject` can create a new instance of a top-level object across a network. Suppose Excel is not installed on the system where the VBA code is running, but is available on a network computer named "BigServer." You can create and use an `Excel.Application` object (which will actually run on the server) as follows:

```
Dim MyExcelApp As Object
Set MyExcelApp = CreateObject("Excel.Appliction", _
                              "BigServer")
```

This assumes, of course, that you have the required permissions on the server, and that the server is set up properly. `CreateObject` can also provide a diagnostic error message if the requested object is not available, which can be useful if you are not sure whether the requested application is installed on the system where your code is running. The following procedure tries to create an `Excel.Application` object, returning the reference to the calling program, and displaying a message to the user if Excel is not found on the current system:

```
Sub CreateExcelApp() As Object

Dim Temp As Object

On Error Resume Next
Set Temp = CreateObject("Excel.Application")
If Err = 429 Then
    MsgBox("Excel not found on this system.")
    Set CreateExcelApp = Nothing
    Exit Function
```

```
Else
    Set CreateExcelApp = Temp
End If

End Function
```

Then you would call this function as shown here:

```
Dim MyExcelApp As Object

Set MyExcelApp = CreateExcelApp
If MyExcelApp Is Nothing Then
    MsgBox ("Could not create Excel application")
Else
    ' Code to use Excel application goes here.
End If
```

Some of the VBA statements used here are new to you, but you should be able to understand how it works. The code is based on the fact that if the `CreateObject` function fails, an error is generated with the code 429. Then the `CreateExcelApp` function returns the special value `Nothing`, indicating that the application was not created.

Invisible Applications

When you create an instance of an Office application from VBA code, using the techniques presented here, that instance will remain hidden and will not display on the screen. This makes sense when you think about it, because in most situations you will be using that application to perform tasks in the background while the user works with the visual interface of the host application. You can, should the need arise, make an application visible by setting its `Visible` property to `True`:

```
Set MyExcelApp = New Excel.Application
. . .
' At this point the Excel application exists but
' is not visible.
. . .
MyExcelApp.Visible = True
' The Excel application is now visible on-screen.
. . .
MyExcelApp.Visible = False
' The Excel application is again hidden.
```

When using `CreateObject` in situations where you are not sure the target application exists, you should always use late binding (as was done in this example). If you use early binding and the target is not found, the code will not work properly.

Referencing Existing Objects

Sometimes the top-level object already exists—the application is already running—and you need to obtain a reference to it in order to manipulate the object. In this situation you use the GetObject function. Since you cannot always be sure that the target application is already running, GetObject is typically used with error-checking code that detects if the application is in fact not running and if so creates a new instance of it (using New or, if required, CreateObject). The code shown here obtains a reference to the running instance of Excel, if one exists, or creates a new instance of Excel:

```
Dim MyExcelApp As Excel.Application

On Error Resume Next
Set MyExcelApp = GetObject( , "Excel.Application")
If Err = 429 Then
    Set MyExcelApp = New Excel.Application
End If
```

The GetObject function can also be used when you need to get a reference to an Office application at the same time as opening a file. The syntax is:

```
Set ObjectVariable = GetObject(FileName, ApplicationName)
```

ObjectVariable is a variable of the proper type for the object reference that you are getting. *FileName* is the name of the Office file to open, and *ApplicationName* is the name of the Office application. Of course, the file that you specify must be an appropriate type for the application. This line of code returns a reference to Excel and opens the workbook Sales.xls:

```
Set MyExcelApp = GetObject("c:\docs\sales.xls", _
                            "Excel.Application")
```

Using GetObject can sometimes be problematic. If more than one instance of the target application is running, you have no control over which instance the returned reference will refer to. Also, if the user has started the application on his or her own, you would not want your VBA code to obtain a reference to that instance and start manipulating its objects. There are times, however, when GetObject is appropriate, such as when your VBA application has used the Shell statement to start an Office application.

Single-Use and Multi-Use Applications

Most Office applications are *single-use,* which means that a new instance is created every time it is requested in code. Thus, the following code creates a new instance of the Word application regardless of whether a copy of Word is already running:

```
Set MyWordApp = New Word.Application
```

Word, Access, Binder, Excel, and FrontPage are all single-use. Only Outlook and PowerPoint are *multi-use,* which means that only a single instance of the application will run at any time, regardless of how many references are requested in code. Look at this code:

```
Set MyOutlookApp = New Outlook.Application
```

If Outlook is already running this will return a reference to the running copy. Only if Outlook is not already running will a new instance be created.

Destroying Objects

An object continues to exist only as long as there is at least one reference to it. When you are finished making use of an application-level object, it is a good idea to explicitly destroy it, which frees up the memory it was using. This is accomplished by setting the object reference to Nothing, a VBA keyword designed specifically to disassociate an object variable from a reference:

```
Set MyExcelApp = Nothing
```

For most application objects you should use the Quit method before setting the object reference to Nothing:

```
MyExcelApp.Quit
Set MyExcelApp = Nothing
```

The Quit method has arguments, which are different from one application to another, that control such things as the saving of open documents. For the OfficeBinder application, use the Close method in place of Quit.

Collections

I have already hinted at the fact that collections are an essential element in the Office object model. Whenever the model requires more than one of something, it uses a collection to keep track of them. An Excel application can contain more than one workbook, for example, and each workbook can contain multiple worksheets. The Excel `Application` object therefore contains the `Workbooks` collection, which contains one `Workbook` object for each open workbook. Each of these `Workbook` objects in turn contains a `Worksheets` collection that contains one `Worksheet` object for each worksheet in the workbook. Recall that the Office naming conventions always name a collection as the plural of the object type it contains.

Because collections and objects are identified not only by their names but also by their location in the hierarchy, you will sometimes find the same name used for different things. One example is the `Windows` collection, which is part of both the `Application` object and the `Document` object. In the former case it contains all windows in the application, while in the latter it represents only those windows that display the specified document.

A `Collection` object has a single property, `Count`, which returns the number of elements in the collection. This is a *read-only* property, which means you can read its value but not change it.

Accessing Collection Members

Each item in a collection has a numerical index associated with it, ranging from 1 to the value of the collection's `Count` property (the number of items in the collection). In some collections, each item also has a unique key, which is nothing more than a string identifying the object. Collections use keys only when it makes sense. For example, in Word's `Documents` collection each `Document` object is assigned its filename as its key. In the `Paragraphs` collections, however, there is no logical key to assign to each `Paragraph` object so they are identified only by a numerical index.

Individual elements in a collection can be accessed by means of the collection's `Item` method. The syntax is:

```
CollectionName.Item(index)
```

in which *index* is the item's numerical index or, when appropriate, it's unique key. Because `Item` is the `Collection` object's default method, you can omit it. Thus, the following statement is equivalent to the one above:

```
CollectionName(index)
```

When you access a member of a collection you can use the reference directly or you can assign it to a variable. For example, the most efficient way to close the Word document named Report.doc is this (using the `Document` object's `Close` method):

```
Documents("Report.doc").Close
```

However, the following code does exactly the same thing:

```
Set DocToClose = Documents("Report.doc")
DocToClose.Close
```

You can easily access all the elements in a collection using the `For Each ... Next` statement. The syntax is:

```
For Each Item In CollectionName
...
Next
```

Item is a variable name that can be used to refer to each object in the collection within the loop, and *CollectionName* is a reference to the collection. The loop repeats once for each item in the collection, and code inside the loop can be used either to perform some action with each item or to look for a particular item. For example, this code prints a copy of each open Excel workbook:

```
For Each B in Workbooks
    B.PrintOut
Next
```

This code closes the Word document Report.doc if it is open, and displays a message to the user.

```
For Each doc In Documents
    If doc.Name = "Report.doc" Then
        doc.Close
        MsgBox("Report.doc was closed.")
    End If
Next
```

Adding and Removing Collection Members

The `Collection` object has `Add` and `Close` methods that are used to add a new member or delete an existing one. Adding an object actually creates a new instance of the object then adds it to the collection. The syntax for `Add` is:

```
CollectionName.Add(arguments)
```

Arguments provides various details about the object to be added. Depending on the type of object in the collection, the details of *arguments* will be different. For example, when adding a member to Word's `Documents` collection you must specify:

- The template that the new document is based on.
- Whether the new document is a regular document or a template.
- The type of the new document (blank document, e-mail message, Web page, etc.).
- Whether the new document is visible.

For most collections there is a default set of arguments that will be applied to the new member of the collection if `Add` is called without *arguments*. The `Add` method returns a reference to the new object, although you are not required to do anything with this reference. For example, the statement

```
Set NewDoc = Documents.Add
```

creates a new Word document based on the default parameters for the `Add` method, and sets `NewDoc` as a reference to that document. You can then use `NewDoc` to manipulate the document as needed, and you could also use the collection. You could also execute the following:

```
Documents.Add
```

This would create a new `Document` object and add it to the `Documents` collection but would create no reference to the object other than the one in the collection.

To remove a member of a collection, use the `Close` method:

```
ObjectReference.Close(arguments)
```

In this syntax, *ObjectReference* is a reference to an object in the collection. You can use the collection syntax or any other reference and the results are the same. The details of *arguments* will differ depending on the specific object being closed, and control things such as whether a document should be saved before closing. Here is code that creates a new Word document, performs some processing on it, then closes it, prompting the user to save changes as needed.

```
Set NewDoc = Documents.Add()
...
' Other code for document processing goes here.
...
NewDoc.Close(wdPromptToSaveChanges)
```

Note that the `Close` method actually belongs to the individual objects—in this case the `Document` object—and not to the collection itself. Some collections have their own `Close` method which has the same effect as executing the `Close` method for each individual object in the collection. For example, in Word the code

```
Documents.Close(wdPromptToSaveChanges)
```

closes all open documents in Word, prompting the user to save changes as needed.

Finding Objects in the Object Hierarchy

A custom Office application usually starts off by creating the top-level application objects it needs. Each of the Office applications has its own complex object model, and accessing an application's child objects is usually a matter of "burrowing down" through the various layers of the object hierarchy to obtain a reference to the desired object. As you learned earlier in this chapter, collections are an important part of all object hierarchies, which means that accessing an individual object often requires accessing the collection it is part of.

VBA provides some shortcut accessors that permit you to access certain objects without having to navigate through the object hierarchy. The use of the shortcut accessors depends on certain factors, including the application the code is executing in and the state of the application. For example, in Excel you can use the accessor `Workbooks` by itself to access the `Workbooks` collection, and do not need to use the more cumbersome `Application.Workbooks` syntax. Outside of Excel, however, the accessor `Workbooks` is meaningless. Word and the other Office application have similar shortcuts.

Some shortcut accessors provide a reference to a currently active part of an application. These accessors have the form `ActiveXXX`; examples include `ActiveDocument` (Word), `ActiveSheet` (Excel), and `ActiveWindow` (various applications). Be aware, however, that references like these may work correctly while you are developing your application but can cause errors down the road because it may not be the case that the active document (or active worksheet) at the time your code is executing is the one you want to refer to. To deal with problems like this, which can occur with either Word or Excel, Office provides the references `ThisDocument` and `ThisWorkbook`, which always refer to the document or workbook in which the code is running, regardless of whether it is currently active.

Early Versus Late Binding

When working with object references in your VBA code, you have the choice of using either early or late binding. As explained earlier in this chapter, late binding makes use of object variables that are declared as the generic `Object` type and can therefore hold a reference to any type of object:

```
Dim MyObjectVariable As Object
...
Set MyObjectVariable = New AnyTypeOfObject
```

In contrast, early binding declares the object variable as a specific type, and the variable can then be used to hold a reference only to that object type:

```
Dim MyObjectVariable As SpecificObjectType
...
Set MyObjectVariable = New SpecificObjectType
```

Remember that to use early binding, your project must contain a reference to the corresponding type library.

Which should you use? With rare exceptions, early binding is preferred. There are three reasons for this. The first is speed. When the project is running, the process of obtaining an object reference with late binding is much slower than with early binding.

The second reason is that only with early binding can you use the Object Browser to obtain reference information about the objects you are using. The use of the Object Browser is covered in the next section.

The third reason, and an important one, is programmer convenience. With early binding, the VBA editor "knows" the details of the object types you are referring to (information obtained from the type library), such as its properties and methods, and can provide lists of items for you to select from. For example, after the statement

```
Dim MyExcelApp As Excel.Application
```

the editor is aware of the type of MyExcelApp and if you type the name of the variable followed by a period, will display a list of the object's properties and methods from which you can select. This is shown in Figure 4–1. The VBA environment can also use the type library information to perform certain types of error checking during compilation, rather than having the errors caught only during program execution, which is what happens with late binding.

If the property and method lists are not being displayed in the VBA editor, it means either that the object's type library is not referenced in the project, or that the VBA editor's Auto List members option is turned off. Both of these were explained in Chapter 3.

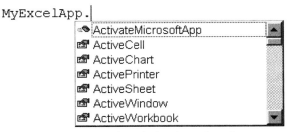

MyExcelApp.

| ActivateMicrosoftApp |
| ActiveCell |
| ActiveChart |
| ActivePrinter |
| ActiveSheet |
| ActiveWindow |
| ActiveWorkbook |

Figure 4–1   *With early binding, the editor can provide lists of properties and methods for known object types.*

When would you prefer late over early binding? It's not all that common, but once in a while you do not know ahead of time what type of object a given variable will refer to. There are also some older Windows applications that support automation but do not support early binding, and if you want to use these applications' objects in your Office application then late binding is your only choice. Otherwise, early binding is definitely the way to go.

The Object Browser

You use the Object Browser to view information about the classes, methods, properties, events, and constants contained in the type libraries that are referenced. By default each Office application automatically references certain type libraries, and you can add references to others using the References dialog box as explained in the previous section of this chapter. You open the Object Browser by pressing F2 from the VBA development editor. The Object Browser window will occupy the editing section of the VBA window.

The Object Browser window is shown in Figure 4–2. Its parts and their uses are described here:

- **Library box.** Select the library whose contents you want to view, or select All Libraries to view contents of all references type libraries.
- **Search box.** To search for specific text, enter it here then click the Search button.
- **Results list.** Displays the results of the most recent search.
- **Show/hide results button.** Click to control the display of the results list.
- **Class list.** Displays all objects and collections in the library.
- **Members list.** Displays all properties and methods of the class selected in the class list.
- **Details pane.** Displays information about the currently selected item. You can select an item in the results list, class list, or members list.

To view a library's defined constants, select Globals in the class list.

Defined Constants

One of the most useful things about type libraries is that they provide an assortment of defined constants that you can use in your VBA code. A defined constant is simply a meaningful name that is assigned to a numerical value. By using the constant instead of the numerical value, your code is easier to read. For example, to close the Word document references by `MyDoc` without saving changes the code is:

```
MyDoc.Close(wdDoNotSaveChanges)
```

The argument used in this case, `wdDoNotSaveChanges`, is a defined constant. It has the numerical value of 0, so the following code would work just as well:

```
MyDoc.Close(0)
```

However, it is not nearly as obvious when you are reading the code what exactly the code is doing. In Office, defined constants have a prefix that identifies the application they are associated with: "wd" for Word, "xl" for Excel, "mso" for shared components, and so on.

The information displayed in the details pane depends on the nature of the selected item. For a method, the details pane displays the method's arguments, its return type (if any), and the name of the object the method belongs to. For a defined constant, it displays the name and numeric value. For a property the pane displays the data type, and whether it is read-only. In Figure 4–2, for example, we can see that the property `BackgroundSavingStatus` is part of the `Word.Application` class, is data type `Long`, and is read-only.

Most type library entries have Help information associated with them. In this case, you can select the item and press F1 to view this information.

Objects and Events

Some of the objects in the Office object hierarchy can respond to events. Many events correspond to something the user does, such as opening a file, modifying some data, clicking with the mouse, or hitting a key. Other events are caused by code or by the system. Events are easy to use because the actual task of detecting them is taken care of automatically. All you need to do is decide which events should be responded to.

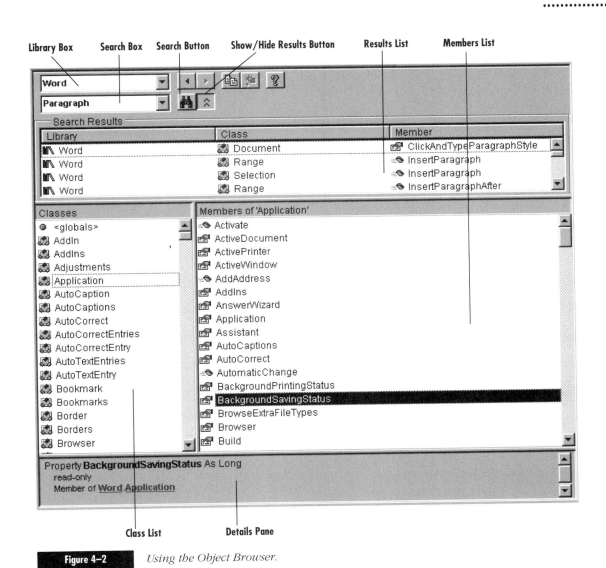

Figure 4-2   *Using the Object Browser.*

To make use of events you use *event handlers* (sometimes called *event procedures*). An event handler is a section of code that is automatically executed when the related event occurs. Events handlers are identified by two things: the name of the object that receives the event, and the name of the event itself. The syntax is as follows:

```
Private Sub ObjectName_EventName()

' Code to be executed when the event occurs goes here.

End Sub
```

For example, Word's `Document` object supports the `Close` event (among others). The event handler for this event looks like this:

```
Private Sub Document_Close()
...
End Sub
```

The code that goes in an event handler depends, of course, on the needs of your application. When you are editing code, you can use the two drop-down lists at the top of the code editing window to create event procedures. The list on the left will contain the names of any objects in the current module, and the list on the right will contain the names of any events supported by the object you have selected in the other box. Select an event and the editor automatically inserts the skeleton of the event procedure for you.

If you do not need to respond to a certain event, simply do not create an event handler for that event (or leave the event handler empty).

Events in Office can happen at two levels. Some events occur at the level of documents or, in some cases, at the level of objects within documents. Other events occur at the level of the application. In some cases, the same event can result in events being detected at both the document and the application level. For example, when a new Word document is created, the `Document` object receives the `New` event while the `Application` object receives the `NewDocument` event.

You will learn more about using events when we cover the details of components for each of the individual Office applications.

Summing Up

Most of the power of the Office development environment comes from the Office object model, which provides objects, or classes, to perform almost any task imaginable. While every object is different from all the others in its details, they all have certain things in common. For example, you must create an object before you can use it, and you also must have a reference to that object. Office often uses collections to manage objects, and a good grasp of collection syntax is essential. Once you have mastered the basics of working with objects, as covered in this chapter, you are ready to start learning the details.

The Office Components

Office provides more than 600 reusable software components (objects) for you to use in your custom solutions. These objects are the "bricks" out of which you will create the functionality required by your clients. You must know what components are available and how to use them if you are to program effectively and efficiently. That's what you'll learn in this section of the book.

Obviously, I cannot cover all 600+ Office components. Fortunately, this is not necessary to give you a good start as an Office developer. A fairly small subset of the components does the bulk of the work in most Office applications, and once you understand how to use these objects it is a relatively easy matter to figure out how to use the others with the help of the online documentation.

The first six chapters in this section each deal with the components exposed by the main Office applications: Word, Excel, Access, PowerPoint, FrontPage, and Outlook. The final chapter explores the shared Office components.

Using Word
Components

Word is a sophisticated word processing program, and whenever your Office application needs to work with text it will almost always call on the services of the objects that Word exposes. A Word document is also the ideal place to combine elements from various Office applications, for example, creating a nicely formatted report that includes text, figures, a chart from Excel, a slide from PowerPoint, and data from Access. In this chapter you will learn how to use the most important elements of the Word object model to create and manipulate documents. In subsequent chapters you'll see how to combine elements from different Office applications in a Word document.

The Word Object Model

At the top of the Word object model is, of course, the `Application` object (as with all Office application object models). Just below that is the `Documents` collection that contains a `Document` object for every open document. The `Document` object is central to almost everything Word can do, and a good part of this chapter will be devoted to it. Most of the other Word components you will work with are subsidiary to the `Document` object.

Remember that to work with an object you must first obtain a reference to it. This may involve creating a new instance of an object, or getting a reference to an existing instance. Techniques for working with object references were presented in Chapter 4.

The `Document` Object

Each open Word document is represented by a `Document` object. There are two ways to get a `Document` object: create a new one or open an existing one. Once you are done working with the document the object must be saved (at least in most cases) and then closed. Let's look at these tasks first, then we will examine the many tools available for manipulating document content.

Opening and Creating Documents

To create a new document, use the `Documents` collection's `Add` method. The syntax is:

```
Dim MyDoc As Word.Document
Set MyDoc = Documents.Add(Template, NewTemplate)
```

The `Template` argument specifies the name of the template that the new document is to be based on. The `NewTemplate` argument specifies whether the new document is a document template (`NewTemplate` = True) or a regular document (`NewTemplate` = False). The two arguments to this method are optional. If omitted, the defaults are to create a new regular document based on the Normal template.

You can create a new document and assign it a name at the same time, as follows:

```
Dim MyDoc As Word.Document
Documents.Add.SaveAs(FileName)
Set MyDoc = Documents(FileName)
```

If you do not name a document when you create it, you must assign a name when you save it, as explained in the next section.

To open an existing document from disk, use the `Open` method:

```
Dim MyDoc As Word.Document
Set MyDoc = Documents.Open(FileName)
```

The *FileName* argument specifies the path and name of the document file to open. If the specified file does not exist, or is not a valid Word document, an error occurs (you'll learn about handling errors such as this in Chapter 20). There are tools available that prevent the "file not found" error. One of them, the `Dialog` object, lets the user select a file, and is covered later in this chapter. The other, the `FileSearch` object, can be used to verify that a specified file exists before trying to open it. The `FileSearch` object will be covered in Chapter 11.

Saving and Closing Documents

You use the `Document` object's `Close` method to close a document. The syntax is (assuming `MyDoc` is a reference to the document):

```
MyDoc.Close(SaveChanges, OriginalFormat, RouteDocument)
```

The *SaveChanges* argument specifies whether the document should be saved. Possible values are wdDoNotSaveChanges, wdPromptToSaveChanges (the default), and wdSaveChanges.

Shortcut Arguments

Many Office methods take multiple arguments, and because most arguments are optional and have default values you often need to specify only a few arguments. One way to do this is by using the argument's position in the list to identify it, marking preceding omitted arguments with commas. Thus, to call the `Close` method using the default values for the first two arguments, and specifying True for the third argument, you would write the following:

```
MyDoc.Close , , True
```

Another approach is to use named arguments with the : = operator. This method identifies an argument by its name rather than by its position. This code is equivalent to the above:

```
MyDoc.Close RouteDocument:=True
```

This latter method is preferred because including the argument names in the call usually makes the code easier to understand.

The *OriginalFormat* argument specifies the format the document is to be saved in. Your choices are wdOriginalDocumentFormat, wdPrompt-User, and wdWordDocument (the default).

The RouteDocument argument is a True or False (the default) value indicating whether the document should be sent to the next recipient in a routing list. A value of True has no effect unless the document has a routing slip attached to it.

You can close all open documents by calling the Documents collection's Close method. The arguments are the same as described above for the Document object's Close method.

Stories in a Document

Each Word document contains a number of *stories* that represent the different parts of the document: main text, first page header, endnotes, etc. Each story is represented by a Range object that contains the entire story. You access the stories via the StoryRanges collection, part of the Document object. Unlike other collections, the StoryRanges collection does not have an Add method. A story is automatically created, and added to the collection, when you place some content in the story. The main text story, however, exists regardless of whether text has been added to it. The following defined constants are used to refer to the various stories:

```
wdCommentsStory
wdEndnotesStory
wdEvenPagesFooterStory
wdEvenPagesHeaderStory
wdFirstPageFooterStory
wdFirstPageHeaderStory
wdFootnotesStory
wdMainTextStory
wdPrimaryFooterStory
wdPrimaryHeaderStory
wdTextFrameStory
```

You can obtain a reference to a particular story as follows:

```
Dim StoryRange As Word.Range
Set StoryRange = MyDoc.StoryRanges(StoryType)
```

in which *StoryType* is one of the defined constants listed above. However if the specified story does not exist in the document, an error will occur. You can trap the error (as explained in Chapter 20) but it's better to avoid this possible problem by looping through the StoryRanges collection to see if the desired story exists before trying to get a reference to it (in this case, the primary header story):

```
Dim StoryRange As Word.Range
Dim R As Word.Range
Dim StoryExists As Boolean

For Each R In MyDoc.StoryRanges
    If R.StoryType = wdPrimaryHeaderStory Then
        Set StoryRange = R
        StoryExists = True
    End If
Next R
If Not StoryExists Then
    MsgBox ("The primary header story does not exist.")
End If
```

Here is code that adds the text "Compiled by R.Smith" to the end of any existing text in the primary footer:

```
Dim R As Word.Range
Dim S As String

For Each R In ActiveDocument.StoryRanges
    If R.StoryType = (wdPrimaryFooterStory) Then
        S = R.Text
    End If
Next R

ActiveDocument.Sections(1).Footers(wdHeaderFooterPrimary). _
    Range.Text = S & "Compiled by R.Smith"
```

Manipulating Document Content

Once you have a document, you can manipulate its contents in just about any way you can imagine. This includes adding, deleting, and moving text, changing formatting, adding footnotes, images, and headers, and so on. In keeping with the object-oriented approach, most everything you do with a document is done with objects—objects that are subsidiary to the Document object. Many of the things you can do with a document's contents require you to specify at what location in, or to what part of, the document you want the actions to take effect. The Selection and Range objects are used for this purpose.

THE Selection OBJECT

The Selection object represents text that is selected (highlighted) in a document. A Selection object is always present, even if no text is selected. The

Selection object can be accessed from the Application, Window, and Pane objects, not the Document object. This may seem strange, but it works this way because the Selection object is related to text that is highlighted on the screen. However, since this is a global object (as described in Chapter 4) you can access it directly within Word.

You can determine the type of the current selection with the Selection object's Type property. This property can have various values, all identified by defined global constants (which you can view in the Object Browser as described in Chapter 3) that are fairly descriptive of the type of selection. For example, wdSelectionRow indicates that a table row is selected. The two selection types you'll use most often are wdSelectionNormal, indicating that some normal text is selected, and wdSelectionIP, meaning than no text is selected (in which case the Selection object correlates with the insertion point).

Things that you do with the Selection object fall primarily into two categories: changing the selection so it includes a different part of the document, and modifying the text within the selection. The Selection object also has properties that provide information about the selected text and methods to manipulate the selection. These properties and methods are described in Tables 5.1 and 5.2.

Now let's look at some examples. To move the insertion point to the end of the main document text:

```
If Selection.StoryType = wdMainTextStory Then
    Selection.Move Unit:=wdStory, Count:=1
End If
```

To move to the start of the document and insert the text "Introduction" followed by a paragraph break:

```
If Selection.StoryType = wdMainTextStory Then
    Selection.Move Unit:=wdStory, Count:=-1
    Selection.TypeText "Introduction"
    Selection.InsertParagraphAfter
End If
```

To select the first paragraph in the active document, copy it to the clipboard, then paste it at the beginning of Report.doc:

```
Selection.Move Unit:=wdStory, Count:=-1
Selection.Expand Unit:=wdParagraph
Selection.Copy
Documents("report.doc").Activate
Selection.Move wdStory, -1
Selection.Paste
```

Table 5.1	Important properties of the `Selection` object.
Property	**Description**
`Active`	True if the selection is active.
`Characters*`	Returns a `Characters` object representing the characters in the selection.
`Document`	Returns a reference to the `Document` object containing the selection.
`End*, Start*`	Returns or sets the character position of the end and the start of the selection.
`ExtendMode`	Sets or returns the status of selection extension mode (True = on). When selection extension mode is on, EXT appears in the status bar and simply moving the insertion point extends the selection (much as if Shift were pressed).
`Font*`	Returns or sets a `Font` object representing the character formatting of the selection.
`ParagraphFormat*`	Returns or sets a `ParagraphFormat` object that represents the paragraph settings for the selection.
`Range`	Returns a `Range` object corresponding to the selection.
`StartIsActive`	Returns True if the start of the selection is active, False if the end of the selection is active. Read/write.
`StoryLength*`	Returns the length, in characters, of the story containing the selection.
`StoryType*`	Returns the story type of the text where the selection is located. Possible return values are descriptive defined constants including `wdMainText-Story` (main document text), `wdFootnotesStory` (a footnote), `wdEndNotesStory` (an endnote), and `wdCommentsStory` (a comment).
`Style*`	Returns or sets the style for the selection. Can be a local custom style name or one of the defined `wdStylexxxx` constants (such as `wdStyleNormal` and `wdStyleHeading1`).
`Text*`	Returns or sets the text in the selection. Setting this property replaces the original text in the selection with the new text.
`Words*`	Returns a `Words` collection representing all the words in the selection.

* Properties also applicable to the `Range` object.

Table 5.2	Important methods of the `Selection` object.
Method	**Description**
`Collapse(Direction)*`	Collapses a selection to its starting position (`Direction = wdCollapseStart`, the default) or its ending position (`Direction = wdCollapseEnd`).
`Copy*`, `Cut*`	Copies or cuts the selection to the clipboard.
`Delete*`	Deletes the selection.
`EndOf(Unit, Extend)*`	Moves or extends the ending character of a selection to the nearest specified unit. Values for `Unit` are `wdCharacter`, `wdWord` (the default), `wdSentence`, `wdParagraph`, `wdSection`, `wdCell`, `wdStory`, `wdColumn`, `wdRow`, and `wdTable`. The `Extend` argument can be either `wdMove` (the default), which collapses the selection and moves it, or `wdExtend`, which extends the end of the selection to the specified location. The method returns the number of characters the selection was extended or moved.
`Expand(Unit)*`	Expands the selection by the specified unit. Values for `Unit` are the same as for the `EndOf` method. The method returns the number of characters the selection was extended.
`Extend(Character)`	Turns extend mode on and extends the selection to the next occurrence of the text specified by `Character`.
`InRange(Range)*`	Returns True if the selection is contained in the specified `Range` object.
`InsertAfter(Text)*` `InsertBefore(Text)*`	Inserts the specified text either before or after the selection. The selection expands to include the new text.
`InsertBreak(Type)*`	Inserts the specified type of break at the selection. The type can be specified by defined constants including `wdPageBreak` (the default), `wdSectionBreak`, and `wdLineBreak`.
`InsertParagraph*`	Inserts a new paragraph at the selection. The selection will be replaced by the new paragraph unless it is collapsed.
`InsertParagraphAfter*` `InsertParagraphBefore*`	Inserts a new paragraph before or after the selection.
`Move(Unit, Count)*`	Collapses the selection and moves it the specified number of units. The `Unit` argument can be any of the global constants listed for the `EndOf` method. If `Count` is positive the selection is collapsed to its end and moved forward. If `Count` is negative the selection is collapsed to its start and moved backwards. The method returns the number of units the selection was moved, or 0 if the move failed.

Table 5.2	Important methods of the Selection object. (Continued)
Method	**Description**
`Paste`*	Inserts the contents of the clipboard at the selection. The selection will be replaced by the clipboard contents unless it is collapsed.
`SetRange(Start, End)`*	Sets the starting and ending character positions for the selection. Has the same effect as setting the `Start` and `End` properties.
`Shrink`	Shrinks the selection to the next smaller unit of text. The units are, in decreasing order: document, section, paragraph, sentence, word, and insertion point.
`TypeBackspace`	If the selection is collapsed, deletes the single character just before it. If the selection is not collapsed, deletes the selection.
`TypeText(Text)`	Inserts the specified text at the selection. Whether or not the selection is replaced by the new text depends on the `ReplaceSelection` option.

* Methods also applicable to the `Range` object.

To insert a page break after the third paragraph in the document:

```
Selection.Move Unit:=wdStory, Count:=-1
Selection.Move Unit:=wdParagraph, Count:=3
Selection.InsertBreak Type:=wdPageBreak
```

The `Selection` object is very much like the `Range` object, which is covered next. Its only real advantages are that you can use the `Selection` object to return the part of the document that the user has selected (highlighted), and that the part of the document represented by the `Selection` object is displayed as highlighted on-screen. If you do not need to make use of either of these features, you can almost always use the `Range` object instead when you need to act on a part of the document. The main advantages are that you can have more than one `Range` object in a window at the same time, referring to different parts of the document, and that operations with the `Range` object are a bit faster because there is no overhead associated with maintaining the screen highlight.

THE Range OBJECT

The `Range` object represents a section of a document. It is defined by the starting and ending characters, and can have any size from being empty to the entire document. As mentioned in the previous section, the `Range` object is very much like the `Selection` object. In fact, many properties and methods are shared by these objects, as indicated by the asterisks in Tables 5.1 and 5.2 on the previous pages.

Paragraphs in Word

A Word document can contain a variety of units: sections, pages, paragraphs, sentences, and so on. However, the paragraph is particularly important in Word, and you need to understand paragraphs to program Word effectively.

In Word, a paragraph is defined as a paragraph mark and all the text that precedes it, up to, but not including, the next preceding paragraph mark. An empty paragraph consists of a paragraph mark immediately following another paragraph mark, or at the start of a document. When working in Word you can see paragraph marks, displayed as ¶, by clicking the Show/Hide ¶ button on the toolbar. When using Word, you insert a paragraph mark by pressing Enter. So far, this sounds simple enough, but a paragraph mark is more than it seems.

Specifically, a paragraph mark contains the information specifying how the paragraph is formatted. If you copy text—say, the last sentence of a paragraph—and include the paragraph mark, then the formatting goes along with the text to its new location. If you copy the text without the paragraph mark, the text will take on the paragraph formatting that is in effect at its new location. For the VBA programmer this means two things.

First, when adding text to a document you must include a paragraph mark at the end and/or at the beginning if you want the text to be a separate paragraph. In VBA the constant vbCRLF represents a paragraph mark. If R is a range, this code inserts the text as a new paragraph, separate from both the preceding and following paragraphs:

```
msg = vbCRLF & "This is a new paragraph." & vbCRLF
R.InsertAfter(msg)
```

In contrast, this code does not create a new paragraph:

```
msg = "This is not a new paragraph."
R.InsertAfter(msg)
```

Second, when working with ranges you need to be aware that the range may include one or more paragraph marks at the end. When working with the range—for example, deleting it or copying it—you need to decide if the paragraph marks should be part of the range or not. The following code checks to see if there is one or more paragraph marks at the end of a range and, if so, shrinks the range to exclude them:

```
Do While Right(MyRange.Text, 1) = Chr$(13)
    MyRange.End = MyRange.End - 1
Loop
```

This code uses the chr$ function with the numerical code 13 to represent a paragraph mark.

To work with a range you must first create a `Range` object. One way to do this is by using the `Document` object's `Range` method. The syntax is:

```
MyDoc.Range(Start, End)
```

The optional arguments `Start` and `End` give the character positions of the start and end of the range. If these arguments are omitted, the method returns a range containing the entire document. This code creates a `Range` object that refers to the first 10 characters in the active document:

```
Dim Range1 As Word.Range
Set Range1 = ActiveDocument.Range(Start:=0, End:=9)
```

You can also obtain a range reference using the `Range` property of various objects. In each case the returned range contains the part of the document—a paragraph, for example—corresponding to the object whose `Range` property was obtained. The following Word objects have the `Range` property:

```
Bookmark
Cell
Comment
Endnote
Footnote
FormField
Frame
HeaderFooter
Hyperlink
Index
InlineShape
List
Paragraph
Revision
Row
Section
Selection
Subdocument
Table
TableOfAuthorities
TableOfContents
TableOfFigures
```

For example, here's how to get a range corresponding to the second paragraph in the document Report.doc:

```
Dim Range1 As Word.Range
Set Range1 = Documents("report.doc").Paragraphs(2).Range
```

The `Range` object has a few properties that are not present in the `Selection` object. They are explained in Table 5.3.

Table 5.3	Additional properties of the `Range` object.	
Property	**Description**	
Bold	Returns True or False indicating whether text in the range is formatted as bold. Returns `wdUndefined` if part of the text is formatted as bold. Set to True or False to change the range's formatting, or to `wdToggle` to toggle between bold and unbold.	
Case	Returns or sets the case of text in the range. Possible values include `wdLowerCase`, `wdUpperCase`, `wdTitleSentence` (first letter of sentences uppercase), `wdTitleWord` (first letter of words uppercase), and `wdToggleCase`.	
Italic	Returns True or False indicating whether text in the range is formatted in italics. Returns `wdUndefined` if part of the text is in italics. Set to True or False to change the range's formatting, or to `wdToggle` to toggle between italics and normal.	
Underline	Returns or sets the type of underlining for the range. Possible settings are descriptive `wdUnderlinexxxx` constants including `wdUnderLineNone`, `wdUnderLine-Single`, `wdUnderLineDotDash`, and `wdUnderlineWords`.	

Most of the code samples given in the previous section for the `Selection` object will also work with a `Range` object. Here are a few range-specific code samples. This code formats the first sentence of each paragraph in the document Letter.doc as bold:

```
Dim R As Word.Range
Dim P As Word.Paragraph
For Each P In Documents("letter.doc").Paragraphs
    If P.Range.Sentences.Count > 0 Then
        Set R = P.Range.Sentences(1)
        R.Bold = True
    End If
Next P
```

This code deletes the second and third paragraphs in the active document:

```
Dim R As Word.Range
Set R = ActiveDocument.Range( _
    Start:=ActiveDocument.Paragraphs(2).Range.Start, _
    End:= ActiveDocument.Paragraphs(3).Range.End)
R.Delete
```

This code changes the font size of the first section of the specified document to 14 points:

```
Documents("Resume.doc").Sections(1).Range.Font.Size = 14
```

USING BOOKMARKS

A bookmark is a part of a document that has been assigned a name. A bookmark can contain no text or other document content, in which case it serves only to mark a location in the document. A bookmark can also contain text. In many ways a bookmark is like a range except that it is saved with the document and can be referred to by name. As you would expect, each bookmark in a document is represented by a `Bookmark` object, and each document has a `Bookmarks` collection containing all of its bookmarks.

To create a new bookmark, use the `Bookmarks` collection's `Add` method:

```
ActiveDocument.Bookmarks.Add(Name, Range)
```

The `Name` argument specifies the bookmark name, and `Range` is a `Range` object that identifies the bookmark location (the `Range` object is covered elsewhere in this chapter). For example, to create a bookmark named "here" at the location of the insertion point:

```
ActiveDocument.Bookmarks.Add Name := "here", _
     Range: = Selection.Range
```

To determine if a bookmark exists, use the `Exists` method, which returns either True or False:

```
If ActiveDocument.Bookmark.Exists("Title page") Then
    ' Process bookmark here.
Else
   MsgBox "The bookmark 'Title page' does not exist"
End If
```

Sometimes you will want to define a range based on an existing bookmark, and then use the `Range` object's methods to work with the text. This is easily done using the `Bookmark` object's `Range` property:

```
Dim R As Word.Range
Set R = ActiveDocument.Bookmarks("SomeBookmark").Range
```

Word has a variety of predefined bookmarks that exist in every document. The ones you'll need most often are described in Table 5.4. For a complete list, open the Help system from the VBA editor and search for "predefined bookmarks."

Table 5.4	Word's predefined bookmarks.
Bookmark	**Description**
\Sel	Insertion point or current selection.
\StartOfSel	Start of the current selection.
\EndOfSel	End of the current selection.
\Line	Current line or the first line of the current selection.
\Char	Current character (the character following the insertion point). If text is selected, the first character of the selection.
\Para	Current paragraph (the paragraph containing the insertion point). If multiple paragraphs are selected, the first paragraph of the selection.
\Doc	Entire contents of the active document, with the exception of the final paragraph mark.
\Page	Current page, including the break at the end of the page, if any. The current page contains the insertion point. If the current selection contains more than one page, the "\Page" bookmark is the first page of the selection.
\StartOfDoc	Beginning of the document.
\EndOfDoc	End of the document.

One of the most powerful uses of bookmarks is to mark locations in documents and document templates. When a document is opened, or a new document is created based on the template, your VBA code can obtain information from the user or from other sources and use the bookmarks to insert the data into the document. The following code creates a new document based on the "ResponseLetter" template. It then prompts the user to enter two pieces of information and inserts them in the document at the locations of the bookmarks RecipientName and ProductName. Then it prints the document and closes it without saving.

```
Dim R As Word.Range
Dim D As Word.Document
Dim Temp As String

Set D = Documents.Add("ResponseLetter.dot")
Set R = D.Bookmarks("RecipientName").Range
Temp = InputBox("Please enter recipient's name: ")
R.InsertAfter Temp
Set R = D.Bookmarks("ProductName").Range
Temp = InputBox("Please enter the product name: ")
R.InsertAfter Temp
D.PrintOut
D.Close SaveChanges:=wdDoNotSaveChanges
```

FINDING AND REPLACING TEXT

The ability to find text and/or formatting in a document, and optionally replace it, is an important part of many custom Office solutions. When using the Word application directly, you use the Find and the Find and Replace dialog boxes to perform these tasks. In a VBA program, the `Find` object provides the same functionality as these dialog boxes.

Both the `Selection` object and the `Range` object have a `Find` property that provides a reference to a `Find` object that you can use with that selection or range. The general procedure is:

1. Define a selection or, more often, a range that includes the part of the document you want the search.
2. Set the `Find` object's properties to specify the search details.
3. Call the `Find` object's `Execute` method to perform the search.

The important properties of the `Find` object are described in Table 5.5.

Table 5.5	The important properties of the `Find` object.
Property	**Description**
`Font*`	Returns or sets a `Font` object identifying the font being searched for.
`Forward`	Specifies whether the search goes forward through the document (True, the default) or backwards (False).
`Found`	True if the last search found a match.
`MatchCase`	Specifies whether the search operation is case sensitive (True) or not (False).
`MatchWholeWord`	Specifies whether the search operation matches whole words only (True) or matches partial words (False).
`ParagraphFormat*`	Returns or sets a `ParagraphFormat` object specifying the paragraph formatting of the find operation.
`Replacement`	Sets or returns a `Replacement` object with the replace criteria for a find and replace operation.
`Style*`	Returns or sets the style for the search and replace operation. Can be a local custom style name or one of the defined `wdStyleXXXX` constants, such as `wdStyleNormal` or `wdStyleHeader`.
`Text*`	Returns or sets the text to find or replace.

* Properties shared by the `Replacement` object.

The Replacement object is used when doing a search and replace. It has properties, marked by asterisks in the table, that you use to specify the replacement text or formatting. You'll see how this works in the examples.

The Find object has two methods you need to know about. The ClearAllFormatting method removes all formatting options that may have been set previously, ensuring that the next find operation will be a pure text-only search. It is a good idea to call this method every time you use the Find object to ensure that any previous formatting settings are cleared. The Execute method performs the search and replace operation according to the options set. The Execute method takes a number of optional arguments that correspond to many of the Find object's properties. In other words, you can specify details of the find operation either by setting properties or by passing arguments to the Execute method (or a combination of both). Thus, the following two code fragments are equivalent (assuming Range1 is a reference to a Range object):

```
With Range1.Find
    .Forward = True
    .Text = "Bill Clinton"
    .Wrap = wdFindContinue
    .Execute
End With

Range1.Find.Execute Forward:=True, Text:="Bill Clinton", _
    Wrap:=wdFindContinue
```

It is essential to remember that a successful search operation changes the selection or range it was applied to. The selection will change to highlight only the found item, and the range will be redefined to include only the found item. Here's an example, which assumes that some text is already selected in the document:

```
With Selection.Find
    .Text = "objects"
    .Execute
End With
```

If the text "objects" is found within the selection, then after this code executes only "objects" will be selected. If the text is not found, the original text will remain selected. If you need to restore the original selection after your search and replace operations are done, you can save it as a Range object and then restore it when done:

```
Dim R As Word.Range

Set R = Selection.Range
With Selection.Find
```

```
    ...
    ' Do search operations here.
    ...
End With

Selection.Start = R.Start
Selection.End = R.End
```

Now let's look at some examples. To select (highlight) the first occurrence of the word "projection" in the second paragraph of the active document:

```
Selection.Start = ActiveDocument.Paragraphs(2).Range.Start
Selection.End = ActiveDocument.Paragraphs(2).Range.End

With Selection.Find
    .ClearFormatting
    .Text = "projection"
    .Execute
End With
```

This code replaces all occurrences of "Chicago" in the document Sales.doc with "Boston":

```
Dim R As Word.Range

Set R = Documents("Sales.doc").Content
With R.Find
    .ClearFormatting
    .Wrap = wdFindContinue
    .Text = "Chicago"
    With .Replacement
        .ClearFormatting
        .Text = "Boston"
    End With
    .Execute Replace:=wdReplaceAll
End With
```

To change all paragraphs formatted with the style Heading1 to the style Heading2:

```
Dim R As Word.Range

Set R = ActiveDocument.Content
With R.Find
    .ClearFormatting
    .Text = ""
    .Style = wdStyleHeading1
    With .Replacement
```

```
          .ClearFormatting
          .Text = ""
          .Style = wdStyleHeading2
     End With
     .Execute Replace:=wdReplaceAll
End With
```

Other Document Properties and Methods

In this section, I describe some other properties and methods of the `Document` object.

SENDING FAXES

If the system is set up to send faxes, you can use VBA code to fax a document using the `SendFax` method. The syntax is (assuming `MyDoc` is a reference to a `Document` object):

```
MyDoc.SendFax(Address, Subject)
```

`Address` is a required argument specifying the recipient's fax number. `Subject` is optional, and specifies the subject of the fax. When this method is executed the document is faxed without any further user interaction.

The `Application` object also has a `SendFax` method, which takes no arguments and starts the Fax Wizard, which the user then completes.

PRINTING

To print a document, use the `PrintOut` method. This method can be applied to the `Application`, `Document`, or `Window` object to print all open documents, the specified document, or the document displayed in the specified window, respectively. This method takes many arguments that correspond to the settings in Word's Print dialog box. All arguments are optional, and if omitted, the current Print dialog box settings will be used. The more commonly used arguments are described in Table 5.6.

SENDING E-MAIL

To send a document using e-mail, use the `SendMail` method. This method takes no arguments and applies only to the `Document` object. When the method executes, a message window opens in which the user must enter the To address and other information. If the `Options.SendMailAttach` property is True, the document is sent as an attachment to the message. If this property is False, the document is sent as text within the message body. For this method to work, the system must be configured for sending e-mail.

Table 5.6	Arguments to the `Printout` method.

Argument	Description
Range	The range of pages to print. Can be one of the following defined constants: `wdPrintAllDocument`, `wdPrintCurrentPage`, `wdPrintFromTo`, `wdPrintRangeOfPages`, `wdPrintSelection`.
From, To	The starting and ending page numbers when Range is `wdPrintFromTo`.
PageType	Specifies which pages to print: `wdPrintAllPages`, `wdPrintEvenPagesOnly`, or `wdPrintOddPagesOnly`.
Collate	True to collate documents when printing multiple copies, otherwise False.
Pages	The page numbers and ranges to be printed. For example, "2, 5-9" prints page 2 and pages 5 to 9.
Item	The specific item to print: `wdPrintAutoTextEntries`, `wdPrintComments`, `wdPrintDocumentContent`, `wdPrintKeyAssignments`, `wdPrintProperties`, or `wdPrintStyles`.

To e-mail a document automatically, without user interaction, you must work with some of the objects exposed by Outlook. These will be covered in Chapter 10.

The `Application` Object

While most of your programming with Word components will probably be centered on the `Document` object and its sub-objects, there are times you will need to deal directly with the `Application` object and other objects that are not subsumed under the `Document` object. This includes setting global options, displaying some useful dialog boxes, and manipulating windows and panes.

If you are working within Word, the `Application` object is automatically available and can be accessed by simply using the `Application` keyword. If you are automating Word from another Office application, then you must create an instance of the Word application and use the reference to it, in this case `MyWordApp`:

```
Dim MyWordApp As Word.Application
Set MyWordApp = New Word.Application
```

Setting Word Options

Word has many option settings that control various aspects of how the program works. When using the program you access these options through the Options dialog box, which has several tabs dealing with different areas of program operation. Many of the options in this dialog box are global, meaning they affect the entire application. Others apply only to the active document. Global options are properties of the Options object, while options that affect single documents are properties of the Document object.

To access application-level options, use the Options object (which is a global property of the Application object). For example:

```
With Options
    .PrintHiddentText = True
    .PrintDrawingObjects = True
End With
```

Generally speaking, it is a good idea to save the original value of any options you are changing, then reset them after your application is done with whatever it is doing. For example, the procedure shown in Listing 5–1 will set the spelling options so that:

- Internet and file addresses are ignored.
- Words containing numbers are ignored.
- Words in all uppercase are not ignored.
- Suggestions are taken only from the main dictionary.
- Corrections are always suggested.

Then a spelling check is performed on the active document. When the spelling check is finished, the spelling options are reset to their original values.

Listing 5–1   *Changing spelling options temporarily.*

```
Sub CheckSpellingIncludeUppercase()
'
' CheckSpellingIncludeUppercase Macro
' Macro recorded 7/19/99 by Peter G. Aitken
'

Dim bIgnoreUppercase As Boolean
Dim bIgnoreMixedDigits As Boolean
Dim bIgnoreInternetAndFileAddresses As Boolean
Dim bSuggestFromMainDictionary As Boolean
Dim bSuggestSpellingCorrections As Boolean

With Options
    bIgnoreUppercase = .IgnoreUppercase
```

```
    bIgnoreMixedDigits = .IgnoreMixedDigits
    bIgnoreInternetAndFileAddresses = .IgnoreInternetAndFileAddresses
    bSuggestFromMainDictionary = .SuggestFromMainDictionaryOnly
    bSuggestSpellingCorrections = .SuggestSpellingCorrections
    .IgnoreUppercase = False
    .IgnoreMixedDigits = True
    .IgnoreInternetAndFileAddresses = True
    .SuggestFromMainDictionaryOnly = True
    .SuggestSpellingCorrections = True
End With

ActiveDocument.CheckSpelling

With Options
    .IgnoreUppercase = bIgnoreUppercase
    .IgnoreMixedDigits = bIgnoreMixedDigits
    .IgnoreInternetAndFileAddresses = bIgnoreInternetAndFileAddresses
    .SuggestFromMainDictionaryOnly = bSuggestFromMainDictionaryOnly
    .SuggestSpellingCorrections = bSuggestSpellingCorrections
End With

End Sub
```

Learning About Options

Word has so many options that it would take a couple of pages to simply list them, let alone explain them. One way to get a feel for what options are available is to use the Object Browser to examine the properties of the `Options` object. Another helpful technique is to turn on Word's macro recorder when changing options in the Options dialog box. An examination of the resulting macro code will reveal which `Options` properties correspond with which dialog box options. You can also tell which options belong to the `Document` object instead of the `Options` object, as they will be recorded as `ActiveDocument.XXXX` in the macro rather than as `Options.XXXX`..

Word Dialog Boxes

The Word application provides an assortment of dialog boxes that you can use in your VBA code. You access these dialog boxes via the `Dialogs` collection, which is a global property of the `Application` object. To use a dialog box you first create a reference to it as follows:

```
Dim MyDialog As Dialog
Set MyDialog = Dialogs(DialogType)
```

The *DialogType* argument specifies the particular dialog box you want. There is a list of defined constants in the Word type library of the form `wdDialogXXXX` in which the `XXXX` identifies the dialog. In many cases (but not all), the name is related to the Word menu commands you would use to display the dialog box: `wdDialogFileOpen`, for example, specifies the file open dialog box. When a dialog box has tabs, the constant has the form `wdDialogXXXXTabYYYY` in which `XXXX` identifies the dialog box and `YYYY` identifies the tab. Thus, `wdDialogFilePageSetupTabPaperSize` specifies the paper size tab in the Page Setup dialog box.

Once you have a reference to the desired dialog box, use the `Show` method or the `Display` method to display the dialog box. The syntax for these two methods is the same (assuming `Dlg` is a reference to the dialog box):

```
Dlg.Show(TimeOut)
Dlg.Display(TimeOut)
```

The `TimeOut` argument specifies how long the dialog box will be displayed before being automatically closed without user intervention. Units are thousandths of a second. If this argument is omitted, the dialog is displayed until the user closes it.

The difference between these two methods is that `Show` results in the settings or actions specified in the dialog box taking effect automatically in the normal manner. In contrast, `Display` puts the dialog box on screen but actions and settings do not automatically take effect. Instead your code must retrieve information from the dialog box after it is closed and then act accordingly. I'll demonstrate this below.

Both methods return a type Long indicating which button the user clicked to close the dialog. Possible values are:

-2	The Close button
-1	The OK button or equivalent (e.g., "Open" in the File open dialog box)
0	The Cancel button (or presses esc, or the dialog times out)
> 0	Another command button; 1 = first button, 2 = second button, etc.

Here's an example that displays the Open dialog box:

```
Dim D As Dialog
Set D = Dialogs(wdDialogFileOpen)
D.Show
```

If the user selects a file and clicks the dialog box's Open button, the file will be opened and a new `Document` object will be created all automatically, with no code required. In contrast, using the `Display` method lets the user select a file but then you must write the code to open it. Typically, this involves the Dialog object's `Execute` method. The following code demonstrates. It assumes the existence of a function named `IsOK`, which can be passed a filename and returns True if the file is OK to open.

```
Dim D As Dialog, R As Long

Set D = Dialogs(wdDialogFileOpen)
With D
    R = .Display
    If R = -1 Then ' The Open button
        If IsOK(.Name) Then
            .Execute
        Else
            MsgBox "That file is not approved for this
                                    application."
        End If
    End If
End With
```

Another way to look at it is that the `Show` method is the same as a `Display` method followed by an `Execute` method. Using `Display` with the built-in dialog boxes can be useful when you want to use one of the built-in dialog boxes to obtain information from the user, but want to check the information before putting it into effect.

Word has some 200 built-in dialog boxes. Unfortunately, the online help is a bit skimpy when it comes to providing details about them. You can find the information that is available by opening Help from the VBA editor, searching for "built-in dialog boxes," then selecting "built-in dialog box argument lists" from the available topics. This Help page lists the available dialog boxes and their properties.

Windows and Panes

If you are manipulating Word through VBA as a hidden application, then you will not be concerned with manipulating screen windows and panes. If your custom solution requires that Word display on-screen for user interaction, then these techniques can be very useful to you.

WINDOWS

The `Application` object contains a `Windows` collection, and in this collection is one `Window` object for each existing window. Likewise, the `Document` object contains a `Windows` collection for those windows displaying that document. Of course, every Windows object in `Document.Windows` is also present in `Application.Windows`.

To access a specific window, use the Windows collection and the name of the document in the window. For example, this code maximizes the window containing Report.doc:

```
Windows("report.doc").WindowState = wdWindowStateMaximize
```

Each window is also identified by an index number, which is the same as the number appearing next to the window's name on Word's Window menu. To create a new window for a specific document, use the `NewWindow` method. Assuming `theDoc` is a reference to the document:

```
theDoc.ActiveWindow.NewWindow
```

To create a new window for the active document, you can use any of the following three syntaxes:

```
ActiveDocument.ActiveWindow.NewWindow
NewWindow
Windows.Add
```

The number of windows associated with a given document can be determined from the `Document` object's `Windows.Count` property. To close a window, use the `Close` method:

```
ActiveDocument.Windows(2).Close
```

Trying to close the last window associated with a document is the same as closing the document. The `Close` method takes the same arguments described earlier in this chapter for the `Document.Close` method to control the saving and routing of the document.

The `Window` object has a number of properties that control the appearance of the window and also are used to work with its contents. The properties you will use most often are described in Table 5.7.

The `Window` object has several methods that let you control the horizontal and vertical scrolling, bringing different parts of the document into view. Use `SmallScroll` to scroll small distances, and `LargeScroll` to scroll larger distances:

```
SomeWindow.SmallScroll (Down, Up, ToRight, ToLeft)
SomeWindow.LargeScroll(Down, Up, ToRight, ToLeft)
```

The four arguments specify the number of units to scroll in the specified direction. For `SmallScroll` a unit corresponds to the distance that is scrolled by clicking the arrow on the scroll bar, approximately one line. For `LargeScroll` a unit corresponds to one screen. If all arguments are omitted, both methods scroll down one unit.

To scroll by pages, use the `PageScroll` method:

```
SomeWindow.PageScroll(Down, Up)
```

Table 5.7	Important properties of the Window object.

Property	Description
Caption	Returns or sets the text displayed in the window's title bar.
ActivePane	Returns a reference to the window's currently active pane.
Active	Returns True if the window is currently active.
DisplayHorizontalScrollBar DisplayVerticalScrollBar DisplayLeftScrollBar DisplayRightRuler DisplayRulers DisplayVerticalRuler	True/False values controlling the display of rulers and scroll-bars in the window.
Height, Width	Returns or sets the height or width of the window. The units are points (1/72 of an inch).
Top, Left	Returns or sets the position of the top left corner of the window, relative to the top left corner of the screen. Units are points. Meaningful only when WindowState = wdWindowStateNormal.
Next, Previous	Returns the next or previous window in the Windows collection.
UsableHeight, UsableWidth	Returns the height or width of the usable (working) area of a window, in points. If none of the working area is visible, returns 1. If any of the working area is visible, the actual working area size is equal to one less than these properties.
WindowState	Returns or sets the state of the window. Possible values are wdWindowStateMaximize, wdWindowStateMinimize, and wdWindowStateNormal.

Use the *Down* or the *Up* argument to specify the number of pages to scroll. If no argument is provided the method scrolls down one page.

To scroll to a specific location in the document use the ScrollInto-View method:

```
SomeWindow.ScrollIntoView(Obj, Start)
```

The *Obj* argument specifies the Range object or the Shape object you want to bring into view. *Start* is optional, and specifies whether the top left corner of *Obj* will be positioned at the top left corner of the window (*Start* = True, the default), or the bottom right corner of *Obj* will be positioned at the bottom right corner of the window (*Start* = False).

Point Measurement Conversions

Many of Word's measurements are by default in units of *points*, a printer's unit that is equal to 1/72 of an inch. If you prefer working with other units, you can use the following VBA conversion functions:

```
PointsToInches
InchesToPoints
PointsToMillimeters
PointsToCentimeters
PointsToLines (1 line = 12 points)
PointsToPicas (1 pica = 12 points)
```

For example, to set a window's height to 5 inches you would write:

```
SomeWindow.Height = InchesToPoints(5)
```

PANES

Each individual window can have more than one pane, represented by `Pane` objects in the window's `Panes` collection. A window has more than one pane if it is split or if it is not in print layout view and information such as footnotes or comments is displayed.

To split a window you can use the `Panes` collection's `Add` method:

```
SomeWindow.Panes.Add(SplitVertical)
```

The optional *SplitVertical* argument specifies the percentage of the window you want above the split. If this argument is omitted the window will be split in half. The following code splits the active document's active window into two panes, 40 percent above the split and 60 percent below:

```
ActiveDocument.ActiveWindow.Panes.Add SplitVertical:=40
```

To open a separate pane for display of headers or other special document content, use the `SplitSpecial` property of the window's `View` object:

```
SomeWindow.View.SplitSpecial = type
```

The *type* argument is a defined constant specifying the type of the new pane. Values include `wdPaneComments`, `wdPaneEndNotes`, and `wdPane-Footnotes`. You can find the other values for this argument in the Object Browser. This code adds a footnote to the active document at the location of the insertion point then displays the footnotes in a separate pane:

```
ActiveDocument.Footnotes.Add Range:=Selection.Range, _
    Text = "I am a footnote."
ActiveDocument.ActiveWindow.View.Type = wdNormalView
ActiveDocument.ActiveWindow.View.SplitSpecial = _
    wdPaneFootnotes
```

THE `View` OBJECT

Every `Window` and `Pane` object has a `View` object associated with it, accessed by the `View` property. You saw the `View` object used above to control pane display. You also use the `View` object to control other aspects of the document display in the window or pane. The properties of the `View` object you'll use most often are described in Table 5.8.

Table 5.8	Important properties of the `View` object.
Property	**Description**
`Draft`	True/False value specifying whether the document is displayed in draft mode.
`FieldShading`	Specifies how document fields are shaded. Possible settings are `wdFieldShadingAlways`, `wdFieldShadingNever`, and `wdFieldShadingWhenSelected`.
`WrapToWindow`	Set to True to wrap lines of text to the window width rather than to the page width.
`ShowAll`	Set to True to display all nonprinting characters, such as tab marks, hidden text, and paragraph marks.

`ShowAnimation`
`ShowBookmarks`
`ShowDrawings`
`ShowFieldCodes`
`ShowFirstLineOnly`
`ShowFormat`
`ShowHiddenText`
`ShowHighlight`
`ShowHyphens`
`ShowObjectAnchors`
`ShowOptionalBreaks`
`ShowParagraphs`
`ShowPicturePlaceholders`
`ShowSpaces`
`ShowTabs`
`ShowTextBoundaries`
	True/False values specifying whether the corresponding document element is displayed.

Table 5.8	Important properties of the `View` object. (Continued)
Property	**Description**
`Type`	Returns or sets the view type. Possible values are `wdMaster-View`, `wdNormalView`, `wdOutlineView`, `wdPrintPreview`, `wdPrintView`, and `wdWebView`.
`Zoom`	References the window or pane's `Zoom` object. Use the `Zoom` object's `Percentage` property to control the size at which the text is displayed.

Events in Word

Part of the Office development model is the automatic detection of events. In Word, the events that are detected occur mostly at the level of the `Application` object, with a few that occur at the level of the `Document` object. If your application needs to respond to a particular event, all you need do is place the code in the corresponding event procedure and it will be executed automatically when the event occurs. The fundamentals of events were covered in Chapter 4. In this section I explain those events available in Word.

Document-Level Events

Document events are detected by individual documents. The event handlers are placed in a module associated with a specific document. If an event handler is placed in a template, then it will be present in all documents based on that template.

When working with document-level events you will need to use the `ThisDocument` module, which is automatically part of every VBA project created from Word. You'll see this module listed in the Project Explorer. Document-level event procedures must be placed in this module for them to work properly. VBA also provides the `ThisDocument` keyword, which you use in code to obtain a reference to the document in which the VBA code is running. You may think that you can use the `ActiveDocument` accessor for this purpose but it does not always work as planned, particularly when you are developing global templates. You cannot be sure that the particular document will be the active document when the code runs, even though it always is while you are developing the application. By using `ThisDocument`, you always refer to the document containing the running code regardless of which document is active. For example, to delete the first paragraph in the document where the code is running:

```
ThisDocument.Paragraphs(1).Range.Delete
```

In contrast, this code deletes the first paragraph in whatever document happens to be active when the code executes:

```
ActiveDocument.Paragraphs(1).Range.Delete
```

THE Close EVENT

The Close event occurs when the document is closed. You can use this event to perform actions such as making backups. This code faxes the document to the specified fax number when the document is closed:

```
Private Sub Document_Close()
    ThisDocument.SendFax("555-555-1212", _
        "Updated document for your approval.")
End Sub
```

THE New EVENT

The New event occurs when a new document is created. The event procedure code must be in the template on which the document is based.

As an example, suppose you have created a template called Report.dot and have written instructions for use of the template in a document called ReportInstructions.doc. Then you could put the following code in the Report template to automatically open the instructions document whenever a new document was created based on this template.

```
Private Sub Document_New()

    Dim AlreadyOpen As Boolean
    Dim D As Word.Document

    For Each D In Documents
        If D.Name = "ReportInstructions.doc" Then _
            AlreadyOpen = True
    Next

    If Not AlreadyOpen Then
        Documents.Open FileName:= "ReportInstructions.doc"
    End If

End Sub
```

THE Open EVENT

The Open event occurs when a document is opened. This code determines if the document contains any comments and, if so, opens a pane displaying the comments.

```
Private Sub Document_Open()

    With ThisDocument
        If .Comments.Count > 0 Then
            .ActiveWindow.View.SplitSpecial = wdPaneComments
        End If
    End With

End Sub
```

Application-Level Events

Working with application-level events is a bit different from using document-level events. Event procedures for application level events must be in a class module that includes an object variable of type `Application` declared using the `WithEvents` keyword. For example, in a class module you could include the declaration

```
Private WithEvents wdApp As Word.Application
```

and then associate the variable with Word in the `Class_Initialize` event procedure:

```
Private Sub Class_Initialize
    Set wdApp = Word.Application
End Sub
```

Then you could write the needed application level event procedures in the class module. Class modules are covered in detail in Chapter 18. Table 5.9 explains the basics of the various application-level events. I will cover one of these events in detail in the next section, and you can refer to online help for details on the others.

An Application-Level Event Example

To give you a feel for how the application-level events can be used, here is an example using the `DocumentBeforePrint` event. The syntax for this event is as follows:

```
Private Sub object_DocumentBeforePrint(ByVal _
    Doc As Document, Cancel As Boolean)
```

`Doc` is a reference to the document being printed. The `Cancel` argument is initially False. If code in the event procedure sets `Cancel` to True, the document is not printed. In this example, code in the event procedure examines the document properties to determine the paper size it uses for printing. If this is not the standard 8.5 × 11 inch size, a warning is displayed and the user is given a chance to cancel the print job. This code would have to be in a class module, as explained earlier, and it assumes that `MyWordApp` is a reference to the running Word application.

Table 5.9	Application-level events in Word.

Application-Level Event	Description
DocumentBeforeClose	Occurs before an open document closes. Is passed a reference to the document being closed, and permits the close operation to be cancelled.
DocumentBeforePrint	Occurs before a document is printed. Is passed a reference to the document being printed, and permits the print operation to be cancelled.
DocumentBeforeSave	Occurs before an open document is saved. Is passed a reference to the document being saved, and permits the save operation to be cancelled.
DocumentChange	Occurs when a new document is created, when a document is opened, or when a different document is made active.
DocumentOpen	Occurs when a document is opened. Is passed a reference to the just-opened document.
NewDocument	Occurs when a new document is created. Is passed a reference to the new document.
Quit	Occurs when the user quits Word.
WindowActivate	Occurs when any document window is activated. Is passed a reference to the just-activated window and a reference to the document displayed in that window.
WindowBeforeDoubleClick	Occurs when the editing area of a window is double clicked, before the default double-click response. Is passed a reference to the window's current selection, and permits the action to be canceled in code.
WindowBeforeRightClick	Occurs when the editing area of a window is right clicked, before the default right-click response. Is passed a reference to the window's current selection, and permits the action to be canceled in code.
WindowDeactivate	Occurs when any document window is deactivated. Is passed a reference to the just-deactivated window and a reference to the document displayed in that window.

....

Listing 5–2   *Demonstrating the DocumentBeforePrint event.*

```
Private Sub MyWordApp_DocumentBeforePrint(ByVal Doc As Document, _
    ByVal Cancel As Boolean)

    Dim retval As Integer
    Dim msg As String

    msg = "This document has a non-standard paper size." & vbCRLF
    msg = msg & "Make sure the printer is loaded with " & vbCRLF
    msg = msg & "the proper size of paper. Continue printing?"

    If Doc.PageSetup.PageWidth <> InchesToPoints(8.5) Or _
        Doc.PageSetup.PageHeight <> InchesToPoints(11) Then
        retval = MsgBox(msg, vbYesNo)
        If retval = vbNo Then Cancel = True
    End If

End Sub
```

Summing Up

All of the power of the Word application program is available to the Office developer through its object model. Anything a user can do sitting at the keyboard, your custom Office application can do in VBA code. Your application can use Word in two ways. Working behind the scenes, Word's objects can carry out your document processing needs without ever displaying on the screen. Or, if the circumstances dictate, you can permit Word to display on the screen for direct user interaction.

Using Excel Components

Excel is a spreadsheet program specialized for analysis and display of numerical data. Excel can store numerical and text data, and can also perform calculations with the data and create charts based on the data. It provides a large number of specialized functions for commonly needed calculations, including financial, statistical, and scientific. When you need numerical processing and charting, you will probably turn to Excel. This chapter provides an overview of the Excel object model and how you can use it in your custom Office applications.

Excel Overview

You can think of an Excel file as an accountant's ledger containing many pages, with each page ruled into rows and columns. It's a truly enormous book, with each page containing 65,536 rows and 256 columns. Columns are identified by letters; the first 26 are A–Z, the second 26 are AA–AZ, and the last one is IV. Rows are identified by numbers starting at 1. The number of worksheets in a workbook is limited only by available memory.

At the intersection of each row and column is a cell. A cell can contain a number, text, or a formula. It is formulas that provide much of Excel's power, permitting you to perform almost any kind of calculation on data in other cells in the same worksheet, or a different worksheet in the same or another workbook.

Excel also has sophisticated charting capabilities, permitting the use of a wide variety of chart types to graphically represent data in the worksheet. When data in a worksheet changes, all of the formula results and charts automatically update to reflect the changes. You can use Excel by itself, but more often Excel will be used in conjunction with other Office programs to provide the numerical analysis and charting components of a custom application.

The Excel Object Model

At the heart of the Excel object model is the `Worksheet` object, representing a single page in the file. Each `Worksheet` object is part of the `Worksheets` collection, which is subsidiary to a `Workbook` object, representing a single Excel file. Because the Excel application can have more than one workbook open at a time, there is also a `Workbooks` collection that contains one `Workbook` object for each open file. As with all Office applications, the `Application` object is at the top of the object hierarchy and is available as an implicit reference if you are working in Excel.

A second kind of "page" in a workbook is a `Chart`, a type of sheet that contains only a chart. The `Workbook` object's `Charts` collection provides access to the existing chart sheets, and the `Sheets` collection provides access to all sheets, both worksheets and charts.

Much of what you do in Excel will involve the `Range` object. Although the name is the same, it is a completely different object than the `Range` object that is part of the Word object model. Its function, however, is essentially the same: indicating a section of the document to operate on. A range can be a single cell, a two-dimension block of cells in a worksheet, or a three-dimensional block of cells spanning two or more worksheets.

Another important part of the Excel object model is the Chart object. There is one Chart object contained in the Charts collection for each chart in a workbook. Subsidiary to each Chart object is a variety of objects representing the parts of a chart, such as the axes, data points, and legend.

The Workbook Object

Each Workbook object represents an open .XLS or .XLA file. When you open Excel as a normal application (not from VBA), it automatically creates a new, blank workbook. When you start Excel from VBA, however, it does not contain any workbooks. The default is for each new workbook to contain three worksheets.

Opening and Creating Workbooks

To create a new workbook, use the Workbooks collection's Add method:

```
Workbooks.Add(Template)
```

The *Template* argument specifies the name of the .XLS file to use as the template for the new workbook, or one of the xlWBATemplate defined constants (viewable in the Object Browser). When you specify a constant, the new workbook contains a single worksheet of the specified type. If the *Template* argument is omitted, a new workbook is created containing the number of worksheets specified by the Application.SheetsInNewWorkbook property (default =3). The Add method returns a reference to the new workbook which can be stored in a variable of the appropriate type, if desired:

```
Dim MyWorkbook As Excel.Workbook
Set MyWorkbook = Workbooks.Add(Template)
```

Use the Open method to open an existing workbook from disk. The simplified syntax is:

```
Workbooks.Open(FileName)
```

FileName is a required argument specifying the path and name of the file to open. The Open method has about a dozen additional optional arguments that you use to specify such things as whether the file is read-only, to give a password if required, and whether to add this workbook to the list of recently used files.

Saving and Closing Workbooks

To save a workbook that already has been assigned a name, use the Work-book object's Save method. This method takes no arguments. To save a newly created workbook for the first time, assigning it a filename, or to save a named workbook under a different filename, use the SaveAs method. The simplified syntax for this method is:

```
MyWorkbook.SaveAs(FileName)
```

The *FileName* argument specifies the name of the file, including path if required. The SaveAs method takes a number of additional, optional arguments that control things such as assigning a password to the file and the file format. You can find details in the VBA online help.

To save a copy of a workbook under a different name without changing the workbook's current name, use the SaveCopyAs method:

```
MyWorkbook.SaveCopyAs(FileName)
```

Before a workbook has been saved and assigned a name, its Name property reflects the default name assigned by Excel (Book1, Book2, etc.). After a name has been assigned, the Name property returns the filename that you assigned. You cannot change the Name property directly, but must use the SaveAs method to change a workbook's name. There are two other properties of the Workbook object that relate to its name: once a workbook has been saved, the FullName property returns the fully qualified filename (path + filename) and the Path property returns the path alone.

To close a workbook use the Close method.

```
MyWorkbook.Close(SaveChanges, FileName, RouteWorkbook)
```

All three arguments are optional. *SaveChanges* specifies what to do if the workbook contains unsaved changes. Possible values are True to save changes and False to discard changes. If this argument is omitted, the user is prompted to save changes.

FileName is the name to save the workbook under. If omitted, the current name is used. If there is no current name, the user is prompted to supply a name.

RouteWorkbook is relevant only if the workbook has a routing slip attached and the workbook has not already been routed. Set to True if you want to route the workbook to the next recipient, otherwise set to False. If omitted, the user is prompted as to whether the workbook should be routed.

ThisWorkbook

Your code usually will use the `ActiveWorkbook` keyword, or a reference to the `Work-books` collection, to specify the Excel workbook that the code is to act upon. You will, however, sometimes want to be sure that your Excel VBA code refers to the workbook in which the code is running regardless of which workbook is currently active. You use the `ThisWorkbook` keyword for this purpose. This situation may arise when you are developing a global workbook template or add-in. This code always refers to the specified range in the workbook where the code is located:

```
Set Menu = ThisWorkbook.Worksheets( _
        "MenuDefs").Range("Menu1")
```

The `ThisWorkbook` keyword is similar in concept to the `ThisDocument` keyword used in Word VBA code, which you learned about in Chapter 5.

Printing Workbook Contents

Excel provides full control of printing workbooks. You use the `PrintOut` method to print; this method is available with the following objects and collections:

```
Chart
Charts
Range
Sheets
Window
Workbook
Worksheet
Worksheets
```

Exactly what is printed, and the relevance of the various arguments to `PrintOut`, will depend of course on the object you use when calling this method. The syntax is:

```
object.PrintOut(From, To, Copies, Preview, ActivePrinter, _
    PrintToFile, Collate, PrToFileName)
```

All of the arguments are optional. If called with no arguments, `Print-Out` prints one copy of the entire contents of the specified object to the default printer.

From and *To* specify the starting and ending page numbers to print. Default values are the beginning and end of the data.

Copies specifies the number of copies to print. The default is 1.

Preview is a True/False value specifying whether the print preview window will be opened before printing. The default is False.

ActivePrinter specifies the name of the printer to use.

PrintToFile is a True/False value specifying whether output should go to a file instead of the printer. The default is False.

Collate is a True/False value specifying whether multiple copy output should be collated.

PrToFileName specifies the name of the file where output is to be placed when *PrintToFile* = True. If omitted, Excel prompts the user for a filename.

E-mailing a Workbook

Use the `Workbook` object's `SendMail` method to e-mail a workbook to one or more recipients. This method uses whatever e-mail system is installed on the computer. The syntax is:

```
SomeWorkbook.SendMail(Recipients, Subject, ReturnReceipt)
```

Recipients is a required argument specifying the name or address of the recipient. If multiple recipients, then *Recipients* is an array of text strings. This code sends the active workbook to the individual identified as "Jane Doe" in your address book:

```
ActiveWorkbook.SendMail Recipient:="Jane Doe"
```

This code sends the active workbook to three recipients with the subject "Sales report" and a return receipt requested

```
Dim r As Variant
r = Array("boris_yeltsin@kremlin.gov", _
          "bill_gates@microsoft.com ", _
          "bill_clinton@whitehouse.gov")
ActiveWorkbook.SendMail Recipients:=r, Subject:= _
    "Sales Report", ReturnReceipt:=True
```

Other Workbook Properties and Methods

It is impossible to cover all of the `Workbook` object's properties and methods; you can use the Object Browser and the online documentation to get details as you need them. Certain properties and methods, however, are needed more frequently than others. I have summarized these in Tables 6.1 and 6.2.

Table 6.1	Commonly used properties of the `Workbook` object.

Property	Description
`BuiltInDocumentProperties`	Returns a `DocumentProperties` collection containing the built-in document properties such as Author, Creation Date, and Last Save Date. These are the properties you see in Excel's properties dialog box.
`CreateBackup`	True to create a backup file when the workbook is saved, otherwise False.
`FullName`	Returns the full name of the workbook, which consists of its path followed by its Name property.
`HasPassword`	True if the workbook is password protected.
`IsAddIn`	True if the workbook is running as an add-in.
`Name`	Returns the workbook's filename.
`Names`	Returns a Names collection containing all the workbook's Name objects. Each Name object represents a named range in the workbook.
`Path`	Returns the path to the workbook file.
`Saved`	True if no changes have been made to the workbook since it was last saved.
`Sheets`	Returns the Sheets collection that contains a Sheet object for every worksheet and chart sheet in the workbook.
`Windows`	Returns a Windows collection that contains a Window object for every workbook window.

Table 6.2	Commonly used methods of the `Workbook` object.

Method	Description
`Activate`	Makes the workbook active.
`AddToFavorites`	Adds a shortcut to the workbook in the Favorites folder.
`NewWindow`	Creates a new window for the workbook.
`SaveCopyAs(`*FileName*`)`	Saves a copy of the workbook under the specified name.

The Worksheet Object

Much of your programming in Excel will deal directly with worksheets, as represented by the Worksheet object. In this section I will cover the important aspects of manipulating worksheets and worksheet data.

Adding and Deleting Worksheets

To add a new worksheet to the Worksheets collection, use the Add method:

```
Dim MySheet As Excel.Worksheet
Set MySheet = Worksheets.Add(Before, After, Count)
```

The arguments are all optional; if omitted, one new worksheet is added before the currently active worksheet. You can use the *Before* or *After* argument to specify the existing worksheet before or after which the new one is to be placed. To add more than one worksheet, specify the desired number in *Count*. If *Count* is more than 1, the Add method returns a reference to the last added worksheet. As always, it is desirable to assign a name to new worksheets that you can use to refer to the sheet in code later:

```
MySheet.Name = "SalesData"
```

To delete a worksheet, use the Worksheet object's Delete method:

```
ActiveWorkbook.Worksheets(SheetName).Delete
```

SheetName is the name of the worksheet to delete. When you try to delete a worksheet in code, Excel's default behavior is to display a prompt to the user. You must set the Application object's DisplayAlerts property to False to prevent the prompt from being displayed. It is important that you return this property to True after the worksheet has been deleted:

```
Application.DisplayAlerts = False
ActiveWorkbook.Worksheets("SalesData").Delete
Application.DisplayAlerts = True
```

Hidden Workbooks

Workbooks created programmatically are hidden. If a user opens the workbook manually, it will still be hidden and the user will have to unhide it in order to view it. This is done by setting the Visible property to True. Visible is a property of individual worksheets and also of the Worksheets collection.

Copying and Moving Worksheets

You can copy and move entire worksheets, either within the same workbook or to a new workbook. To copy a worksheet to a new location in the same worksheet, or to a new workbook, use this syntax:

```
Sheet.Copy(Before, After)
```

Sheet is a reference to the sheet being copied. If you want the sheet copied to a new location in the same workbook, use the *Before* or *After* argument to specify the existing worksheet before or after which the copy is to be placed. If you omit these arguments, the worksheet is copied to a new workbook. The following code copies the worksheet SalesData to the last position in the workbook:

```
Worksheet("SalesData").Copy
After:=Worksheets(Worksheets.Count)
```

To move a worksheet, use the Move method. The syntax is the same as for Copy. For example, this code copies the worksheet SalesData to the position following the worksheet named "Projections":

```
Worksheet("SalesData").Copy After:="Projections"
```

The Range Object

You cannot do much with VBA and Excel without using the Range object. A Range object is used to specify the target for some action. A range can represent a single cell, an entire row or column in a worksheet, or an arbitrary two- or three-dimensional block of cells in a workbook. While a workbook can have multiple ranges in existence at the same time, there is no Ranges collection providing access to all of these objects.

You can obtain a Range object from the Range property of an Application, Worksheet, or Range object. The way these work is slightly different. The Application.Range property refers to the currently active worksheet. Thus, after this code executes:

```
Dim Range1 As Range
Set Range1 = Application.Range("A2")
```

the range Range1 refers to cell A2 in whatever worksheet is active when the code executes. In contrast, the Worksheet.Range property refers to a specific worksheet. This code sets Range2 to refer to cell B2 in the worksheet SalesData, regardless of which worksheet is active:

```
Dim Range2 As Range
Set Range2 = Worksheets("SalesData").Range("A2")
```

The `Range.Range` property is different in that it returns a range whose position is relative to the first range. Look at this code:

```
Dim Range3 As Range, Range4 As Range
Set Range3 = Worksheets("SalesData").Range("B2")
Set Range4 = Range3.Range("C4")
```

This does not result in R4 referring to cell C4, but rather to cell D5. This is because the range is relative to Range3, which is cell B2, so the result is that the Range4 reference is shifted accordingly—in this case, one column to the right and one row down.

Other properties and methods that return a `Range` object are listed in Table 6.3. Some of these properties and methods are explained in more detail following the table.

Table 6.3	Other properties and methods returning Range objects.
Property	**Returns a Range Object Referring To**
`ActiveCell` (Application object)	The active cell in the currently active window.
`ActiveCell` (Window object)	The active cell in the specified window.
`CurrentRegion` (Range object)	A range bounded by, but not including, the nearest blank rows, blank columns, and worksheet edges.
`Selection` (Application object)	The current selection in the active window.
`Selection` (Window object)	The current selection in the specified window.
`SpecialCells` (Range object)	All the cells that match the specified type and value.
`UsedRange` (Worksheet object)	The smallest rectangular region that includes all of the used cells in the worksheet.

THE `CurrentRegion` PROPERTY

The `CurrentRegion` property is one of Excel's most useful properties. Its use is based on the fact that worksheets are almost always arranged with blank rows and columns separating blocks of data. You can use this property to obtain a `Range` object that references such a region. What this property does in effect is to start at the specified location and expand in all directions—up, down, left, and right—until a blank row, a blank column, or the edge of the worksheet is reached. To see what this means, suppose that this line of code was executed in the worksheet in Figure 6–1:

```
Dim rng As Range
Set rng = ActiveCell.CurrentRegion
```

If the active cell is A2 (or B4, or B6, etc.) when this code executes, then rng will refer to cells A2:B7. If, on the other hand, the active cell is D5 (or E7, or F8, etc.) then rng will refer to D5:F9.

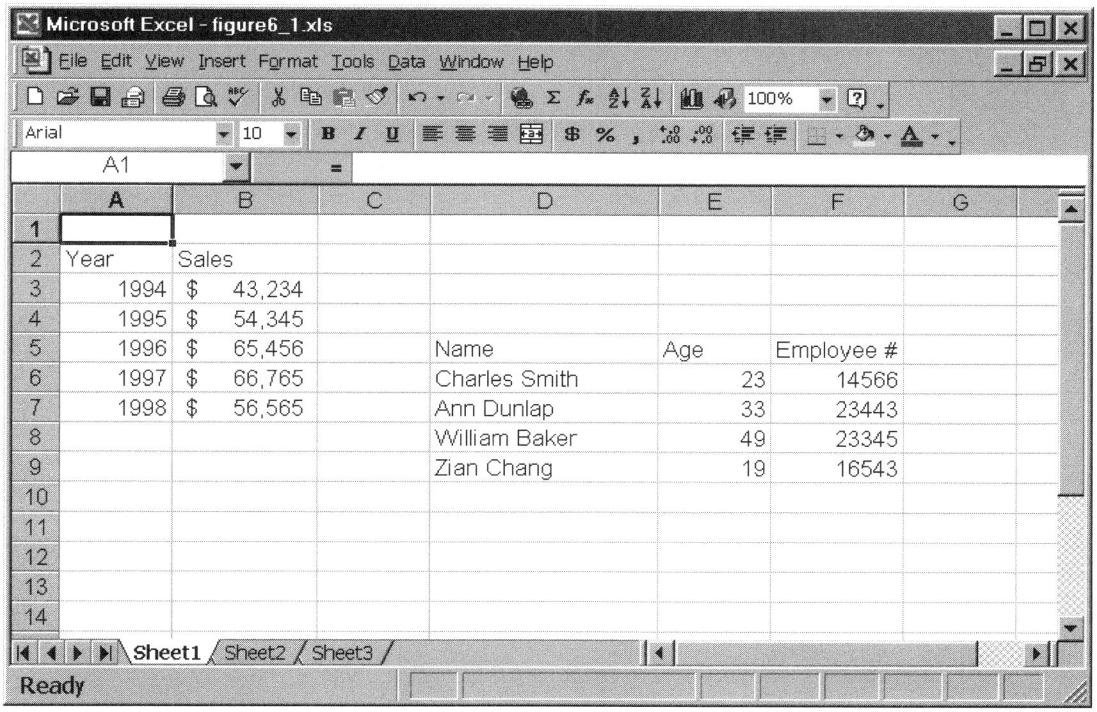

Figure 6–1   *Demonstrating the CurrentRegion property.*

The UsedRange property returns the used region of a worksheet. If applied to the worksheet in Figure 6–1, the returned range would refer to A2:F9.

THE SpecialCells METHOD

The SpecialCells method lets you pick out certain types of cells in an existing range. The syntax is:

```
SomeRange.SpecialCells(Type, Value)
```

The Type argument is required, and can be one of the xlCellType constants shown in Table 6.4.

The *Value* argument is optional, and is used only when *Type* is either `xlCellTypeConstants` or `xlCellTypeFormulas`. Possible values are listed in Table 6.5. If the *Value* argument is omitted, `SpecialCells` returns all formula cells or all constant cells, regardless of type.

Table 6.4	Type arguments for the `SpecialCells` method.
Constant	**Cell Type in Returned Range**
`xlCellTypeAllFormatConditions`	Cells of any format.
`xlCellTypeAllValidation`	Cells containing validation criteria.
`xlCellTypeBlanks`	Blank cells.
`xlCellTypeComments`	Cells containing notes.
`xlCellTypeConstants`	Cells containing constants (numbers or text).
`xlCellTypeFormulas`	Cells containing formulas.
`xlCellTypeLastCell`	The last cell in the used range.
`xlCellTypeSameFormatConditions`	Cells having the same format.
`xlCellTypeSameValidation`	Cells having the same validation criteria.
`xlCellTypeVisible`	Cells that are visible.

Table 6.5	Value arguments for the `SpecialCells` method.
Constant	**Meaning**
`xlErrors`	Formula cells with an error.
`xlLogical`	Cells containing logical formulas.
`xlTextValues`	Cells containing text.
`xlNumbers`	Cells containing numbers.

The following code deletes the contents of all cells that contain text in the current region surrounding the active cell in Sheet1:

```
Dim r As Range
Worksheets("Sheet1").Activate
Set r = ActiveCell.CurrentRegion
r.SpecialCells(xlCellTypeConstants, xlTextValues).Value = ""
```

This code activates the last cell (lower right corner) in the current region:

```
ActiveCell.CurrentRegion.SpecialCells( _
    xlCellTypeLastCell).Activate
```

THE Selection PROPERTY

The Selection property returns the currently selected object in either the active worksheet (Application.Selection) or a specific window (Window.Selection). Note that the selection is often a range of one or more worksheet cells, but there are other Excel objects, such as a chart, that can be selected. To make sure that the selection is a range, you can use the Type-Name function as follows:

```
If TypeName(Selection) = "Range" Then
    ' Selection is a range.
Else
    ' Selection is not a range.
End If
```

Assuming that one or more worksheet cells are selected, then Selection returns a Range object representing the selected cell(s). This corresponds to cells selected by the user by dragging with the mouse, which are displayed on-screen with a different color background. If only a single cell is selected, then Selection returns the same range as the ActiveCell property. If more than one cell is selected, the Range object returned by Selection represents all the cells. Note that in the latter case, when there is more than one cell selected, there is still a single active cell that will be at one corner of the selected range depending on how the cells were selected.

Most of the time you will use the Range object when specifying sections of a worksheet to act on. It is a lot more flexible than the Selection object, and you can have as many defined at once as you need. In contrast, there can be only one selection at a time. One time when the Selection object is useful is when your code needs to interact with the user in some way, such as asking whether a particular block of cells is the proper one to act on. You could, assuming Excel is visible on-screen of course, select the cells and then prompt the user:

```
Range("B2:C3").Select
Do
    reply = MsgBox("Is this the correct range?", vbYesNo)
    If reply = vbYes Then
        ' Code to process range goes here.
    Else
        ' Code to select another range goes here.
    End If
Loop While reply <> vbYes
```

Or, you could simply prompt the user to select the cells and then run the macro that processes the cells:

```
Public Sub SomeMacro()

Dim rng As Range

Set rng = Selection.Range
' Code to process rng goes here.

End Sub
```

RANGE OFFSETS, UNIONS, AND INTERSECTIONS

Use the Offset property to obtain a range that is offset by a specific amount with respect to another range. This is similar to the offset obtained using the Range.Range property, as discussed previously, but has the advantage of using a numerical offset rather than an alphanumeric column/row designator. The syntax is:

```
SomeRange.Offset(RowOffset, ColumnOffset)
```

The two arguments specify the number of rows or columns to offset by. Positive values are down and right, negative values are up and left. If either argument is omitted the default value of 0 is used. This example activates the cell that is three columns to the right of the current active cell on the worksheet SalesData:

```
Worksheets("SalesData").Activate
ActiveCell.Offset(columnOffset:=3).Activate
```

Use the Application object's Union method to create a range that refers to two or more discontinuous regions of a worksheet. The syntax is:

```
Application.Union(Range1, Range2, ..., Rangen)
```

The various Range arguments (there must be at least two) are the individual ranges to combine into the new range. The ranges must all be in the same worksheet or the Union method will fail. Here's an example that results in the cells B10, C12, and E14 all containing the text Hello:

```
Dim r1 As Range
Set r1 = Union(Range("B10"), Range("C12"), Range("E14"))
r1.Value = "Hello"
```

The Intersect method returns a range referencing the intersection of two or more ranges—in other words, the rectangular region where the ranges overlap. The syntax is:

```
Application.Intersect(Range1, Range2, ..., Rangen)
```

The various *Range* arguments (there must be at least two) are the individual ranges to intersect. The following code puts the text Hello in cells C12, C13, and C14:

```
Dim r1 As Range
Set r1 = Intersect(Range("B10:C14"), Range("C12:F15"))
r1.Value = "Hello"
```

If the ranges passed to `Intersect` do not overlap, the method returns the special value `Nothing`. This is illustrated in this code fragment, which selects the region where the ranges `rng1` and `rng2` overlap or, if they do not overlap, displays a message:

```
Dim r1 As Range
Set r1 = Intersect(Range("rng1"), Range("rng2"))
If r1 Is Nothing Then
    MsgBox("The two ranges do not overlap.")
Else
    r1.Select
End If
```

USING THE `Cells` PROPERTY

`Cells` is a property of the `Application`, `Worksheet`, and `Range` objects. It returns a `Range` object that references all of the cells (not just the used cells) in the active worksheet, the specified worksheet, or the specified range, respectively. The value of this property comes from the fact that you can use it to loop through the cells in a range, examining or performing some action on each cell. This is done using the `Range` object's `Item` property, which has two available syntax forms:

```
object.Cells.Item(RowIndex, ColumnIndex)
object.Cells.Item(RowIndex)
```

Object is a reference to the `Application` object or to a `Worksheet` or `Range` object. In the first syntax, *RowIndex* and *ColumnIndex* specify the location of a cell with respect to the top left corner of the range. In the second syntax, `RowIndex` is the offset of the cell in the range counting across then down. Suppose that `rng` is a range that is 4 columns wide and 3 rows high. The following two expressions both return a range that references the first cell in the second row of that range:

```
rng.Item.Cells(2,1)
rng.Item.Cells(5)
```

Because `Item` is the default property for the `Range` object, you can omit the `Item` keyword. The following two statements are equivalent:

```
Worksheets("Sheet1").Cells.Item(5,5)
Worksheets("Sheet1").Cells(5,5)
```

Let's look at some examples. This code sets the font to Arial and the font size to 12 for every cell in the active worksheet:

```
With Application.Cells.Font
    .Name = "Arial"
    .Size = 12
End With
```

This code fills cells B1:B10 in Sheet1 with the values 10, 20, ... 100:

```
Dim i As Integer
For i = 1 To 10
    Worksheets("Sheet1").Cells(2, i).Value = i * 10
Next i
```

This code looks at all the cells in the current region surrounding the active cell. The cell containing the largest value is formatted to display in red.

```
Dim row As Integer, col As Integer
Dim row_largest As Integer, col_largest As Integer
Dim largest_value As Double
Dim r As Range

Set r = ActiveCell.CurrentRegion
largest_value = r.Cells(1, 1).Value
row_largest = 1
col_largest = 1
For row = 1 To r.Width
    For col = 1 To r.Height
        If r.Cells(row, col) > largest_value Then
            largest_value = r.Cells(row, col).Value
            row_largest = row
            col_largest = col
        End If
    Next col
Next row

r.Cells(row_largest, col_largest).Font.Color = _
    RGB(255, 0, 0)]
```

NAMING RANGES

You can assign meaningful names, such as Sales1999 or IncomeTotal, to ranges in a workbook. Once you assign a name, you can refer to the range by this name. One way to define a named range is with the `Range` object's `Name` property:

```
Dim r As Range
Set r = Range("A2")
r.Name = "MyRange1"
```

Then you can refer to the range as follows:

```
Range("MyRange1").Value = 12
```

Range names assigned in this way have the limitation that they exist only as long as the code is running, and are not saved with the workbook. To create persistent named ranges that will be saved, use the `Name` object. A workbook has a `Names` collection containing one `Name` object for each named range. Use the `Add` method to define a named range:

```
ActiveWorkbook.Names.Add(Name, RefersTo)
```

Name is the name assigned to the range. *RefersTo* is the range specification in either relative or absolute format, using A1-style notation. Relative format refers to a cell or range relative to the currently active cell. For example, the *RefersTo* argument

```
=sheet1!b2
```

refers to the cell one column to the right and one row down from the active cell on sheet1. It will actually refer to cell b2 only if the active cell is a1. The same is true of multiple cell ranges, as shown in Table 6.6.

Table 6.6	Examples of relative range addresses.
If the Active Cell Is ...	**Then `=sheet1!b2:c3` Refers to Cells ...**
a1	b2:c3
b3	c4:d5
c1	d2:e3

A1-Style and R1C1-Style Notation

Excel uses two different notations to refer to worksheet ranges. A1-style notation uses the column letter followed by the row number, with absolute references indicated by dollar signs. R1C1-style notation has the form RxCy in which x is the row number and y is the column number. x and/or y are omitted if there is no relative offset, and relative references are indicated by brackets. The following R1C1 and A1 style references are equivalent:

$A$1	R1C1
A1	RC
A2	R[1]C
A1:C3	RC:R[2]C[2]
A2:C3	R[1]C:R[2]C[2]
$A$2:$C$3	R2C1:R3C3

To refer to a specific range of cells that is not relative to the active cell, use the absolute addressing format which places a dollar sign in front of the row and column references. The *RefersTo* argument

```
=sheet1!$b$2:$c$3
```

refers to cells b2:c3 in sheet1 regardless of the position of the active cell. This code creates a named range "Total" that refers to cell c2w2 on sheet1:

```
Names.Add Name:="Total", RefersTo:="=sheet1!$C$22"
```

Now you can refer to this range by its name:

```
If Range("Total").Value < 0 Then
...
```

The Names collection uses standard collection syntax. The Name object has the properties listed in Table 6.7.

Table 6.7   Properties of the Name object.

Property	Description
RefersTo	Specifies the range that the Name object refers to, in A1-style notation.
RefersToR1C1	Specifies the range that the Name object refers to, in R1C1-style notation.
RefersToRange	Returns a Range object that references the range that the Name object refers to.

The following code creates a new worksheet and then displays in it a list of all the named ranges in the workbook, and the addresses they refer to.

```
Dim r, w As Worksheet

Set w = Worksheets.Add
For r = 1 To Names.Count
    w.Cells(r, 1).Value = Names(r).Name
    w.Cells(r, 2).Value = Names(r).RefersToRange.Address
Next r
```

Manipulating Worksheet Contents

You have already seen some examples of manipulating worksheet contents. For the most part, the manipulations consist of either putting something into worksheet cells, or reading something out of worksheet cells. The Range object's Value property is used to both set and read cell data. For example, the statement

```
SomeRange.Value = data
```

puts *data* in the specified range. If SomeRange refers to more than one cell, then *data* is put into each of the cells in the range. Existing data is overwritten without warning. *Data* can be a number, text, a formula, or one of Excel's built in functions:

```
Range("A1").Value = 1234.56
Range("A2").Value = "Sales data"
Range("A3").Value = "=A1/2"
Range("B11").Value = "=sum(B1:B10)"
```

You use the Value property to obtain the value in a cell as well. If the specified range refers to a single cell, then the Value property returns whatever data—blank, number, or text—that is in the cell. If the range refers to more than one cell, Value returns an array containing the data in all the cells. You can use the IsArray function to test for this condition. Here's an example:

```
Dim x
x = Range("SalesTotals").Value
If IsArray(x) Then
    ' Code here to deal with x being an array.
Else
    ' Code here to deal with x being a single value.
End If
```

The array returned under these conditions is a two-dimensional array of type `Variant`. You can use the `UBound` and `LBound` functions to determine the size of the array (which of course is the same as the size of the range). Chapter 12 presents more information about VBA arrays.

Note that while a blank cell's `Value` property seems to return an empty string, it actually returns the special value `Empty`. You can test for this using the `IsEmpty` function:

```
If IsEmpty(Range("A1").Value) Then
    ' Cell A1 is empty.
Else
    ' Cell A1 is not empty.
End if
```

If you want to obtain the formula in a cell, use the `Formula` property. While `Value` will return the results of the formula, `Formula` returns the formula itself. For cells that do not contain formulas, `Formula` works just like `Value`. Look at this code:

```
Dim f, v
Range("A1").Value = 5
Range("A2").Value = 7
Range("A3").Value = "=A1+A2"
v = Range("A3").Value
f = Range("A3").Formula
```

After this code executes, the variable `v` contains the value 12 while the variable `f` contains the string "=A1+A2".

Table 6.8 describes some additional methods of the `Range` object.

Finding and Replacing Data

You can search a range for data using the `Find` method. This method returns a single cell range that refers to the cell where a match is found, or to the special value `Nothing` if there is no match. The syntax is:

```
SomeRange.Find(What, After, LookIn, LookAt, SearchOrder, _
    SearchDirection, MatchCase, MatchByte)
```

What is the data to find. It can be any Excel data type. This is the only required argument of the `Find` method.

After specifies the single cell in the range after which the search is to start. If omitted the search starts in the top left cell of the range.

LookIn specifies what data is to be searched. Possible values are `xlFormula`, `xlValues` (the default), and `xlComments`.

Table 6.8	Range object methods.
Method	**Action**
AddComment(*Text*)	Adds the specified comment to the range.
AutoFit	Adjusts the width of columns in the range to fit their data.
Calculate	Recalculates all formulas in the range.
Clear	Clears cell contents and formatting from the range.
ClearComments	Clears cell comments from the range.
ClearContents	Clears cell contents from the range, but retains formatting.
ClearFormats	Clears cell formats from the range.
ClearNotes	Clears notes and sound notes from the range.
Delete(*Shift*)	Deletes cells in the range along with their contents. Adjacent cells are shifted up or to the left to replace the deleted cells. Set *Shift* to either xlShiftToLeft or xlShiftUp to specify the shift direction. If *Shift* is omitted, Excel decides based on the shape of the range.
Insert(*Shift*)	Inserts new empty cells, shifting the existing range down or to the right to make room. Set *Shift* to either xlShiftToRight or xlShift-Down to specify the shift direction. If *Shift* is omitted, Excel decides based on the shape of the range.
Justify	Rearranges text in the range so it fits evenly.

LookAt can be either xlPart or xlWhole specifying whether the entire data item or only part of it is to be matched.

SearchOrder can be either xlByColumns or xlByRows specifying the order in which the cells in the range are searched.

SearchDirection is either xlNext (the default) or xlPrevious specifying the direction of the search.

MatchCase is True or False (the default) specifying whether the search is case-sensitive.

MatchByte is relevant only when double-byte language support is installed. True means that double-byte characters match only double-byte characters, while False means that double-byte characters will match the single-byte equivalents.

When you call the Find method, values specified for the *LookIn*, *LookAt*, *SearchOrder*, and *MatchByte* arguments are saved and will be in effect the next time you call Find unless you explicitly change them.

After calling Find you can call FindPrevious or FindNext to continue the search. The syntax is:

```
SomeRange.FindNext(After)
SomeRange.FindPrevious(After)
```

The optional *After* argument has the same meaning as the `Find` method. Typically, you will pass the range that was returned by the previous `Find` or `FindNext` so that the search continues from where it left off. Note that these methods do not keep track of where they have already searched, and will loop back and search the range again if left to themselves. It is up to the programmer to keep track, typically by storing the address of the first cell where a match is found and comparing subsequent matches with it. Listing 6–1 shows a function that returns the number of times the specified text is found in the specified range.

Listing 6–1   *CountStrings returns the number of times text is found in a range.*

```
Public Function CountStrings(rng As Range, template As String)

Dim count As Long
Dim r As Range
Dim FirstAddress

count = 0
'Find the first instance.
Set r = rng.Find(template)

' If not found, return 0.
If r Is Nothing Then
    CountStrings = 0
    Exit Function
' If found, loop to find any other instances.
Else
    ' Save the first location's address.
    FirstAddress = r.Address
    Do
        count = count + 1
        ' Find next instance starting where we left off.
        Set r = rng.FindNext(r)
    ' Loop until we return to the first location.
    Loop While r.Address <> FirstAdress

End If

CountStrings = count

End Function
```

To replace data in a range, use the `Replace` method. The syntax is:

```
SomeRange.Replace(What, Replacement, LookAt, SearchOrder, _
    MatchCase, MatchByte)
```

What is the string to be replaced, and *Replacement* is the string to replace it with. The other arguments have the same meanings as they do for the `Find` method. The `Replace` method always returns True. Here are some examples. To replace every instance of "New York" with "Illinois" in column B of Sheet2:

```
Worksheets("Sheet1").Columns("B").Replace _
    What:="New York", Replacement:="Illinois"
```

To replace every instance of "SALES" with "Sales" in the range A1:C100:

```
Range("A1:C100").Replace What:="SALES", _
    Replacement:="Sales" _
    MatchCase:=True
```

The Active Cell and Current Selection

None of these methods—`Find`, `FindNext`, `FindPrevious`, **or** `Replace`—**has any effect on the active cell or the current selection in a worksheet.**

Sorting Data

You can sort the data in a range using the `Sort` method. You can sort worksheet rows into order based on the data in one, two, or three columns. The syntax for `Sort` is:

```
SomeRange.Sort(Key1, Order1, Key2, Order2, _
               Key3, Order3, Header)
```

Key1, *Key2*, and *Key3* specify the columns on which the sort is to be based. Only *Key1* is required; *Key2* and *Key3* are optional and are used only when there is a tie in the *Key1* sort order. You can specify these arguments as a cell address or range name.

Order1, *Order2*, and *Order3* specify the sort order for the corresponding keys. Possible settings are `xlAscending` (0–9, a–z) and `xlDescending` (z–a, 9–0), with the default being `xlAscending`.

Header specifies whether the range has a header row—a row of labels identifying the data in the columns. You want a header row to remain at the top of the range and not be sorted with the other data. Possible settings are `xlYes`, `xlNo` (the default), and `xlGuess`. Use the last setting to have Excel try to determine if there is a header by examining the data.

This code sorts the data in the current region surrounding the active cell based on the data in the leftmost column, in ascending order:

```
With ActiveCell
    .CurrentRegion.Sort Key1:=.CurrentRegion.Cells(1, 1)
End With
```

This code sorts the data in range A1:D400 in descending order based on the data in column A as the first key and column C as the second key. A header row is assumed.

```
Range("A1:D400").Sort Key1:=Range("A1"), _
    Order1:=xlDescending, Key2:=Range("C1"), _
    Order2:=xlDescending, Header:=xlYes
```

Working with Charts

Creating charts is one of Excel's strong points. You can choose from a wide variety of chart types suitable to just about any data you can imagine. You have the common types such as bar charts, line charts, and pie charts, as well as more specialized types such as scatter charts, radar charts, doughnut charts, and stock quote charts. You have full control over many aspects of chart display, including colors, backgrounds, titles, legends, and axes. I strongly recommend that you spend some time working with Excel charts to gain some familiarity with the options available, as it is impossible to present all the details within the space limitations of this chapter.

Chart Sheets Versus Embedded Charts

An Excel workbook has two ways of displaying charts. One method has each individual chart on its own worksheet, called a chart sheet. A chart sheet contains only a chart, and does not have rows and columns for data. The second method displays a chart embedded on a standard data worksheet. In both cases the charts are essentially the same, they differ only in how they are displayed. Figures 6–2 and 6–3 show the differences.

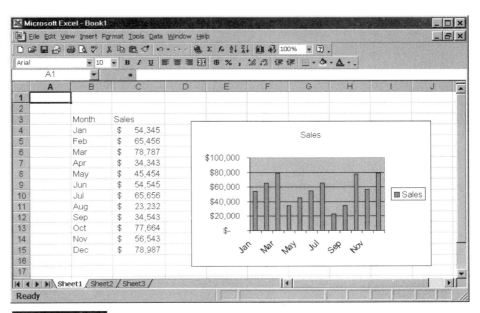

Figure 6–2   *This chart is embedded on a worksheet.*

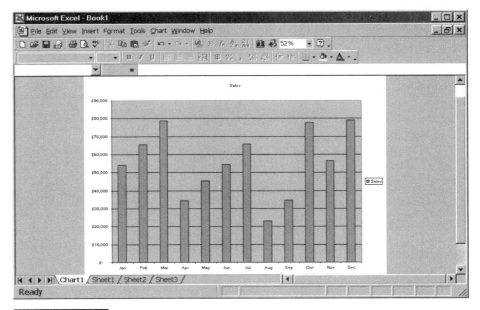

Figure 6–3   *This chart is displayed on a chart sheet.*

Chart sheets are represented by the `Charts` collection, which contains a `Chart` object for each chart sheet in the specified workbook (`Workbook` object) or the active workbook (`Application` object). Thus, this code prints all the chart sheets in the workbook Sales.xls:

```
Workbooks("Sales.xls").Charts.Printout
```

This code adds a new chart sheet to the active workbook:

```
Charts.Add
```

As with other collections, you can assign a name to each chart in the `Charts` collection and then use that name to refer to the object later:

```
Dim ch As Excel.Chart
Set ch = Charts.Add
ch.Name = "Sales"
```

Each chart that is embedded on a worksheet is also represented by a `ChartObject` object that serves as a container for a `Chart` object. This may seem unnecessarily complex but is required because an embedded chart can be displayed with different sizes and positions, unlike a chart on a chart sheet. The properties of the `ChartObject` object control the appearance and size of the embedded chart. Each `Worksheet` object has a `ChartObjects` collection that contains one `ChartObject` object for each embedded chart on the worksheet. To add an embedded chart to a worksheet, use the `Add` method:

```
Chartobjects.Add(Left, Top, Width, Height)
```

Left and *Top* specify the position of the top left corner of the chart, with respect to the top left corner of the worksheet. *Width* and *Height* specify the chart size. All four arguments are required and are in units of *points*, (1 point = 1/72 inch). You can use the `InchesToPoints` function to convert measurement units. We'll look at the `ChartObject` object in more detail soon, but first we need to understand the `Chart` object.

The Chart Object

Each chart in a workbook, whether embedded in a worksheet or on a chart sheet, is represented by a `Chart` object. The data the chart displays is specified using the `Chart` object's `SetSourceData` method. The syntax is:

```
MyChart.SetSourceData(Source, PlotBy)
```

Source is a reference to a `Range` object representing the data to be charted; this argument is required. The optional *PlotBy* specifies whether data series are in rows (`xlRows`, the default) or in columns (`xlColumns`). The data to be charted is typically arranged in a rectangular table, with the left column and the top row containing labels that identify the data. Figure 6–4 shows a range of data arranged in this manner. Other arrangements are possible, but not common.

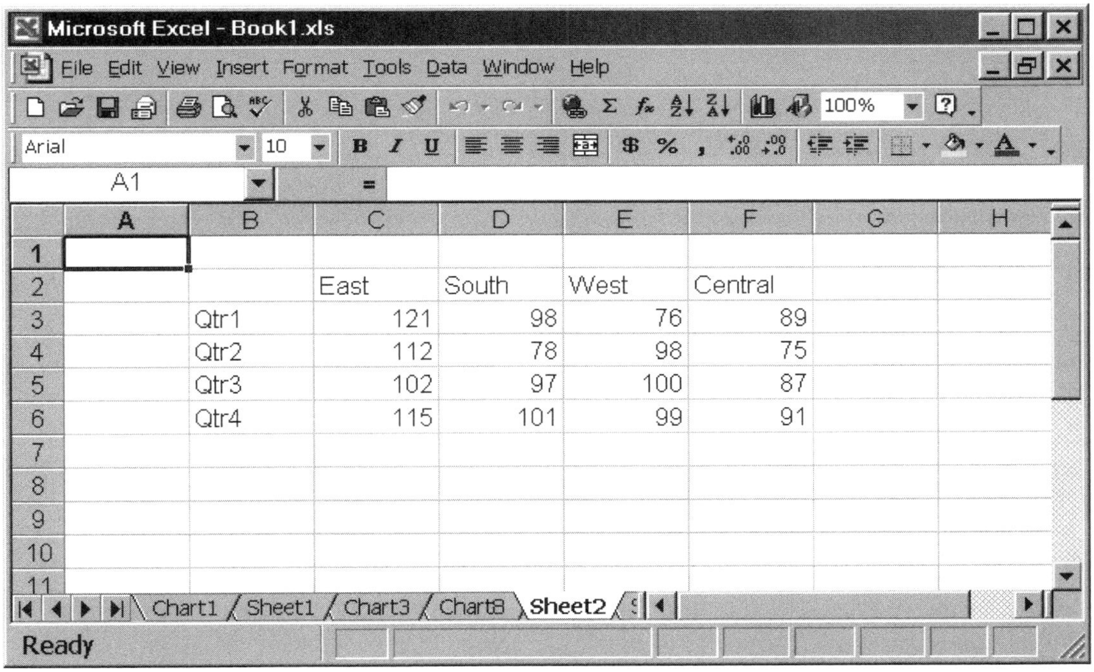

Figure 6–4 *Data arranged in an appropriate format for charting.*

In addition to specifying the data range, the one other fundamental part of creating a chart is specifying the chart type. This is set by means of the `Chart` object's `ChartType` property, and the possible values are `xlChart-Type` constants. Excel has 14 basic chart types, such as bar, line, and column. Each of these fundamental types then has several subtypes. For example, `xlColumnClustered` specifies a clustered column chart, `xlColumnStacked` specifies a stacked column chart, and so on. Rather than listing the several dozen chart type constants here, I suggest you use the Object Browser to identify them.

Before we get to additional details, let's look at a couple of examples. The following code creates a new chart sheet, creates a clustered column chart using the data shown in Figure 6–4, then activates the chart sheet. The resulting chart is shown in Figure 6–5.

```
Dim c As Excel.Chart

Set c = Charts.Add
c.ChartType = xl3DColumnClustered
c.SetSourceData Source:=Worksheets("Sheet2").Range("B2:F6")
c.Activate
```

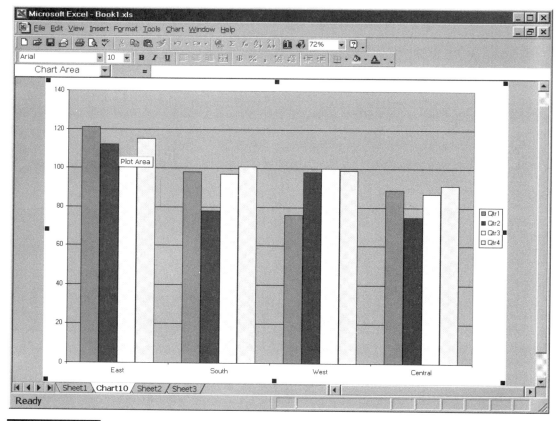

Figure 6–5   *The chart sheet created by the sample code.*

To create an embedded chart on the same worksheet as the data, use the following code. The result is shown in Figure 6–6.

```
Dim co As Excel.ChartObject

With Application
```

```
Set co = _
    .ActiveWorkbook.Worksheets("Sheet2").ChartObjects.Add( _
        .InchesToPoints(4.2), _
        .InchesToPoints(0.25), _
        .InchesToPoints(3.5), _
        .InchesToPoints(3))
End With
co.Chart.ChartType = xlColumnClustered
co.Chart.SetSourceData Source:=Worksheets( _
    "Sheet2").Range("B2:F6")
co.Activate
```

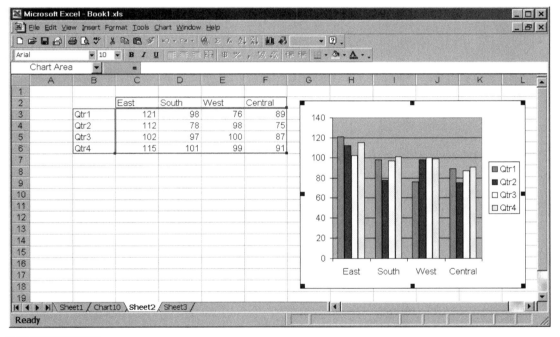

Figure 6–6   *The embedded chart created by the above code fragment.*

Most Excel charts work with categories and data series. Take a look at the chart in Figure 6–5. Because this chart was plotted with the default *PlotBy* setting of xlRows, each row in the data range is used as a data series while the categories are represented by the columns. Thus Qtr1, Qtr2, Qtr3, and Qtr4 are the data series while East, South, West, and Central are the categories. You can see from the chart that categories are plotted on the horizontal axis, while the data series are differentiated by different bar colors or symbols in the graph. In a chart like this, the horizontal axis is the *category* axis and the vertical axis is the *value* axis.

Active Charts

When a chart is active you can use the `ActiveChart` property to refer to it. This property is available with three objects:

- `Application`. The active chart in the active workbook.
- `Window`. The active chart in the specified window.
- `Workbook`. The active chart in the specified workbook.

If the `ActiveChart` keyword is used without an object qualifier, it returns a reference to the active chart in the active workbook. A chart on a chart sheet is active if its sheet is active. An embedded chart is active if it has been selected by the user or activated with the `Activate` method. If no chart is active, this property returns `Nothing`.

The ChartWizard Method

The `ChartWizard` method is used to modify the appearance of a chart. It is easier to use than changing individual properties of a chart one at a time (although you will use that method sometimes as well). The syntax is:

```
ChartToModify.ChartWizard(Source, Gallery, Format, PlotBy, _
    CategoryLabels, SeriesLabels, HasLegend, Title, _
    ValueTitle, ExtraTitle)
```

- *Source*. A Range object referencing the data to be plotted.
- *Gallery*. An xlChartType constant specifying the type of chart: xlArea, xlBar, xlColumn, xlLine, xlPie, xlRadar, xlXYScatter, xlCombination, xl3DArea, xl3DBar, xl3DColumn, xl3DLine, xl3DPie, xl3DSurface, xlDoughnut, or xlDefaultAutoFormat.
- *Format*. A numerical value in the range 1-*n* specifying the built-in autoformat, or chart subtype. The type and number of autoformats, and hence the maximum value of *n*, depends on the *Gallery* argument.
- *PlotBy*. Either xlRows (the default) or xlColumns specifying whether data should be plotted by rows or by columns.
- *CategoryLabels*. The number of columns (if *PlotBy* = xlRows) or the number of rows (if *PlotBy* = xlColumns) containing category labels.
- *SeriesLabels*. The number of rows (if *PlotBy* = xlRows) or the number of columns (if *PlotBy* = xlColumns) containing data series labels.

- *HasLegend*. True to include a legend, otherwise False.
- *Title*. The text of the chart's title.
- *CategoryTitle*. The text of the category axis label.
- *ValueTitle*. The text of the value axis label.
- *ExtraTitle*. The text of the series axis title for 3D charts or the second value axis for 2D charts.

All of the arguments to the `ChartWizard` method are individually optional, but of course it makes no sense to call the method with no arguments. Note, however, that the method will fail and generate an error if *Source* is omitted and an existing chart is not currently active.

You can use the `ChartWizard` method to define the details of a chart at the same time it is created. Using the data shown in Figure 6–4, the following code creates the new chart sheet shown in Figure 6–7.

```
With Charts.Add
    .ChartWizard Source:= _
        Worksheets("Sheet2").Range("B2:F6"), _
        Gallery:=xlLine, _
        PlotBy:=xlRows, _
        CategoryLabels:=1, _
        SeriesLabels:=1, _
        Title:="Quarterly units by region", _
        ValueTitle:="Units in thousands"
End With
```

You can also use the `ChartWizard` method to modify an existing chart. This code prompts the user to enter the title for the existing chart named "SalesData":

```
Charts("SalesData").ChartWizard _
    title:=InputBox("Title for chart?")
```

Using the `ChartWizard` method to modify a chart is of course limited to those aspects of a chart that the method deals with. Working with other aspects of chart appearance is covered next.

Controlling Chart Appearance

The `Chart` object is a complex structure. It has a number of properties and methods that control various aspects of its appearance. It also contains some subobjects that represent components of the chart, such as the axes. Some chart manipulations, therefore, require setting the properties of one or more of these subobjects. A simplified diagram of the `Chart` object structure is shown in Figure 6–8.

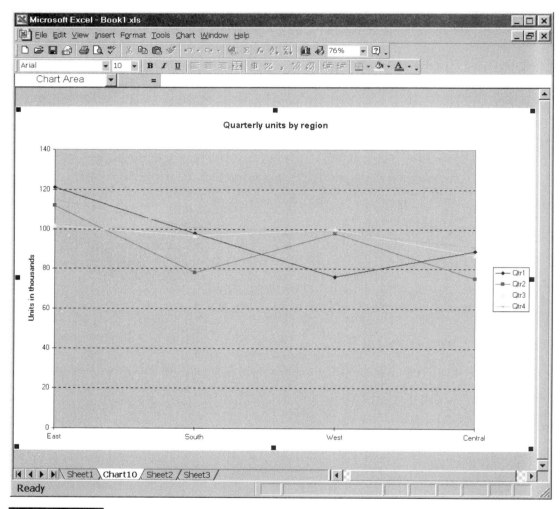

Figure 6–7 *A chart created using the ChartWizard method.*

The Legend object represents the chart's legend. Properties of the Legend object control the overall appearance of the legend, such as its font and border. Each individual entry in the legend is represented by a LegendEntry object in the LegendEntries collection. Display of the legend is controlled by the Chart object's HasLegend property, which can be set to True or False.

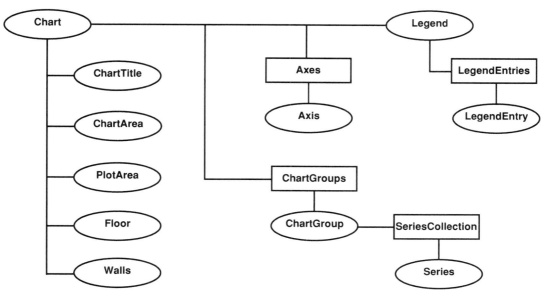

Figure 6–8   *A simplified diagram of* Chart *object structure, with collections represented by rectangles and objects by ovals.*

Each of the chart's axes is represented by an Axis object in the Axes collection. The appearance of an individual axis is controlled by the settings of the corresponding Axis object. Which axes, if any, the chart has is controlled by the Chart object's HasAxis property.

A ChartGroup object represents one or more data series that are plotted on the chart using the same format. Each data series in a ChartGroup object is represented by a Series object in the SeriesCollection collection. In most charts, a single ChartGroup object contains only a single data series.

The ChartTitle object represents the chart title. Properties of the ChartTitle object specify the text and appearance of the title.

On a 2D chart the ChartArea object represents the area containing the axes, axis titles, chart title, and legend. On a 3D chart it represents the area including the chart title and legend. Properties of the ChartArea object control such things as the size and background pattern of the chart area.

The PlotArea object represents the plot area of a chart, the area where the data is plotted. On both 2D and 3D charts the plot area contains the data markers, gridlines, data labels, and trendlines. On 3D charts it also contains the walls, floor, axes, and tick mark labels.

The Floor and Walls objects represent the floor and walls, respectively, of a 3D plot. Properties of these objects control the color and other aspects of the appearance of a 3D plot's walls and floor.

THE ChartObject OBJECT

A chart that is embedded on a worksheet is contained within a ChartObject object. The ChartObject object controls the size of the chart and certain aspects of its appearance. Each worksheet has a ChartObjects collection that contains all of the ChartObject objects corresponding to the worksheet's embedded charts, in the order they were created. The properties and methods listed in Tables 6.9 and 6.10 are used to control the display of the chart, as well as to perform some other tasks.

Table 6.9	Properties of the ChartObject object.
Property	**Description**
Border	Returns a Border object representing the ChartObject's border.
BottomRightCell	Returns a Range object representing the worksheet cell that lies under the chart's bottom right corner. Read only.
Chart	Returns a Chart object representing the chart displayed.
Enabled	True/False value specifying whether the chart is enabled.
Height, Width	The height and width of the ChartObject, in points.
Interior	Returns an Interior object that controls the formatting of the interior of the ChartObject.
Left, Top	The distance in points of the top corner of the ChartObject from the top left corner of the worksheet.
Placement	Specifies how the ChartObject is attached to the worksheet cells beneath it. Possible settings are xlMoveAndSize, xlMove, and xlFreeFloating.
PrintObject	True if the ChartObject is to be printed when the worksheet is printed; otherwise False.
RoundedCorners	True/False value specifying whether the ChartObject has rounded corners.
TopLeftCell	Returns a Range object representing the worksheet cell that lies under the chart's top left corner. Read only.
Visible	True/False value specifying whether the ChartObject is visible.

Table 6.10	Methods of the `ChartObject` object.
Method	**Description**
`BringToFront`	Brings the `ChartObject` to the top of the z-order, which means it will be displayed "on top" of any overlapping charts.
`Copy`	Copies the `ChartObject` to the clipboard.
`CopyPicture`	Copies the chart to the clipboard as a picture.
`Cut`	Cuts the `ChartObject` to the clipboard.
`Delete`	Deletes the `ChartObject`.
`Duplicate`	Duplicates the `ChartObject` and returns a reference to the duplicate. The new `ChartObject` is located on top of the original.
`Select`	Selects the `ChartObject`.
`SendToBack`	Sends the `ChartObject` to the bottom of the z-order, which means it will be displayed "behind" any overlapping charts.

Let's look at some examples of working with the `ChartObject` object. This code reduces the size of the first embedded chart on Sheet2 by 50 percent:

```
With Worksheets("Sheet2").ChartObjects(1)
    .Height = .Height / 2
    .Width = .Width / 2
End With
```

This code copies the first embedded chart on Sheet1 to the clipboard, and then pastes the copy into Sheet3 with the top left corner located in cell G4:

```
Worksheets("Sheet1").ChartObjects(1).Copy
Worksheets("Sheet3").Activate
Worksheets("Sheet3").Range("G4").Activate
Worksheets("Sheet3").Paste
```

This code makes a duplicate of the second embedded chart on Sheet1, then moves it to display just below the original chart and changes the chart type to Line:

```
With Worksheets("Sheet1").ChartObjects(2).Duplicate
    .Top = .Top + .Height + 14
    .Chart.ChartType = xlLine
End With
```

Here's something a bit more involved. The procedure `PrintAll-Charts`, shown in Listing 6–2, is passed a reference to a workbook. The procedure goes through all the worksheets in the workbook, copying every embedded chart to a new worksheet. The copied charts are arranged in a single column down the left side of the new worksheet. The new worksheet containing all the charts is printed, and then deleted. Comments in the code explain how things work.

Listing 6–2	*PrintAllCharts prints all embedded charts in a workbook.*

```vba
Public Sub PrintAllCharts(wb As Excel.Workbook)

Dim ws As Excel.Worksheet
Dim co As Excel.ChartObject
Dim NewSheet As Excel.Worksheet
Dim TopCoordinate As Long
Dim OldDisplayAlertsSetting As Boolean

' Initial top coordinate.
TopCoordinate = 10
' Add a new worksheet.
Set NewSheet = wb.Worksheets.Add

' Loop for each worksheet in the workbook.
For Each ws In wb.Worksheets
    ' Skip the newly added worksheet.
    If ws.Name <> NewSheet.Name Then
        ' Loop once for each ChartObject on the worksheet.
        For Each co In ws.ChartObjects
            ' Copy the Chartobject to the clipboard.
            co.Copy
            With NewSheet
                ' Paste the ChartObject into the new worksheet.
                .Paste
                ' Move it to the proper position.
                .ChartObjects(.ChartObjects.Count).Top = _
                    TopCoordinate
                .ChartObjects(.ChartObjects.Count).Left = 0
                ' Update the TopCoordinate value to indicate
                ' 10 points below the just-added chart.
                TopCoordinate = TopCoordinate + _
                    .ChartObjects(.ChartObjects.Count).Height + 10
            End With
        Next co
    End If
Next ws

' Print the new worksheet.
```

```
NewSheet.PrintOut
' Turn off alerts, saving the original setting, so the new
' worksheet can be deleted without a prompt being dislayed.
OldDisplayAlertsSetting = Application.DisplayAlerts
Application.DisplayAlerts = False
' Delete the worksheet.
NewSheet.Delete
' Return the DisplayAlerts property to its original value.
Application.DisplayAlerts = OldDisplayAlertsSetting

End Sub
```

The **Application** Object

If your VBA code is running within Excel, then the Excel application object is automatically available to you by using the `Application` keyword. If you are automating Excel from another Office application you must explicitly create an instance of Excel and use a reference to that instance to access the `Application` object. For example, this code could be run from any other Office application to start a hidden copy of Excel, create a new workbook, and put the value 12 in cell A1 of Sheet1:

```
Dim MyXLApp As Excel.Application
Set MyXLApp = New Excel.Application
MyXLApp.Workbooks.Add
MyXLApp.Worksheets("Sheet1").Cells(1,1).Value = 12
```

Note that when Excel is started programmatically, it does not automatically have a new workbook—you must explicitly create a new workbook, if you need one, as is done in the third line of the code fragment above. The number of worksheets in a new book is specified by the `Application.SheetsInNewWorkbook` property, which has the default value of 3. This is one of the Excel options that I will cover in more detail in the next section.

Object References

When VBA code is running within Excel, the `Application` object is available implicitly. Thus, you could write the following:

```
Workbooks.Add
```

and the implicit reference causes the "Workbooks" keyword to automatically apply to the `Excel.Application` object. When your code is running in another Office application, however, you must create a reference to the Excel application and reference it explicitly. For example, in a procedure that will run in Word you could write the following:

```
Dim xlApp As Excel.Application
Set xlApp = New Excel.Application
xlApp.Workbooks.Add
```

The `Application` object makes several useful object references available to you, most of which you have seen used earlier in this chapter. They are `ActiveCell`, `ActiveChart`, `ActivePrinter`, `ActiveSheet`, `ActiveWindow`, and `ActiveWorkbook`.

Excel Options and Settings

When you are using Excel, you can use the options dialog box to set options that control various aspects of program operation. You can also set these options in code. In Excel, options are properties of the `Application` object. This is different from Word which, as you learned in the previous chapter, has the `Options` object whose properties represent the individual options. The options you'll probably need to change most often are explained in Table 6.11.

Table 6.11 Excel `Application` option properties.

Property	Description
Calculation	Specifies when workbook formulas are recalculated. Possible settings are `xlCalculationManual`, `xlCalculationAutomatic`, and `xlCalculationSemiAutomatic`.
Caption	Specifies the name that appears in Excel's title bar.
Columns, Rows	Returns a range containing all of the columns or rows on the active worksheet.
Cursor	Specifies the appearance of the mouse pointer. Possible values are `xlDefault`, `xlWait` (hourglass), `xlNorthwestArrow`, and `xlIBeam`.
DefaultFilePath	Specifies the folder where files are opened from and saved to by default.
Dialogs	Returns a `Dialogs` collection that contains Excel's built-in dialog boxes. See Chapter 5 for an explanation of using Word's built-in dialog boxes, which work in the same manner as Excel's.
Interactive	True/False value specifying whether Excel will respond to keyboard and mouse input.
Height, Width	Specifies the size of the Excel window, in points.
Left, Top	Specifies the position of the Excel window, in points, with respect to the top left corner of the screen.
Path	The path of the active workbook.
UsableHeight, UsableWidth	The size of the usable window area, in points.
Visible	True/False value specifying whether Excel is visible on-screen.

Using the WorksheetFunction Object

As you probably know, Excel has a wide variety of built-in functions that perform calculations on data in a worksheet. You can use VBA code to insert these functions into worksheet cells, and then retrieve the result of the function calculation. Suppose, for example, that cells A1:A10 contain numbers, and you want to know what the largest value is. The max function returns the largest value in a range, so you could put the function in another cell and then retrieve the result:

```
Worksheets("Sheet1").Range("A11").Value = "=max(A1:A10)"
LargestValue = Worksheets("Sheet1").Range("A11").Value
```

If, however, the worksheet itself does not need this value displayed, but you need only the value for calculation in your VBA code, you can use the WorkSheetFunction object to obtain the result of applying an Excel function to a worksheet range without actually inserting the function in the worksheet. The WorkSheetFunction object is obtained from the Application object's WorkSheetFunction property. The syntax is:

```
Application.WorksheetFunction.FunctionName(FunctionArguments)
```

FunctionName is the name of the worksheet function, and *FunctionArguments* are the arguments required by that function. This example replaces the code shown above:

```
LargestValue = _
   Application.WorksheetFunction.Max(Range("A1:A10"))
```

Windows and Panes in Excel

Excel offers the same windowing flexibility as other Office applications. Of course windows are not relevant if you are automating Excel as a hidden application, but some situations require that Excel be visible to the user and you may need to work with the windows and panes. For the most part, Excel windows and panes work the same as windows and panes in Word, and you can refer to Chapter 5 for the details.

Events in Excel

Most of the events you will be working with occur at the level of the Workbook, Worksheet, or Chart objects. A good number of the events are detected by two or three of these objects, so you have a great deal of flexibility as to how you use the events. Table 6.12 describes those events that are detected by two or all three of these objects.

	Table 6.12	Events detected by two or three of the `Workbook`, `Worksheet`, and `Chart` objects.

Event	Detected By	Description
`Activate`	Ch, Wb, Ws	Occurs when the object is activated.
`BeforeDoubleClick`	Ch, Ws	Occurs when the object is double-clicked, before the default double-click event. See below for details.
`BeforeRightClick`	Ch, Ws	Occurs when the object is right-clicked, before the default right-click event. See below for details.
`Calculate`	Ch, Ws	Occurs after the worksheet recalculates its formulas, and after the chart plots new data.
`Deactivate`	Ch, Wb, Ws	Occurs when the object is deactivated.

The `BeforeDoubleClick` and `BeforeRightClick` events can be used to intercept these actions and modify or cancel Excel's default actions that occur in response to these user actions. For the `Worksheet` object, the syntax is:

```
Sub Worksheet_BeforeRightClick(ByVal Target As Range, _
    Cancel As Boolean)
Sub Worksheet_BeforeDoubleClick(ByVal Target As Range, _
    Cancel As Boolean)
```

Target is a Range object referring to the cell nearest the location of the mouse pointer when the event occurs. *Cancel* is initially False; if set to True by code in the event procedure, then Excel's default response to the event is cancelled. The event procedure shown in Listing 6–3 demonstrates.

	Listing 6–3	*Using the BeforeRightClick event to cancel right-click events in the range A1:B10.*

```
Private Sub Worksheet_BeforeRightClick(ByVal Target As Range, _
    Cancel As Boolean)

Dim r As Range

Set r = Application.Intersect(Target, Range("A1:B10"))
If Not r Is Nothing Then Cancel = True

End Sub
```

For the `Chart` object, the syntax for these event procedures is:

```
Private Sub Chart_BeforeRightClick(Cancel As Boolean)
Private Sub Chart_BeforeDoubleClick( _
    ByVal ElementID As Long, ByVal Arg1 As Long, _
    ByVal Arg2 As Long, Cancel As Boolean)
```

In both cases *Cancel* is initially False; if set to True by code in the event procedure, the default response to the user input is cancelled. The additional arguments for the `BeforeDoubleClick` event procedure provide details about which element of the chart was double-clicked. You can find additional information about these arguments in the online help documentation.

WithEvents

Objects that will respond to events must be declared in a class module with the `WithEvents` keyword. Otherwise, the events described here will not be available.

Table 6.13 describes events detected by the `Workbook` object.

Table 6.13	Events detected by the `Workbook` object.

Event	Description
`BeforeClose(Cancel As Boolean)`	Occurs before the workbook closes. If code in the event procedure sets *Cancel* to true, the close operation is cancelled.
`BeforePrint(Cancel As Boolean)`	Occurs before the workbook is printed. If code in the event procedure sets *Cancel* to true, the print operation is cancelled.
`BeforeSave(SaveAsUI As Boolean, Cancel As Boolean)`	Occurs before the workbook is saved. *SaveAsUI* is True if the SaveAs dialog box will be displayed. If code in the event procedure sets *Cancel* to true, the save operation is cancelled.
`NewSheet(Sh As Worksheet)`	Occurs when a new sheet is created in the workbook. *Sh* is a reference to the new `Worksheet` object.
`Open`	Occurs when the workbook is opened.
`SheetActivate(Sh As Worksheet)`	Occurs when any sheet is activated (worksheet or chart sheet). *Sh* is a reference to the just-activated sheet.

Table 6.13	Events detected by the `Workbook` object. (Continued)
Event	**Description**
`SheetBeforeDoubleClick(Sh As Worksheet Target As Range, Cancel As Boolean)` `SheetBeforeRightClick(Sh As Worksheet, Target As Range, Cancel As Boolean)`	Occurs when any worksheet is double-clicked or right-clicked, before the default click action. `Sh` is a reference to the sheet, and `Target` is a reference to a `Range` object representing the clicked cell. Setting `Cancel` to True cancels the default action.
`SheetCalculate(Sh As Worksheet)`	Occurs after any worksheet is recalculated or any changed data is plotted on a chart. `Sh` is a reference to the sheet.
`SheetSelectionChange(Sh As Worksheet, Target As Range)`	Occurs when the selection changes in a worksheet. `Sh` is a reference to the sheet, and `Target` is a reference to the newly selected range.
`WindowActivate(Wb As Workbook, Wn As Window)`	Occurs when any workbook window is activated. `Wb` is a reference to the workbook, and `Wn` is a reference to the window.
`WindowDeactivate(Wb As Workbook, Wn As Window)`	Occurs when any workbook window is deactivated. `Wb` is a reference to the workbook, and `Wn` is a reference to the window.
`WindowResize(Wb As Workbook, Wn As Window)`	Occurs when any workbook window is resized. `Wb` is a reference to the workbook, and `Wn` is a reference to the window.

Let's look at some examples of using Excel events. This event procedure selects cell A1 whenever the worksheet is activated:

```
Private Sub Worksheet_Activate()

Range("A1").Select

End Sub
```

This code prevents the default double-click action from occurring in Sheet1:

```
Private Sub Workbook_SheetBeforeDoubleClick(ByVal _
    Sh As Object, _ByVal Target As Range, Cancel As Boolean)
```

```
If Sh.Name = "Sheet1" Then Cancel = True

End Sub
```

This code displays a warning message if the user selects a block of cells on Sheet1 that is less that 4 columns wide:

```
Private Sub Workbook_SheetSelectionChange( _
    ByVal Sh As Object, ByVal Target As Range)

If Sh.Name = "Sheet1" And Target.Columns.Count < 4 Then
    MsgBox ("Range must be at least 4 columns wide.")
End If

End Sub
```

This code activates Sheet3 whenever the workbook is opened:

```
Private Sub Workbook_Open()

Sheet3.Activate

End Sub
```

This code puts the current date and time in cell A1 of any new worksheet that is added to the workbook:

```
Private Sub Workbook_NewSheet(ByVal Sh As Object)

Sh.Range("A1").Value = Now

End Sub
```

Summing Up

Excel provides you with a great deal of power and flexibility when it comes to storing and manipulating numerical data. In addition, it provides sophisticated charting capabilities for visual presentation of data and built-in functions for performing a variety of calculations. You can be sure that information in Excel is up-to-date, because any changes to the data are automatically reflected in calculations and charts. Once you understand the Excel object model and its capabilities, you can start putting them to work in your custom applications.

Using Data Access Components

The term data *is often used in a generic sense to refer to almost any kind of information. In some contexts, however, it has a more specific meaning and refers to data maintained by database programs. Access is the database component of Office designed to work with databases. A database is a specific format for maintaining data that uses a record and field format. Each individual entry in a database table is a record, and each piece of information contained in a record is a field. In a mailing list database, for example, each person's entry is a record, and each piece of information—name, address, city, and so on—is a field. Sometimes you will hear records referred to as rows, and fields as columns. Vast amounts of information are kept in databases, ranging from financial records to warehouse inventories to airline schedules. Database programming is one of the most common tasks faced by Office developers, and this chapter will get you on your way to being able to use Office's data access capabilities in your custom applications.*

Access Fundamentals

Access is a *relational* database program, meaning that it can work not only with single database tables, but also with relationships between the data in two or more database tables. A relationship is created when two database tables have one or more fields in common. Suppose, for example, you have an inventory database table where each record contains, in addition to fields for information about the item, another field holding a number that identifies the supplier for that item. Then you have a second database table that contains information about your suppliers. Each record contains the supplier name, address, etc., as well as a field for the supplier number. The two database tables are linked by the presence of the common field, supplier number. This relationship lets you perform tasks such as determining the supplier for a particular item, or listing all the items that come from a particular supplier. A single set of records, all of which contain the same fields, is called a *database table*. In the previous example, Inventory and Suppliers would each be a database table. The set of all related database tables is called a *database* or *database file*.

Database activities usually fall into one of three categories:

1. Entering and editing data,
2. Performing *queries* or asking questions about the data, and
3. Creating reports to summarize the data.

Access has powerful capabilities for each of these activities. As with the other Office applications, you can use Access alone in a custom application to perform many tasks, but more often it is used in conjunction with other Office applications to create an integrated solution. For example, you might use Access to extract the needed data from a large database table, use Excel's charting capabilities to create summary charts of the data, and then include those charts in a report formatted in Word.

As a developer, you will find that the database that your custom application will be working with often exists already. If it does not, then you'll need to create it. The process of creating a database means defining what tables the database will have, what fields will be present in each table, the relationships between the tables, what reports and forms the user will need, and so on. In general, you will use the tools available in the Access application to perform these tasks, then distribute the completed database, forms, etc., as part of your application. It is possible to define databases, forms, and other such objects by means of automation, but this approach is rarely used except in special circumstances such as creating a wizard.

Throughout this chapter I will be referring to the Northwind database and using it in code samples. This database is a sample file that is installed along with Microsoft Office.

SQL

SQL (pronounced ess-cue-ell) is Structured Query Language, a language that IBM originated and that has become the *de facto* standard for accessing and manipulating databases. SQL is a non-procedural language that contains no statements to control the progress of program execution, nor does it have named procedures. In SQL you specify *what* you want done. In plain English, for example, you might request "a list of all records in the Addresses database table where the state is California, sorted by last name." In SQL this request would be written as follows:

```
SELECT * FROM Addresses WHERE State='Ca' ORDER
     BY LastName
```

The basic syntax of this type of SQL statement is:

```
SELECT Fields FROM Tablename WHERE Condition ORDER
     BY SortField
```

`Fields` is a list of the fields that you want in the result. Use the wildcard character `*` to return all fields in the table.

`Tablename` is the name of the database table or recordset you are using.

`Condition` specifies the criteria for returning records. Use the AND and OR operators for complex selection criteria. If `Where Condition` is omitted all records are returned.

`SortField` specifies the field whose data is used to sort the results. If ORDER BY `SortField` is omitted, the order is based on the order of records in the table, or the active table index if one exists.

This is an extremely simple introduction to SQL, but should be enough for you to understand the SQL statements you'll see in this book.

Data Access Technologies

Data access under the Windows operating system is somewhat more complex than the model used by other Office applications. With Word and Excel, for example, there is a straightforward relationship between program and data: Word provides the tools for working with document files, and Excel provides the tools for working with spreadsheet files.

When dealing with the Access application and database technologies, things are not so simple. The direct manipulation and modification of a database is done by a *database engine* and not directly by Access or whatever database application is being used. One reason for this approach is the variety of database file formats that are commonly in use. The database engine can be thought of as an interpreter that translates your general commands (for example, "sort this table alphabetically") into the specific command required by the particular database format in use. Translation occurs in the other direction as well, when the database engine takes data or messages from the database file and sends them to the application.

The database engine you will use depends primarily on the format of the database file you are using. For Access-format files (.MDB), the Microsoft Jet database engine is used. For .ADP databases, the Microsoft SQL Server engine is used. Other engines exist as well. Fortunately, you as a developer rarely have to give any thought to database engine details beyond sometimes having to select which one to use. The operation of the engine is largely transparent from the developer's and the user's perspective.

As the Windows operating system has evolved over the years, data access technologies have changed as well. Microsoft's long-term strategy is a technology called Universal Data Access, which is currently supported by Office 2000. Universal Data Access is implemented at two levels. The low-level data access component architecture—the part of Universal Data Access that interacts directly with the database file—is called OLE DB. The higher-level programming interface, which sits between applications programs and OLE DB, is ActiveX Data Objects, or ADO. Any programming language can use ADO as long as the language supports the Component Object Model, or COM. Languages with this support include Visual Basic Scripting Edition, Visual C++, Visual J++, Visual Basic, and most important for our purposes, Visual Basic for Applications.

The Office 2000 installation includes the latest versions of OLE DB and ADO. Unless you have a specific reason to do otherwise, I recommend that you use these technologies when creating new database projects. This is a case in which newer definitely is better, as Universal Data Access offers a simpler yet more powerful programming interface and support for more database file formats than its predecessor, Data Access Object (DAO). Office still supports DAO, which makes it possible for you to integrate existing DAO applications into your custom Office applications.

ADO and DAO can be automated via VBA code without going through the Access application. In general, if your Office application needs only to access the data in a database, and does not need to use Access objects such as forms and reports, you will bypass the Access application and use ADO or DAO directly.

The Access Object Model

At the top of the Access object model is, of course, the `Application` object. At the next level down in the hierarchy are the three objects you'll be working with most. While these objects have much in common they are designed for different tasks:

- The `Form` object is used for the entry and editing of data.
- The `Report` object is used to display formatted data that cannot be edited.
- The `DataAccessPage` object combines the abilities of forms and reports for data entry, editing, and display. It is designed for use in a Web browser.

In most cases, the forms, reports, and data access pages you work with will already exist, whether created by you or someone else. Your task as a developer is to automate these existing objects to achieve the goals of your application. While it is possible to use VBA to create these objects from scratch, this is a specialized approach that will not be covered further in this chapter. Chapter 26 presents a sample application that generates a custom report in VBA code.

Opening and Closing Access Applications

When you are automating Access from another Office application, you will usually need to open and possibly close the Access application, or database file, that you need to work with. To open an existing .mdb type database, use the `OpenCurrentDatabase` method. The syntax is:

```
AccessApp.OpenCurrentDatabase dbname, exclusive
```

This example assumes that `AccessApp` is a reference to an `Access.Application` object. *dbname* is a string specifying the full name, including path, of the database file to open. The optional *exclusive* argument specifies whether the database should be opened in exclusive mode (True) or shared mode (False, the default). The following code opens the Northwinds database and prints the report named "Products by Category." Note that the default action of the `OpenReport` command is to print the report, that's why you do not see an explicit print command in this code.

```
Dim AccessApp As Access.Application
Set AccessApp = New Access.Application

Const PATH = _
    "c:\program files\microsoft office\office\samples\"

With AccessApp
    .OpenCurrentDatabase PATH & "northwind.mdb"
    .DoCmd.OpenReport "Products by Category"
End With

AccessApp.Quit
```

ADP Versus MDB Files

An ADP file (Access Data Project) provides access to a Microsoft SQL Server database through OLE DB technology. The ADP file contains only code—or HTML-based database objects, such as forms and reports—it does not contain the actual data or any data-definition-based objects, such as tables or stored procedures. An MDB file (Microsoft DataBase) contains not only the database objects, such as forms and reports, but also the actual data, and uses the Jet database engine for access. An MDB database may contain all the relevant data, but linked data can also exist externally in, for example, an Excel file or a dBase database.

To open an ADP file use the `OpenAccessProject` method:

```
AccessApp.OpenAcessProject projname
```

Projname is the name, including path, of the ADP file.

To close the currently open database, whether an MDB or an ADP file, use the `Application` object's `CloseCurrentDatabase` method. This method takes no arguments.

The AccessObject Object

The `AccessObject` object is a generic object type that is used by Access to keep track of a variety of different types of objects. For example, `Form`, `DataAccessPage`, and `Query` are three of the specific object types that are subsumed under the generic `AccessObject` umbrella. The following Access collections, which are available as properties of the `CurrentData` and `CurrentProject` objects (discussed below), contain `AccessObject` properties:

```
AllDataAccessPages **
AllDataBaseDiagrams *
AllForms **
AllMacros **
AllModules **
AllQueries *
AllReports **
AllStoredProcedures *
AllTables *
AllViews *
```

---

* Property of `CurrentData` object.
** Property of `CurrentProject` object.

Each of these collections contains one `AccessObject` object for each item in the collection. Each `AccessObject` object in turn contains an object of the specific type. For example, in the `AllDataAccessPages` collection each `AccessObject` object contains a reference to a `DataAccessPage` object.

These collections are all 0-based, and contain existing (saved) instances of the corresponding object type. This means that you cannot use standard collection syntax to add and delete objects from these collections; rather you use the collections to access the existing objects (if any) of the specified type.

An `AccessObject` object has the properties listed in Table 7.1.

Table 7.1	Properties of the `AccessObject` object.
Property	**Description**
`IsLoaded`	True if the object is loaded (open in any view), otherwise False.
`Name`	The name of the object.
`Properties`	Returns an `AccessObjectProperties` collection that contains the object's properties.
`Type`	Returns an `acObjectType` value specifying the type of the object (for example, `acDataAccessPage`, `acQuery`, or `acReport`). See the Object Browser for details.

The procedure in Listing 7–1 can be run from any Office application to display a list of all reports that are available in the Northwind database, and whether each one is loaded or not.

Listing 7–1   *Subroutine to list all available reports in Northwind.mdb.*

```
Public Sub ListAllReports()

Dim AccessApp As Access.Application
Dim ao As AccessObject
Dim buf As String
Const DB_PATH = "c:\program files\microsoft office\office\samples\"

Set AccessApp = New Access.Application
AccessApp.OpenCurrentDatabase DB_PATH & "northwind.mdb"

For Each ao In AccessApp.CurrentProject.AllReports
    buf = buf & ao.Name
    If ao.IsLoaded Then
        buf = buf & " is loaded."
```

```
    Else
        buf = buf & " is not loaded."
    End If
    buf = buf & vbCrLf
Next

MsgBox buf
AccessApp.Quit

End Sub
```

These `All****` collections provide information about various objects, but do not permit you to manipulate them beyond determining which ones exist, whether they are loaded or not, and setting and reading custom properties. You must load an object before you can really use it, something that is covered in the next section.

Note that these collections refer to objects that contain data, but do not provide access to the data itself. You use ADO or DAO to actually work with the data, as will be covered later in the chapter.

Opening Reports, Forms, and Data Access Pages

Before you can work with an object such as a report or form, you must load it. You use the `DoCmd` object for this purpose (as well as for many other tasks, as we will see later in this chapter). To open a form, use the `OpenForm` method. Its simplified syntax is:

```
DoCmd.OpenForm formname, view, filtername, wherecondition
```

Formname is the only required argument, and is the name of the form to open.

View is an optional constant specifying how the form is to be opened. Possible values are `acDesign` (design view), `acFormDS` (datasheet view), `acNormal` (normal view, the default), and `acPreview` (print preview).

Filtername is the name of a valid query in the current database to be applied to the form data.

Wherecondition is a valid SQL WHERE clause, without the `WHERE` keyword.

You would not use both the *filtername* and *wherecondition* arguments at the same time because they serve the same purpose. Here's an example: the following code opens the Northwind database, then opens the form named Employees in normal view, showing only records in which the Title field contains "Sales Representative." Finally, the application is made visible, permitting the user to work with the form. This code assumes that `gAccessApp` is a global variable of type `Access.Application`.

```
Const DB_PATH = _
    "c:\program files\microsoft office\office\samples\"
Set gAccessApp = New Access.Application
gAccessApp.OpenCurrentDatabase DB_PATH & "northwind.mdb"
gAccessApp.DoCmd.OpenForm FormName:="Employees", _
    WhereCondition:="Title='Sales Representative'"
gAccessApp.Visible = True
```

Use the `OpenReport` method to open a report. The syntax is:

`DoCmd.OpenReport` *reportname, view, filtername, wherecondition*

Reportname is the name of the report to open, and is the only required argument. *View* specifies how the report is opened. Possible values are `acViewDesign` (design view), `acViewNormal` (normal view, the default), and `acViewPreview` (print preview).

Filtername is the name of a valid query in the current database to be applied to the form data.

Wherecondition is a valid SQL WHERE clause, without the `WHERE` keyword.

With reports, "normal" view is not what you might expect. The report is immediately printed without being displayed on the screen. Use print preview mode to display the report to the user without printing it. This code opens the report named Invoices in print preview mode, displaying only invoices for the customer ID "RATTC".

```
Const DB_PATH = _
    "c:\program files\microsoft office\office\samples\"
Set gAccessApp = New Access.Application
gAccessApp.OpenCurrentDatabase DB_PATH & "northwind.mdb"
gAccessApp.DoCmd.OpenReport View:=acViewPreview, _
    ReportName:="Invoice", _
    wherecondition:="CustomerID='RATTC'"
gAccessApp.Visible = True
```

To open a data access page, use the `OpenDataAccessPage` method:

`DoCmd.OpenDataAccessPage` *datapagename, datapageview*

Datapagename is the name of the data access page to open; this argument is required. *Datapageview* specifies whether to open the page in browse mode (`acDataPageBrowse`, the default) or in design mode (`acDataPageDesign`).

This code opens the data access page named "Analyze Sales" and displays it on screen.

```
Const DB_PATH = _
    "c:\program files\microsoft office\office\samples\"
Set gAccessApp = New Access.Application
gAccessApp.OpenCurrentDatabase DB_PATH & "northwind.mdb"
gAccessApp.DoCmd.OpenDataAccessPage
    datapagename:="Analyze Sales"
gAccessApp.Visible = True
```

You also use `DoCmd` methods to open queries, tables, stored procedures, and other Access objects. The general approach is similar to what you have seen in this section for forms, reports, and data access pages. Please refer to online VBA help for the details.

To close an object you use the `Close` method. The syntax is:

`DoCmd.Close objecttype, objectname, save`

Objecttype is a constant specifying the type of the object being closed. Possible values are `acDataAccessPage`, `acDefault` (the default), `acDiagram`, `acForm`, `acMacro`, `acModule`, `acQuery`, `acReport`, `acServerView`, `acStoredProcedure`, and `acTable`.

Objectname is the name of the object to close. If the *Objecttype* argument is specified then the type of the object specified by *Objectname* must match that type.

Save is relevant only for objects in which data and/or design may have been changed. Possible values are `acSaveNo`, `acSavePrompt` (the default), and `acSaveYes`.

If the first two arguments are omitted, the object in the active window is closed. If you try to close an object that is not open, or does not exist at all, no error occurs.

Referring to Open Objects

Access maintains a set of collections containing the open objects of various types. For example, the `Reports` collection contains all currently open reports; there are also `Forms` and `DataAccessPages` collections. These collections are accessed as properties of the `Application` object, and they differ from the `All****` collections covered earlier in this chapter in that the `All****` collections contain all existing objects of the specified type, not just open objects. Remember that you can determine if an object is open by examining the `IsLoaded` property of the object in the corresponding `All****` collection.

As with all collections, you can access members of the `Forms`, `Reports`, and `DataAccessPages` collections by index number or by name. You should use the index number only when iterating through the collection, as an individual collection member's index may change as other objects are added to and removed from the collection. This code, for example, saves and closes all open data access pages (assuming `AccessApp` is a reference to the Access `Application` object):

```
Dim Index As Integer
With AccessApp
For Index = 0 To .DataAccessPages.Count - 1
    .DoCmd.Close acDataAccessPage, _
        .DataAccessPages(Index).Name, acSaveYes
Next Index
```

This code verifies that the Employees form is open and, if so, obtains a reference to its recordset:

```
Dim rsEmployees As ADODB.Recordset
With AccessApp
    If .AllForms("Employees").IsLoaded Then
        Set rsEmployees = .Forms("Employees").recordset
    End if
End With
```

The *CurrentProject* Object

The `CurrentProject` object returns a reference to the current project. You use this object to access and manipulate the application components of a database project. You have already been introduced to some of this object's properties, the `All****` collections, earlier in this chapter. Table 7.2 lists the properties of the `CurrentProject` object.

The *CurrentData* Object

The `CurrentData` object is used to refer to the data elements of the current database. These are elements that are part of the database itself, as opposed to elements that are part of your application (which are accessed with the `CurrentProject` object). The `CurrentData` object has only five properties: `AllDatabaseDiagrams`, `AllQueries`, `AllStoredProcedures`, `AllTables`, and `AllViews`. Each of these properties references a collection that contains all available objects of the specified type. You learned about using these collections earlier in the chapter in the section on the `AccessObject` object.

Table 7.2	Properties of the `CurrentProject` object.
Property	**Description**
`AllDataAccessPages` `AllForms` `AllMacros` `AllModules` `AllReports`	Reference collections containing `AccessObject` objects for all the available objects of the specified type (forms, reports, etc.).
`BaseConnectionString`	Returns the base connection string that was used to connect to an external database. Read-only.
`Connection`	Returns a reference to the current ADO `Connection` object. Read-only.
`FullName`	The full name, including path and filename, of the current database project. Read-only.
`IsConnected`	True if the current project is connected to its data source, otherwise False.
`Name`	Returns the filename, without path, of the current project.
`Path`	Returns the path, without filename, of the current project.
`ProjectType`	Returns the type of the current project: `acADP` for .ADP projects and `acMDB` for .MDB projects.
`Properties`	Returns a reference to an `AccessObjectProperties` collection containing the object's custom properties.

The Screen Object

In Access, you use the `Screen` object to obtain a reference to the form, report, or control that currently has the focus. The `Screen` object, which is accessed via the `Application` object's `Screen` property, has the following properties, each of which returns a reference to the currently active object of the specified type:

```
ActiveControl
ActiveDataAccessPage
ActiveDatasheet
ActiveForm
ActiveReport
```

If you try to read one of these properties, and an object of the specified type is not currently active, an error occurs.

The `Screen` object's `MousePointer` property controls the appearance of the mouse pointer over the entire screen. Possible settings are:

0   Default (appearance determined by Access)
1   Normal select (arrow)
3   Text select (I-beam)
7   Vertical resize
9   Horizontal resize
11   Busy (hourglass)

The DoCmd Object

`DoCmd` permits you to carry out Access actions from VBA code. Actions perform a variety of tasks such as opening reports and data access pages, closing windows, and working with controls. The `DoCmd` object is available as the `DoCmd` property of the `Application` object. The syntax is:

```
AccessApp.DoCmd.action [arg1, arg2, ...]
```

`AccessApp` is a reference to an `Access.Application` object. `Action` is the name of a supported method. `Arg1` etc. represent the arguments of the specific method being called. The `DoCmd` object has many actions, or methods, available to it, and we will deal with many of these as needed. Three of the most frequently needed tasks for `DoCmd` are opening and closing reports, forms, and data access pages, as you saw earlier in this chapter.

Access Options

When you are using Access, options that affect the behavior of the entire application are modified using the Options dialog box (Select Tools, Options from the Access menu). These settings control such things as whether a status bar is displayed, the printing margins, the default data file directory, and the default font for datasheets. To work with these options in code you use the `Application` object's `GetOption` and `SetOption` methods. The syntax is:

```
Application.GetOption(OptionName)
Application.SetOption OptionName, Setting
```

`OptionName` is the name of the option, and `Setting` is the new setting for the Option. `GetOption` returns the current setting of the specified option, as a type `Variant`. The way the setting is returned depends on the type of option:

- Yes/No. The return value is True or False depending on the option setting.
- User-specified string or number. A string containing the option setting as it would appear in the options dialog box.

- A selection from a list or an option group. A number specifying the position of the current setting in the list or group, with the first position being 0.

The values you pass when setting options work the same way. If your VBA code does need to change Access options, it is a good idea to store the original option settings and restore them before exiting. To view a list of Access names, open Visual Basic help and display the page for the `GetOption` and `SetOption` methods, then click the Set Options from Visual Basic link.

Startup Properties

Access has another category of options called *startup properties*. Rather than affecting the Access application itself, these options control how a particular database application appears when it is opened. For example, startup options include the application's title, its icon, and which form or page is displayed initially. In Access, the startup options are viewed in the Startup dialog box (Select Tools, Startup from the menu). Startup properties are kept in the `Properties` collection of the database. For .mdb databases this collection is a property of the `Database` object; for .adp databases it is a property of the `CurrentProject` object. Before you can set the value of a startup property in code, you must add the property to the `Properties` collection. This is done by trying to set the property value. If no error occurs then you know the property was already in the `Properties` collection and the change of value was successful. If the property was not already in the collection an error will occur; you must trap this error and create the property. You can use the `Properties` collection to add your own custom properties to a database project, in addition to those startup properties recognized by Access.

The code in Listing 7–2 shows a procedure that will set the value of a custom property, creating the property if it does not already exist. You can see that properties are represented by the `Property` object, which must first be created and then appended to the `Properties` collection. This code assumes that the property being added is a string (text), as indicated by the second argument to the `CreateProperty` method, `dbText`. Properties can be a variety of types in Access, including date, (`dbDate`), currency (`dbCurrency`), and Boolean (`dbBoolean`). For a complete list of types, and the associated constants, view online help for the `Type` property.

Listing 7–2   *Setting a custom startup property.*

```
Public Function SetCustomProperty(PropertyName As String, _
    PropertyValue As String) As Boolean

Dim db As Object
```

```
Dim prop As Property

' Error handling for property not found error.
On Error GoTo PropNotFound

' Get the current database.
Set db = CurrentDb
' Try to set the property value.
db.Properties(PropertyName) = PropertyValue
' If successful, return True.
SetCustomProperty = True

Done:
    Exit Function

PropNotFound:
    If Err = 3270 Then ' Error code for "property not found"
        ' Create the property object.
        Set prop = db.CreateProperty(PropertyName, dbText, _
                PropertyValue)
        ' Append it to the Properties collection.
        db.Properties.Append prop
        Resume
    Else
        SetCustomProperty = False
        Resume Done
    End If

End Function
```

Working with Forms and Reports

Access forms and reports are similar in that they both display data to the user. They differ in that a form permits the user to enter and edit the data, while a report is for display only and does not permit changes to the data. If, for example, your users needed to enter order information into a database, you would design a form for that purpose. For printing the invoices to send to customers, you would use a report. Reports also let you take *snapshots* of them, so the report can be viewed outside of Access. Once a snapshot is taken, the report stops being dynamic—that is, it will no longer change to reflect changes in the data.

There are two steps to using a form or report in your custom Office application. First, the form or report must be created. While it is possible to create forms and reports directly from VBA code, it is much easier, and therefore much more common, to create the form or report in Access and then save it for use in your VBA project. It is beyond the scope of this book to delve into the details of form and report design, but I will explain some of the basic concepts that you should know in order to effectively use forms and reports in your custom Office applications.

To create a form or report, start Access and open the database project you are working with. Select Form or Report from the Insert menu. The New Report dialog box is shown in Figure 7–1, and the New Form dialog box is similar. In either case, Access provides you with several options for creating your new form or report, including Wizards. At this point you also select the source of the data that the form will use, from the drop-down list in the dialog box. This list will let you select from all the tables and queries that are in the project.

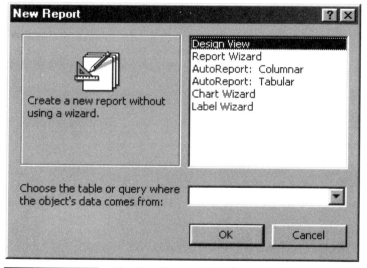

Figure 7–1   *The New Report dialog box is the first step in designing a new report in Access.*

Queries

A query is a way of returning a subset of the records in a database table. For example, you could design a query based on an Address table that includes only those people from the list who live in California. In some ways, a query does the same thing as an SQL WHERE clause, but queries are much more powerful. For example, a query can perform calculations on data, display summaries, update table data and more. Often, forms and reports are based on a query. The query selects and manipulates the data, and the form or report displays it. Queries are also essential when you are working with relational databases, permitting you to select and manipulate data located in two or more related tables.

Access provides powerful tools for designing reports and forms. For example, Figure 7–2 shows a new, blank report open in the report designer. The white area with the grid represents the report itself, with areas for headers, footers, and report details. One of the small windows lists all the fields that are present in the data source that you selected for this report.

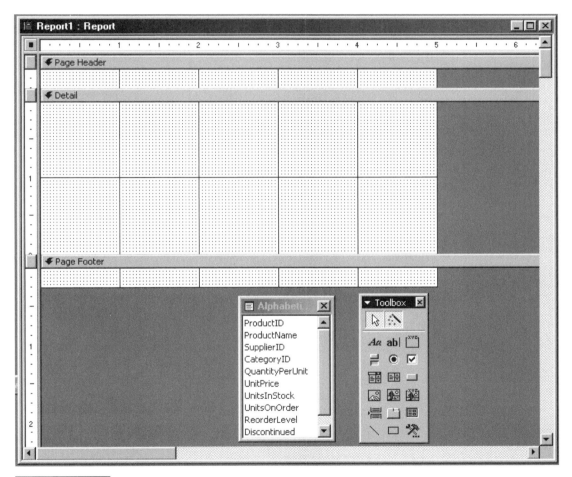

Figure 7–2   *Designing an Access report in the report designer.*

The second small window, called the Toolbox, lets you select from the controls that Access provides. These controls provide great flexibility in arranging and displaying the data on the report. Some of the more useful ones are:

- The text box displays text that the user can edit.
- The label displays text that cannot be edited.
- The check box and option button display True/False data.
- The list box lets the user select from a list of items.
- The image control displays a graphical image.

The Toolbox displays only those controls that are part of Access. The button in the lower right corner of the Toolbox is the More Controls button. Click it and you'll see a list of all the available controls on your system. The beauty of controls is that you can bind them to your data. By setting a control property you specify that data from a specific field in the data source be automatically displayed by that control. A control can display text, pictures, etc., and can also display summary data such as totals.

The end result is that an Access form or report is largely automatic. The links, or bindings, between the control on the form or report and the underlying data source are all built into the form or report, and work automatically, usually without the need for any intervention from the VBA programmer. For a report, this is a one-way street—data comes from the data source to the report and is displayed by the controls. For a form it can be a two-way street, with data coming from the data source for display on the form, and then new or edited data moving back from the form to the data source.

In almost all cases, forms and, to a lesser extent reports, also contain VBA code. Much of this code functions internally to the form or report, performing tasks such as doing summary calculations for data display in a report, or validating data entered onto a form. Other VBA code may interact with external elements, such as opening another form when a form is closed. The need for such code differs depending on the intended use of the form. If a set of forms and reports is designed to run within Access, then you are more likely to need this sort of code that controls the user's "flow" from one form or report to the next. On the other hand, if the forms are designed to be automated using VBA in a custom Office application, then you are more likely to want the workflow to be controlled by your VBA code and not by code internal to the forms and reports. If you are adapting existing forms and reports to a custom VBA application you will need to be on the lookout for such code, which can cause unexpected results.

Using Controls

Even though an Access form or report handles most things automatically, you will sometimes need to work directly with the controls on the form or report. You can access individual controls by means of the Controls collection, which contains one item for each control on the form or report. As always with collections, you can access individual items by the Name property or by their index, which ranges from 0 to Controls.Count - 1. More typically, you will use the `For Each` loop when you need to iterate through all the controls in the collection.

Each control has the `ControlType` property which specifies the type of control. You cannot change this property, but only read it in code. Possible values for `ControlType` are listed in Table 7.3.

Table 7.3   Possible values for the `ControlType` property.

Constant	Type of control
acBoundObjectFrame	Bound object frame
acCheckBox	Check box
acComboBox	Combo box
acCommandButton	Command button
acCustomControl	ActiveX (custom) control
acImage	Image
acLabel	Label
acLine	Line
acListBox	List box
acObjectFrame	Unbound object frame or chart
acOptionButton	Option button
acOptionGroup	Option group
acPage	Page
acPageBreak	Page break
acRectangle	Rectangle
acSubform	Subform/subreport
acTabCtl	Tab
acTextBox	Text box
acToggleButton	Toggle button

Bang and Dot Notation

You have seen dot notation used to indicate an object property, as follows:

```
Object.Property
```

The `.` operator indicates that what follows is an item defined by Access. For example, in this code the identifiers "Controls" and "Text" are both Access-defined items:

```
buf = Forms("Sales").Controls("txtName").Value
```

You can use the `!` operator, sometimes called the bang operator, to refer directly to user-defined items. Thus, the following code is equivalent to the above:

```
buf = Forms!Sales.Controls!txtName.Value
```

Furthermore, while not directly related to the `!` operator, the fact that `Controls` in the default property of the `Form` object, the code above could be further simplified like this:

```
buf = Forms!Sales!txtName.Value
```

In all three cases the meaning is the same: The `Value` property of the control named "txtName" on the form named "Sales."

For example, this code retrieves the value in the text box named "txt-CompanyName" on the form named "Customers":

```
buf = Forms!Customers!txtCompanyName.Value
```

The code in Listing 7–3 is an example of looping through all controls on a form and acting only on controls of a certain type. Passed a form reference as an argument, the code in the procedure loops through all the controls on the form and sets every text box to a blank string.

Listing 7–3	*The procedure `ClearAllTextBoxes` sets all text boxes on the specified form to a blank string.*

```
Sub ClearAllTextBoxes(f As Form)
    Dim c As Control

    For Each c In f.Controls
        If c.ControlType = acTextBox Then c.Value = ""
    Next c

End Sub
```

Me

> The Me keyword returns a reference to the form, report, or class module where the running code is located. Thus, code running inside a form could clear all the text boxes on the form, using the procedure in Listing 7–3, as follows:
>
> ```
> Call ClearAllTextBoxes(Me)
> ```

The Controls collection is not restricted to Form and Report objects. Forms and reports consist of several sections, such as headers and footers, page headers and footers, and a main detail section. Individual sections are accessed through the Section property, as follows:

obj.Section(*SectionType*)

Obj is a reference to a form or report. The *SectionType* argument specifies the section of interest, as shown in Table 7.4.

Table 7.4   Constants for specifying section type.

Constant	Description
acDetail	Detail section
acHeader	Header section
acFooter	Footer section
acPageHeader	Page header section
acPageFooter	Page footer section
acGroupLevel1Header	Group level 1 header section *
acGroupLevel1Footer	Group level 1 footer section *
acGroupLevel2Header	Group level 2 header section *
acGroupLevel2Footer	Group level 2 footer section *

* Reports only

For example, this code loops through the controls in the detail section of the specified form:

```
Dim c As Control
For Each c In Forms!Personnel.Section(acDetail).Controls
...
Next c
```

Two controls also have their own `Controls` collection. The option group control, which is used to group related controls, has a `Controls` collection that contains the option button, check box, toggle button, and/or label controls in the group. The tab control, used to create multiple page dialog boxes, has a `Pages` collection. Each `Page` object has its own `Controls` collection containing the controls on that page of the tab control.

Working with Data Access Pages

Data access page technology is specifically designed to provide Web-based access to data. A data access page is, in fact, a Hypertext Markup Language (HTML) document that contains HTML codes, HTML intrinsic controls, and ActiveX controls. Microsoft Internet Explorer version 5 is the preferred browser for use with data access pages. Other Web browsers can display data access pages but do not permit users to interact directly with the data. Figure 7–3 shows a data access page displayed in Internet Explorer. This page makes use of the Pivot Table control, one of many controls that can be used on data access pages.

In some ways you can think of a data access page as a Web-based combination of a form and a report. Data access pages are like reports in that they can display summary data and offer great flexibility as to how you sort, group, and filter data. They are similar to forms in that users can edit, delete, and add records. While specifically designed for use on the Web, data access pages can also be viewed and used within Access.

How do data access pages fit into your custom Office solutions? Sometimes one or more data access pages will *be* the solution, particularly when your needs are for a data-centric solution that does not use the other Office applications and must be based on the Internet or an Intranet. Because such a project uses only Access, it is really more a topic of Access development and not Office development, where elements from two or more Office applications are used together. Data access pages have their uses, however, even in non-Web-based custom Office projects. Because a data access page can be viewed and used either in Access or in a browser, you have a choice as to how it is presented to the user. Data access pages have many capabilities that you may want to use in your projects, even when their "Web awareness" is not used at all.

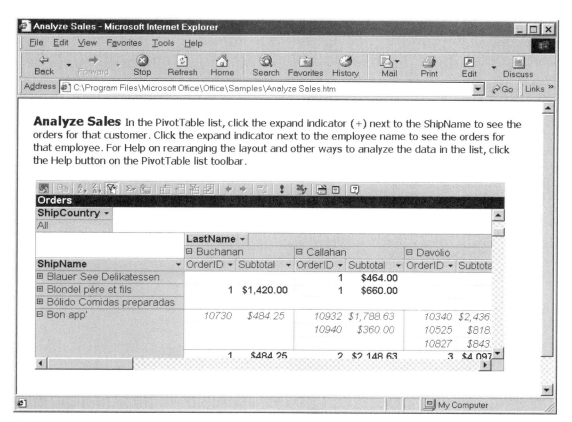

Figure 7–3   *A data access page displayed in the Internet Explorer browser.*

Security Considerations

Data access pages present a double-edged security problem. You not only have to be concerned with database security, but also with Internet security. These topics are covered later in this chapter.

Creating Data Access Pages

You can create data access pages programmatically, but just as with forms and reports, it is much easier to use the design tools that are part of Access. You have three choices: to use a wizard to create a data access page, to open a blank data access page in design view, or to open an existing Web page on which you want to base the new data access page. Figure 7–4 shows a blank data access page in design view. As with forms and reports, you have a toolbox of controls that you can place on the page, although the selection of controls is somewhat different when you are creating a data access page. Some of the controls are Web-related, such as hyperlinks that are bound to your data. There are some very sophisticated controls available for use on a data access page, including a self-contained chart for graphical display of data and a miniature spreadsheet for row and column display. Web-related controls are covered in more detail in Chapter 23.

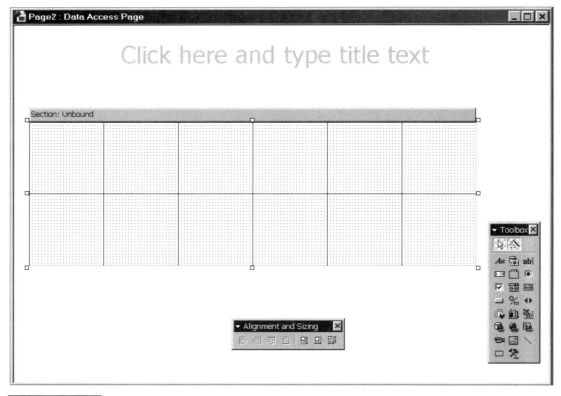

Figure 7–4   *Using design view to create a data access page..*

When you design a data access page, you specify the database that the page is linked to, and also specify the tables and/or fields that individual controls are bound to. When the page is viewed by the user, either in the Internet Explorer browser or in Access, the data link is automatically established between the database and the page, and data is transferred to and from the page as needed.

Using Data Access Pages

You learned earlier in this chapter how to use the `DoCmd` object's `Open-DataAccessPage` method to open a data access page in either browse mode or design mode. Briefly, the syntax is:

```
DoCmd.OpenDataAccessPage datapagename, datapageview
```

in which *datapagename* is the name of the data access page to open, and *datapageview* specifies whether to open the page in browse mode (`acDataPageBrowse`, the default) or in design mode (`acDataPageDesign`). While it is possible to open a data access page in design mode and manipulate it using VBA code, you will most often be opening pages in browse mode and making them visible so the user can work with them. The following code opens the Northwind database and displays the data access page "Review Products" in browse mode:

```
Dim AccessApp As Access.Application
Set AccessApp = New Access.Application
Const PATH = _
    "c:\program files\microsoft office\office\samples\"

AccessApp.OpenCurrentDatabase PATH & "northwind.mdb"
AccessApp.DoCmd.OpenDataAccessPage "Review Products"
AccessApp.Visible = True
```

You can also open the data access page in Internet Explorer, which is sometimes preferable. This is done using the VBA `Shell` command, which takes the program command line as its argument plus a second argument indicating the window state. This code opens Internet Explorer in a maximized window and loads the data access page named "review orders.htm":

```
Const IE_PATH = _
    "C:\Program Files\Internet Explorer\IEXPLORE.EXE "
Const DAP_PATH = _
    "c:\program files\microsoft office\office\samples\"
Const DAP_NAME = "review orders.htm"
Shell IE_PATH & DAP_PATH & DAP_NAME, vbMaximizedFocus
```

Securing Databases

Database security is a complex topic, but can be broken down into two broad areas. One area involves the security of the data. Many databases contain sensitive information and in today's world of networked computers it is essential to protect such data against unauthorized snooping and modification. Securing databases against unauthorized access involves techniques such as establishing user-level security and database encryption, topics that are beyond the scope of this book.

The second area of security is protecting the implementation of your custom solution. You may want to protect your intellectual property by preventing others from seeing the details of your objects and code. You will also want to prevent users from tampering with your solution by inadvertently (or maliciously) modifying your code and objects. There are several approaches to protecting your custom solution, and the one you use will depend on the nature of your solution and the level of security desired. Note also that techniques used to protect the database, such as user-level security, can also assist in protecting your code and objects.

Startup Options

When only a moderate level of security is required you can use Access's startup options to limit the extent to which users can access the program's menus, toolbars, the database window, and special keys. You can use this technique only if your solution has a startup form and a custom menu that contains the commands the user needs. You can set the required startup options from VBA code, as explained earlier in this chapter, or directly from Access as follows:

1. Select Startup from the Tools menu to display the Startup dialog box.
2. Click the Advanced button to display all startup options.
3. Select the desired startup form in the Display Form box.
4. Select the desired menu bar in the Menu Bar box.
5. Turn off all the dialog box options except for Display Status Bar.

In your solution's VBA code, set the application's `AllowBypassKey` property to False, so that users will not be able to use the Shift key to bypass the startup options. Using startup options for security can be used with both .mdb and .adp files.

Database Passwords

By assigning a password to a database file, you can limit access to authorized users. Note, however, that a password does not limit what a user can do with your solution, such as viewing your source code, once they open the file. When a database has a password, users are prompted for the password when they try to open the database. Here are the steps to set a password directly from Access. It's always a good idea to create a backup of the database file before assigning a password. Passwords can be used only with .mdb files.

1. Select File, Open to display the Open dialog box.
2. Locate the database file and highlight its name.

3. Click the arrow next to the Open button and select Open Exclusive.
4. Select Tools, Security, Set Database Password.
5. In the dialog box, enter the password twice, then click OK. Note that passwords are case-sensitive.

To remove a password, follow steps 1 through 3, but in step 4 select Tools, Security, Unset Database Password. Enter the existing password to remove password protection from the database file.

Setting, changing, or removing a database password using VBA code is possible using the older Data Access Objects (DAO) technology, but cannot be done using the newer ActiveX Data Objects (ADO). Since the many benefits of ADO dictate that it be used for new database projects, you'll have to work directly from Access, as described above, to set and change passwords. You can, however, open password-protected databases from ADO code without requiring the database engine itself to prompt for the password. The password can be hard-coded into your VBA code, or you can use VBA code to prompt the user for the password as required.

To open a password-protected database, you give the password as the provider-specific `Jet OLEDB:Database Password` property. There are two ways to do this: as a property of the `Connection` object used to connect to the database, or as a part of the connection string passed as an argument to the `Open` method. This code demonstrates the first technique, with the database file c:\data\employees.mdb with the password BANANA:

```
Dim adoCon As ADODB.Connection
Set adoCon = New ADODB.Connection

With adoCon
    .Provider = "Microsoft.Jet.OLEDB.4.0"
    .Mode = adModeReadWrite
    .Properties("Jet OLEDB:Database Password") = "BANANA"
    .Open "c:\data\employees.mdb"
End With
```

Hiding VBA Source Code

Access lets you save your database files in a format where the VBA code is compiled and can be run but not viewed or modified. This works for both .mdb files and .adp files, which are saved as .mde and .ade files respectively. This technique can be used alone or along with other forms of database security. Saving a database as an .mde or .ade file prevents the user from:

- Viewing or editing your VBA source code.
- Creating or modifying forms, reports, and modules.
- Adding or deleting references to object libraries.
- Opening the Object Browser.

To save a project as an .mde or .ade file, start Access and open the .mdb or .adp file, making sure no other users have the file open if it is shared on a network. From the menu select Tools, Database Utilities, Make MDE (or ADE) File. Specify the filename and location, and click Save. Your original file remains unchanged and the new .mde or .ade file is saved.

An .mde or .ade file cannot be converted back into a .mdb or .adp file. If you want to make any changes to the project, whether to the VBA code or your reports and forms, you will have to work with the original .mdb or .adp file and then save the modified project again as a .mde or .ade file. This means you must keep the original file.

Creating an .mde file is usually not a good approach with .mdb files that contain the database tables. If you make modifications to the original .mdb file later, you will face problems reconciling different versions of the data as the tables in the .mde file will likely have been modified. This means that saving an .mdb project as an .mde file is really appropriate only in those cases in which the solution has been implemented in a front end/back end configuration.

Summing Up

Database programming is the most complicated aspect of Office development that you will encounter. In many situations, it is also the most important and dangerous. It is important because many organizations keep a lot of information in databases, and providing custom solutions to use that data is a common task asked of Office developers. It is dangerous because the data you are working with is usually important, if not essential, and if you foul something up it has the potential to cause big problems. More so than with any other area of Office programming, I recommend that you get a good grounding in database technologies in general, and in Access programming specifically, before taking on any but the most simple database programming tasks.

Using PowerPoint Components

The PowerPoint Application is designed for creating presentations that consist of a series of pictures, or slides, each containing graphs, text, graphics, and other visual elements. A presentation can contain sound and animation, and you can also use PowerPoint to create handouts and notes to accompany a presentation. From the perspective of the VBA programmer, PowerPoint will most often be automated to create new presentations, to create and design new slides, and to run slide shows.

As always in Office, the `Application` object is at the top of the object hierarchy in PowerPoint. Each presentation is represented by a `Presentation` object, and each slide in a presentation is represented by a `Slide` object.

The `Presentation` Object

When you work with PowerPoint you will mostly be manipulating presentations and the slides they contain. Slides are covered in the next section. The PowerPoint `Application` object maintains a `Presentations` collection that contains one `Presentation` object for each open presentation. You use standard collection syntax to access individual members of the collection, referring to them by name or index number. This code applies the design template located in the file professional.pot to the presentation named "Sales Results":

```
Presentations("Sales Results").ApplyTemplate _
    "professional.pot"
```

This code loops through all the open presentations and prints two copies of each one:

```
For Index = 1 To Presentations.Count
    With Presentations(Index)
        .PrintOptions.NumberOfCopies = 2
        .PrintOut
    End With
Next Index
```

Creating and Opening Presentations

There are two ways to create a new presentation. To create a blank presentation, use the `Presentations` collection's `Add` method. The syntax is:

```
Presentations.Add(WithWindow)
```

The optional *`WithWindow`* argument is a Boolean value indicating whether the new presentation will be visible (the default) or not. You should use the Office constants `msoTrue` and `msoFalse` for this argument. Here's an example that creates a non-visible presentation (assuming `ppApp` is a reference to the PowerPoint application):

```
Dim newPres As PowerPoint.Presentation
Set newPres = ppApp.Presentations.Add(msoFalse)
```

You can also create a new presentation based on an existing file. PowerPoint has the ability to open a variety of different file formats, such as Word documents, Harvard Graphics presentations, and Freelance presentations, and to convert their content into a PowerPoint presentation. To create a new presentation based on an existing file, use the `Presentations` collections's `Open` method. The simplified syntax is:

```
ppApp.Presentations.Open(FileName, WithWindow)
```

FileName is the name of a file in one of the supported formats. See the PowerPoint documentation for information on what file formats PowerPoint can open, and the rules used for converting the data to a PowerPoint presentation. *WithWindow* is a True (the default) or False value indicating whether the new presentation will be visible. The following code creates a new presentation based on the contents of the Harvard Graphics file sales.sh3:

```
ppApp.Presentations.Open Filename:="c:\data\sales.sh3", _
    WithWindow:=False
```

To open a PowerPoint presentation that has been previously saved to disk, you also use the Open method:

```
ppApp.Presentations.Open(FileName, ReadOnly, _
    Untitled, WithWindow)
```

FileName is the name of a PowerPoint presentation file (*.ppt). *ReadOnly* is an optional Boolean value indicating whether the file is opened in read-only mode; the default is False. *Untitled* is an optional Boolean value indicating whether the file should be opened without a title. The default setting of False results in the filename becoming the title of the presentation. Setting *Untitled* to True in effect makes a copy of the presentation, which you can then assign another name to. *WithWindow* is a Boolean value that specifies whether the presentation is displayed or not.

Saving and Closing Presentations

To save a presentation that has never been saved, or to save a presentation under a new filename, use the SaveAs method:

```
obj.SaveAs(FileName, FileFormat, EmbedFonts)
```

Obj is a reference to a Presentation object. *FileName* is the name, including path, of the file to be saved. *FileFormat* is an optional value specifying the format to save; the default is ppSaveAsPresentation, which saves the file as a PowerPoint presentation. You can view the ppSaveAs-FileType constants in the Object Browser for information on other possible settings. *EmbedFonts* specifies whether TrueType fonts are embedded in the saved file (True); the default is False.

To save a presentation that has been saved previously, use the Presentation object's Save method, which takes no arguments. To determine whether a presentation has been saved previously, examine its Path property, which will be blank if the presentation has never been saved. You can use the Saved property to determine if the presentation has been changed since its last save, and then save it only if required. This code saves all open presentations that have been modified since they were last saved:

```
Dim p As PowerPoint.Presentation
For Each p In Presentations
    If Not p.Saved And p.Path <> "" Then p.Save
Next p
```

To close a presentation, use the `Close` method, which takes no arguments. If the presentation contains unsaved data, the user will not be prompted and the data will be lost. You should always check a presentation's `Saved` property, and save it if needed, before applying `Close` (unless, of course, you specifically want to discard unsaved changes).

Presentation Templates

A PowerPoint presentation can have a *template* associated with it. Each template contains a master slide that specifies the basic formatting and layout of slides, controlling things such as the background color or image, font style and color, and bulleted/numbered list format. A template can also contain masters for handouts, titles, and notes. By applying a template to a presentation you ensure a consistent appearance throughout the presentation. You can always modify individual slides as needed, or assign a different template at any time.

Templates sometimes contain regular slides as well as a master slide. Regular slides in a template usually contain boilerplate text that you replace with your own text. PowerPoint refers to templates that contain only a master slide as *design templates* and templates that contain regular slides as *content templates*. The two types, however, are saved as the same type of file (with the .pot extension) and differ only in what they contain.

PowerPoint comes with a selection of ready-to-use templates, and you can also create your own templates using procedures explained in the PowerPoint online help. To determine which template is associated with a presentation, use the `TemplateName` property. This read-only property returns the filename, without path information, of the presentation's template. To assign a different template to a presentation, use the `ApplyTemplate` method. This code checks to see what the active presentation's template is. If it is not modern.pot, then that template is assigned.

```
With ActivePresentation
    If .TemplateName <> "modern.pot" Then
        .ApplyTemplate "c:\templates\modern.pot"
    End If
End With
```

Slide Shows

The term *slide show* refers to displaying a presentation to your audience. Certain aspects of a slide show are controlled by the presentation's `SlideShow-Settings` object (accessed via the `SlideShowSettings` property). Other aspects of a slide show are determined by individual slide settings, which will be covered later. Properties of the `SlideShowSettings` object are described in Table 8.1.

Table 8.1	Properties of the `SlideShowSettings` object.
Property	**Description**
`AdvanceMode`	Specifies how the show advances from slide to slide. Possible settings are `ppSlideShowManualAdvance` (slide advances when user presses a key), `ppSlideShowRehearseNewTimings` (for rehearsing), and `ppSlideShowUseSlideTimings` (each slide is shown for the time specified in the slide's `AdvanceTime` property).
`EndingSlide`	The number of the last slide to be shown.
`LoopUntilStopped`	Set to True if you want the slide show to repeat continuously until the user presses Esc. Otherwise the show plays once then stops.
`PointerColor`	References a `ColorFormat` object that specifies the color of the pointer.
`ShowType`	Specifies the type of slide show. Possible settings are `ppShowType-Kiosk` (unattended full-screen presentation), `ppShowTypeSpeaker` (presentation given by a live speaker), and `ppShowTypeWindow` (presentation in a screen window).
`ShowWithAnimation`	Specifies whether any animations in the presentation are displayed (True/False).
`ShowWithNarration`	Specifies whether narration (if any) is played during the presentation (True/False).
`StartingSlide`	The number of the first slide to be shown.

The `SlideShowSettings` object has a single method, `Run`, which runs the specified slide show. The following code runs a slide show for the active presentation. It runs as an unaccompanied full-screen show, starts at slide 2 and ends at slide 12, uses the individual slide timings, and loops repeatedly until interrupted:

```
With ActivePresentation.SlideShowSettings
    .RangeType = ppSlideShowRange
    .StartingSlide = 2
    .EndingSlide = 12
    .LoopUntilStopped = True
    .ShowType = ppShowTypeKiosk
    .AdvanceMode = ppSlideShowUseSlideTimings
    .Run
End With
```

The `Slide` Object

At the heart of any PowerPoint presentation is the `Slide` object, representing one slide or screen in the presentation. The `Presentation` object has a `Slides` collection containing one `Slide` object for every slide in the presentation. To add a new slide to the collection, use the `Add` method:

```
Slides.Add(Index, Layout)
```

Both arguments are required. *Index* is the index number of the new slide within the Slides collection, and can range from 1 to Slides.Count + 1. If you add a new slide at any index below Slides.Count + 1, existing slides at that and higher index positions are "bumped up" to make room for the new slide.

Layout is a constant specifying the layout of the new slide. It can be one of the defined `ppSlideLayout` constants, which you can view in the Object Browser. A layout provides placeholders in a slide for various elements such as text, charts, and clipart. For example, `ppLayoutChartAndText` creates a chart with one placeholder for text and another for a chart. Use the argument `ppLayoutBlank` to create a blank slide. Note that a slide's layout can be changed at any time after it is created.

New slides are automatically assigned a name in the form `Sliden` in which *n* is the index number of the slide at the time it was added. You can assign a more meaningful name to the `Slide` object's `Name` property.

Slides in the `Slides` collection can be accessed by index number and by their `Name` property. `Slide` objects also have a `SlideID` property that contains a unique number that is assigned when the slide is created. More important, unlike the index value, the `SlideID` property does not change when slides are added to or removed from the `Slides` collection. You can retrieve a slide from the `Slides` collection based on its `SlideID` property, by using the `Slides` collection's `FindSlideByID` method. The following code creates a new slide and saves its `SlideID` property, then later uses that property to retrieve the slide from the `Slides` collection:

```
Dim SpecificSlideID As Long

With ActivePresentation.Slides
    SpecificSlideID =.Add(.Count + 1, _
        ppLayoutChart).SlideID
End With
...
With _
ActivePresentation.Slides.FindBySlideID(SpecificSlideID)
    .SlideShowTransition.EntryEffect = ppEffectCoverLeft
    .SlideShowTransition.AdvanceTime = 5
    .SlideShowTransition.Speed = ppTransitionSpeedMedium
End With
```

Shapes on Slides

Anything and everything that is displayed on a PowerPoint slide is a `Shape` object. This is true of text, charts, graphics, and so on. It follows, therefore, that the process of editing a slide consists of adding, removing, and modifying `Shape` objects. In keeping with the general structure of the Office object model, all the shapes on a slide are represented in the `Slide` object's `Shapes` collection. Many of the slides you work with in PowerPoint will have shapes already on them, as specified by the *Layout* argument used when you created the slide.

You can refer to individual shapes in the `Shapes` collection by their index number or name. When a shape is created, it is assigned a name in the form *shapetype n* where *shapetype* is the type of the shape and *n* is the number of shapes on the slide when the new shape was added, plus 1.

The `Shapes` collection differs from the typical Office collection in that it does not have an `Add` method. Rather, it has a whole series of `Addxxxx` methods for individual types of shapes. For example, the `AddTextEffect` method adds a WordArt shape while the `AddTextbox` method adds a text box shape. The various add methods are listed below; each method name describes the type of shape it adds. Each of these methods has a set of arguments that specifies characteristics such as shape size, position, and appearance. The arguments differ for the various methods, and you can find the details in the online help.

```
AddCallout
AddComment
AddConnector
AddCurve
AddLabel
AddLine
AddMediaObject
AddOLEObject
```

```
AddPicture
AddPlaceHolder
AddPolyLine
AddTable
AddTextBox
AddTextEffect
AddTitle
```

A particularly flexible type of shape is called an `AutoShape`, and you add it to the `Shapes` collection with the `AddShape` method. An `AutoShape` can take on many different forms and can be changed from one form to another. For example you could create an `AutoShape` in the form of a 5-point star and then later change it to an 8-point star. The syntax for the `AddShape` method is:

`obj.AddShape(Type, Left, Top, Width, Height)`

All arguments are required. *Type* is an `msoAutoShapeType` constant that specifies the type of the shape. You can view these constants in the Object Browser; they are part of the Office object library.

Left and *Top* specify the position of the shape's top left corner with respect to the top left corner of the slide. The units are points (1/72 of an inch).

Width and *Height* specify the size of the shape, in points.

Let's look at an example of creating a blank slide and putting some shapes on it. The procedure in Listing 8–1 performs the following tasks:

1. Starts PowerPoint and creates a new presentation.
2. Adds a blank slide to the new presentation.
3. Adds a WordArt shape to the slide with the text "Company Goals."
4. Adds a text box shape and puts a bulleted list of four items in it.
5. Positions the shapes on the slide.

The resulting slide is shown in Figure 8–1.

Listing 8–1   *Creating a new PowerPoint slide.*

```
Public Sub CreateNewSlide()

Dim newPres As PowerPoint.Presentation
Dim newSlide As PowerPoint.Slide
Dim newShape As PowerPoint.Shape
Dim slideWidth As Long, slideHeight As Long

' ppApp declared globally elsewhere.
Set ppApp = New PowerPoint.Application
```

```
Set newPres = ppApp.Presentations.Add
Set newSlide = newPres.Slides.Add(1, ppLayoutBlank)

slideWidth = newPres.PageSetup.slideWidth
slideHeight = newPres.PageSetup.slideHeight

With newSlide
    Set newShape = .Shapes.AddTextEffect(msoTextEffect8, _
        "Company Goals", "Arial", 72, msoFalse, msoFalse, 50, 50)
    With newShape
        .Left = (slideWidth - .Width) / 2
        .Top = (slideHeight - .Height) / 8
        .Name = "Heading"
    End With
    ' Create a text box at an arbitrary position and
    ' a size we know will be bigger than needed.
    Set newShape = .Shapes.AddTextbox(msoTextOrientationHorizontal, _
        10, 10, 500, 200)
    ' Add text to the text box, format it as a
    ' left aligned bulleted list, and set its font.
    With newShape
        With .TextFrame.TextRange
            .Text = "Improve morale" _
                & vbCrLf & "Reduce accidents" _
                & vbCrLf & "Increase productivity" _
                & vbCrLf & "Increase market share"
            With .ParagraphFormat
                .Alignment = ppAlignLeft
                .Bullet = msoTrue
            End With
            With .Font
                .Italic = msoTrue
                .Name = "Arial"
                .Size = 38
            End With
        End With
        ' Size the text box to fit the text in it.
        .Width = .TextFrame.TextRange.BoundWidth
        .Height = .TextFrame.TextRange.BoundHeight
        ' Center the text box horizontally.
        .Left = (slideWidth - .Width) / 2
        ' Center it vertically under the WordArt shape.
        .Top = ((newSlide.Shapes("Heading").Height + _
            slideHeight - .Height) / 2)
    End With
End With

End Sub
```

Figure 8–1   *The slide created by the VBA code in Listing 8–1.*

WORKING WITH TEXT ON SHAPES

Most of PowerPoint's shapes, including most of the AutoShape types, can contain text. If a shape can display text then its `HasTextFrame` property will be True and it will have a `TextFrame` property that returns the `TextFrame` object, which controls various aspects of the text display, such as orientation, margins, and word wrap. The `TextFrame` object in turn contains a `Text-Range` object that contains the actual text, in its `Text` property, as well as controlling other aspects of the text display such as the font, bulleted and numbered list formatting, and alignment. The `TextFrame` and `TextRange` objects' properties are listed in Table 8.2 and 8.3.

There is one exception to the rule that all objects that can contain text have an associated `TextFrame` object: a WordArt shape, which is created with the `AddTextEffect` method (as you saw in the example in Listing 8–1). Instead, the `TextEffect` property references the `TextEffectFormat` object that contains the properties and methods that you use to manipulate WordArt shapes.

Table 8.2	Properties of the `TextFrame` object.
Property	**Description**
`AutoSize`	Specifies whether the shape size is automatically changed to accommodate the text. Possible settings are `ppAutoSizeMixed`, `ppAutoSizeNone`, and `ppAutoSizeShapeToFitText`.
`HasText`	True if the shape has text in it, otherwise False.
`MarginBottom` `MarginTop` `MarginLeft` `MarginRight`	Specify, in points, the size of the indicated margin. A margin is the distance between the edge of the text frame and the edge of the inscribed rectangle of the shape that contains the text.
`TextRange`	Returns a reference to the `TextRange` object.
`WordWrap`	Specifies whether lines of text break automatically to fit within the shape. True/False value.

Table 8.3	Properties of the `TextRange` object.
Property	**Description**
`BoundHeight` `BoundWidth`	Return the size, in points, of the text bounding box.
`Font`	Returns a reference to the `Font` object that controls certain aspects of the appearance of the text in the frame, such as the typeface, size, underlining, and italics.
`Length`	Returns the number of characters in the text.
`ParagraphFormat`	Returns a reference to the `ParagraphFormat` object that controls certain aspects of the appearance of text in the frame, such as bulleted lists and alignment.
`Text`	Specifies the text displayed in the shape.

Slide and Shape Ranges

When you need to work with more than one slide at a time, you can define a range of slides that contains two or more slides in a presentation. A similar technique is available for shapes, permitting you to define a range of shapes containing two or more shapes on a slide. To create a range of slides, you use the `Slides` collection's `Range` method, which returns a `SlideRange` object representing the specified slides. The syntax is:

```
obj.Slides.Range(Index)
```

Obj is a reference to a PowerPoint presentation. *Index* is an optional type `Variant` specifying the slides to include in the range. If this argument is omitted, the resulting range contains all the slides in the presentation. You can specify a single slide by using its index number or name:

```
Dim sr1 As PowerPoint.SlideRange
Dim sr2 As PowerPoint.SlideRange
Set sr1 = ActivePresentation.Slides.Range(3)
Set sr2 = ActivePresentation.Slides.Range("Sales Totals")
```

You can also use the VBA `Array` function to create a range of two or more slides based on their individual index numbers or names:

```
Dim sr1 As PowerPoint.SlideRange
Dim sr2 As PowerPoint.SlideRange
Set sr1 = ActivePresentation.Slides.Range _
    (Array(1, 3, 4, 5, 6))
Set sr2 = ActivePresentation.Slides.Range _
    (Array("Sales ", "Profits", "Expenses"))
```

Once you have created a `SlideRange` object you can refer to its properties just as if it were a single slide. The changes you make will affect all the slides in the range. For example, this code sets the title color to blue for slides 3 through 8 in the active presentation:

```
Dim sr1 As PowerPoint.SlideRange
Set sr1 = ActivePresentation.Slides.Range _
    (Array(3, 4, 5, 6, 7, 8))
sr1.ColorScheme.Colors(ppTitle).RGB = RGB(0, 0, 255)
```

This long line of code sets the title color for all slides in the active presentation:

```
ActivePresentation.Slides.Range.ColorScheme.Colors _
    (ppTitle).RGB = RBG(0, 0, 255)
```

To create a range of shapes, use the `Shapes` collection's `Range` method, which has the same syntax as the `Range` method for the `Slides` collection explained previously:

```
obj.Shapes.Range(Index)
```

Obj is a reference to a PowerPoint slide. *Index* is an optional type `Variant` specifying the shapes to include in the range. If this argument is omitted, the resulting range contains all the shapes on the slide. This code sets the fill pattern for shapes 2 through 5 on slide 1 in the active presentation:

```
Dim shapeRange As PowerPoint.ShapeRange
Set shapeRange = ActivePresentation.Slides(1).Shapes. _
    Range(Array(2, 3, 4, 5))
shapeRange.Fill.Patterned msoPatternDottedGrid
```

The PowerPoint Application Object

Unlike all other Office applications (except Outlook), PowerPoint is a *single-use application*. This means that there can be only one instance of PowerPoint running at a time. If you use the New keyword to create an instance of PowerPoint, and PowerPoint is already running, then the reference that New returns points to the existing instance of the program.

If you are writing VBA code in PowerPoint, then the Application object is automatically available to you. To automate PowerPoint from other Office applications, you must create an instance of the object and a reference to it:

```
Dim ppApp As PowerPoint.Application
Set ppApp = New PowerPoint.Application
```

Because of PowerPoint's single-use nature, there is never a need to use GetObject when you want to reference the existing instance of the program.

The Application object's Presentations property returns the Presentations collection, which contains one Presentation object for each open presentation. You learned about this collection earlier in this chapter. The Application object has some other properties, as listed in Table 8.4.

Table 8.4   Properties of the PowerPoint Application object.

Property	Description
Active	Returns True or False indicating whether the PowerPoint window is active.
ActivePresentation	Returns a reference to the active presentation.
ActivePrinter	Returns the name of the active printer.
ActiveWindow	Returns a DocumentWindow object representing the active window.

Table 8.5	Properties of the PowerPoint Application object. (Continued)
Property	**Description**
Height, Width	Specifies the height or width of the PowerPoint window, in points.
Left, Top	Specifies the distance, in points, of the top left corner of the PowerPoint window from the top left corner of the desktop.
SlideShowWindows	Returns a collection of SlideShowWindow objects representing the open slide shows.
Visible	Specifies whether the PowerPoint window is visible (True) or not (False).
Windows	Returns a collection of DocumentWindows objects representing all open document windows.
WindowState	Specifies the state of the PowerPoint window. Possible values are ppWindowMaximized, ppWindowMinimized, ppWindow-Mixed, and ppWindowNormal.

Summing Up

PowerPoint is a presentation program. It does not have any data manipulation capabilities, but once your data is ready to show, PowerPoint is often the best way to create clear, eye-catching graphics. You can create individual slides, which can be exported to other applications, and you can also create entire slide shows with automatic timing and narration. In my experience, Office developers do not need to turn to PowerPoint all that often, but when you do need its presentation features, you'll be glad to have it.

Using FrontPage Components

Microsoft FrontPage is an application designed for creating, deploying, and managing Web sites and for editing individual Web pages. While FrontPage has been around for a while, it is a new part of Office with the Office 2000 release. If you have worked with earlier versions of FrontPage, you will find that the language elements have changed drastically with FrontPage 2000. The older language elements are still supported, but only for purposes of backward compatibility.

FrontPage Overview

An individual Web site that is open in FrontPage is represented by a `Web` object. The `Webs` collection contains one `Web` object for each open Web. Each `Web` object has a `WebWindow` object that represents the FrontPage window the Web is displayed in. In turn, the `WebWindow` object has a `PageWindows` collection which contains a `PageWindow` object for each individual Web page that is open. Finally, each `PageWindow` object has `Document` property that references the `Document` object for that Web page.

A Web exists on disk as a set of files and folders. Each folder in the Web is represented by a `WebFolder` object, and the Web's root folder is represented by the `RootFolder` object. Every `WebFolder` object has `WebFolders` and `WebFiles` collections that contain all the folders (as `WebFolder` objects) and files (as `WebFile` objects) in that folder. Note that the `WebFolders` and `WebFiles` collections are accessed via the `Folders` and `Files` properties of the `WebFolder` object and not the `WebFolders` and `WebFiles` properties that you might expect.

A Web contains a navigation structure that consists of all the hyperlinks between the various Web pages. In terms of the Web's navigation structure, each page in the Web is represented by a `NavigationNode` object. The `NavigationNode` object has a `Children` property that returns a `NavigationNodes` collection containing one `NavigationNode` object for each page that the current page is linked to.

The `Web` Object

Before you can work on a Web you must open it. This is done with the `Webs` collection's `Open` method. The syntax is:

```
Webs.Open(WebUrl, UserName, Password)
```

`WebURL` is the base URL of the Web to open. It can specify a local Web root folder, such as c:\MyWebs\Products, or the URL of a remote Web, as in http://www.YourFirm.com. The `UserName` and `Password` arguments are optional, and provide the user name and password required to access the Web server, if required.

To create a new Web, use the `Webs` collection's `Add` method. The syntax is:

```
Webs.Add(WebUrl, UserName, Password)
```

WebURL is the base URL where the Web will be stored. The *UserName* and *Password* arguments are optional, and provide the user name and password required to access the Web server, if you want to use them.

Both the `Open` and `Add` methods return a reference to the newly opened or created Web. Tables 9.1 and 9.2 describe the properties and methods of the `Web` object.

Table 9.1	Properties of the `Web` object.
Property	**Description**
`ActiveWebWindow`	Returns an `ActiveWebWindow` object representing the Web's current active Web window.
`AllowsLongFilenames`	Returns True if the operating system on the computer where the Web is located permits the use of long filenames.
`HomeNavigationNode`	Returns a `NavigationNode` object representing the Web's home page.
`Properties`	Returns a `Properties` collection that contains the Web's custom properties.
`RootFolder`	Returns a `Folder` object representing the Web's root.
`RootNavigationNode`	Returns a `NavigationNode` object representing the abstract navigation root. The first child node of the abstract navigation root is the Web's home page.
`Title`	Specifies the title of the Web.
`Url`	Returns the URL of the Web. Read-only.
`WebWindows`	Returns a collection of `WebWindow` objects each representing an open window.

The term *publishing* means to copy the Web from its local location on your disk to the Web server where it will be available to others. When FrontPage publishes a Web it can compare the files on the remote Web with the files in your local Web and copy only new and changed files. You use the `Web` object's `Publish` method to publish a Web. The syntax is as follows.

```
obj.Publish(DestinationURL, PublishFlags, UserName, _
        Password)
```

DestinationURL is a string containing the entire target URL for the Web.

Table 9.2	Methods of the `Web` object.
Method	**Description**
`Activate`	Makes the Web active.
`ApplyNavigationStructure`	Applies changes that have been made to the Web's navigation structure.
`Close`	Closes the Web.
`LocateFile(String)`	Returns a `WebFile` object representing the file whose name is specified by `String`. If the file is not in the root folder then `String` must include path information as well as the filename.
`LocateFolder(String)`	Returns a `WebFolder` object representing the folder whose name is specified by `String`. If the folder is not in the root folder then `String` must include path information as well as the folder name.
`Publish`	Publishes the Web. See below for arguments and details.
`RecalcHyperlinks`	Recalculates the Web and updates FrontPage's information about hyperlinks, titles, and so on.

PublishFlags can be `fpPublishIncremental` to publish only new and changed files, or `fpPublishAddToExistingWeb` to add to an existing Web.

UserName and *Password* specify the user's name and password, and are required only if the Web server requires logon.

The following line of code publishes the active Web to the URL http://www.somewhere.com, assuming the Web has been published previously and the Web server does not require logon.

```
ActiveWeb.Publish("http://www.somewhere.com", _
    fpPublishAddToExistingWeb)
```

Working with Folders

To add a new folder to the Web, use the `WebFolders` collection's `Add` method. The syntax is:

obj.Add(*FolderURL*)

Obj is a reference to a `WebFolders` collection. *FolderURL* is the absolute path or URL of the new folder. The following code adds the folder named c:\myweb\images to the Web:

```
ActiveWeb.RootFolder.Folders.Open("c:/myweb/images")
```

If you do not specify a path for the folder, it is created in the specified folder. For example, if c:\myweb is the active Web's root folder then this code has the same effect as the previous example:

```
ActiveWeb.RootFolder.Folders.Add("images")
```

To delete a folder, use the `WebFolders` collection's `Delete` method:

```
obj.Delete(index)
```

Obj is a reference to a `WebFolders` collection, and *index* is the index number or name of the folder to delete. Deleting a folder also deletes any folders and files it contains. The following code deletes the folder named images from the active Web's root folder:

```
ActiveWeb.RootFolder.Folders.Delete("images")
```

To move a folder, use the `WebFolder` object's `Move` method:

```
obj.Move(DestinationURL, UpdateLinks, ForceOverwrite)
```

Obj is a reference to a `WebFolder` object representing the folder to be moved. *DestinationURL* is the location the folder is to be moved to. *UpdateLinks* is an optional True/False value indicating whether links are to be updated as part of the move process; the default is False. *ForceOverwrite* is an optional True/False value specifying whether duplicate folders or files should be overwritten if encountered; the default is False. The following code moves the folder "cars" from its original location in the active Web's root folder into the folder named "images":

```
Dim f As WebFolder, s As String

Set f = ActiveWeb.RootFolder.Folders("cars")
s = ActiveWeb.RootFolder.Folders("images").Url & "/cars"
f.Move (s)
```

You can rename a folder using the `Move` method by specifying only a different name but the same path.

Working with Web Pages

The tasks involved in working with Web pages fall into two categories:

1. Creating, opening, moving, and deleting pages, and
2. Working with the page content.

You also need to understand how FrontPage represents an open Web page by a `PageWindow` object. I will cover these in turn.

Creating, Opening, Moving, and Deleting Web Pages

To create a new, blank, Web page and add it to the Web, use the `Files` collection's `Add` method. This method returns a reference to the new page. The syntax is:

```
obj.Files.Add (Filename)
```

Obj is a `WebFolder` object specifying the folder where the new file is to be placed. *Filename* is the name of the file, including the .htm or .html extension. If a file of the specified name already exists, an error occurs. This code adds a new page with the name "travel.htm" to the root folder of the active Web, then sets the new page's `Title` property:

```
Dim newPage As FrontPage.WebFile
Set newPage = ActiveWeb.RootFolder.Files.Add("travel.htm")
newPage.Title = "Travel Destinations"
```

To open an existing Web page so you can edit it, use the `WebFile` object's `Open` method. The syntax is:

```
obj.Open
```

Obj is a reference to a `WebFile` object that represents the desired file. The following code opens the file named "welcome.htm" in the active Web's root folder:

```
Dim myPage As WebFile

Set myPage = ActiveWeb.RootFolder.Files("welcome.htm")
myPage.Open
```

If the FrontPage application is visible, opening a Web page will display it on-screen for editing. You can also open a page by adding it to the `PageWindows` collection, as explained in the next section.

To move a Web page, use the `WebFile` object's `Move` method:

```
obj.Move (DestinationURL, UpdateLinks, ForceOverwrite)
```

Obj is a reference to a `WebFile` object representing the file to be moved. *DestinationURL* is the location the file is to be moved to. *UpdateLinks* is an optional True/False value indicating whether links are to be updated as part of the move process; the default is False. *ForceOverwrite* is an optional True/False value specifying whether a duplicate file should be overwritten if encountered; the default is False. The following code moves the Web page aquarium.htm from the Web's root folder to the folder named "hobbies":

```
Dim f As WebFile, s As String

Set f = ActiveWeb.RootFolder.Files("aquarium.htm")
s = ActiveWeb.RootFolder.Folders("hobbies").Url _
    & "/aquarium.htm"
f.Move (s)
```

To delete a Web page, use the `WebFile` object's `Delete` method:

```
obj.Delete
```

Obj is a reference to a `WebFile` object that represents the file to be deleted. The following code deletes the file named "welcome.htm" in the active Web's root folder.

```
ActiveWeb.RootFolder.Files("welcome.htm").Delete
```

If you try to delete a file that does not exist, an error occurs.

Working with PageWindows

A Web page that has been opened is represented by a `PageWindow` object. You access individual `PageWindow` objects via the `PageWindows` collection, which is a property of the `WebWindow` object. Each `WebWindow` object represents an open Web, and is a member of the `WebWindows` collection. As you can see, the FrontPage application can have one or more Webs open, and each of those Webs can have multiple Web pages open.

You can access a specific `PageWindow` object by referring to the `PageWindows` collection of the Web that contains the opened page. This code, for example, returns a reference to the first open page in the first open Web:

```
Dim myPageWindow As PageWindow
Set myPageWindow = WebWindows(0).PageWindows(0)
```

You can open a Web page by adding it to the `PageWindows` collection, and obtain a reference to it all in one step. This code opens the file c:\myweb\prices.htm and adds it to the active Web's `PageWindows` collection:

```
Dim myPageWindow As PageWindow
Set myPageWindow = ActiveWeb.WebWindows(0).PageWindows. _
    Add("c:\myweb\prices.htm")
```

You can also refer to a member of the `PageWindows` collection by its `Caption` property:

```
Set myPageWindow = _
    ActiveWebWindow.PageWindows("prices.htm")
```

To save a `PageWindow` object, use the `Save` method. You can determine if the object needs to be saved—that is, if it has been modified since the last time it was saved—by examining its `IsDirty` property. The following code saves the page referenced by `myPageWindow` only if it has been modified:

```
If myPageWindow.IsDirty Then myPageWindow.Save
```

Working with Web Page Content

To work with the content of a Web page, you must work with the Dynamic Hypertext Markup Language (DHTML) `Document` object. You access this object as the `Document` property of a `PageWindow` object that references the open Web page that you want to work with. For example, the following code opens the Web page welcome.htm, works with its contents, then saves and closes it.

```
Dim myPageWindow As PageWindow

Set myPageWindow = _
    ActiveWebWindow.PageWindows.Add("welcome.htm")

With myPageWindow.Document
' Code to manipulate document contents here.
End With

myPageWindow.Save
myPageWindow.Close
```

The `Document` object is specifically the Dynamic HTML document, and is based on the model developed by the World Wide Web Consortium. This model is designed to permit *dynamic* Web pages that can interact with the user, and also presents a comprehensive object model through which all of the HTML elements on the page are exposed and can be manipulated by means of its properties and methods. A DHTML document is based on the standard HTML tags, and you should be familiar with both HTML and DHTML in order to work with this model.

An *element* on a DHTML page is the part of the page represented by an HTML tag. HTML tags are enclosed in angle brackets and, with few exceptions, come in pairs that mark the beginning and end of an element. The ending tag is the same as the starting tag with the addition of a slash. Thus, for example, <TITLE> and </TITLE> mark the start and end of the page's title element. Listing 9–1 shows the HTML code for a very simple Web page.

Listing 9–1   *HTML for a very simple Web page.*

```
<HTML>
<HEAD>
<TITLE>HTML TAGS EXAMPLE</TITLE>
</HEAD>
<BODY>
<CENTER>
<H1>This is a centered first level heading</H1>
</CENTER>
<P>This is a paragraph</P>
<P>This is another paragraph</P>
<H2>This is a second level heading</H2>
</BODY>
</HTML>
```

In this page, the elements that are exposed as objects include the title, the headings, and the paragraphs. When you are working with the DHTML object programmatically, your VBA code can add, change, and remove elements from a page. This includes not only the basic page elements, such as text and headings, but also HTML controls, such as buttons and text boxes, style sheets, and so on.

The Document object exposes several collections that represent elements on a page. Most important is the all collection that represents all of a page's elements. Each element in the all collection has a tagName property that returns its tag. For example: "p" for a paragraph element <P></P>, "h1" for a first level heading <H1></H1>, and so on. The following code prints (in the Immediate window) the tags for all the elements in the page "welcome.htm":

```
Dim p As PageWindow, i

Set p = ActiveWebWindow.PageWindows.Add("welcome.htm")
With p.Document
    For i = 0 To .all.Length - 1
        Debug.Print .all(i).tagName
    Next i
End With
```

You can use the `all` collection's `tags` method to return a collection containing all page elements of a specified kind. The syntax is:

```
document.all.tags(tag)
```

The *tag* argument is the tag of the type of element you want to retrieve. The following code creates a collection containing all of the paragraph elements on the specified page and then prints each paragraph's text:

```
Dim p As PageWindow
Dim AllParagraphs
Dim ob As Object

Set p = ActiveWebWindow.PageWindows.Add("welcome.htm")
Set AllParagraphs = p.Document.all.tags("p")
For Each ob In AllParagraphs
    Debug.Print ob.innerText
Next
```

Dynamic HTML—Should You Use It?

The DHTML document object model is indeed powerful, and I have only touched the surface of its capabilities in this chapter. You should be aware, however, that this model is not always the most appropriate one to use when your custom Office application needs to manipulate Web pages. DHTML was designed primarily as a method for Web pages to be manipulated actively in real time, as they are being viewed. It is less well suited for creation and editing of Web pages, which is often what you need to do from a custom Office solution.

Remember that a Web page is a plain text file, and that VBA provides a powerful set of statements for manipulating text. I have often found that the best approach is to create or modify a Web page using this approach, rather than FrontPage's DHTML document object. Then, if the Web page is part of a FrontPage Web, you can automate FrontPage to refresh the Web to integrate the page changes into the Web.

Summing Up

FrontPage is specialized for creating and managing Web sites. Given the ever increasing reliance on the Web, it is more and more common for custom Office applications to include some connection with Web publishing. FrontPage offers all the capabilities you'll need, accessible from your VBA code. The ability to combine the various Office applications to create Web content, then to use FrontPage to publish and manage it, is indeed a powerful tool for Office developers.

Using Outlook Components

Microsoft Outlook is a program of many talents. Its main job is sending and receiving e-mail, but it also provides a calendar, task list, address book, and notebook. As a VBA programmer, you will probably use Outlook's e-mail capabilities most often, but its other features are exposed for automation as well. For the most part, this chapter will be limited to coverage of Outlook's e-mail capabilities.

Outlook Overview

Outlook is organized around items and folders. An item is an object that holds information. Mail messages, appointments, and notes are examples of Outlook items. A folder is a place to keep things, and an Outlook folder can hold items and also other folders. Outlook folders are arranged hierarchically in a manner than is analogous to folders on a disk; however, an Outlook folder is not the same thing as a disk folder.

As with all Office applications, the `Application` object is at the top of the Outlook object model. One level down, the `NameSpace` object is used to access Outlook items and folders. We'll look at these two objects first, then explore the details of working with folders and items, with an emphasis on e-mail messages.

The `Application` and `NameSpace` Objects

If you are working within Outlook, the `Application` object is always available to your VBA code as an implicit reference. If you are automating Outlook from another Office application, you must create a reference to the Outlook Application. If you have selected the Outlook 9 object library in the References list, you can use the `New` keyword as follows:

```
Dim myOutlookApp As Outlook.Application
Set myOutlookApp = New Outlook.Application
```

You can also use the `GetObject` function, which does not require a reference to the Outlook 9 object library to be present:

```
Dim myOutlookApp As Object
Set myOutlookApp = GetObject(Outlook.Application)
```

Outlook is one of only two Office applications that are *single-use*, meaning that there is never more than one instance of the application running (PowerPoint is the other single-use Office application). This means that whether you use `New` or `GetObject`, the result it same: If Outlook is not running, a new hidden instance is created. If Outlook is running, a reference to the existing instance is returned.

Any existing data in Outlook is accessed via the `NameSpace` object. Currently, the only data source supported by Outlook is MAPI. To obtain a reference to the `NameSpace` object, use the `Application` object's `GetNameSpace` method:

```
Dim myNameSpace As Outlook.NameSpace
Set myNameSpace = Application.GetNameSpace("MAPI")
```

Because Outlook is a single-use application, it is sometimes useful to use a global variable to hold the reference to the Outlook application, as well as to the NameSpace object. Then, these variables can be used within the various VBA procedures that need to automate Outlook. Listing 10–1 presents a function that initializes global variables for the Outlook Application and NameSpace objects, and returns True on success and False on failure.

| Listing 10–1 | *The* StartOutlook *function initializes global variables for the* Application *and NameSpace objects.* |

```
Public Function StartOutlook() As Boolean

' Initializes global variables for the Outlook application
' and the Namespace object. Returns True on success
' and False on failure. The variables myOutlookApp and
' myOutlookNameSoace must be globally declared elsewhere as
' types Outlook.Application and Outlook.NameSpace, respectively.
' Returns True on success and False on failure.

    On Error GoTo CannotInitialize

    StartOutlook = True
    Set myOutlookApp = New Outlook.Application
    Set myOutlookNameSpace = myOutlookApp.GetNamespace("MAPI")

Done:
    Exit Function

CannotInitialize:
    StartOutlook = False
    Resume Done

End Function
```

To make use of this function, the code would need to first check if Outlook is already initialized, then call StartOutlook only if it is not. For example:

```
If myOutlookApp Is Nothing Then
    If StartOutlook = False Then
        MsgBox "Error initializing Outlook application."
        Exit Function
    End If
End If
```

Manipulating Folders and Items

Folders in Outlook are represented by the `MAPIFolder` object. You can obtain a reference to the default folder for a built-in Outlook item by using the `NameSpace` object's `GetDefaultFolder` method. The syntax is:

`obj.GetDefaultFolder(itemtype)`

Obj is a reference to the `NameSpace` object, and *item* is a constant identifying the type of item whose default folder you want to retrieve. Possible settings for this argument are described in Table 10.1.

| **Table 10.1** | Constants for the `GetDefaultFolder` method's *itemtype* argument. |

Constant	Item
`olFolderContacts`	Contacts—the address book.
`olFolderDeletedItems`	Items that have been deleted.
`olFolderDrafts`	Drafts of incompleted items.
`olFolderInbox`	Received e-mail messages.
`olFolderJournal`	Journal entries.
`olFolderNotes`	Note entries.
`olFolderOutbox`	E-mail messages waiting to be sent.
`olFolderSentMail`	E-mail messages that have been sent.
`olFolderTasks`	Task entries.

The following code obtains a reference to the Inbox folder:

```
Dim folderInbox As MAPIFolder
Dim ns As NameSpace

Set ns = GetNamespace("MAPI")
Set folderInbox = ns.GetDefaultFolder(olFolderInbox)
```

Folders that are not default Outlook folders are obtained from the `Folders` collection. Each top-level folder is a member of the `NameSpace` object's `Folders` collection. Each of these top-level folders in turn has its own `Folders` collection, and so on until you reach a folder that does not contain any subfolders. To return a reference to a specific folder, given that you know its name, you can use the function in Listing 10–2. This function is passed the name of the desired folder and returns a reference to the desired folder, if it exists. If the folder does not exist, the value `Nothing` is returned. This function makes use of the function `StartOutlook` from Listing 10–1. Note that this code looks at all the folders present in Outlook's top-level folders, but does not go deeper. To find subfolders at the deeper level the code would have to be modified. Be aware that folder names in Outlook are case-sensitive.

Listing 10–2   *Returning a reference to a specific folder.*

```
Public Function GetOutlookFolder(FolderName As String) As _
    Outlook.MAPIFolder

' Passed the name of an Outlook folder, returns a reference
' to that folder, or Nothing if the folder is not found.

Dim f1 As Outlook.MAPIFolder
Dim f2 As Outlook.MAPIFolder
Dim foundFolder As Outlook.MAPIFolder

If myOutlookApp Is Nothing Then
    If StartOutlook = False Then
        MsgBox "Error initializing Outlook application."
        Set GetOutlookFolder= Nothing
        Exit Function
    End If
End If

For Each f1 In myOutlookNameSpace.Folders
    For Each f2 In f1.Folders
        If f2.Name = FolderName Then
            Set foundFolder = f2
        End If
    Next
    If Not f2 Is Nothing Then Exit For
Next

Set GetOutlookFolder = foundFolder

End Function
```

To get access to an existing Outlook item, use the `MAPIFolder` object's `Items` collection. For a given folder, the `Items` collection contains one entry for every item in the folder. Individual items can be identified by their index number or by their default property, which in the case of mail messages is their subject. This code retrieves a reference to the first message in the Inbox folder in which the subject is "Sales figures":

```
Dim myMessage As Outlook.MailItem
Set myMessage = myOutlookNameSpace.GetDefaultFolder _
    (olFolderInbox).Items("Sales figures")
```

The function in Listing 10–3 returns the number of unread mail messages in the Inbox.

| Listing 10–3 | *This function returns the number of unread mail messages.* |

```
Public Function NumberOfUnreadMessages() As Integer

' Returns the number of unread mail messages in the Inbox.
' Returns -1 on error.

Dim count As Integer
Dim mailItem As Outlook.mailItem

If myOutlookApp Is Nothing Then
    If StartOutlook = False Then
        MsgBox "Error initializing Outlook application."
        NumberOfUnreadMessages = -1
        Exit Function
    End If
End If

count = 0
For Each mailItem In myOutlookNameSpace. _
    GetDefaultFolder(olFolderInbox).Items
        If mailItem.UnRead = True Then count = count + 1
Next

NumberOfUnreadMessages = count

End Function
```

Another way to determine the number of unread messages is to look at the MAPIFolder object's UnReadItemCount property.

Working with Mail Messages

E-mail messages in Outlook are represented by the MailItem objects. When creating custom Office applications you will need to deal with messages in two ways: retrieving information from received messages, and creating and sending new messages.

Using Received Messages

By default, Outlook places received messages in the Inbox folder. If you need to know as soon as new mail has arrived, you can use the `NewMail` event (covered in detail later in this chapter). You can use the `GetDefaultFolder` method to obtain a reference to the Inbox folder, then use the `Items` collection to access all the messages in the Inbox.

The `MailItem` object has a large number of properties. Those properties that are of interest when you are dealing with received messages are described in Table 10.2. By accessing these properties you can determine for each message who sent it and when, who it was sent to, what its subject is, its content, and so on. Examples of dealing with received messages are given following the table.

Table 10.2	`MailItem` properties relevant for received messages.
Property	**Description**
`Attachments`	A collection of `Attachment` objects each representing a document or link attached to the message.
`Body`	Specifies the text of the message (if plain text).
`CreationTime`	Returns a type `Date` specifying when the message was created.
`HTMLBody`	Specifies the text of the message (if HTML).
`Importance`	Returns the importance level of the message. Possible values are: `olImportanceHigh`, `olImportanceLow`, and `olImportanceNormal`.
`ReceivedTime`	Returns a type `Date` specifying when the message was received.
`Recipients`	A collection of `Recipient` objects representing the message recipients.
`Saved`	True if the message has been saved since it was last modified.
`SenderName`	Returns the display name of the message sender.
`SentOn`	Returns a type `Date` specifying when the message was sent.
`Subject`	Specifies the message subject.
`To`	Returns a semicolon delimited list of the message recipients' display names.
`UnRead`	Returns True if the message has not been opened.

Let's look at some examples of working with the messages in the Inbox folder. The function presented in Listing 10–4 examines all messages in the Inbox folder. All messages in which the subject contains the specified text are moved to the specified folder. This function makes use of the `GetOutlook-`

Folder function presented in Listing 10–2 earlier in this chapter. The return value is True on success and False if an error occurs (for example, if the destination folder does not exist).

Listing 10–4	*Moving selected messages from the Inbox folder.*

```
Public Function MoveMessagesBySubject(Subject As String, _
    DestinationFolder As String) As Boolean

' Moves all messages where the subject contains the Subject
' argument from the Inbox folder to the folder specified by
' DestinationFolder. Returns True on success, False on error.

    Dim f As Outlook.MAPIFolder
    Dim m As Outlook.mailItem

    On Error GoTo ErrorHandler

    If myOutlookApp Is Nothing Then
        If StartOutlook = False Then
            MsgBox "Error initializing Outlook application."
            Exit Function
        End If
    End If

    Set f = myOutlookNameSpace.GetDefaultFolder(olFolderInbox)
    For Each m In f.Items
        If InStr(m.Subject, Subject) > 0 Then
            m.Move GetOutlookFolder(DestinationFolder)
        End If
    Next

    MoveMessagesBySubject = True

ErrorExit:
    Exit Function

ErrorHandler:
    MoveMessagesBySubject = False
    Resume ErrorExit

End Function
```

The code in Listing 10–5 shows how you can look through received messages and create a summary document, which contains the text of all messages that were sent by a certain sender and received since a certain date and time. The code looks through all messages in the Inbox, and processes only those sent by the specified sender and received since the specified date. The

ReceivedDate argument can include a time as well. The body text of all matching messages is combined and written to a disk file.

Listing 10–5   *Creating a summary of selected messages.*

```
Public Sub CombineMessagesBySender(SenderName As String, _
    OutputFile As String, ReceivedSince As Date)

' Combines the body text from all messages that have
' been received from SenderName since ReceivedDate.
' The resulting text is saved in OutputFile, and
' the original messages are deleted.
' If there are no matching messages, no file is written.

    Dim f As Outlook.MAPIFolder
    Dim m As Outlook.mailItem
    Dim buf As String
    Dim fn As Integer

    If myOutlookApp Is Nothing Then
        If StartOutlook = False Then
            MsgBox "Error initializing Outlook application."
            Exit Sub
        End If
    End If

    Set f = myOutlookNameSpace.GetDefaultFolder(olFolderInbox)
    For Each m In f.Items
        If m.SenderName = SenderName And m.ReceivedTime > _
            ReceivedSince Then
                buf = buf & vbCrLf & m.Body
                m.Delete
        End If
    Next

    If Len(buf) > 0 Then
        fn = FreeFile
        Open OutputFile For Output As #fn
        Print #fn, buf
        Close #fn
    End If

End Sub
```

The MailItem object has a set of methods that let you do things such as deleting, copying, and moving messages, as well as replying to and forwarding messages. Table 10.3 describes these methods.

Table 10.3	MailItem object methods.
Method	**Description**
Copy	Creates a copy of the message and returns a reference to it.
Delete	Deletes the message.
Display	Opens a new Inspector object and displays the message.
Forward	Creates a copy of the message for forwarding.
Move(*Destination*)	Moves the message to the indicated folder. *Destination* is a reference to a MAPIFolder object representing the destination.
PrintOut	Prints the message.
Reply	Creates a copy of the message pre-addressed to the original sender.
ReplyAll	Creates a copy of the message pre-addressed to the original sender and all recipients.
SaveAs(Path, Type)	Saves the message to the file indicated in *Path*. The optional *Type* argument specifies the file format. Values you will use most often are olDoc (Word document), olHTML, olMSG (message format, the default), olRTF (rich text format), and olTXT (text).

To forward a message, execute the Forward method to obtain a copy of the message. Fill in its Recipient and other properties as needed, then execute the Send method. The following code forwards the first message in the Inbox to the recipient "Bill Clinton."

```
Dim myNameSpace As Outlook.NameSpace
Dim InboxFolder As Outlook.MAPIFolder
Dim myForwardMsg As MailItem
Set myNameSpace = Application.GetNameSpace("MAPI")
Set InboxFolder = _
    myNameSpace.GetDefaultFolder(olFolderInbox)
Set myForwardMsg = InboxFolder.Items(1).Forward
myForwardMsg.Recipients.Add "Bill Clinton"
myForwardMsg.Send
```

To reply to a message, execute the Reply method to obtain a copy of the message. The copy's Recipients collection will already have the original message senders added, and the copy's body will contain the text of the original message, formatted as specified in the Outlook options (e.g., each line preceded by >). Then, you can add text to the body as desired and send the message. The following code replies to the first message in the Inbox:

```
Dim myNameSpace As Outlook.NameSpace
Dim InboxFolder As Outlook.MAPIFolder
Dim myReply As MailItem
Dim temp As String
Set myNameSpace = Application.GetNameSpace("MAPI")
Set InboxFolder = _
    myNameSpace.GetDefaultFolder(olFolderInbox)
Set myReply = InboxFolder.Items(1).Reply
temp = myReply.Body
temp = temp & vbCRLF & "Thanks for the message!"
myReply.Body = temp
myReply.Send
```

Creating and Sending Messages

Outlook makes the process of creating and sending an e-mail message simple. The basic steps are:

1. Create a new `MailItem` object.
2. Add one or more recipients to its `Recipients` collections.
3. Put the message subject in its `Subject` property.
4. Put the message text in it `Body` property.
5. Execute its `Send` method.

We will look at some examples soon. First, let's look at the `MailItem` object's properties that are relevant when creating and sending messages. They are described in Table 10.4.

Table 10.4	`MailItem` properties relevant for sending messages.
Property	**Description**
`Attachments`	A collection of `Attachment` objects representing files attached to the message.
`BCC`	A semicolon-delimited list of display names for the blind carbon copy recipients.
`Body`	The text of the message for plain text messages.
`CC`	A semicolon-delimited list of display names for the carbon copy recipients.
`HTMLBody`	The text of the message for HTML format messages.
`ReadReceiptRequested`	True to request a read receipt for the message.

Table 10.4	MailItem properties relevant for sending messages. (Continued)
Property	**Description**
Recipients	A collection of Recipient objects representing the message recipients.
SaveSentMessageFolder	Specifies the Outlook folder where a copy of the message will be saved when it is sent. The default is the Sent Items folder.
Sent	True if the message has been sent, otherwise False.
To	A semicolon-delimited list of display names for the message recipients.

Working with Message Recipients

Each recipient of a message is represented by a Recipient object in the Recipients collection. This is true whether the recipient is a regular "to" recipient or is a CC or BCC recipient; these different recipient types are distinguished by the Type property. To add a recipient to the collection, use the Add method. The syntax is:

```
obj.Recipients.Add(Name)
```

Obj is a MailItem object, and *Name* is the display name of the recipient. Note that the display name of the recipient is not the same as the e-mail address, which is set as the Address property of the Recipient object. The following code illustrates how to add a recipient and specify both its display name and e-mail address:

```
myMessage.Recipients.Add("Bill Gates")
myMessage.Recipients("Bill Gates").Address = _
    "bill_gates@microsoft.com"
```

You can specify a recipient by Name property only and later resolve its e-mail address against an address book. This will be explained later. The important properties of the Recipient object are described in Table 10.5.

To delete a recipient, use the Delete method. The following code deletes the recipient "Bill Gates" from the message's Recipients collection:

```
myMailMessage.Recipients("Bill Gates").Delete
```

To resolve a recipient, use the Resolve method. The Resolve method looks through the address book for a match to the recipient's display name. If a match is found, the corresponding e-mail address is placed in the Address property and the Resolved property is set to True. The Resolve method returns True on success and False on failure. The following code adds a recipient to a message, attempts to resolve it, and if the resolution is not successful, displays the mail item for the user to resolve manually:

```
Set myNewMailItem = myOutlookApp.CreateItem(olMailItem)
Set myNewRecipient = myNewMailItem.Add("Bill Clinton")
If Not myNewRecipient.Resolve Then myNewMailItem.Display
```

If you explicitly set the `Address` property of a recipient there is no need to resolve it.

Table 10.5	Properties of the `Recipient` object.
Property	**Description**
Address	The e-mail address of the recipient.
Name	The display name of the recipient.
Resolved	True if the recipient has been resolved, or validated, against the address book.
Type	Specifies the type of the recipient. Possible settings are `olBCC`, `olCC`, `olTo`, and `olOriginator`.

Working with Address Books

An Outlook application will have one or more address books associated with it. You access these address books by means of the `NameSpace` object's `AddressLists` collection, which contains one `AddressList` object for each available address book. You can get a list of available address books as shown in this code:

```
Dim ab As Outlook.AddressList

For Each ab In myOutlookNameSpace.AddressLists
    Debug.Print ab.Name
Next
```

Likewise, each `AddressList` object has an `AddressEntries` collection that contains one `AddressEntry` object for each entry in the address book. Each `AddressEntry` object has a set of properties, the most important of which are `Name` and `Address`, which contain the display name and e-mail address of the entry. There is also the `DisplayType` property, which determines the type of the entry. The two types of interest are `olUser`, which means the entry is an individual, and `olDistList` which means the entry is a distribution list. When the `DisplayType` is `olDistList` the "entry" is a distribution list, which is in effect a sublist of individual entries, and has its own `AddressEntries` collection. A distribution list lets you keep related address book entries together and quickly send a message to everyone on the list.

The procedure in Listing 10–6 sends the specified message to everyone in the specified address book, and the procedure in Listing 10–7 does the same, but for the members of a distribution list.

Listing 10–6   *Sending a message to all entries in an address book.*

```
Public Sub SendMessageToAll(MessageBody As String, _
    MessageSubject As String, AddressBookName As String)

' Creates a message with the specified body and subject
' and sends it to everyone in the specified address book.

Dim adrBook As Outlook.AddressList
Dim adrEntry As Outlook.AddressEntry
Dim newMessage As Outlook.MailItem
Dim newRecipient As Outlook.Recipient

If myOutlookApp Is Nothing Then
    If StartOutlook = False Then
        MsgBox "Error initializing Outlook application."
        Exit Sub
    End If
End If

Set adrBook = myOutlookNameSpace.AddressLists(AddressBookName)
Set newMessage = myOutlookApp.CreateItem(olMailItem)
newMessage.Subject = MessageSubject
newMessage.Body = MessageBody

For Each adrEntry In adrBook.AddressEntries
    Set newRecipient = newMessage.Recipients.Add(adrEntry.Name)
    newRecipient.Resolve
Next

newMessage.Send

End Sub
```

Listing 10–7   *Sending a message to all members of a distribution list.*

```
Public Sub SendMessageToList(MessageBody As String, _
    MessageSubject As String, _
    AddressBookName As String, _
    ListName As String)

Dim adrBook As Outlook.AddressList
Dim adrList As Outlook.AddressEntry
Dim adrEntry As Outlook.AddressEntry
Dim newMessage As Outlook.MailItem
Dim newRecipient As Outlook.Recipient

If myOutlookApp Is Nothing Then
    If StartOutlook = False Then
        MsgBox "Error initializing Outlook application."
        Exit Sub
    End If
End If

Set adrBook = myOutlookNameSpace.AddressLists(AddressBookName)
Set newMessage = myOutlookApp.CreateItem(olMailItem)
newMessage.Subject = MessageSubject
newMessage.Body = MessageBody

Set adrList = adrBook.AddressEntries(ListName)

For Each adrEntry In adrList.Members
    Set newRecipient = newMessage.Recipients.Add(adrEntry.Name)
    newRecipient.Resolve
Next

newMessage.Send

End Sub
```

Working with Attachments

An e-mail message can have one or more attachments, files, or links to files that are part of the message. A `MailItem` object has the `Attachments` collection that contains one `Attachment` object for each message attachment. You can determine whether a message has attachments by examining the collection's `Count` property:

```
If myMailItem.Attachments.Count > 1 Then
' Deal with message attachments here.
End If
```

Each `Attachment` object has a set of properties, as described in Table 10.6.

Table 10.6	Properties of the `Attachment` object.
Property	**Description**
`DisplayName`	The name displayed below the attachment's icon when the message is displayed on-screen. Not necessarily the same as the filename.
`FileName`	The filename of the attachment.
`PathName`	The full path to an attached linked file. This property is valid only for linked attachments.
`Type`	The type of the attachment. Possible settings are `olByValue` (an attached file), and `olByReference` (a link to a file).

To save an attachment from a received message, use the `SaveAsFile` method. The syntax is:

```
obj.SaveAsFile(Path)
```

Obj is a reference to an `Attachment` object, and *Path* is the path where the file is to be saved. The following code saves all the attachments from the specified message, using the original filename and the path specified in the `SAVEPATH` constant:

```
Dim atc As Outlook.Attachment

For Each atc in myMailMessage.Attachments
    If atc.Type = olByValue Then
        atc.SaveAsFile(SAVEPATH & atc.FileName)
    End If
Next
```

To add an attachment to a message, use the `Attachments` collection's Add method. The syntax is:

```
obj.Attachments.Add(Source, Type, Position, DisplayName)
```

Obj is a reference to a `MailItem` object. *Source* is a required argument specifying the path to the file to attach. *Type* is an optional argument specifying the type of the attachment: `olByValue` (for an attached file) or `olByReference` for a link (shortcut) to a file. *Position* is an optional argument specifying the position of the attachment in the message. The default is for attachments to be placed at the end of the message. *DisplayName* is an optional argument giving the attachment's display name. If this argument is omitted, the name of the file will be used as the display name.

Microsoft recommends that a message be saved before adding or removing attachments. The following code adds two file attachments, an Excel workbook and a Word document, to the specified message:

```
myMailMessage.Save
With myMailMessage.Attachments
    .Add "c:\sales\summary.xls", olByValue, , _
        "Sales Summary Worksheet"
    .Add "c:\sales\Report.doc", olByValue, , _
        "Sales Report"
End With
```

VBA in Outlook

Outlook differs from most other Office applications in the way VBA projects are handled. Word, Excel, Access, and PowerPoint permit a VBA project to be associated with a specific document and/or template. Since Outlook does not have documents *per se*, the VBA project is associated with the Outlook application. For a given user, therefore, there can be only a single Outlook project, which is stored in a file named VbaProject.OTM. For Windows 95/98/2000 this file is stored in c:\windows\application data\Microsoft\outlook when there are not multiple users set up, and in c:\windows\profiles*username*\application data\microsoft\outlook when multiple users are set up. In Windows NT, this file is stored in c:\winnt\profiles*username*\application data\Microsoft\outlook.

The one Outlook project can contain multiple modules, including class modules and user forms. It always contains a class module called ThisOutlookSession which is pre-bound to the Outlook Application object. Application-level events (covered in the next section) are automatically available to you in this class module. The ThisOutlookSession module is analogous to the ThisDocument and ThisWorkbook objects in Word and Excel.

Events in Outlook

Some of the events exposed in Outlook are *application-level* events which are automatically available in the ThisOutlookSession module. These events are associated with the Outlook application or with top-level objects in the application. You can write VBA procedures to respond to these events, as needed. A description of these events follows.

ItemSend occurs whenever an item is sent, either by the user or by the Send method. The syntax is:

```
Sub Application_ItemSend(Item As Object, Cancel As Boolean)
```

Item is a reference to the object being sent. *Cancel* is initially False. If code in the event procedure sets it to True the send operation is cancelled.

Using Events

Remember that, like other Office applications, you must declare an instance of the Outlook application in a class module (in this case, the `ThisOutlookSession` module) using the `WithEvents` keyword, in order for events to be available.

NewMail occurs whenever e-mail is received. The syntax is:

```
Sub Application_NewMail()
```

The code shown in Listing 10–8 will display the Inbox folder whenever new mail arrives. This code must be in the `ThisOutlookSession` module, and the `myOutlookApp` variable must be initialized by other code. This procedure makes use of the Outlook `Explorers` collection, which I will cover soon.

Listing 10–8 *Displaying the Inbox folder whenever new mail arrives.*

```
Dim WithEvents myOutlookApp As Outlook.Application

Private Sub myOlApp_NewMail()
    Dim exp As Outlook.Explorers
    Dim fld As Outlook.MAPIFolder
    Dim i As Integer
    Set exp = myOlApp.Explorers
    Set fld = myOlApp.GetNamespace("MAPI"). _
            GetDefaultFolder(olFolderInbox)
    If exp.Count <> 0 Then
        For i = 1 To exp.Count
            On Error GoTo continue
            If exp.Item(i).CurrentFolder.Name = "Inbox" Then
                exp.Item(i).Display
                exp.Item(i).Activate
                Exit Sub
            End If
continue:
        Next i
    End If
    On Error GoTo 0
    fld.Display

End Sub
```

Quit occurs when Outlook is about to close, and Startup occurs when Outlook loads, after any add-in programs are loaded. The syntax is as follows:

```
Sub Application_Quit()
Sub Application_Startup()
```

Code in your VBA project can use these events for initialization on startup and to perform any required cleanup and data saving upon quitting.

Summing Up

Of Outlook's many capabilities, e-mail is certainly the most important. These days it's a rare enterprise that does not depend heavily on e-mail communication. Many people complain about the inordinate amount of time they spend dealing with e-mail messages—reading, replying, and organizing. The ability to automate Outlook from VBA code, and to integrate it into a custom Office solution, seems to have endless possibilities. Given the power and flexibility of its object model, Outlook is up to any task you can throw at it.

Using the Office Shared Components

Some of the components that are provided by Office are shared, meaning that they do not belong to any specific Office application. These components perform commonly needed tasks, such as providing user feedback and locating files. The shared components are available in any Office application, and can be very useful when you are creating a custom Office solution. This chapter covers the most commonly needed shared components.

Shared Components Overview

There are several Office shared components. In brief summary, they are:

- The Office Assistant provides an animated character that can interact with your users.
- The `FileSearch` object lets you locate disk files that meet certain criteria.
- Command Bars let you create custom toolbars and menus for your project.
- Document properties keep track of information about any Office document.
- The `HTMLProject` object represents HTML code in an Office document.
- Scripts let you use VBScript code in an Office document.

The first four items on this list are needed most often, and will be covered in this chapter. You can find information about the other shared components in the Office Developer online help.

Shared components do not have to be created, using the `New` keyword, before being used. They are always available by using the `Application` object's relevant property. For example, if `myWordApp` is a reference to a `Word.Application` object, then you access the `FileSearch` object as `myWordApp.FileSearch`. The type library for the shared components is the Microsoft Office 9.0 Object Library. With the exception of Access, all of the Office applications automatically include a reference to this library in the VBA References dialog box. In Access, you must set this reference manually to work with the shared components.

The Office Assistant

With the single exception of FrontPage, the Office Assistant is available in all Office applications. It shows on-screen as a small animated character, such as a paper clip, and its default function is to provide an interface between the user and Office's online help. It can be programmed, however, and you can customize the Office Assistant to do things such as providing special context-sensitive help, gathering information from the user, or pointing out specific items on-screen.

Displaying and Animating the Office Assistant

To program the Office Assistant, you must first create a reference to it. Then, by accessing the Assistant's properties and methods you can make it do what you want. Programmatically, the Office Assistant consists of three things: the

Office Assistant itself (the animated character), the balloon, and the material inside the balloon.

Save Office Assistant Properties

Most Office users will have customized their Office Assistant to operate as they want when they are using the Office applications. Therefore, you should always be sure to save the Office Assistant property values before you change them, then set them back to the original values when you are done using the Assistant.

The most basic properties of the Office Assistant control whether it is on and whether it is visible, and are controlled by the On and Visible properties, respectively. To animate the Assistant, you set its Animation property to one of the msoAnimation constants, each of which has a descriptive name. For example, msoAnimationCheckingSomething makes the Assistant character act as if it is examining something, and msoAnimationGestureDown makes it point downward. You can find a full list of these constants in the Object Browser.

If you are performing several animations in sequence, you need to give each one time to complete before the next one starts. Suppose you ran this code, which does not provide for a pause:

```
Dim Office Assistant As Assistant

Set Office Assistant = Application.Assistant

With Office Assistant
    .On = True
    .Visible = True
    .Animation = msoAnimationGestureDown
    .Animation = msoAnimationCharacterSuccessMajor
End With
```

You would only see the second animation as there was no time for the first one to complete. You can use the Pause procedure, shown in Listing 11–1, to pause the program for a specified period. With a little experimentation you can determine the amount of time needed to pause for the various animations.

| Listing 11–1 | *The Pause function lets the program pause for the specified number of seconds.* |

```
Public Sub Pause(delayInSeconds As Single)

' Pauses by the specified number of seconds.

Dim t As Single
t = Timer
Do
    DoEvents
Loop While (Timer - t) < delayInSeconds

End Sub
```

The position of the Office Assistant is controlled by its `Top` and `Left` properties, which specify the position of the Assistant with respect to the top left corner of the screen, in pixels. The code in Listing 11–2 shows how to save original Office Assistant properties, locate the Assistant at the top left corner of the application window, perform several animations, and return the Assistant to its original state.

| Listing 11–2 | *Animating the Office Assistant.* |

```
Public Sub AnimateAssistant()

Dim Office Assistant As Assistant
Dim oldVisible As Boolean
Dim oldOn As Boolean

Set Office Assistant = Application.Assistant

With Office Assistant
    oldVisible = .Visible
    oldOn = .On
    .On = True
    .Visible = True
    .Top = Application.ActiveWindow.Top
    .Left = Application.ActiveWindow.Left
    .Animation = msoAnimationGestureDown
    Call Pause(3)
    .Animation = msoAnimationListensToComputer
    Call Pause(4)
    .Animation = msoAnimationCharacterSuccessMajor
    Call Pause(4)
    .On = oldOn
    .Visible = oldVisible
End With

End Sub
```

The character displayed by the Office Assistant is determined by its `FileName` property, which specifies the .acs file to use. Several characters are supplied with Office, and you can create your own using the Microsoft Agent ActiveX control's character editor. To display a different character, set the `Assistant.FileName` property to the desired file. If the .acs files are in their default location you do not need to specify a path.

Using Balloons

The Office Assistant can display a balloon, as shown in Figure 11–1. The balloon lets you display information to, and obtain information from, the user. You can create multiple balloon objects, although only one can be displayed at a time. A balloon can contain text, labels, check boxes, icons, and bitmaps.

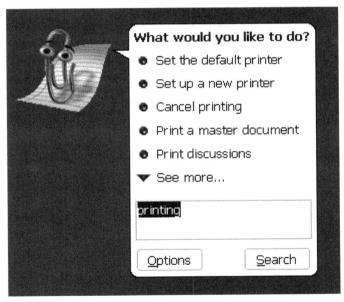

Figure 11–1   *The Office Assistant displaying a balloon.*

To create a balloon, call the Office Assistant's `NewBalloon` method. Set the balloon's properties as desired, then display it with the `Show` method. The procedure in Listing 11–3 shows how to create and display a simple balloon that has a title, a message, an icon, and an OK button.

| Listing 11-3 | *Creating and displaying a simple balloon.* |

```
Public Sub BasicBalloon()

Dim myBalloon As Balloon
Dim title As String
Dim message As String

With Application.Assistant
    .On = True
    .Visible = True
    Set myBalloon = .NewBalloon
End With

title = "Your first balloon!"
message = "Click OK after reading this message."

With myBalloon
    .BalloonType = msoBalloonTypeButtons
    .Button = msoButtonSetOK
    .Icon = msoIconAlertInfo
    .Heading = title
    .Text = message
    .Show
End With

End Sub
```

Limited formatting of the balloon message is possible by including codes in brackets within the text. You can control underlining and text color. Use {ul 1} to turn underlining on, and {ul 0} to turn it off. To change text color, use {cn *n*} in which *n* is a number specifying one of the 16 system colors:

0	Black	248	Medium gray
1	Dark red	249	Red
2	Dark green	250	Green
3	Dark yellow	251	Yellow
4	Dark blue	252	Blue
5	Dark magenta	253	Magenta
6	Dark cyan	254	Cyan
7	Light gray	255	White

Here's an example of text formatted with these codes:

```
This is normal text, {ul 1}this is underlined{ul 0}, this
is normal again, {cf 254}this is magenta{cf 0} and this is
black (the default color).
```

The `Button` property determines which buttons are displayed in the balloon. You can display a single OK button, as in the example above, or a Cancel button, or no button at all. Your choices are enumerated as msoButtonSet constants, which can be viewed in the Object browser.

DISPLAYING CONTROLS IN A BALLOON

A balloon can display labels and/or check boxes. A label can be selected, or clicked, by the user and your code can determine which label was selected. To add labels to a balloon, use its `Labels` property. To "create" a label all you need do is assign text to a label's `Text` property. The procedure in Listing 11–4 displays a list of choices to the user, then responds to the choice that was made. The balloon displayed by this code is shown in Figure 11–2.

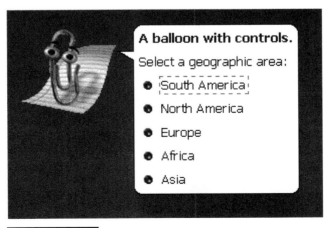

Figure 11–2   *The Office Assistant displaying a balloon.*

| **Listing 11–4** | *Using labels to get user selections.* |

```
Public Sub BalloonWithLabels()

Dim myBalloon As Balloon
Dim title As String
Dim message As String
Dim choice As Integer

With Application.Assistant
    .On = True
    .Visible = True
    Set myBalloon = .NewBalloon
End With

title = "A balloon with controls."
message = "Select a geographic area:"

With myBalloon
    .BalloonType = msoBalloonTypeButtons
    .Button = msoButtonSetNone
    .Heading = title
    .Text = message
    .Labels(1).Text = "South America"
    .Labels(2).Text = "North America"
    .Labels(3).Text = "Europe"
    .Labels(4).Text = "Africa"
    .Labels(5).Text = "Asia"
    choice = .Show
    If choice > 0 Then
        MsgBox "You selected " & .Labels(choice).Text
    End If
End With

End Sub
```

If you need to let the user make more than one selection, you can use checkboxes. They work pretty much the same as labels except that the balloon is not automatically closed when the user clicks a checkbox, as is the case with labels. Therefore a balloon that uses checkboxes must have a button to close the balloon after the user had made his or her selections. The procedure in Listing 11–5 shows how to use checkboxes; this code creates the balloon shown in Figure 11–3.

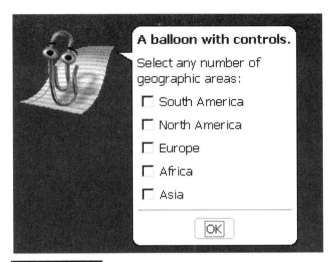

Figure 11–3   *Getting multiple choices with checkboxes.*

Listing 11–5   *Displaying a balloon with checkboxes.*

```
Public Sub BalloonWithCheckBoxes()

Dim myBalloon As Balloon
Dim title As String
Dim message As String
Dim choice As Integer
Dim buf As String
Dim chkBox

With Application.Assistant
    .On = True
    .Visible = True
    Set myBalloon = .NewBalloon
End With

title = "A balloon with controls."
message = "Select any number of geographic areas:"

With myBalloon
    .BalloonType = msoBalloonTypeButtons
    .Button = msoButtonSetOK
    .Heading = title
    .Text = message
    .Checkboxes(1).Text = "South America"
    .Checkboxes(2).Text = "North America"
```

```
            .Checkboxes(3).Text = "Europe"
            .Checkboxes(4).Text = "Africa"
            .Checkboxes(5).Text = "Asia"
            choice = .Show
            buf = "You selected "
            For Each chkBox In .Checkboxes
                If chkBox.Checked Then
                    buf = buf & chkBox.Text & "; "
                End If
            Next
            MsgBox buf
        End With

        End Sub
```

USING MODELESS BALLOONS

The balloons we have seen so far are modal, meaning that the user cannot continue working in the application until the balloon is closed. You can also create *modeless* balloons, which remain displayed while the user continues working. Modeless balloons can be used, for example, to display instructions for the user to follow.

To create a modeless balloon, set its `Mode` property to `msoModeModeless`. You must also display at least one button, provide the name of a procedure to call when the balloon is closed, and supply a unique identifier for the balloon's `Private` property. This property will identify the balloon should the same callback procedure be used for more than one balloon.

The callback procedure must be written to take three arguments. The syntax is as follows:

```
Sub CallbackProc(bln As Balloon, button As Long, lPriv As Long)
```

While you can select the argument names as desired, their types must be as shown here. When the balloon is closed, the associated callback procedure is called and the callback procedure arguments contain the following information:

- `bln` contains a reference to the balloon that was closed.
- `button` contains a numerical code indicating which button was clicked in the balloon.
- `iPriv` contains the value in the balloon's `Private` property.

At a minimum, the callback procedure should close the balloon by calling its `Close` method. It can also perform other actions as needed, based on information entered by the user in the balloon. Listing 11–6 shows a callback function that closes the associated balloon then displays a message indicating which button was clicked. Listing 11–7 shows the code to display the associated modeless balloon.

Listing 11-6   *Demonstrating a callback function for a modeless balloon.*

```
Public Sub BalloonClosed(bln As Balloon, lbtn As Long, lPriv As Long)

bln.Close
If lbtn = -6 Then
    MsgBox "The balloon has been closed with the Next button."
ElseIf lbtn = -12 Then
    MsgBox "The balloon has been closed with the Cancel button."
End If

End Sub
```

Listing 11-7   *Displaying a modeless balloon.*

```
Public Sub ModelessBalloon()

Dim myBalloon As Balloon
Dim title As String
Dim message As String
Dim choice As Integer
Dim buf As String
Dim chkBox

With Application.Assistant
    .On = True
    .Visible = True
    Set myBalloon = .NewBalloon
End With

title = "Printing a document."
message = "Here are the steps to print a document:"

With myBalloon
    .BalloonType = msoBalloonTypeNumbers
    .Button = msoButtonSetNextClose
    .Mode = msoModeModeless
    .Callback = "BalloonClosed"
    .Heading = title
    .Text = message
    .Labels(1).Text = "Select File from the main menu."
    .Labels(2).Text = "Select Print from the File menu."
    .Labels(3).Text = "Check the options in the dialog box."
    .Labels(4).Text = "Click the OK button."
    .Show
End With

End Sub
```

The **FileSearch** Object

You use the `FileSearch` object to search for files that meet certain criteria. The functionality of this object is the same as you see in the Open dialog box and the Advanced Find dialog box, part of all Office applications. The basics of searching are as follows:

1. Create a reference to the `FileSearch` object.
2. Clear data from any previous search.
3. Specify where—which folder—you are searching in.
4. Specify the file name you are looking for, which may include wildcards.
5. Specify whether subfolders should be searched.
6. Execute the search.
7. Retrieve the results.

Here's a simple example. The following code prints, in the Immediate window, the names of all document files (*.doc) in the folder c:\documents and its subfolders:

```
Dim myFSO As FileSearch
Dim foundFile

Set myFSO = Application.FileSearch

With myFSO
    .NewSearch
    .LookIn = "c:\documents"
    .SearchSubFolders = True
    .FileName = "*.doc"
    If .Execute() > 0 Then
        For Each foundFile In .FoundFiles
            Debug.Print foundFile
        Next
    End If
End With
```

In addition to specifying the name to search for, you can restrict the search to files that were last modified in a certain timeframe, or files of a certain type. The most commonly needed properties of the `FileSearch` object are described in Table 11.1.

Table 11.1	FileSearch object properties.

Property	Description
FileName	The name of the file to find. Can include the wildcards ? (to match any single character) and * (to match any sequence of 0 or more characters).
FileType	Specifies the type of files to search for. Can be one of the following MsoFileType constants: msoFileTypeAllFiles, msoFileTypeBinders, msoFileTypeDatabases, msoFileTypeExcelWorkbooks, msoFileTypeOfficeFiles (the default), msoFileTypePowerPointPresentations, msoFileTypeTemplates, or msoFileTypeWordDocuments.
FoundFiles	Returns a FoundFiles object containing the names of all files found.
LastModified	Specifies the amount of time since the file was last modified and saved. Can be one of the following MsoLastModified constants: msoLastModifiedAnyTime (the default), msoLastModifiedLastMonth, msoLastModifiedLastWeek, msoLastModifiedThisMonth, msoLastModifiedThisWeek, msoLastModifiedToday, or msoLastModifiedYesterday.
LookIn	Specifies the folder where the search is to start.
SearchSubfolders	Specifies whether subfolders will be searched. True/False value.

The FileSearch object has two methods. The NewSearch method, which takes no arguments, resets all of the FileSearch object's properties to their default value (except for LookIn, which retains its value). The Execute method executes the currently defined search. Its syntax is:

```
fso.Execute(SortBy, SortOrder, AlwaysAccurate)
```

Fso is a reference to a FileSearch object. All of the methods are optional. SortBy specifies how the returned list of files is to be sorted. Possible values are msoSortbyFileName (the default), msoSortbyFileType, msoSortbyLastModified, or msoSortbySize. SortOrder specifes the order of the sort: msoSortOrderAscending (the default) or msoSortOrderDescending. AlwaysAccurate is a True/False value specifying whether the search should be limited to the file index (False) or whether files added since the index was last updated should be included as well (True, the default). The Execute method returns a value greater than 0 if one or more files were found, and 0 if no files were found.

After a successful search the FoundFiles property lets you access the files that were found. The FoundFiles.Count property tells you how many files were found, and you can use the `For Each...Next` loop to access the entire list of files (as in the previous example).

Let's look at a concrete example. The procedure `SendNewWoksheets` in Listing 11–8 uses the `FileSearch` object to locate all Excel workbooks in c:\documents that were modified today, then includes all the matching files as attachments in an e-mail message to the specified recipient.

Listing 11–8	*This procedures sends all new worksheets to the specified recipient.*

```
Public Sub SendNewWorksheets(Recipient As String)

Dim olApp As Outlook.Application
Dim fso As FileSearch
Dim msg As Outlook.mailItem
Dim foundFile

Set olApp = New Outlook.Application
Set fso = Application.FileSearch

With fso
    .NewSearch
    .FileType = msoFileTypeExcelWorkbooks
    .LastModified = msoLastModifiedToday
    .LookIn = "c:\documents"
    .SearchSubFolders = True
    .Execute
    If .FoundFiles.count > 0 Then
        Set msg = olApp.CreateItem(olMailItem)
        msg.To = Recipient
        msg.Subject = "Latest figures"
        msg.Body = "The latest worksheets are attached."
        For Each foundFile In .FoundFiles
            msg.Attachments.Add (foundFile)
        Next
        msg.Send
    End If
End With

End Sub
```

Command Bars

Office commands bars are of three types: menu bar, toolbar, and pop-up menu. The Office application use many built-in command bars, and you can create custom command bars as well. In all Office applications, you can create custom toolbars using the Customize dialog box on the Tools menu.

Access lets you also create menu bars and pop-up menus from this dialog box, while all other Office applications require that menu bars and pop-up menus be created from VBA code.

Command bars are represented as `CommandBar` objects in the `Application` object's `CommandBars` collection. To create a new command bar, use this collection's `Add` method:

```
Application.CommandBars.Add(Name, Position, MenuBar, _
                            Temporary)
```

Name is the optional name of the command bar. If omitted a default name of the form Custom1 is used.

Position specifies the type and/or position of the command bar. Settings are as follows:

`msoBarLeft,` `msoBarTop,` `msoBarRight,` `msoBarBottom`	A toolbar docked at the indicated position in the application window.
`msoBarFloating`	A floating toolbar.
`msoBarPopup`	A pop-up menu.
`msoBarMenuBar`	A menu bar.

MenuBar specifies whether the new command bar will replace the active menu bar. The default is False.

Temporary indicates whether the command bar is temporary (True), meaning it will be deleted when the application is closed. The default is False.

Once you have created a command bar you need to add controls to it. The controls on a command bar are represented by the `CommandBarControls` collection, accessed via the `CommandBar` object's `Controls` property. You use this collection's `Add` method to add a control to the command bar:

```
obj.Controls.Add(Type, Id, Parameter, Before, Temporary)
```

Obj is a reference to a `CommandBar` object.

Type specifies the type of control. Possible settings are:

```
msoControlButton
msoControlEdit
msoControlDropdown
msoControlComboBox
msoControlPopup
```

ID specifies an existing control to add to the command bar. If ID is 1 or omitted, a blank control of the kind specified by Type is added.

Parameter is an optional type `Variant` argument that lets you associate some custom information with the control (much like the `Tag` property of Visual Basic controls). Neither VBA nor Office makes any use of the *Parameter* argument.

Before is a value indicating the position of the new control on the command bar. The control will be placed before the existing control at the specified position. If this argument is omitted, the control will be placed at the end of the command bar.

Temporary specifies whether the control will be deleted when the application closes. The default is False.

By using the *ID* argument you can add existing buttons to a command bar, such as the buttons found on Word's built-in toolbars. When you place an existing button on a command bar, its original functionality comes with it—you do not need to program its action. You obtain an existing button's ID by referring to its toolbar and its name. This line, for example, returns the ID of the Cut button on the Editing toolbar:

```
CommandBars("Edit").Controls("Cut").ID
```

The code in Listing 11–9 creates a custom toolbar that contains the Cut, Copy and Paste buttons from the Editing toolbar and the Bold, Italic, and Underline buttons from the Formatting toolbar.

Listing 11–9	*Creating a custom toolbar.*

```
Public Sub CreateCommandBar()

Dim myCB As CommandBar

Set myCB = CommandBars.Add("Custom Editing")

With myCB.Controls
    .Add msoControlButton, CommandBars("Edit").Controls("Cut").ID
    .Add msoControlButton, CommandBars("Edit").Controls("Copy").ID
    .Add msoControlButton, CommandBars("Edit").Controls("Paste").ID
    .Add msoControlButton, _
        CommandBars("Formatting").Controls("Italic").ID
    .Add msoControlButton, _
        CommandBars("Formatting").Controls("Bold").ID
    .Add msoControlButton, _
        CommandBars("Formatting").Controls("Underline").ID
End With
myCB.Visible = True

End Sub
```

Much of the power of creating custom command bars comes from the ability to restrict what the user can do in the application. You can create a command bar that contains buttons for only those commands you want the user to have access to, then display your custom command bar while hiding the default command bars and menus.

Document Properties

Every document created in Office has a set of properties associated with it. In this context, the term *document* refers to any Office application file and not just to Word documents. Document properties include a set of built-in properties, and you can add your own custom properties as well.

Word, Excel, and PowerPoint use Office's shared `DocumentProperties` collection to store both built-in and custom properties. From within these applications you access document properties by selecting Properties from the File menu. The `DocumentProperties` collection is accessed by means of the `BuiltInDocumentProperties` and `CustomDocumentProperties` properties of a document. Each individual property is stored as a `DocumentProperty` object.

Access, FrontPage, and Outlook do things differently. The properties of a database are stored as part of the database, and not in the `DocumentProperties` collection. Custom and built-in properties in FrontPage are kept in the `MetaTags` and `Properties` collections of the `WebFile` object. Outlook does not use document properties. The remainder of this section is applicable only to Word, Excel, and PowerPoint.

To access a built-in property, use the `BuiltInDocumentProperties` collection, referring to the property by name. This line of code obtains the Title property of the active document:

```
docTitle = _
    ActiveDocument.BuiltInDocumentProperties("Title")
```

You set a property value in the same way. This code prompts the user for his or her name and sets the document's `Author` property accordingly.

```
ActiveDocument.BuiltInDocumentProperties("Author") = _
    InputBox("Please enter your name")
```

To create a custom property, use the `CustomDocumentProperties` collection's `Add` method. The syntax is:

```
obj.Add(Name, LinkToContent, Type, Value, LinkSource)
```

Obj is a reference to the `CustomDocumentProperties` collection.

Name is a required argument giving the name of the property.

LinkToContent is a required True/False value specifying whether the property is linked to the contents of the document.

Type is a required argument specifying the data type of the property. Possile settings are:

```
msoPropertyTypeBoolean
soPropertyTypeDate
msoPropertyTypeFloat
msoPropertyTypeNumber
msoPropertyTypeString
```

Value is the property value. This argument can be omitted, or is ignored, if *LinkToContent* is True.

LinkSource is required only if *LinkToSource* is True. It specifies the document source for the linked property. The types of source linking are determined by the document, and you can find details in the documentation for each application.

Linked Properties

Linked properties are updated only when the document is saved.

The following code adds two custom properties to the active Excel workbook.

```
With ActiveWorkbook.CustomDocumentProperties
    .Add Name:="Employee Code", LinkToContent:=False, _
        Type:=msoPropertyTypeNumber, Value:=1234
    .Add Name:="Employee Name", LinkToContent:=False, _
        Type:=msoPropertyTypeString, Value:="Ned Smith"
End With
```

Once you have created a custom property, you change or read its value as described above for built-in properties.

Summing Up

Some Office projects do not use any of the shared components, but when you need the functionality of these objects you'll be glad to have them. Using the Office Assistant to provide feedback and instructions to the user, for example, can make the difference between an ordinary custom application and one that really shines and impresses your clients. Likewise, the use of Command Bars to provide easy access to your application's features can make a custom application much easier to use.

The VBA Language

You have seen a lot of the VBA language used in the previous chapters, and you probably have a good idea how certain parts of it work. To be an efficient Office developer, however, you need to have a good command of all the language elements. VBA is a powerful and flexible tool, and like all tools, you need to learn how to use it properly if you are to get the best results.

This section contains eight chapters. The first six deal with the fundamental language elements: storing data, controlling program execution, making decisions, manipulating text and number data, working with dates and times, and accessing disk files. These topics are the "meat and potatoes" of VBA programming, and while there is a good amount of information to learn, VBA was designed to be relatively easy to grasp. The final two chapters explore some more advanced areas of VBA: defining your own classes and designing custom screen windows.

Data Storage and Operators

One of the most fundamental things any VBA program does is work with information, or data. Clearly, a program needs some place to keep data while the program is executing. It also needs tools to manipulate the data as needed by the particular application. VBA stores data in variables, and uses operators for many data manipulations. This chapter starts you off with a look at the basics of VBA syntax, and then provides detailed coverage of variables and operators.

Basic VBA Syntax

A VBA program is made up of statements. Each statement is a discrete instruction telling the system to perform a specific action—add two numbers, write some text to a disk file, display a graphic on screen, and so on. For the most part, each statement is on its own line. There are two exceptions to this general rule. As we will see in Chapter 13, VBA has some compound statements that span two or more lines. Also, it is possible to put two or more VBA statements on the same line if they are separated by a colon. However, I advise against doing this because it offers no real advantage and can make your source code difficult to read.

The Line Continuation Character

Some VBA statements can be quite long. The VBA code editor does not care how long a statement is, but if a line of code disappears off the right edge of your screen it can make editing cumbersome. You can use the *line continuation character* to split a single line of code over two or more lines in the editor. To do so, type a space followed by an underscore where you want the line to break, then hit Enter. Here is a long line broken into three lines:

```
ActiveWorkbook.CustomDocumentProperties.Add _
    Name:="Employee Code" LinkToContent:=False, _
    Type:=msoPropertyTypeNumber, Value:=1234
```

Note than the second and subsequent continued lines are indented with respect to the first line (by pressing Tab). This is not required but makes the code easier to read by visually indicating that the second and third lines are subsidiary to the first. You can use the line continuation character anywhere in a line of code except inside double quotes. The following, for example, would not be permitted:

```
ActiveWorkbook.CustomDocumentProperties.Add Name:="Employee _
    Code" LinkToContent:=False, _
    Type:=msoPropertyTypeNumber, Value:=1234
```

Comments

VBA code can also contain *comments*. Comments are ignored when the program runs, and serve only for you to document how the code works, add reminders to yourself, and so on. There are two ways to create a comment. Any line that starts with Rem is a comment, and anything on a line after the ' (single quote) character is a comment. The ' can be at the start of the line or following a VBA statement; Rem, however, can only be at the start of a line. For example:

```
Rem This is a comment.
' this is another comment
Dim X As Integer ' This too is a comment.
```

You can see that comments are displayed in a different color in the VBA editor. I advise you to get into the habit of liberally commenting your code. What seems clear to you when you write the code may not be so clear when you return to it next month! Also, if you will be sharing code with others in a development team, comments are almost a necessity.

Commenting Out Code

When you are developing VBA code there will be times when you want to temporarily remove or turn off one or more statements. Rather than erasing them and later typing them back in, simply convert them to comments.

Formatting Source Code

VBA does not care about white space in your code—spaces, tabs, and blank lines. You can use white space to format your source code for easy readability. Commonly used formatting conventions include separating sections of code with different purposes by blank lines, and indenting statements with respect to other statements to which they are logically subsidiary. If you follow the style you see in this book's listings you cannot go wrong.

VBA Editor Options

If you have worked with the VBA editor at all, you have probably noticed that it helps you as you work, performing actions such as formatting code and correcting capitalization as well as displaying comments and code in different colors. You may or may not find these actions helpful. Fortunately, you can control which of these automatic aids are active as well as other aspects of how the editor works. To do so, select Tools, Options and then make the desired settings in the Options dialog box. The details of setting VBA editor options were covered in Chapter 3.

Storing Data

A variable is a place where your program can store data while it is running. As the name implies, the data in a variable can change as often as needed. VBA provides a complete set of different types of variables suited for different kinds of data. Let's look first at naming and declaring variables, then we will examine the different variable types.

Naming and Declaring Variables

Each variable in a program needs its own unique name (but see the section on variable scope later in this chapter). You can name a variable pretty much anything you like as long as you follow these rules:

- Do not use one of VBA's keywords.
- The maximum length is 255 characters.
- The first character must be a letter.
- The name cannot contain a period, space, or any of these characters: ! @ # & % $

The case of names does not matter, although you will see that the VBA editor automatically adjusts case to be the same for all instances of a given name. Thus, if the first time you use a variable you call it `Total`, and the second time you type in `TOTAL`, the second entry will be changed to `Total`.

It's an excellent idea to use descriptive variable names—names that describe the data the variable is holding. For example, a variable that holds a telephone number might be called `PhoneNumber` or `TelNum`. You could call it `Banana` or `X55` and VBA would not care, but clearly, the descriptive names make your code a lot easier to read and debug.

While not required, it is common practice to use a combination of upper- and lowercase letters for variable names. Here are some examples:

```
TotalOfSales
AverageCost
RecipientName
```

Names in all uppercase are traditionally reserved for constants, which are covered later in the chapter.

Variables should be declared before being used for the first time. A variable declaration takes the following form:

```
Dim varname As type
```

Varname is the name of the variable, and *type* is the data type (as covered in the following sections). If you omit the `As type` part of the declaration, the variable is created as VBA's default type, `Variant`. You can place multiple declarations on the same line:

```
Dim varname1 As type1, varname2 As type2, varname3 As type3
```

Note that I say variables *should* be declared, not that they *must* be declared. As a holdover from earlier versions of the Basic language, VBA gives you the option of not requiring variable declaration—you can simply use new variable names as needed. This may sound convenient, but it is a very bad idea. When variable declaration is required, misspelling a variable name results in an error message when you run the program, so the misspelling can be easily corrected. If variable declaration is not required, then misspellings go undetected and can cause lots of problems. To make sure variable declaration is required, select Tools, Options and ensure that the Require Variable Declaration option is checked. You can obtain the same effect by placing the `Option Explicit` statement at the start of every VBA module.

Numbers

VBA provides six different types of variables for storing numeric values. These types differ in two ways: whether the number can have a fractional part (a floating point value) or can only be a whole number (an integer value), and the range of values permitted—that is, the largest and smallest values that can be stored. The three floating point data types also differ in their precision, or the number of accurate digits. Table 12.1 lists VBA's six numeric data types.

Table 12.1	VBA's numeric data types.			
Name	**Type**	**Range**	**Precision**	**Size**
Byte	Integer	0 to 255	N/A	1 byte
Integer	Integer	-32,768 to 32,767	N/A	2 bytes
Long	Integer	-2,147,483,648 to 2,147,483,647	N/A	4 bytes
Single	Floating point	-3.4×10^{38} to 3.4×10^{38} *	6 digits	4 bytes
Double	Floating point	-1.79×10^{308} to 1.79×10^{308} *	14 digits	8 bytes
Currency	Floating point	-9.22×10^{11} TO 9.22×10^{11} *	4 digits	8 bytes

* Approximate values.

Note that the VBA online help mentions a `Decimal` data type for numbers, but this type has not been implemented yet.

Which type should you use? It depends, of course, on the data you are storing. The `Currency` type is specialized for holding currency values, and is ideal for that purpose. For other types of numeric data, first determine whether you need an integer type or a floating point type. Then, choose a specific type based on the range of values the data will need. When in doubt, it is always advisable to err on the side of caution, using a type `Long` rather than a type `Integer`, for example. If you try to store an out of range value in a variable, VBA generates an Overflow error, as in this example:

```
Dim x As Integer
x = 100000   ' Causes overflow error.
```

If you assign a floating point value to an integer variable, no error occurs but the value is rounded to the nearest integer. Look at this code:

```
Dim x As Integer, y As Integer
x = 1.1
y = 1.7
```

After this code executes, the variable x contains the value 1 and y contains the value 2.

Text

Text, or *strings* as it is called in VBA, can be stored in two ways. A variable length string can hold any amount of text from one to about two billion characters. Because a variable length string expands and contracts automatically to fit the data you put in it, you do not need to specify the size when declaring it:

```
Dim Name As String
```

In contrast, a fixed length string has a fixed size that is specified when the variable is declared. This size can range from 1 up to approximately 64,000 characters. For example:

```
Dim ZipCode As String * 5
Dim City As String * 16
```

If you assign text that is too long to a fixed length string variable, the extra part of the text is lost:

```
Dim Name As String * 6
Name = "Alexander"     ' Name contains "Alexan"
```

It's important to be aware of the difference between a number and a text representation of a number. Thus,

```
12345
```

is a number, while

```
"12345"
```

is text. VBA is actually pretty clever when it comes to figuring out what you mean. For example, look at this code:

```
Dim s As String, y As Integer
```

```
s = "12"
y = s / 2
```

The result is that y equals 6. VBA is able to figure out what you mean, and temporarily treat s as a number. However, it is best not to rely on VBA to make the necessary string/number conversions for you, as unexpected errors are still possible. You can use the `Variant` data type, discussed later in this chapter, when string/number confusion is possible. There are also some functions to convert between strings and numbers, which will be covered in Chapter 15.

Constants

VBA has two types of constants, literal and symbolic. A literal constant is a number or string typed directly into your code. String literals are typed in double quotation marks. Numeric literal constants are typed without special formatting. In this code, the `"Arthur"` and the `99.1` are literal constants.

```
Dim Max As Single
Dim Name As String
Max = 99.1
Name = "Arthur"
```

A symbolic constant is like a variable in that it has a name, but different in that its value does not change during program execution. You create a symbolic constant using the `Const` keyword:

```
Const constname As Type = value
```

The rules for constant names are the same as for variables. Many programmers like to use all uppercase names with underscore separators for constants, to make them easily distinguishable from variables in the code (which are commonly done with a combination of upper- and lowercase). Thus, INTEREST_RATE is easily identified as a constant, while InterestRate is clearly a variable. The `As type` part of the declaration is optional and is required only if you want the constant to be stored as a specific data type. *Value* is the constant value. Here are two examples:

```
Const INTEREST_RATE As Double = 0.055
Const DATA_SAVE_PATH = "c:\my documents\databases\"
```

If you do not specify a type for a constant, VBA uses the data type most appropriate for the value you specify. The major advantage of using symbolic constants is that you can change the value of a constant throughout the program simply by editing its declaration statement. Another advantage is that the constant's name can help in making the program easier to read.

Objects

The `Object` data type can hold a reference to an object. You have seen such references used often in previous chapters. There are two ways to declare variables to hold an object reference. The preferred method, which is called *early binding*, requires that you declare the variable as a specific type, or class. For example:

```
Dim myXLApp As Excel.Application
Dim myMailMessage As Outlook.MailItem
```

To use early binding, your project must include a reference to the relevant type library, as explained in Chapter 4. Early binding is the preferred method of declaring object variables. However, you can also use *late binding* in which a variable is declared as a generic object type that allows it to hold a reference to any type of object:

```
Dim AnyObject As Object
```

Using a generic object type like this is referred to as late binding because the program does not know what type of object the variable will refer to until the program runs. In my experience you need late binding only rarely, such as when you do not know ahead of time what object the variable will refer to. With late binding the project does not need a reference to the corresponding type library.

To initialize an object reference variable you use either the `New` keyword or the `CreateObject` or `GetObject` functions. Remember that declaring an object variable and initializing it are two distinct steps. They can be done separately, as shown here:

```
Dim myXLApp As Excel.Application
Set myXLApp = New Excel.Application
```

When using the `New` keyword, declaration and initialization can be done at the same time, as follows:

```
Dim myXLApp As New Excel.Application
```

You'll find more details on object initialization in Chapter 4.

Once you are done using the object referenced by the type `Object` variable, you should set the variable equal to the special value `Nothing`, which destroys the link between the variable and the object it references:

```
Set myXLApp = Nothing
```

Once all references to an object have been destroyed, the memory used by the object is released.

True/False Values

To hold data that can take only two values—true/false, yes/no, on/off—you use a type `Boolean` variable. To assign values to `Boolean` variables you can use the VBA keywords `True` and `False`. Boolean variables are sometimes referred to as *flags*. Here's an example:

```
Dim TodayIsWeekday As Boolean
TodayIsWeekday = True
```

Dates

In VBA, the term *date* refers to time of day as well as calendar date. Dates are stored as floating point numbers in which the part to the left of the decimal point represents the number of days since December 30, 1899, with negative numbers representing prior dates. The part to the right of the decimal point represents the time, as a fraction of a day, so that .25 is 6 A.M., .5 is noon, and so on. The range of dates that can be represented is January 1, 100 to December 31, 9999.

You use the `Date` data type to hold date values. When displayed, a type `Date` displays the date in the proper format as set on the system's short date format, and times are displayed as either 12- or 24-hour times, again in accordance with the system settings.

Date literals can be written in just about any recognizable format, but must be enclosed in # signs before assignment to date variables. Here are some examples:

```
Dim d1 as Date, d2 As Date, d3 As Date

d1 = #January 1, 1999#
d2 = #1 Jan 99#
d3 = #1/1/1999#
```

The VBA editor will automatically convert date literals to a standard format. VBA has a wide range of tools for working with dates and times, and they will be covered in Chapter 16.

The Variant Type

The data type `Variant` is VBA's default variable type, and also its most flexible. By default I mean that if you declare a variable without a type specification, it is created as a `Variant`. For example, these declarations create two type `Variant` variables:

```
Dim x
Dim y As Variant
```

This data type's flexibility comes from its ability to hold any type of data (with the single exception of fixed length strings). Thus, a type `Variant` can hold numbers, text, object references, user defined types, and arrays. One common use for this data type is when data needs to be treated either as text or as a number depending on circumstances. Another use is as an argument to procedures that can take different kinds of data. You should not, however, simply use type `Variant` as a convenience to avoid the necessity of thinking about what data type should be used for specific variables. The `Variant` data type requires more memory to store, and more processor time to manipulate, than other data types.

A type `Variant` can also hold a one-dimensional array. To create the array you use the `Array` function, then assign the return value to a type `Variant` variable. For example:

```
Dim va As Variant
va = Array(1, 2, 3, 4, 5)
```

You can also create an array using the syntax explained previously in this chapter, then assign it to the type `Variant`. The following code has the same result as the previous example:

```
Dim v, x(4)
x(0) = 1
x(1) = 2
x(2) = 3
x(3) = 4
x(4) = 5
v = x
```

You access the elements of a type `Variant` array using the usual syntax:

```
Dim AWeek, ADay
AWeek = Array("Mon", "Tue", "Wed", "Thu", "Fri", _
              "Sat", "Sun")
ADay = AWeek(2)      ' ADay contains "Wed"
```

Note that a type `Variant` array cannot contain fixed length strings or user defined types as its elements.

When working with the `Variant` data type there are some functions you can use to tell what kind of data a given variable contains. They return either True or False, and are described in Table 12.2.

Table 12.2	Data classification functions.
Function	**Returns True If**
IsArray(x)	X contains an array.
IsDate(x)	X contains a date.
IsEmpty(x)	X has not been initialized.
IsNull(x)	X contains Null.
IsNumeric(x)	X can be evaluated as a number.
IsObject(x)	X contains an object reference.

Variable Initialization

After you declare a variable, but before you explicitly initialize it by assigning a value to it, it will contain the default initialization value assigned by VBA. These are:

- Numeric variables: 0
- String variables: the null string (a string containing no characters)
- Boolean variables: False
- Variants: the special value Empty
- Dates: the time 12:00:00 A.M.

Arrays

An array lets you store multiple data items under the same name, using a numerical index to access individual items. VBA offers two types of arrays: static and dynamic.

STATIC ARRAYS

A static array has a fixed number of elements that is specified when the array is declared. You declare a static array using the following syntax:

```
Dim ArrayName(n) As type
```

ArrayName is the name of the array, which follows the same naming rule as regular VBA variables. n specifies the number of elements in the array. *type* can be any of VBA's built in data types as well as UDT's. Here's an example:

```
Dim MyArray(100) As Integer
```

This statement creates an array of integers. Because VBA's default is to start array indexes at 0, this array actually contains 101 elements, at indexes 0 through 100. Once an array exists, you access its elements using any expression to specify the index. For example:

```
MyArray(0) = 12
x = 1
MyArray(x) = 15   ' Same as MyArray(1)
MyArray(MyArray(0)) = 5   ' Same as MyAray(12)
```

It is often useful to use loops (covered in Chapter 13) to work with arrays. This code, for example, fills the array above with the values 0, 2, 4 ...

```
For i = 0 To 100
    MyArray(i) = i * 2
Next i
```

If you do not want the array index to start at 0, you can take either of two approaches. Putting the `Option Base 1` statement in the module, before declaring any arrays, makes the default starting index 1. More flexible, however, is the `To` keyword, which lets you specify any starting index you like. The format is as follows:

```
Dim MyArray(start To stop)
```

Start and *stop* are the desired starting and ending indexes. For example,

```
Dim Months(1 To 12)
```

The arrays we have seen so far are one-dimensional, meaning that they have a single index. You can also create multidimensional arrays that have two or more indexes by including the information about the additional indexes in the `Dim` statement. This statement creates a two-dimensional array:

```
Dim DaysOfYear(1 To 12, 1 To 31) As Integer
```

There is no limit to the number of dimensions in an array, or to the number of elements per dimension, other than limitations imposed by available memory and disk space.

DYNAMIC ARRAYS

A dynamic array has a variable number of elements and can be enlarged or shrunk while the program is running. The syntax for declaring a dynamic array is the same as for static arrays except that no indexes are specified—the parentheses are left blank:

```
Dim arrayname() As type
```

Before you can use the array, you must set its size using the ReDim statement:

```
ReDim arrayname(indexes)
```

The *indexes* argument specifies both the number of dimensions and the number of elements, using the same syntax as you learned above for declaring static arrays. Here are some examples:

```
Dim Array1()
Dim Array2()
Dim Array3()
...
Redim Array1(10)     ' 1 dimension, 11 elements 0-10.
Redim Array2(5 to 20)   ' 1 dimension, 16 elements 5-20.
ReDim Array3(1 To 5, 1 to 10)   ' 2 dimensions,
                                  50 total elements.
```

Subsequently, you can change the array size as many times as needed. The syntax is:

```
ReDim Preserve arrayname(indexes)
```

Indexes specify the new array size, as above. The optional Preserve keyword is used when you want the existing data in the array to be kept. Without Preserve the array will be reinitialized and existing data lost when you execute ReDim. There are some limitations on the use of Preserve:

- If you make an array smaller, the data in the part of the array that is "trimmed off" will be lost.
- You cannot change the number of dimensions of the array.
- If the array is multidimensional, you can change only the upper bound of the last dimension.

Dynamic arrays are very useful when you do not know how much data you will have. The following example uses a dynamic array to store names entered by the user, expanding the array as needed. Then, all the name are printed. This procedure uses the Ubound function, one of VBA's built-in functions, to determine the upper bound of the array.

Listing 12–1   *Using a dynamic array.*

```
Public Sub GetNames()

Dim Names() As String
Dim count As Integer
Dim temp As String

Do
    temp = InputBox("Next name (blank when done):")
    If temp <> "" Then
        count = count + 1
        ReDim Preserve Names(count)
        Names(count) = temp
    End If
Loop Until temp = ""

For count = 1 To UBound(Names)
    Debug.Print Names(count)
Next count

End Sub
```

User Defined Types

A *user defined type* or UDT, lets you define your own data structures that contain two or more elements. UDT's must be defined at the module level—that is, outside of any procedures. You use the `Type ... End Type` statement to define a UDT:

```
Type UDTName
    Element1 As type
    Element2 As type
    ....
    Elementn As type
End Type
```

Each individual element can be any of VBA's data types: `Byte`, `Boolean`, `Integer`, `Long`, `Currency`, `Single`, `Double`, `Date`, variable length or fixed length `String`, `Object`, `Variant`, another UDT, or an object type. Each element can be a single variable or an array. The rules for naming the elements are the same as the rules for naming VBA variables.

Let's look at an example. This code defines a UDT that could be used for keeping track of books in a library:

```
Type BookItem
    AuthorName As String
    Title As String
    Cost As Currency
```

```
      PubDate As Date
      CopiesOnHand As Integer
      CallNumber As String * 10
End Type
```

Once you have defined a UDT it will be available as a data type for declaring variables, including arrays. You then declare variables of that type using the usual syntax:

```
Dim OneBook As BookItem          ' A single BookItem variable.
Dim ManyBooks(1000) As BookItem  ' An Array of BookItem
                                   variables.
```

To access the elements of a UDT variable, use the *VarName.Element-Name* syntax as illustrated here:

```
OneBook.AuthorName = "Thomas Mann"
OneBook.Cost = 22.95
...
ManyBooks(1).AuthorName = "John Updike"
ManyBooks(2).AuthorName = "Philip Roth"
```

A UDT can contain arrays and other UDT's, in almost any imaginable combination. For example:

```
Type Person
    LastName As String * 20
    FirstName As String * 12
    UniformNumber As Integer
    FavoriteFoods(10) As String
End Type

Type SoccerTeam
    TeamName As String
    Members(10) As Person
    CoachName As String
    GamesWon As Integer
    GamesLost As Integer
End Type

Dim YouthLeague(10) As SoccerTeam

YouthLeague(1).CoachName = "Linda Smith"
YouthLeague(1).TeamName = "Hornets"
YouthLeague(1).Members(1).LastName = "Chang"
YouthLeague(1).Members(1).FirstName = "Liu"
YouthLeague(1).Members(1).UniformNumber = 12
YouthLeague(1).Members(1).FavoriteFoods(1) = "Bananas"
YouthLeague(1).Members(1).FavoriteFoods(2) = "Chocolate"
```

```
YouthLeague(1).Members(2).LastName = "O'Malley"
YouthLeague(1).Members(2).FirstName = "Kathy"
...
YouthLeague(2).CoachName = "Belinda Washington"
YouthLeague(2).TeamName = "Sharks"
YouthLeague(2).Members(1).LastName = "Gomez"
YouthLeague(2).Members(1).FirstName = "Gail"
```

Enumerations

An *enumeration* creates a user-defined data type that consists of a predefined set of symbolic constants. To create an enumeration, you use the Enum keyword. Here's a simple example:

```
Enum Fabrics
     Wool
     Silk
     Cotton
     Polyester
     Rayon
End Enum
```

This creates an enumeration called Fabrics with the constants Wool equal to 0, Silk equal to 1, and so on. If you do not want the enumeration values assigned sequentially starting at 0, you can specify the values:

```
Enum Fabrics
     Wool = 2
     Silk = 3
     Cotton = 6
     Polyester = 12
     Rayon = 21
End Enum
```

Enumerations can be defined only at the module level. Once an Enum is defined, it becomes available as a data type you can use to declare variables:

```
Dim SuitCoatFabric As Fabric
```

A variable declared as an enumerated type can only take on the set of values defined in the enumeration. A real convenience is that VBA displays autolist members for enumerated types, permitting you to select from a list of the associated constants.

Variable Scope

The *scope* of a variable refers to the parts of a program in which the variable is visible. A variable can be used only where it is in scope. In other parts of the program, it is out of scope and might as well not exist. It might seem a lot simpler to just have all variables visible throughout the entire program, but this turns out to be a bad idea. The ability to limit variable scope has two important advantages:

- By limiting a variable's scope to those sections of code where it is needed, you remove the possibility that the variable will be inadvertently modified in other parts of the program.
- Variables whose scopes do not overlap can have the same name yet be totally independent of each other.

In your VBA programs you control a variable's scope in two ways: by where the variable is declared, and by using certain keywords. There are three levels of scope available:

- A variable declared within a procedure is visible only within that procedure.
- A variable declared at the module level using the Private keyword or the Dim keyword is visible throughout its own module but nowhere else.
- A variable declared at the module level using the Public keyword is visible throughout all modules in all projects, unless the Option Private Module statement is in effect, in which case the variable is visible only in modules that are part of the same project.

The following code provides some examples, which are explained in the following list.

```
Option Private Module
Dim x As Integer
Private y As Long
Public z As Single

Public Sub MySub()

Dim q As Single

End Sub
```

- The variables x and y are visible throughout the module where the code is located.
- The variable z is visible throughout all modules in the project. If the Option Private Module statement were omitted, it would be visible throughout all loaded projects.
- The variable q is visible only within the procedure MySub.

If two variables of the same name are in scope at the same location, the one with the most restrictive scope takes precedence. For example, look at this code:

```
Dim total As Single    ' Module level declaration
...

Public Sub MySub()

Dim total As Single    ' Procedure level declaration.

End Sub
```

In this case, there are two variables named total—one inside the procedure, and the other outside of it. Look at the code in Listing 12–2. It has three declarations of a variable named X. One declaration is global, at the module level. The other two are local, inside procedures. When you run this code (starting with Proc1) it produces the following output in the Immediate window:

```
At the start of Proc1 the global x =  111
In Proc2, the local x =  99
In Proc3, the local x =  0
At the end of Proc1 the global x =  111
```

This clearly illustrates that the three variables, even though they have the same name, are completely independent of each other because they have different scopes.

Listing 12–2	*Demonstrating variable scope.*

```
Option Explicit

Dim x As Integer

Sub Proc1()

x = 111
Debug.Print "At the start of Proc1 the global x = "; x
Call Proc2
Call Proc3
Debug.Print "At the end of Proc1 the global x = "; x

End Sub

Sub Proc2()

Dim x As Integer
x = 99
Debug.Print "In Proc2, the local x = "; x

End Sub
```

```
Sub Proc3()

Dim x As Integer
x = 0
Debug.Print "In Proc3, the local x = "; x
End Sub
```

There is one general rule for deciding on variable scope in your projects: use the most restrictive scope possible. This means that, if possible, all variables and arrays should be declared locally inside procedures. When a procedure needs access to data that is kept outside the procedure, it is almost always better to pass the data to the procedure as an argument rather than to store the data in a global variable. The rules of variable scope apply to UDT's and enums as well as regular data types, except of course UDT and enums cannot be declared inside procedures.

Expressions

An expression is anything that evaluates to a valid piece of data. The data can be a number, a string, a Boolean value, an object reference—it does not matter, as long as it is meaningful to VBA.

Operators

An operator is a symbol that instructs VBA to manipulate data in some manner. Adding two numbers together is an example. VBA operators fall into several categories.

The Assignment Operator

Perhaps the most fundamental operator is the assignment operator, represented by the equal sign. When the assignment operator is used in a statement, the value of the expression on the right side of the operator is assigned to the variable on the left side of the operator. For example, the statement

```
x = y + z
```

adds the values in variables y and z and assigns the result to x.

Mathematical Operators

The mathematical, or arithmetic, operators perform the common operations such as addition and division. They are summarized in Table 12.3.

Table 12.3	The mathematical operators.	
Operator	**Description**	**Example**
+	Addition	4 + 7 evaluates to 11
–	Subtraction	12 – 5 evaluates to 7
*	Multiplication	2 * 12.5 evaluates to 25
/	Division	39 / 3 evaluates to 13
\	Integer division with rounding	10 \ 3 evaluates to 3
^	Exponentiation (to the power of)	3 ^ 2 evaluates to 9
mod	Modulus (remainder after division)	20 mod 6 evaluates to 2

The following should be kept in mind when using the mathematical operators:

- For both kinds of division, the divisor must not be equal to 0 or an error occurs.
- Integer division does not round off but simply discards the fractional part of the answer. Thus, both 31\10 and 39\10 evaluate to 3.
- Exponentiation requires that if the number being raised is negative, then the exponent must be an integer. If not, no error occurs but the exponent is rounded off before the calculation is performed.
- If floating point numbers are used with mod, they are rounded to integers before the calculation is performed.

String Operators

There is a single string operation called *concatenation*. The operator for this is &. Concatenation combines two strings. For example, after this code:

```
MyString = "Apple " & "pie"
```

the variable MyString contains "Apple pie." There are lots of other things you can do with strings, but they do not involve operators. You'll learn more in Chapter 15.

Comparison Operators

The comparison operators perform comparisons between two expressions. The result of a comparison is either True or False depending on whether the comparison was true or not. One group of comparison operators, which are used primarily with numeric expressions, is listed in Table 12.4.

Table 12.4	The numerical comparison operators.
Operator	**Comparison**
=	Is equal to?
>	Is greater than?
<	Is less than?
>=	Is greater than or equal to?
<=	Is less than or equal to?
<>	Is not equal to?

For example, the expression

```
x > y
```

asks the question "is x greater than y?" and returns either True or False depending on the values of the two variables.

These operators can also be used to perform string comparisons. Strings are compared character by character, with order determined alphabetically for letters and by ASCII value for other characters. Text comparisons can be in binary mode, in which uppercase letters are "less than" the corresponding lowercase letters, or in text mode where case does not matter. The string comparison mode is binary by default, so the expression

```
"AAA" = "aaa"
```

will evaluate to False. To turn on text mode comparisons, place the statement Option Compare Text at the beginning of the module.

There are two other special comparison operators. The Is operator is used to compare two object references and determine if they refer to the same object. The expression

```
obj1 Is obj2
```

returns True if obj1 and obj2 refer to the same object, False if they do not. You can use Is in conjunction with the Nothing keyword to determine if an object reference has been initialized. The expression

```
obj1 Is Nothing
```

evaluates as True if obj1 has not been initialized to refer to an object, False if obj1 refers to any object.

The Like operator compares a string with a pattern and returns True or False depending on whether there is a match. The syntax is:

```
result = string Like pattern
```

String is the string being compared, and *pattern* is a combination of special characters representing the pattern to be matched. These characters are listed in Table 12.5.

Table 12.5	Elements of the Like operators pattern.
Element	**Matches**
A single character	The character
?	Any single character
*	Any sequence of 0 or more characters
#	Any digit
[*list*]	Any character in *list*. Use a hyphen to indicate character ranges, such as a–z.
[!*list*]	Any character not in *list*.

The operation of Like as regards comparing upper and lowercase letters is controlled by the Option Compare setting, as described earlier. Table 12.6 shows some examples, assuming Option Compare Text is in effect.

Table 12.6	Examples of using the Like operator.	
Pattern	**Examples of Matches**	**Examples of Nonmatches**
p[ao]t	pat, pot	pet, pit
[a-z]*	apple, zebra, at, q145	1A, b, $400
f?t	fit, fat, fqt, f9t	foot, feat, ft
###-###-####	phone numbers	anything else
John [!Q]. Public	John A. Public, John J. Public, John 7. Public	John Q. Public

There are more details to using the Like operator, which can be found in the VBA online help.

Logical Operators

The logical operators are used to manipulate logical (True/False) expressions. Most of the logical operators combine two logical expressions into a single logical value. There are plenty of examples of this in your daily life. Suppose you want to buy a car that has a sunroof, costs less than $20,000, and has leather seats. Your decision could be stated logically like this:

```
BuyCar = (Has sunroof?) and (less than $20,000?)
    and (has leather seats?)
```

In other words, `BuyCar` will be True only if all three of the conditions are True. This makes use of the `And` operator. This and the other logical operators are described in Table 12.7.

Table 12.7	The logical operators. X and Y are both assumed to be logical expressions.	
Operator	**Example**	**Evaluation**
And	X And Y	True if both X and Y are True; False otherwise.
Or	X Or Y	True if X or Y, or both of them, are True; False only if both X and Y are False.
Xor (exclusive Or)	X Xor Y	True if X and Y are different (one True and the other False); False if both are True or both are False.
Eqv (Equivalence)	X Eqv Y	True if X and Y are the same (both True or both False); False otherwise.
Imp (Implication)	X Imp Y	False only if X is True and Y is False; True otherwise.
Not	Not X	True if X is False, False if X is True.

The logical operators are often used in conjunction with the comparison operators. For example, the following expression evaluates as True only if a is equal to 2 and b is not equal to 0.

```
(a = 2) And (b <> 0)
```

Operator Precedence and Parentheses

If an expression contains more than one operator, it may not always be clear how the expression evaluates. Here is an example:

```
15 + 3 * 4
```

If the addition is performed first, it evaluates to 72 (15 plus 3 is 18, 18 times 4 is 72); but if the multiplication is performed first, the result is 27 (3 times 4 is 12, 12 plus 15 is 27). Such potentially ambiguous expressions are resolved by VBA's rules of operator precedence. These rules specify the order in which operations are performed The precedence of VBA's operators is given in Table 12.8. Operators with lower precedence numbers are performed first.

Table 12.8	VBA Operator precedence.
Operator	**Precedence**
Exponentiation ^	1
Multiplication (*), division (/)	2
Integer division (\)	3
Modulus (Mod)	4
Addition (+), subtraction (−)	5
String concatenation (&)	6

Returning to the original example, you can see that because multiplication has a higher precedence than addition, the expression will evaluate to 27. For operators that have the same precedence level, such as multiplication and division, the order of execution is always left to right.

You can modify the order of execution by using parentheses in an expression. Parts of an expression within parentheses are always evaluated first regardless of operator precedence. Thus,

```
(15 + 3) * 4
```

evaluates to 72 because the parentheses force the addition to be performed before the multiplication. You can use as many parentheses in an expression as you like, as long as they always come in pairs; each left parenthesis must have a matching right parenthesis. When parentheses are nested (one set inside another set), execution starts with the innermost set and proceeds outward.

Summing Up

Perhaps the most fundamental task of any VBA program is to deal with data. As you saw in this chapter, VBA provides a rich set of tools for storing and manipulating both numerical and text data. It's important that you understand how to use VBA variables, arrays, and operators so you can write the most efficient and error-free code to handle your data.

Conditional and Loop Statements

An important part of VBA programming has to do with program control. It is not sufficient to simply write the code that performs the required tasks—you must also control which code is executed, when it is executed, and how many times it is executed. Conditional statements control which code is executed. Defined blocks of code may be executed, or not executed, based on conditions in the program as it is executing. Loop statements execute blocks of code zero, one, or more times as required. You'll see that VBA provides you with complete control over code execution, using the statements covered in this chapter.

Conditional Statements

Conditional statements are used to control the execution of other VBA statements. You can specify that certain statements in your program either are executed, or are not executed, depending on conditions in the program—hence the term *conditional*. VBA offers two conditional statements.

If...Then...Else

The `If...Then...Else` statement executes a block of statements only if a specified logical condition is True. Optionally, a second block of statements is executed only if the condition is False. The syntax is as follows:

```
If condition Then
    block1
Else
    block2
End If
```

Condition is a logical expression. If *condition* is True, the statements in *block1* are executed. If *condition* is False, the statements in *block2* are executed. The `Else` keyword and the second block of statements are optional; you can write an If statement like this:

```
If condition Then
    block1
End If
```

In this case, no statements are executed when *condition* is False. If you have only a single statement to be executed when *condition* is True, you can place it on the same line as the `If` keyword and omit the `End If`:

```
If condition Then statement
```

You can use the `ElseIf` keyword in an `If` statement to test multiple conditions. The syntax is as follows:

```
If condition1 Then
    block1
ElseIf condition2 Then
    block2
ElseIf condition3 Then
    block3
....
Else
    block4
End If
```

You can have as many ElseIfs as you like. The various conditions are tested one at a time, starting at the top. As soon as one is found that is True, the associated block of statements is executed and execution exits the If statement. If no true condition is found the block following the Else keyword is executed. Note that at most, one block of statements will be executed regardless of how many of the conditions are true. Note also that the Else keyword is again optional.

When you have multiple conditions to be tested, it is usually easier to use the Select Case statement, covered next. The short procedure in Listing 13–1 illustrates use of the If...Then...Else statement.

Listing 13–1   *Demonstrating the If...Then...Else statement.*

```
Public Sub DemonstrateIf()

Dim buf As String

buf = InputBox("Enter a word 5 or 6 characters long:")

If Len(buf) = 5 Then
    MsgBox ("That's 5 characters - thank you!")
ElseIf Len(buf) = 6 Then
    MsgBox ("That's 6 characters - thank you!")
Else
    MsgBox ("What's the matter, can't you count to 5?")
End If

End Sub
```

Select Case

The Select Case statement evaluates a single expression, then executes one of several blocks of statements depending on the expression evaluation. The syntax is:

```
Select Case expression
    Case template-1
        statements-1
    Case template-2
        statements-2
    ....
    Case template-n
        statements-n
    Case Else
        statements-else
End Select
```

First, *expression* is evaluated. The result is matched against the various templates, in order from top to bottom. When a match is found, the following block of statements is executed. If no match is found, the statements following the `Case Else` are executed. The `Case Else` keyword is optional. At most, a single block of statements will be executed—the block following the first matching template.

Each template in a `Select Case` statement can contain one or more of the following elements:

- Any expression. The test expression must match exactly.
- Two expressions separated by the `To` keyword. The test expression must fall within the range specified by the two expressions. For example, `5 To 10`.
- The `Is` keyword followed by a comparison operator and an expression. For example, `Is > 10`.

If you use multiple elements in a template, they must be separated by commas. Here's an example that would match if the text expression evaluated to 5, to any value between 10 and 15, or to any value greater than 20:

```
Case 5, 10 To 15, Is > 20
```

You can use string expressions as part of the template, too. The `To` keyword is interpreted alphabetically, and the comparison operators work as described for strings earlier in this chapter. Look at this template:

```
Case "apple", Is < name, "cat" To "dog"
```

This test expression would match:

- The string `"apple"`
- Any string that is less than the value of the variable `name`.
- Any string that falls between `"cat"` and `"dog"`—in other words, is equal to or greater than `"cat"` and is also less than or equal to `"dog"`. Listing 13–2 shows an example of using `Select Case`.

Listing 13–2   *Demonstrating the `Select Case` statement.*

```
Public Sub DemonstrateSelectCase()

Dim x As Single

x = InputBox("Enter any number:")

Select Case x
    Case Is < 0
        MsgBox ("You entered a negative number.")
```

```
        Case 0 To 10
            MsgBox ("You entered a number between 0 and 10.")
        Case Is > 10
            MsgBox ("You entered a number greater than 10.")
End Select

End Sub
```

Loop Statements

VBA's loop statements are used to execute a block of statements a certain number of times. The For...Next and For Each...Next loops specify in advance the number of times the statements will be executed. The Do...Loop statement executes statements repeatedly until a specified logical condition is met.

For...Next

The For...Next statement executes a block of VBA statements a specified number of times. The syntax is:

```
For counter = start To stop Step step
...
statements
...
Next counter
```

Counter is a numeric variable used as the loop counter. *Start* and *stop* are the starting and ending values of *counter*. *Step* is a numerical expression that specifies the increment for *counter*. The Step *step* part of the statement is optional; if omitted, an increment of 1 is used. Including the name of the counter variable with the Next keyword is optional. If it is omitted, VBA automatically associates the Next with the preceding For. Here's how the For...Next statement operates:

1. When execution reaches the For statement, *counter* is set equal to *start*.
2. *Counter* is compared to *stop*. If *counter* is less than or equal to *stop*, the statement in the loop are executed. If not, the loop terminates.
3. *Counter* is incremented by the value of *step* or by 1 if *step* is omitted.
4. Return to step 2.

For example, this simple loop sets the values of the array to 0, 2, 4, ... 200:

```
Dim MyArray(100) As Integer
Dim i As Integer
```

```
For i = 0 To 100
    MyArray(i) = i * 2
Next i
```

Code inside the loop should never change the value of *counter*. If you use a fractional *step* value, then the counter variable must be a floating point type. This loop prints the values 1.0, 1.1, ... 1.9 in the Immediate window:

```
Dim i As Single

For i = 1.0 to 1.9 Step 0.1
    Debug.Print i
Next i
```

You can use the For...Next loop to count down by making *step* negative. In this case, *start* must be greater then *stop*, and the loop terminates when *counter* is less than *stop*. This loop fills the elements of the array with the values 100, 99, ... 0.

```
Dim MyArray(100) As Integer
Dim i As Integer

For i = 100 To 0 Step -1
    MyArray(i) = 100 - i
Next i
```

To exit from a For...Next loop early (before the counter variable reaches its final value), use the Exit For statement. You can have as many Exit For statements in the loop as you like. As soon as any one of them is executed, the loop terminates immediately. This loop determines if there is at least one element equal to "Chicago" in a string array named Cities. Note the use of the UBound and LBound functions to determine the array boundaries.

```
Dim found As Boolean
found = False
For i = LBound(Cities) To UBound(Cities)
    If Cities(i) = "Chicago" Then
        found = True
        Exit For
    End If
Next i
```

You can nest For...Next loops within each other. The only requirement is that each inner loop be totally within the outer loop. Here's an example:

```
For i = 1 To 100
    For j = 10 To 20
        For k = 50 to 30 Step -1
        ....
        Next k
    Next j
Next i
```

For Each...Next

The For Each...Next loop executes a group of statements once for each member of a collection. The syntax is:

```
For Each item in collection
...
statements
...
Next item
```

Item is the variable used to iterate through the collection. It must be declared as a data type appropriate for the members of the collection—a type Variant, a type Object, or a specific object type. *Collection* is the name of the collection. The statements are executed once for each element in the collection. Here's an example that sets the Color property of all objects in the collection to Blue:

```
Dim obj As Object

For Each obj In MyCollection
    obj.Color = Blue
Next obj
```

To exit a For Each...Next loop early, use the Exit For statement, as described above for the For...Next loop.

Do...Loop

The Do...Loop statement executes a block of statements zero, one, or more times depending on a specified logical condition. There are several variants of this statement. In one variant, the condition is tested at the start of the loop. To execute statements repeatedly as long as a logical condition is True, use the While keyword:

```
Do While condition
...
statements
...
Loop
```

To execute statements repeatedly as long as a condition is False, use the `Until` keyword:

```
Do Until condition
   ...
   statements
   ...
Loop
```

When execution reaches the `Do` statement, `condition` is evaluated. If it is True (if using `While`) or False (if using `Until`) the statements are executed and then `condition` is evaluated again. This continues until the value of `condition` changes. Note that depending on the initial value of `condition`, the statements in the loop may not be executed at all.

The other variant of the `Do...Loop` statement tests the condition at the end of the loop. Again, you have the choice between the `While` or `Until` keywords:

```
Do
   ...
   statements
   ...
Loop While condition
```

```
Do
   ...
   statements
   ...
Loop Until condition
```

In this case, the statements are executed once and then `condition` is evaluated. If it is True (for `While`) or False (for `Until`), the statements are executed again, and the process repeats. When the condition is tested at the end of the loop, you are guaranteed that the statements in the loop will be executed at least once.

To exit a `Do...Loop` early, use the `Exit Do` statement. The following loop executes until either X or Y is greater than 100:

```
Do Until X > 100
    ....
    If Y > 100 Then Exit Do
    ....
Loop
```

Note that the same result could be obtained as follows:

```
Do Until X > 100 Or Y > 100
    ....
Loop
```

The `While...Wend` Loop

The `While...Wend` loop is a holdover from earlier versions of the Basic language. I mention it here only because you might see it in old code. Its syntax is:

```
While condition
...
statements
...
Wend
```

The statements in the loop are executed repeatedly as long as `condition` is True. Note that exactly the same thing can be accomplished with a Do...Loop statement:

```
Do While condition
...
statements
...
Loop
```

Because of its greater flexibility, the `Do...Loop` statement should be used in preference to `While...Wend`.

When writing `Do...Loop` statements, be aware of the danger of *infinite loops*. If, once a loop starts executing, there is nothing to change the value of the test condition, the loop will run forever. Here's an example:

```
Dim index As Integer
Dim Array(50) As Single
index = 0
Do
    Array(index) = -22
Loop Until index = 50
```

Do you see the problem? There is no code in the loop to increment the variable index, so the loop will run forever and the program will stop responding. Here's the solution:

```
Do
    Array(index) = -22
    index = index + 1
Loop Until index = 50
```

Listing 13–3 illustrates a use of the Do...Loop statement.

Listing 13–3	*Demonstrating the Do...Loop statement.*

```
Public Sub DemonstrateDoLoop()

Dim buf As String

Do
    buf = InputBox("What continent is France located in?")
Loop Until buf = "Europe"

End Sub
```

Using DoEvents

VBA has a function named DoEvents that temporarily passes control from your program back to the operating system. This permits the operating system to process its event queue and respond to keystrokes and mouse actions. When you have a loop that is dependent on some outside factor to terminate, and you cannot be 100 percent sure this will always occur, be sure to put a call to DoEvents in the loop. In the event of a non-terminating condition, this will permit users to break out by pressing Ctrl+Break.

The GoTo Statement

There's one more program control statement to be covered, the GoTo statement. GoTo is VBA's unconditional branch statement. The syntax is as follows:

```
GoTo label
```

Label is a program label that identifies the location where execution is to go, consisting of an identifier followed by a colon. A label can be on a line by itself, or be followed by another VBA statement. *Label* must be located within the same procedure or method as the GoTo statement. Here's an example of using GoTo, which assumes MyArray is an array of strings. The code sets found to True if the string "Smith" is found in the array:

```
Dim found As Boolean
Dim i As Integer

i = LBound(MyArray)
found = False
```

```
LookAgain:

If MyArray(i) = "Smith" Then found = true
i = i + 1
If found = True Then GoTo Done
If i <= UBound(MyArray) Then GoTo LookAgain

Done:
....
```

I think you can see how the same result could be obtained a lot easier using other VBA statements. That's almost always the case with GoTo—there's a better way to do it. For this reason, the use of GoTo is frowned upon by most programmers, and my advice is that you avoid it altogether.

Summing Up

An essential aspect of VBA programming is controlling program execution: which lines of code execute and which do not, when they execute, and how many times they execute. VBA's conditional and loop statements, covered in this chapter, provide you with complete control over program execution. With a good understanding of these statements, you'll be able to write VBA code that does just what you want it to do.

Writing Procedures

Almost all of the VBA code you write will be contained in procedures. It's a pretty good idea, therefore, to know how to create procedures! A procedure is a section of code that has been assigned a name. When you need to execute that code, you refer to its name in your program. This is referred to as calling the procedure. Good programming practice dictates that the functionality of a program be broken up into relatively small and independent units of code, with each such "unit" contained in its own procedure. In this chapter we will first look at the five different kinds of procedures that VBA supports, then learn the details of how to write your own.

Types of Procedures

VBA provides you with five different types of procedures.

- A sub procedure is an independent, named section of code that performs some action.
- A function procedure is identical to a sub procedure except it also returns data to the calling program (which a sub procedure does not do).
- A method is a sub or function procedure that is located in a class module.
- A property procedure is used to access properties in user-defined classes. These are covered in Chapter 18.
- An event procedure is executed automatically when the corresponding event, such as a mouse click, occurs.

Event procedures are a special case. You, the programmer, do not create event procedures but only add the code to them that you want executed when the event occurs. Event procedures are defined as part of the various objects that are part of the Office development environment. You have seen some event procedures in previous chapters, and they will be covered in more detail in Chapter 19.

Methods are different from other procedures only in terms of their location. Regular sub and function procedures are located in code modules, which include specialized modules such as Word's `ThisDocument` module. Methods, in contrast, are located in class modules, which will be covered in Chapter 18.

What code can you put in a procedure? Just about anything, including variable declarations. The only major exclusion is that you cannot define one procedure within another.

Defining a Procedure

The syntax for defining a procedure is quite similar for both sub and function procedures. For a sub procedure, the basic syntax is as follows:

```
Sub subname(argumentlist)
...
' Code goes here
...
End Sub
```

Subname is the name of the sub procedure, following the same VBA naming rules that you learned in Chapter 5. The name must be unique within the project. The *argumentlist* specifies arguments (data) that are passed to the procedure. The details of passing arguments will be explained below. A procedure can take no arguments, in which case the name should be followed by an empty set of parentheses.

The syntax for defining a function procedure is quite similar:

```
Function functionname(argumentlist) As type
...
' Code goes here
functionname = returnvalue

End Function
```

Functionname uniquely identifies the function, and again follows the same VBA naming rules. The *argumentlist* specifies arguments (data) that are passed to the procedure. *Type* specifies the data type of the function's return value. This can be any of VBA's data types, including `Object`. It can also be a specific object type, a user-defined type, or an enumerated type. If the `As` *type* clause is omitted, the function's return type defaults to `Variant`.

The actual data that is returned by the function is specified by assigning a value to the function name within the body of the function. If the return type is an object type, then you must use the `Set` statement to assign the return value:

```
Set functionname = returnobjectreference
```

If you do not explicitly assign a return value to a function, the return value will depend on the data type of the function declaration, as follows:

A numeric type: 0.
A string type: a null string.
Variant: the value `Empty`.
An object type: the value `Nothing`.

Passing Arguments

A procedure can be defined to accept as many arguments as required. Each argument represents a piece of data that is passed to the procedure when it is called. Argument syntax is identical for sub and function procedures. The *argumentlist* has the following basic syntax:

```
argname1 As type, argname2 As type, .....
```

Each *argname* is a unique name that follows VBA's standard naming rules. *Type* specifies the data type of the argument. An argument can be any of VBA's built-in data types, a user-defined type, or an enumeration. If the `As type` clause is omitted, the argument will default to type `Variant`. Within the procedure, each argument is available as a regular variable. Here's an example of a function that takes one type `Double` argument:

```
Function HalfOf(x As Double) As Double

HalfOf = x / 2

End Function
```

You can pass arrays as procedure arguments by using an empty set of parentheses in the argument list. Here's a procedure that prints all elements of an integer array.

```
Sub PrintArray(array() As Integer)

Dim i As Long

For i = LBound(array) To UBound(array)
    Debug.Print array(i)
Next i

End Sub
```

Optional and `ParamArray` Arguments

VBA lets you use optional arguments with a procedure. An optional argument is one that may or may not be passed when the procedure is called. With an optional argument, you can also define a default value that will be used if a value is not included in the procedure call. The syntax for an optional argument is:

```
Optional argname As type = defaultvalue
```

The *argname* and *type* are used the same as for non-optional arguments. If included, the `= defaultvalue` clause specifies the argument's default value. Any optional arguments must be placed at the end of the argument list, after any non-default arguments. Here is a procedure declaration that specifies one non-optional argument and one optional argument with a default value of 0.

```
Sub MyProcedure(Name As String, Optional YearsEmployed _
    As Integer = 0)
...
End Sub
```

Another way to pass a variable number of arguments to a procedure is to use the `ParamArray` keyword in the argument list. There can be only one, it must be the last argument in the list, and it cannot be used with the `Optional` keyword. Arguments passed this way are always type `Variant`, so a *type* specification is not used. Here's an example:

```
Sub MySub(ParamArray OtherArgs())
...
End Sub
```

Then, in the procedure, any arguments passed by the calling program are available as elements in the array. For example, suppose this procedure was called as follows:

```
Call MySub(1, "hello", -99.9)
```

Then within the procedure, `OtherArgs(0)` equals 1, `OtherArgs(1)` equals "hello", and `OtherArgs(2)` equals `-99.9`. Using the `ParamArray` keyword can be very useful in those situations where you do not know the number of arguments being passed. For example, Listing 14–1 presents a function named `Average` that returns the average of the numbers passed to it, and can accept any number of values.

Listing 14–1   *Using `ParamArray` to pass a variable number of arguments.*

```
Public Function Average(ParamArray pa())

Dim i, total, count
total = 0
count = 0
For i = LBound(pa) To UBound(pa)
    count = count + 1
    total = total + pa(i)
Next

Average = total / count

End Function
```

Passing Arguments `ByVal` and `ByRef`

An argument to a procedure can be passed in one of two ways. *By reference* passes a reference to where the original argument is stored in memory, whereas *by value* creates a copy of the argument and passes the copy. The main practical difference between these two methods of passing arguments is that by reference provides the code in the procedure with access to the original copy of the argument, while by value does not. As a result, procedure code can change the value of a variable that is passed by reference, but cannot do so when it is passed by value. Note that this distinction applies only when a variable is passed as an argument, and is irrelevant when a constant or literal is passed. VBA's default is to pass arguments by reference. To pass an argument by value, precede the argument name with the `ByVal` keyword:

```
Sub MySub(ByVal X As Integer)
...
End Sub
```

To see this in action, look at the code in Listing 14–2. There are two procedures here. The procedure `Test` creates a variable X, sets it equal to 11, then passes it to `Test1` by value. Code in `test1` changes the value of X to 99. However, when execution returns to `Test`, and the value of X is displayed, it still has the original value of 11. Because it was passed `ByVal`, the code in `Test1` could not change the value of X.

Next, remove the `ByVal` keyword from the definition of `Test1`, and rerun the procedure `Test`. Now you will see that the value of X is indeed changed to 99. Because it was passed by reference, the default, the code in `Test1` could access and therefore change the value of the original variable.

| Listing 14–2 | *Demonstrating ByVal.* |

```
Public Sub test()

    Dim x
    x = 11
    Call test1(x)
    Debug.Print x

End Sub

Public Sub test1(ByVal c)

    c = 99

End Sub
```

In general, procedure code should not change the value of arguments passed to them. If you need to return data to the calling program, use a function. However for specialized programming situations you can use by reference arguments to "return" multiple data items from a procedure.

Procedure Type Checking

When an argument is passed by reference, and you use a variable as the argument, VBA checks to see that the variable type is the same as the declared type of that argument. If it is not, a "ByRef Argument Type Mismatch" error occurs. For example, this code will not work because it tries to pass a type `Integer` to a procedure that requires a type `Double`.

```
Dim i As Integer
...
Call Test(i)

Sub Test(X As Double)
...
End Sub
```

You can sidestep this problem by enclosing the argument in parentheses, which has the effect of converting it into a typeless expression. This code works fine:

```
Dim i As Integer
...
Call Test((i))

Sub Test(X As Double)
...
End Sub
```

Variables in Procedures

You can declare variables inside a procedure without any limitations. You cannot define a user-defined type or an enumeration in a procedure, but if a UDT or an enum is defined elsewhere, you can declare a variable of that type in a procedure. Variables declared within a procedure are called *local* variables because they are not visible outside the procedure. Normally, local variables are created and initialized each time the procedure is called, and destroyed when the procedure terminates. Even if a procedure calls itself (a technique called *recursion*), each instance of the procedure is separate and has its own independent set of local variables.

Sometimes it is useful to have a local variable retain its value between calls to the procedure. This is done by using the `Static` keyword. You can make individual variables static by including the keyword with the variable declaration, in place of `Dim`. For example:

```
Sub MySub()

Static X As Integer, MyObj As Object
Dim Y As Integer
...
End Sub
```

In this case, X and MyObj are static while Y is not. To make all of a procedure's local variables static, use the Static keyword in the procedure definition:

```
Static Function MyFunc()
...
End Function

Static Sub MySub()
...
End Sub
```

The Static keyword has no effect on a function's return value. The use of static variables is illustrated by the code in Listing 14–3. The procedure Test1 has one static variable X and one non-static variable Y. Code in the procedure prints the values of both variables, then sets both to the value 999. The procedure Test calls test1 two times. If you run Test, you'll see that the first time test1 executes, both X and Y are initially 0. The second (and subsequent) times Test1 is run, X has retained the value 999 while Y has been recreated and initialized to 0.

Listing 14–3   *Demonstrating static local variables.*

```
Public Sub test()

Call test1
Call test1

End Sub


Public Sub test1()

Static X As Integer
Dim Y As Integer

Debug.Print "X="; X
Debug.Print "Y="; Y

X = 999
Y = 999

End Sub
```

A static local variable retains its value until the module it is in is reset or restarted.

Calling a Procedure

To execute the code in a procedure—in other words, to *call* the procedure— you use a different syntax for sub and function procedures. Because a function returns a value, it is in effect an expression, and you call it by referring to it anywhere an expression could be used. Perhaps most commonly, a function is called by referring to it on the right side of an assignment statement. If you have a function named HalfOf, for example, you could call it and assign the return value to X as follows:

```
x = HalfOf(y)
```

Or, you could call the function and display the return value in the Immediate window:

```
Debug.Print HalfOf(104)
```

Calling sub procedures is different. Because they do not return a value, they cannot be treated as an expression. You use the Call keyword to call a sub procedure:

```
Call ProcedureName(argumentlist)
```

You can omit the Call keyword, in which case the argument list is not enclosed in parentheses:

```
ProcedureName argumentlist
```

You can use either of these Call syntaxes to call a function procedure. In this case the function's return value is discarded.

Named Arguments

In the standard syntax for the argument list, when calling a procedure, the arguments must be passed in the exact order they are listed in the procedure definition. Also, no arguments (other than optional arguments) can be omitted. It is sometimes more convenient to use named arguments, particularly when a procedure has many optional arguments that are often not passed. You have seen named arguments used many times in earlier chapters when dealing with VBA's built-in procedures. To pass a named argument, use this syntax:

```
argname:=value
```

in which *argname* is the name of the argument in the procedure definition, and *value* is the argument value. Note the special := operator that is used only for named arguments. Suppose you have a procedure that uses optional arguments, as follows:

```
Sub MyProc(Optional Country As String = "USA", _
    Optional City As String = "New York", _
    Optional Sex As String = "Female")
```

Then, to call it passing only the City argument, accepting the defaults for the other arguments:

```
MyProc City:="San Francisco"
```

You can use named arguments regardless of whether the argument is optional or required, and regardless of whether you are passing all the arguments or only some of them. When you use named arguments, the order of the arguments in the list does not matter.

Procedure Scope

Just like variables, procedures have scope, which controls the parts of the project from where the procedure can be called. Procedure scope is controlled by the use of the Public and Private keywords in the procedure definition, and by the Option Private statement. There are three possibilities:

- A public procedure is visible to code in all other modules in all projects. To make a procedure public, use the Public keyword in the procedure definition, or use no keyword as public is the default scope:

  ```
  Public Sub MySub()
  ```

- A private procedure is visible only to code within its own module. To make a procedure private, use the Private keyword in the procedure definition:

  ```
  Private Sub MySub()
  ```

- If the Option Private statement is present in the module, then all public procedures in that module are visible to all other modules in the same project, but not in other projects.

Planning and Storing Procedures

The way you organize your code into procedures has a major influence on the structure of your project, and also on how easy your code is to reuse, maintain, and debug. When planning how to create your procedures, the best rule to keep in mind is that each procedure should perform a single, discrete, and self-contained task. What the tasks are will, of course, be decided by the nature of your application. However, by breaking your code into procedures based on this rule you cannot go too far wrong.

For example, suppose your application needs to download some data from the Internet, perform some calculations on the data, then display the data on screen. Rather than include all this functionality in a single procedure, you should break it into three: one to download the data, another to do the calculations, and a third to display the results.

Procedures are stored in code modules, and as your programming experience grows you may want to create special purpose modules for certain types of procedures. Text processing procedures can be kept together in one module, financial planning procedures in another, and so on. Then, as other projects require certain types of procedures, you can simply add the relevant modules to your project.

Summing Up

There's no getting away from procedures in VBA programming for the simple reason that 99.9% of VBA code is located in procedures. Proper programming practice dictates that independent sections of code performing specific tasks be separated each into its own procedure. Some procedures execute automatically in response to certain events—these are called event procedures. Others are called from your code, and still others are associated with class properties. Proper use of procedures is an essential part of creating efficient, error-free VBA programs.

Working with Strings

• •

It's a rare VBA program that does not work with strings, or text, in one way or another. We Office programmers are fortunate in that VBA has an extremely powerful set of text processing tools built right in. If there's anything you cannot do with text in VBA, I have yet to hear about it! This chapter is organized in reference fashion, starting with a table that summarizes VBA's string functions, which is followed by detailed descriptions of the functions in alphabetical order.

String Processing Summary

Table 15.1 summarizes the string manipulation statements and functions in VBA, based on the type of task they perform. Then, each of these statements and functions is covered separately in the chapter. Items are in alphabetical order.

Table 15.1	Summary of VBA's string-related statements and functions.
Task	**Statement(s)/Functions(s)**
Compare two strings	StrComp
Convert strings	StrConv, Str, Val
Convert to lowercase or uppercase	LCase, Ucase
Create string of repeating character	Space, String
Display messages to user	MsgBox
Extract part of a string	Mid function, Left, Right
Find one string in another	InStr, InStrRev
Find length of a string	Len
Input text from user	InputBox
Insert one string within another	Mid statement
Set string comparison rules	Option Compare
Trim leading and/or trailing spaces	LTrim, RTrim, Trim
Work with ASCII and ANSI values	Asc, Chr

Asc

The Asc function returns an integer specifying the character code of the first character in its argument. The syntax is:

Asc(*string*)

See the Chr function for converting a code into a character.

Chr

The Chr function returns the character represented by a specific numerical code. The syntax is:

Chr(*code*)

Code is a character code in the range 0–255. See the VBA online help for a list of characters and their codes (as shown in Figure 15–1).

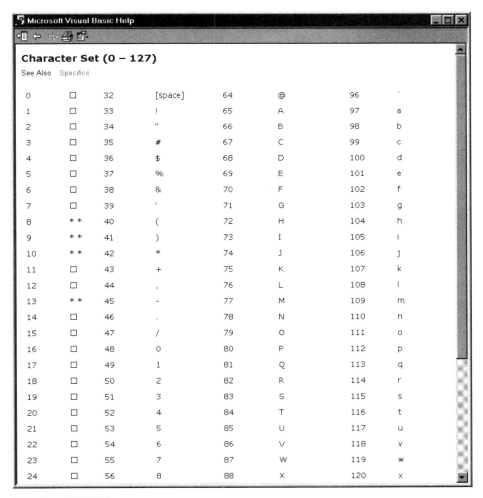

Figure 15–1 *The VBA Help system displaying part of the character code list.*

InputBox

The InputBox function returns a string entered by the user from the keyboard. The syntax is:

```
InputBox(prompt, title, default, xpos, ypos, _
    helpfile, context)
```

Prompt is the text displayed in the dialog box as a prompt to the user.

Title is an optional argument that specifies the title displayed in the dialog box's title bar. If this argument is omitted, the application name is used as the title.

Default is an optional string expression that specifies the default response if the user takes no action. If omitted, the default response is an empty string.

Xpos and *ypos* are optional numerical values specifying the horizontal and vertical position of the dialog box, in twips (1,440 twips equal 1 inch), from the left top edge of the screen. If *xpos* is omitted, the dialog box is centered horizontally. If *ypos* is omitted, the dialog box is positioned about one-third of the distance from the top of the screen.

Helpfile and *context* are optional arguments that specify the *helpfile* and the context for the dialog box's context sensitive help. If you provide one of these arguments you must include the other as well.

This code uses the InputBox function to get the user's country of residence, with "United States" being the default response.

```
Country = InputBox("Your country of residence?", _
    "Country", "United States")
```

InStr, InStrRev

To find the first occurrence of one string within another, use the InStr function. InStrRev does the same thing but starts looking at the end of the string rather than at the beginning. The syntax is:

```
InStr(start, stringcheck, stringmatch, compare)
InstrRev(stringcheck, stringmatch, start, compare)
```

Stringcheck is the string being searched.

Stringmatch is the string you are looking for.

Start is an optional argument specifying the character position in *stringcheck* where the search is to begin. If omitted, InStr starts at the first character (position 1) and InStrRev starts at the last character.

Compare is an optional constant that specifies the type of comparison. Possible settings are vbTextCompare, where upper- and lowercase letters match, and vbBinaryCompare, where different case letters (e.g., "A" and "a") do not match. If this argument is omitted, the search is done based on the Option Compare setting.

The return value of these functions is the character position at which the first match was found, or 0 if there is no match. The function returns Null if either *stringcheck* or *stringmatch* is Null. Table 15.2 shows some examples of using these functions, assuming that Option Compare has been set to vbTextCompare).

Table 15.2	Using InStr and InStrRev.

Example	Return Value
InStr(, "Mississippi", "ss")	3
InStrRev(, "Mississippi", "ss")	6
InStr(, "MISSISSIPPI", "ss", vbCompareBinary)	0
InStr(5, "abcabcabcabc", "abc")	7

InStrRev

See Instr on page 288.

LCase, UCase

These functions convert a string to all uppercase (UCase) or all lowercase (LCase). The syntax is:

```
LCase(string)
UCase(string)
```

The return value is *string* with all letters converted to the designated case. Non-letter characters in *string* are not modified.

Left, Mid (function), Right

These functions extract a portion of a string. Left extracts characters from the start of a string, Mid extracts them from the middle of a string, and Right extracts them from the end of a string. The syntax is:

```
Left(string, n)
Right(string, n)
Mid(string, start, n)
```

String is the string to extract from.

N is the number of characters to extract. If *n* is greater than or equal to the length of *string*, then the entire string is returned.

Start is the character position at which to start extracting.

Table 15.3 Illustrates the use of these functions.

Table 15.3	Examples of the Left, Mid, and Right functions.
Example	**Return Value**
Left("Microsoft", 5)	"Micro"
Right("Software", 2)	"re"
Mid("Microsoft", 2, 3)	"icr"

Len

Returns the number of characters in a string. The syntax is:

```
Len(string)
```

If *string* contains Null, then Null is returned.

LTrim, RTrim, Trim

These functions remove leading and/or trailing spaces from a string. The syntax is:

```
LTrim(string)
RTrim(string)
Trim(string)
```

The return value is *string* minus any leading spaces (LTrim), trailing spaces (RTrim), or both leading and trailing spaces (Trim). Here are some examples.

```
RTrim("     Hello     ") returns "     Hello"
LTrim("     Hello     ") returns "Hello     "
Trim("     Hello     ") returns "Hello"
```

Mid (function)

See Left on page 289.

Mid (statement)

The Mid statement replaces characters in one string with characters from another string. The syntax is:

```
Mid(stringvar, start[, length]) = string
```

    Stringvar is the string variable to modify.

    Start is the character position in *stringvar* where the replacement is to begin.

    Length is an optional argument specifying how many characters in *stringvar* are to be replaced. If this argument is omitted, the number of characters replaced is equal to the length of *string*.

    String is a string expression that replaces the characters in *stringvar*.

    Table 15.4 shows some examples of using the Mid statement. Note that the original length of *stringvar* is never changed.

Table 15.4   Examples of using the Mid statement.

Example	S Contains
s = "abcdefghijk" Mid(s, 2, 5) = "123456789"	a12345ghijk
s = "abcdefghijk" Mid(s, 2) = "123"	a123efghijk
s = "abcde" Mid(s, 2, 5) = "123456"	a1234

MsgBox

The MsgBox function displays a dialog box to the user with a message and one or more buttons. The return value specifies which of the buttons the user must click to close the dialog box. The syntax is:

```
MsgBox(prompt, buttons, title, helpfile, context)
```

Prompt is a string expression specifying the message to display.

Buttons is an optional argument specifying what buttons and/or icons to display in the dialog box and, when there is more than one button, which one is the default. If omitted, only an OK button is displayed. Possible settings for this argument are given in Table 15.5. To combine settings, use the Or operator.

Title is an optional argument that specifies the title displayed in the dialog box's title bar. If this argument is omitted, the application name is used as the title.

Helpfile and *context* are optional arguments that specify the help file and the context for the dialog box's context sensitive help. If you provide one of these arguments you must include the other as well.

Table 15.5	Predefined constants for the MsgBox function's *buttons* argument.	
Constant	**Value**	**Description**
vbOKCancel	1	Display OK and Cancel buttons
vbAbortRetryIgnore	2	Display Abort, Retry, and Ignore buttons
vbYesNoCancel	3	Display Yes, No, and Cancel buttons
vbYesNo	4	Display Yes and No buttons
vbRetryCancel	5	Display Retry and Cancel buttons
vbCritical	16	Display Critical Message icon
vbQuestion	32	Display Warning Query icon
vbExclamation	48	Display Warning Message icon
vbInformation	64	Display Information Message icon
vbDefaultButton2	256	Second button is default
vbDefaultButton3	512	Third button is default

The possible return values for the MsgBox function are also defined by constants, which are listed in Table 15.6.

Here's an example of using the MsgBox function. The following code displays a message asking the user whether they want to delete a file, then takes action based on whether they select the Yes or No button. The dialog box displays a question mark icon, and the second button ("No") is the default button.

```
Temp = MsgBox("Do you really want to delete that file?", _
    vbYesNo Or vbQuestion Or vbDefaultButton2)
```

```
If Temp = vbYes Then
    'Code to delete file goes here.
End If
```

Table 15.6	Constants for the MsgBox function's return value.

Constant	Value	Button Selected
vbOK	1	OK
vbCancel	2	Cancel
vbAbort	3	Abort
vbRetry	4	Retry
vbIgnore	5	Ignore
vbYes	6	Yes
vbNo	7	No

Option Compare

The Option Compare statement sets the default text comparison method that will be used by VBA. This statement must appear in a module before any procedures. The syntax is:

```
Option Compare method
```

Method can be set to Binary or to Text. The default setting is Binary. Binary comparisons do not consider upper- and lowercase letters to be the same, so the strings "Apple" and "apple" would not be considered equal. Text comparisons do not consider the case of letters.

Right

See Left on page 289.

RTrim

See LTrim on page 290.

Space

The Space function returns a string containing a specified number of spaces. The syntax is:

Space(*n*)

N is the number of spaces to include in the string.

Str

The Str function converts a numeric value into its string representation. The syntax is:

Str(*val*)

Val is any numeric expression. If *val* is positive, the returned string includes a leading space. If *val* is negative the returned string includes a leading minus sign and no leading space.

String

The String function returns a string containing a specified number of a specified character. The syntax is:

String(*n*, *char*)

N is the number of characters to put in the string.

Char is a string specifying the character to use. If *char* contains more than one character, the first character is used. For example, String(8, "XYZ") returns "XXXXXXXX."

StrComp

This function compares two strings. The syntax is:

StrComp(*string1*, *string2*, *compare*)

String1 and *string2* are the string expressions being compared.

Compare is an optional constant that specifies the type of comparison. Possible settings are vbTextCompare, in which upper- and lowercase letters match, and vbBinaryCompare, in which different case letters (e.g., "A" and "a") do not match. If this argument is omitted the search is done based on the Option Compare setting.

The return value of this function is:

-1	if *string1* is less than *string2*.
0	if *string1* and *string2* are equal.
1	if *string1* is greater than *string2*.
Null	if either *string1* or *string2* is Null.

StrConv

This function can perform a variety of conversions on a string. The syntax is:

StrConv(*string, conversion, LCID*)

String is a string expression to be converted.

Conversion is the type of conversion or conversions to perform, as specified in Table 15.7.

LCID is an optional argument specifying the LocaleID to use in making the conversion. The default setting is the system LocaleID.

Table 15.7   Settings for the StrConv function's *conversion* argument.

Constant	Value	Conversion
vbUpperCase	1	Converts the string to uppercase characters.
vbLowerCase	2	Converts the string to lowercase characters.
vbProperCase	3	Converts the first letter of every word in string to uppercase, and subsequent letters to lowercase.
vbWide	4	Converts narrow (single-byte) characters in string to wide (double-byte) characters. Far East locales only.
vbNarrow	8	Converts wide (double-byte) characters in string to narrow (single-byte) characters. Far East locales only.
vbKatakana	16	Converts Hiragana characters in string to Katakana characters. Japan only.
vbHiragana	32	Converts Katakana characters in string to Hiragana characters. Japan only.
vbUnicode	64	Converts the string to Unicode.
vbFromUnicode	128	Converts the string from Unicode.

Trim

See `LTrim` on page 290.

UCase

See `LCase` on page 289.

Val

The `Val` function converts a string representation of a number to a numeric value. The syntax is:

`Val(string)`

> *String* is the string expression to convert.

`Val` reads *string* from the first character until it reaches a character that is not recognized as part of a number. Valid characters are the digits 0–9, plus and minus signs, decimal point, and the radix prefixes &O (octal) and &H (hexadecimal). Blanks, tabs, and newline characters are ignored. The valid characters are converted to a numeric value and returned as the appropriate type. If no valid characters are read, 0 is returned.

Table 15.8 Shows some examples of using `Val`.

Table 15.8	Examples of using `Val` to convert strings to numbers.
Example	**Numeric Value Returned**
`Val("12 Oak Street")`	12
`Val("-0.5xyz")`	-0.5
`Val("A15")`	0

Summing Up

This chapter taught you how to use VBA's powerful string manipulation functions. Because many custom Office applications work heavily with text data, you'll find these functions extremely useful. When these functions are combined with the text processing capabilities of the Office object model, you'll find there are no text manipulation tasks beyond your abilities.

Working with Dates and Times

It is very common for custom Office applications to need to work with dates and times. VBA provides a special data type for this purpose, as well as a rich set of tools for working with dates and times. The way that VBA represents dates and times may seem strange to you at first, but with a little experience you will realize that this method provides a great deal of flexibility.

The `Date` Data Type

You learned in Chapter 12 that VBA uses the `Date` data type to store dates and times. The `Date` type is a floating point data type. The integer part of the value represents the date as the number of days since December 30, 1899, with dates before then represented by negative values. The decimal part of the value represents the time as a fraction of the 24-hour day. Thus, .25 is 6A.M., .5 is noon, and so on. A date value with no integer part represents a time without a date.

The fact that 36495.4375 represents 10:30A.M. on December 1, 1999, may not seem particularly useful to you! Don't worry, because VBA makes it easy to display dates and times in the formats we are accustomed to. The advantage of representing dates and times in this manner is that they can be added and subtracted in many useful ways. For example, you can subtract two dates to determine the number of days in between. You'll learn about these and other programming techniques in this chapter.

The Current Date and Time

To obtain the current date and time, as set on the system clock, use the `Now`, `Date`, and `Time` functions. These functions returns the current date and time, the current date, or the current time, respectively. For example:

```
Dim d As Date
d = Now
Debug.print "The current date and time are: ", d
```

Creating Dates and Times

VBA offers you several options for creating date values. VBA can recognize date literals in just about any standard format. To indicate that it is a date and not something else, enclose the literal in # characters. For example, in the following statement the # characters make it clear you are not performing a division:

```
Dim d As Date
d = #10/5/99#
```

You can also use the `DateValue` function, which converts a string into a date value:

```
Dim d As Date
d = DateValue("March 7, 2000")
```

If the argument contains time information, it is ignored. If, however, the time information is invalid, an error occurs. Note that the `DateValue` function does not offer any advantage over assigning the date directly, as you saw earlier.

To assemble a date from day, month, and year information, use the `DateSerial` function. The syntax is:

```
DateSerial(year, month, day)
```

The three arguments are integer expressions specifying the year (100–9999), the month (1–12), and the day (1–31). If the year argument is omitted, the current system year is used. If the *day* or *month* values are outside these ranges, the resulting date "wraps" to the next larger unit. For example, this statement evaluates as June 4, 2000:

```
dateserial(00,5,35)
```

Under Windows 98/00/NT, two-digit years for the *year* argument are interpreted based on user-defined settings. The default settings are that values in the range 0–29 are interpreted as the years 2000–2029, and values 30–99 are interpreted as the years 1930–1999. For all other *year* arguments, use a four-digit year. Earlier versions of Windows interpret two-digit years based on the defaults described above. To be sure the function returns the proper value, use a four-digit year.

VBA has similar functions for creating time values. To create a time value (`Date` data type) from a string representation of a time, use the `Time-Value` function. You can represent the time in either 12- or 24-hour style. The following two statements return the same value:

```
TimeValue("6:45PM")
TimeValue("18:45")
```

If the argument to `TimeValue` includes date information, it is ignored. If the date information is invalid, however, an error occurs.

To construct a time from hour, minute, and second information, use the `TimeSerial` function:

```
TimeSerial(hour, minute, second)
```

The three arguments are integer expressions specifying the hour, minute, and second of the time. *Hour* must be in the range 0–23. *Minute* and *second* are normally in the range 0–59 but can be outside that range and are then "wrapped" to the next larger unit. A minute value of 75, for example, is interpreted as 1 hour and 15 minutes. Likewise, a second value of 125 is interpreted as 2 minutes and 5 seconds. Thus, these two statements are equivalent:

```
TimeValue(12, 15, 0)
TimeValue(11, 75, 0)
```

Adding and Subtracting Dates and Times

To add or subtract a specified interval to or from a date, use the `DateAdd` function. It can be useful to add dates and for performing tasks such as determining what day of the week a particular future date falls on. You can add any date interval to an existing date: years, quarters, months, weeks, or days. You can also add time intervals of hours, minutes, or seconds. The syntax is:

```
DateAdd(interval, number, date)
```

Interval specifies the type of interval being added. It is a string expression, as shown in Table 16.1. *Number* is the number of intervals to add. Use a negative value to subtract intervals. *Date* is the date being added to or subtracted from.

Table 16.1	Values for the `DateAdd` function's `interval` argument.
Argument	**Interval**
yyyy	Year
q	Quarter
m	Month
y	Day of year (equivalent to "d")
d	Day
w	Weekday (equivalent to "d")
ww	Week
h	Hour
n	Minute
s	Second

Here's an example of using `DateAdd`. Suppose, when filling an order, you want to store a "payment due" date that is one month from the present day. This statement will do it:

```
Dim DateDue As Date
DateDue = DateAdd("m", 1, Date)
```

The `DateAdd` function will never return an invalid date. If, for example, you add one month to January 31, the return value is February 28 if it is not a leap year, and February 29 if it is a leap year.

Getting Date and Time Information

Sometimes you need to obtain information about a date or a time, such as what day of the week a specified date falls on. VBA has several functions for this purpose. The most flexible of them is `DatePart`. The syntax is:

`DatePart(interval, date, firstdayofweek, firstweekofyear)`

Interval is a string specifying the interval of interest. The possible values are the same as shown in Table 16.1. *Date* is the date value you are getting information about. *Firstdayofweek* is an optional argument indicating which day is to be considered the first day of the week. Settings are shown in Table 16.2. *Firstweekofyear* is an optional argument indicating which week is to be considered the first week of the year. Settings are shown in Table 16.3.

Table 16.2	Settings for the *Firstdayofweek* argument.	
Constant	**Value**	**Description**
vbUseSystem	0	Use the system setting.
vbSunday	1	Sunday (this is the default)
vbMonday	2	Monday
vbTuesday	3	Tuesday
vbWednesday	4	Wednesday
vbThursday	5	Thursday
vbFriday	6	Friday
vbSaturday	7	Saturday

Table 16.3	Settings for the *Firstdayofyear* argument.	
Constant	**Value**	**Description**
vbUseSystem	0	Use the system setting.
vbFirstJan1	1	The week in which January 1 occurs (this is the default).
vbFirstFourDays	2	The first week that has at least four days in the new year.
vbFirstFullWeek	3	The first full week of the year.

The `DatePart` function returns an integer value (as a type `Variant`) that specifies the interval of interest. For example,

```
DatePart("q", #5/10/2000#)
```

returns the value 2 because May 5 is in the second quarter. Note that the interval specifiers "w," "d," and "y" work differently in this function, as follows:

- "w" returns the day of the week, 1 for the first day (Sunday, by default), 7 for the last day (Saturday by default).
- "d" returns the day of the month.
- "y" returns the day of the year (days since January 1).

This code, for example, calculates the number of days from today until the end of the year:

```
days = DatePart("y", #12/31#) - DatePart("y", Date)
```

To calculate the number of time intervals between two dates, use the `DateDiff` function. The syntax is:

```
DateDiff(interval, date1, date2, firstdayofweek, _
        firstweekofyear)
```

Interval is a string specifying the interval of interest, as described in Table 16.1. *Date1* and *date2* are the two dates of interest. *Firstdayofweek* and *firstweekofyear* are optional arguments that work the same as was described for the `DatePart` function. The `DateDiff` function returns an integer (as a type `Variant`) specifying the number of intervals between the two dates. We can repeat the previous example, calculating the number of days to the end of the year, using this function:

```
days = DateDiff("y", Date, #12/31#)
```

Note that *date1* is subtracted from *date2*, so if *date1* is after *date2* the function will return a negative value.

Some additional VBA functions that return specific information about date and time values are listed in Table 16.4. Each of these functions takes as its one argument any expression that represents a valid date or time. The return value is an integer value (as a type `Variant`).

Table 16.4	Other date and time information functions.

Function	Returns
`Year(date)`	A value representing the year.
`Month(date)`	A value 1–12 representing the month.
`Weekday(date, firstdayofweek)`	A value representing the day of the week (default, Sunday = 1). The *firstdayofweek* argument is optional. Possible settings are given in Table 16.2.
`Day(date)`	A value 1–31 representing the day of the month.
`Hour(date)`	A value 0–23 representing the hour of the day.
`Minute(date)`	A value 0–59 representing the minute of the hour.
`Second(date)`	A value 0–59 representing the second of the minute.

Formatting Dates and Times

When you need to display date or time values, you will often want the data formatted in a specific way. When displaying type `Date` data, VBA is pretty good at displaying the information in an appropriate format, based on the system settings. In the United States, for example, the system settings typically result in the display of a date/time value as follows:

```
10/16/99 10:07:32 AM
```

System Settings

Under the Windows operating system, default formats for displaying dates and times (as well as other items such as currency) are set in the Control Panel, under the Regional Settings icon. When you write code to display a date or time using the system settings, it is the end user's system settings that are used, not yours.

For greater control over the display of dates and times, use the `Format` function. The syntax is:

`Format(expression, format, firstdayofweek, firstweekofyear)`

Expression is the date value to format. *Format* is a string expression specifying how the date should be formatted. *Format* can be a named format or a custom format. The named formats are described in Table 16.5, and the custom formats are explained in Table 16.6. The *firstdayofweek* and *firstweekofyear* arguments are optional, and the possible settings were given earlier in the chapter in Tables 16.2 and 16.3.

Note that the `Format` function can be used to format numbers as well as dates, but that is not covered here.

Table 16.5	Named formats for the `Format` function.
General Date	Shows date and time if *expression* contains both. Date display is determined by the system settings.
Long Date	Uses the Long Date format specified by user's system settings.
Medium Date	Uses the *dd-mmm-yy* format (for example, 13-Dec-99). Date display is determined by the system settings.
Short Date	Uses the Short Date format specified by the system settings.
Long Time	Displays a time including hours, minutes, and seconds using the system long-time format.
Medium Time	Shows the hour, minute, and AM or PM using the *hh:mm AM/PM* format.
Short Time	Shows the hour and minute using the *hh:mm* format.

To construct a custom format, use the characters shown in Table 16.6.

Table 16.6	Characters used to construct custom date and time formats.	
Character(s)	**Displays**	**Example of Output**
m	A number representing the month or minute.	1 (for January), 5 (for 5 minutes after the hour)
mm	A number representing the month or minute, with a leading 0 for 1-9.	01 (for January), 05 (for 5 minutes after the hour)
mmm	The abbreviated name of the month.	Jan
mmmm	The full name of the month.	January
d	A number representing the day.	5
dd	A number representing the day with a leading 0 for 1-9.	05
ddd	The abbreviated weekday.	Wed
dddd	The full weekday.	Wednesday
ddddd	The date according to the regional settings.	Depends on settings
AM/PM	AM or PM for morning or afternoon.	AM
a/p	a or p for morning or afternoon.	a
h	A number representing the hour.	2 (for 2 hours past midnight)
hh	A number representing the hour, with a leading 0 for 0-9.	02 (for 2 hours past midnight)
s	A number representing the second.	5 (for 5 seconds past the minute)
ss	A number representing the second, with a leading 0 for 0-9.	05 (for 5 seconds past the minute)
ttttt	The time according to the regional settings.	Depends on settings
/ : - (and most other characters)	The character itself.	/ : -

Table 16.7 gives some examples of using the named and custom date and time formats. In all cases, the date and time were May 5, 2000, 12:15 PM. These examples were generated on a system with regional settings for the United States.

Table 16.7	Examples of named and custom date and time formats.
Format Argument to the Format Function	**Result**
Short Date	5/12/00
Long Date	Friday, May 12, 2000
Medium Time	12:15 PM
dddd, mm/dd	Friday, 05/12
dddd, mmmm dd	Friday, May 12
ttttt, mmmm dd, yyyy	12:15:00 PM, May 12, 2000
mm-dd-yyyy	05-12-2000
hh:mm a/p	12:15 p

Summing Up

VBA's method of storing dates and times as floating point numbers offers several advantages, such as making it easy to calculate intervals. VBA provides a rich set of functions for converting dates and times between this numerical representation and the common formats we are used to working with. Given the importance of dates and times in many custom Office applications, you'll probably find yourself making use of these capabilities on a regular basis.

Working
with Files

If you want to save data permanently, you have pretty much only one choice: to write it to a disk file. Then, to use the data again you must read it from a disk file. The Office applications all have their own dedicated file formats: .DOC files for Word, .XLS files for Excel, and so on. To read and write these dedicated file formats, you use the methods that are provided by the application's object model, as was covered in Chapters 5 through 11. However there will be times when these dedicated file types simply don't meet your needs. When this happens, you'll find that VBA provides a powerful set of tools for flexible writing and reading of files.

Overview

Working with files has two aspects: file *access* and file *management*. File access refers to methods for reading data from and writing data to files, while file management refers to tasks such as moving and deleting files and creating folders.

There are two approaches a programmer can take to file access and management in Visual Basic. One approach, which might be called the traditional approach, uses statements that have been part of the Basic language for a long time. The second, newer, approach is object-oriented, and treats the file system as a File System Object, or FSO, that has properties and methods that are used to manipulate the files. Which of these two methods you use does not affect the end result, but affects only how you go about writing the code. The FSO model provides for file management, and for reading and writing text files. The traditional approach can also perform those tasks and adds the capability to read and write binary files. You can mix traditional and FSO methods in the same program.

This chapter is divided into three parts. The first covers file access using the traditional methods. You need to know these traditional methods as there are some file access tasks you simply cannot do using the newer object-oriented techniques. The second part deals with text files, and how to work with them using both traditional and FSO methods. Finally, we will look at file management techniques, concentrating on the newer FSO methods but including basic coverage of the traditional methods as well.

File Access

In broad outline, all Visual Basic file access consists of the same three steps: opening the file, reading from or writing to the file, and closing the file. However, there are three different types of files available, with each type suited for different kinds of data. The three types are sequential, random, and binary.

A sequential file is a text file, meaning that the data in the file consists of characters. The data in a sequential file is stored as a series of variable-length units, called *records*. If you store a number in a sequential file, that's one record. If you store a string, that's another record. The records are *variable length* because each record's length is not fixed but is determined by its contents. The end of one record, and the beginning of the next, is marked by a carriage return/line feed (CRLF) character. A CRLF character on a line by itself indicates an empty record. Sequential files are so called because their records must always be read in sequence, from the beginning of the file. There's no way to jump directly to a record in the middle of the file. A sequential file stores numbers as text. Thus, the value 99.9 is stored as characters 99.9 and not in a binary representation. Text is also stored as characters, and is differentiated from numbers by being enclosed in double quotation marks.

A random file stores data as a series of fixed-size records. Each record in the file is the same size as all the others, with the record size being defined when the file is first created. The records in a random access file are numbered sequentially starting at 1. As the name suggests, a random access file permits a program to directly access each record by its number, without having to first read previous records. In a 1,000 record file, for example, you could access record 755 without first having to read records 1 through 754. You can store both text and numbers in a random access file. Text is stored as characters, and numbers are stored in a binary format.

Each record in a random access file contains a fixed number of bytes, or characters. Each record contains one or more fields, and each field also has a fixed length. Obviously, the record size is equal to the sum of the field sizes. The sizes of a file's records and fields are defined by the program when the file is created. Random files do not use delimiters to mark the end of each field. Because the fields and records are a fixed length, it is possible to determine exactly where a given record or field begins. For example, if the record size is 122 bytes, you know that the 20th record in the file begins at byte position 2441.

Binary files store data as an unformatted sequence of bytes. There are no records or fields, and no delimiter character. Binary files allow you to manipulate the individual bytes of a file without any assumptions about what the bytes represent. Binary files are not limited to ASCII text or VBA variables. You can use binary access to read and modify any kind of disk file, as well as to store program data. Because a binary file has no records or other structure, the program is completely responsible for keeping track of what is stored where.

Opening Files

Before you can write to or read from a file, you must open it. Files are opened with the Open statement, which has the following syntax:

```
Open filename For mode Access access lock _
    As #filenum LEN=reclen
```

Filename is a string expression specifying the name of the file to be opened. If *filename* does not include drive and path information, the file is opened in the current folder.

Mode is an optional argument that specifies the file access mode. Possible settings are shown in Table 17.1.

Access is an optional argument that specifies the operations permitted on the open file. Possible settings are shown in Table 17.2.

Lock is an optional argument that controls access to a file by other processes. Possible settings are explained in Table 17.3.

Table 17.1	Values for the Open statement's Mode argument.
Mode Argument	**File Access Mode**
APPEND	Sequential file access. If *filename* already exists, new data is appended at the end of the file. If *filename* does not exist, it is created.
BINARY	Binary file access, for both reading and writing data. If *filename* does not exist, it is created.
INPUT	Sequential file access, for reading data only. If *filename* doesn't exist, an error occurs.
OUTPUT	Sequential file access, for writing data only. If *filename* exists, it is deleted and a new file created. If *filename* does not exist, it is created.
RANDOM	Random file access, for both reading and writing data. If *filename* does not exist, it is created. This is the default file access mode if the *mode* argument is omitted.

Table 17.2	Settings for the Access argument to the Open statement.
Setting	**Description**
READ	File opened for reading only.
WRITE	File opened for writing only.
READ WRITE	File opened for reading and writing. This mode is valid only for random mode files, binary mode files, and sequential mode files opened for APPEND.

Table 17.3	Settings for the Lock argument to the Open statement.
Setting	**Description**
SHARED	Any process may read or write the file.
LOCK READ	No other process may read the file. A program can open a file in LOCK READ mode only if no other process already has read access to the file.
LOCK WRITE	No other process may write to the file. A program can open a file in LOCK WRITE mode only if no other process already has write access to the file.
LOCK READ WRITE	No other process may read or write the file. A program can open a file in LOCK READ WRITE mode only if no other process already has read or write access to the file, and a LOCK READ or LOCK WRITE is not already in place.

Filenum is an integer expression with a value between 1 and 511. The next section gives more information on file numbers.

Reclen is an integer expression that specifies the record length, in bytes, for random access files, and the buffer size for sequential access files. The maximum is 32,767, and the default is 128 for both. *Reclen* is not applicable to binary mode files.

File Numbers

When you open a file in VBA, it must have a unique file number associated with it. This is the *filenum* argument that you include in the Open statement. Once the file is open, you use this number to refer to the file for read and write operations, and also to close it. The file number must be within the range 1 through 511, and only one open file can be associated with a given number at a time. This refers not only to files opened by VBA, but by other processes on the system as well. After the file has been closed, the file number is free to be used with another file.

To ensure that you obtain an unused file number, you use the Free-File function. This function returns the lowest unused file number. The syntax is:

```
FreeFile(arg)
```

The function returns an integer value containing an unused file number. If called with no argument or an argument of 0, FreeFile returns a value within the range 1–255. With an argument of 1, the return value is within the range 256–511.

This code fragment shows the basic procedure for opening a file:

```
Dim filenum As Integer
filenum = FreeFile
OPEN "c:\my documents\sales.txt" FOR APPEND AS #filenum
```

Closing Files

You should close each file when the program is finished using it. Closing a file flushes the file's buffer (a temporary storage area in memory), ensuring that all data has been physically written to disk, and also frees up the file number that was associated with the file, allowing it to be used for another file. To close a specific file, execute the Close statement with the file number or numbers as argument. To close all open files, execute Close with no argument:

```
Close #filenum
Close #f1, #f2, #f3
Close
```

All open files are automatically closed when a VBA program terminates. Even so, develop the habit of closing individual files as soon as the program is finished with the file. This technique avoids the possibility of data loss in the event of a system crash or power failure.

Using Sequential Files

To write one record of data to a sequential file, use the `Write #` statement. The syntax is:

```
Write #fn, list
```

The `fn` argument is the file number that was used to open the file, using the `Open` statement as explained previously. The file must have been opened in APPEND or OUTPUT mode. `List` is a comma-delimited list of one or more expressions to be written to the file. If you omit `list`, an empty record (in other words, a blank line) is written to the file. The `Write #` statement automatically inserts the required comma delimiters and quotation marks. Because the double quotation mark is used as a field delimiter, it cannot be included in the data saved with `Write #`.

To read data from a sequential file, use the `Input #` statement. Its syntax is:

```
Input #fn, varlist
```

The `fn` argument is the number that was associated with the file when it was opened in INPUT mode. `Varlist` is a list of one or more program variables to be assigned the data that is read from the file. If `varlist` contains more than one variable name, separate them by commas. `Input #` reads as many fields from the file as there are variables in `varlist`. This statement reads data from the sequential file on a field-by-field basis, and assigns data read from the file to variables that appear in the `Input #` statement's argument list, in order. The next time you call `Input #`, it reads the next field(s).

Here's an example. This statement reads the first three fields from the specified file and assigns them to V1, V2, and V3, in that order:

```
Input #fn, V1, V2, V3
```

The exact same result would be obtained by this code:

```
Input #fn, V1
Input #fn, V2
Input #fn, V3
```

How does the `Input #` statement break the data into fields? It depends on the type of variable in the statement's argument list. If `Input #` is reading data into a string variable, the end of a field is marked by one of the following:

- A double quotation mark if the field begins with a double quotation mark.
- A comma if the field does not begin with a double quotation mark.
- A carriage return/line feed (CR/LF) character.

If Input # is reading data into a numeric variable, the end of the field is marked by a comma, one or more spaces, or CR/LF.

The procedure in Listing 17.1 shows how to read and write sequential files. The code prompts the user to enter a series of names and ages, storing the data in a two-dimensional array. Then, the data is written to a sequential file. Finally, the file is opened for reading and the data is read in and displayed in the Immediate window.

Listing 17–1   *Writing and reading sequential files.*

```
Public Sub DemoSequentialFile()

' Demonstrates writing and reading sequential files.

Dim fn As Integer, index As Integer, count As Integer
Dim Data(100, 1)
Dim temp1, temp2

' Get the data from the user.
count = 0
Do While True
    temp1 = InputBox("Enter person's name, a blank to quit:")
    If temp1 = "" Then Exit Do
    Data(count, 0) = temp1
    Data(count, 1) = InputBox("Enter person's age:")
    count = count + 1
Loop

' Write the data to a sequential file.
fn = FreeFile
Open "demo.dat" For Output As #fn
For i = 0 To count
    Write #fn, Data(i, 0), Data(i, 1)
Next i
Close #fn

' Read the data from the file and display it.
fn = FreeFile
Open "demo.dat" For Input As #fn
For i = 0 To count
```

```
     Input #fn, temp1, temp2
     Debug.Print temp1, temp2
Next i

Close #fn

End Sub
```

Using Random Files

Like a sequential file, a random file consists of records. The difference lies in that the records in a random file are all the same size, and the program differentiates one record from the next by its position in the file. No special characters are used to delineate records. For instance, if a file's records are each 200 bytes long, bytes 1 through 200 contain the first record (byte positions in a file always start at position 1), and record 4 is at positions 601 through 800. The records in a random file are numbered sequentially starting at 1, and the maximum number of records in a file is 2,147,483,647.

Each record in a random file consists of one or more fields. Like the records, the fields have a fixed size. This means that each record in a random file has the same number of fields and the same field sizes. You define a random file's structure when you first create the file. This is typically done by reference to a user-defined type, or UDT, which you learned about in Chapter 12 (which you should refer to for details). Briefly, a UDT is a data structure that contains two or more elements, or fields. For example, you could create a UDT called `Employee` as follows:

```
Type Employee
    LastName As String * 16
    FirstName As String * 12
    EmpNumber As Long
    HireDate As Date
End Type
```

Perhaps you have noticed a correspondence between a UDT and the structure of a random file. There is indeed a relationship, and random files are usually used to store arrays of UDTs. Each UDT is a record in the file, and each UDT element is a field. When you open a random file, you must specify the record length, which is, of course, the same as the UDT size.

Let's continue using the `Employee` UDT defined above to see how random files work. You would need an array of type `Employee` to store all your employee records, and you want to be able to save that data to disk. This code declares the array and opens the random file (the code to permit the user to enter the data into the array is not shown):

```
Dim OurEmployees(500) As Employee
...
fn = FreeFile
Open "c"\data\employees.dat" For RANDOM As #fn _
    Len = Len(OurEmployees(0))
```

The Len function returns the length, in bytes, of the item passed to it. By passing it a single element of the array, it returns the length of a single Employee UDT. As a result, the random file is set up with the proper record length.

Once the random file is open, it is available for reading and writing. To write data to a random file, use the Put statement. The syntax is:

```
Put #fn, recnum, item
```

Fn is the number associated with the random file when it was opened.

Recnum is an optional argument specifying the record number in the file where the data is to be placed. If *recnum* is omitted, the data is put in the next record (following the previous record that was written or read from the file). If the file has just been opened, record 1 is used. If *recnum* points to an existing record in the file, that record's data is overwritten with the new data.

Item is an instance of the associated UDT that is to be written to the file.

Continuing with the example above, the following code would write the entire contents of the OurEmployees array to the open file (then closes the file):

```
For i = 0 To 500
    Put #fn, , OurEmployees(i)
Next i
Close #fn
```

Since Put automatically increments the record number each time it is called, this code writes the entire array, in order, to the file.

If you want to add records to an existing file, without overwriting data that is already in the file, you must add the new records at the end of the file. To determine how many records are in the file, use the Lof function, which returns the length of the entire file in bytes. Since you know the length of each record, a simple division gives you the number of records in the file. If fn is the file number of the open random file, you would write as follows:

```
NumRecords = Lof(fn) \ Len(item)
```

in which *item* is an instance of the UDT associated with the file. Then, to add a new record at the end of the file:

```
Put #fn, NumRecords + 1, item
```

To read data from a random file, use the Get statement. The syntax is:

```
Get #fn, recnum, item
```

Fn is the number associated with the random file when it was opened.

Recnum is an optional argument specifying the record number in the file to be read. If *recnum* is omitted, the data is put at the next record (following the previous record that was written or read from the file). If the file has just been opened, record 1 is read.

Item is an instance of the associated UDT where the data read from the file is to be placed.

This code reads the 55th record from the open employees file into its proper position in the array:

```
GET #fn, 55, OurEmployees(55)
```

You can use a loop to read all the records from a random file, starting at the beginning. This would be similar in concept to the loop used to write the entire array to disk, shown earlier in this section. However, you may not know ahead of time how many records are in the file. You can calculate the number of records, as explained above, or you can use the Eof function, which returns True only when the last record in the file has been read. Here's an example:

```
i = 0
Do Until Eof(fn)
    Get #fn, , OurEmployees(i)
    i = i + 1
Loop
```

This code example assumes that the array OurEmployees is large enough to hold all the records. You can always use a dynamic array, as covered in Chapter 12, expanding it as needed to hold all the data.

The File Pointer

Visual Basic maintains a file pointer for each open random access file. This pointer keeps track of where you are in the file—in other words, the next record to be written or read. When you first open a random file, the file pointer is at 1, indicating the first record. Then, as you read and write data, the file pointer changes as follows:

- A call to Get or Put without a *recnum* argument increments the file pointer by 1.
- A call to Get or Put with a *recnum* argument sets the file pointer to *recnum* + 1.

Table 17.4 shows some other ways VBA lets you work with file pointers in random files.

Table 17.4	File pointer information and manipulation.
Statement or Function	**Description**
Seek(*fn*) (the function)	Returns the current file pointer position for file *fn*.
Seek *fn*, *position* (the statement)	Sets the file pointer for file *fn* to *position*. If *position* is beyond the end of the file, the file is extended as needed. If *position* is 0 or negative, an error occurs.
Loc(*fn*)	Returns the position of the last record that was read or written. If the file has just been opened, returns 0.

Using Binary Files

A binary file stores data as an unformatted sequence of bytes. There are no records and no fields. Binary files are very flexible, but this flexibility requires that the programmer do more work to keep track of what is stored where in the file. As with random files, binary files each have a file pointer associated with them. Instead of indicating record number, however, a binary file's pointer indicates the byte position where the next read or write operation will occur. A file that contains *n* bytes has positions numbered from *1* through *n*.

You work with the file pointer in much the same way in binary files as with random files. The pointer is at position 1 when a file is first opened, and after any read or write operation (which is explained below) the pointer is located just after the data that was read or written. You can change the file pointer and determine its value using the same Seek statement and Seek and Loc functions that you learned about in the previous section on random files. VBA knows the access mode in which a given file was opened, and interprets Seek or Loc correctly when you use them, working with bytes for a binary file and records for a random file. You can also use the Eof function with a binary file to detect when the end of the file has been reached.

To write data to a binary file, use the Put statement. To read data from a binary file, use the Get statement. These are the same statements that are used for random files; they are interpreted differently depending on the mode the file was opened in. The syntax is:

```
Get #fn, pos, var
Put #fn, pos, var
```

Fn is the number associated with the file when it was opened in binary mode. *Pos* is an optional argument specifying the byte position where the read or write operation is to take place. If *pos* is omitted, the current file pointer position is used. *Var* is any VBA variable. Get reads data from the file into *var*, while Put writes data from *var* to the file. These statements automatically read or write the number of bytes contained in var. If *var* is a variable length string, the number of bytes transferred is equal to the number of characters currently in *var*.

Here's an example of using binary files. The code in Listing 17–2 creates an array of type Currency, then puts a value into the 122nd element of the array. The entire array is then written to a binary file named "currency.dat." The file is then closed and then re-opened—though this is not strictly necessary, because unlike sequential files, a binary file can be written to and then read without having to close and re-open it. Finally, the 122nd element in the file is read and displayed.

Listing 17–2   *Demonstrating binary file input and output.*

```
Public Sub TestBinaryFileIO()

Dim fn As Integer, count As Integer
Dim MyData(1000) As Currency, OneValue As Currency

' Put some data in one array element.
MyData(122) = 99.99

' Open the file.
fn = FreeFile
Open "currency.dat" For Binary As #fn
'
 Write the entire array to the file.
For count = 0 To 1000
    Put #fn, , MyData(count)
Next count
Close #fn

' Re-open the file.
fn = FreeFile
Open "currency.dat" For Binary As #fn

' Get the 122nd element.
Get #fn, 122 * Len(OneValue) + 1, OneValue
Close #fn

' Display the input value.
Debug.Print OneValue

End Sub
```

The flexibility of binary files makes them suitable for just about any kind of data storage. They do require some extra programming work to keep track of what is stored where. If you "lose track" of how the data is organized in a binary file, you are likely to get strange results. If, for example, your file pointer is off by even a single byte, the data you read in is likely to be gibberish. For example, the data written to the file in Listing 17–2, which originated as an array of type `Currency`, could just as easily be read back in as an array of type `Double` or any other data type. You would not get an error message or warning, but the results would be meaningless.

Here are some important things to keep in mind when working with binary files;

- To add new data at the end of an existing binary file, execute `Seek #fn, Lof(fn) + 1` to move the file pointer to the end of the file.
- If you write data to an existing binary file at a position before the end of the file, the new data will overwrite existing data.
- If you write data at a file pointer position that is past the end of a file, the file will be extended to the new length but the part of the file between the original end of the file and the newly written data will contain garbage (undefined values).
- If you read data at a file pointer position that is beyond the end of a file, no error occurs, but the returned data will be garbage.

Working with Text Files

Disk files are often used to store text, and as an Office developer you'll probably find yourself needing to read and write text files on a regular basis. When it comes to text files, VBA gives you two choices. You can use the traditional methods, more specifically the sequential file type that was covered earlier in this chapter. Or, you can use the new object-oriented file system. In this part of the chapter I will show you how to use the object-oriented file system, as well as provide some specifics for using sequential files for text.

Object-Oriented Text File Manipulation

To use object-oriented methods to work with text files, you always start with the `FileSystemObject` class, usually referred to as FSO. This class is at the top of the hierarchy of objects that are used with text files. Thus, any program that wants to use these objects must start by creating an instance of the FSO class:

```
Dim fso As Scripting.FileSystemObject
Set fso = New Scripting.FileSystemObject
```

To use early binding, the recommended technique for working with objects in your code, you must select "Microsoft Scripting Runtime" in the VBA References dialog box. Remember that selecting a type library in the References dialog box not only permits early binding, but also gives you access to the library's classes, methods, and properties in the Object Browser. Use of the Object Browser was covered in Chapter 4.

After creating an instance of the `FileSystemObject` class, you must next create a `TextStream` object. You can think of a `TextStream` object as a regular text file enclosed in an FSO wrapper. The FSO has two methods for creating a `TextStream` object:

- `CreateTextFile` creates a new text file, overwriting an existing file of the same name if it exists.
- `OpenTextFile` opens a text file for reading and/or writing. If the file already exists, new data is appended to existing data.

The syntax for these two methods is similar. In these examples, assume that `fso` is a `FileSystemObject`.

```
Dim ts As Scripting.TextStream
Set ts = fso.CreateTextFile(filename, overwrite, unicode)
Set ts = fso.OpenTextFile(filename[, iomode[, create[, _
                          format]]])
```

Filename is a string expression specifying the name, including path information, of the file.

Overwrite is an optional True/False value specifying whether an existing file of the same name will be overwritten. If this argument is omitted, the default is False. If *overwrite* is False and *filename* already exists, an error occurs. You can trap this error to permit the user to verify file overwrites.

Unicode is True to create a Unicode file, False (the default) for an ASCII file.

IOMode is an optional argument. Possible values are `ForReading` to open the file in read-only mode, `ForAppending` to write new data to the end of the file, and `ForWriting` to write data without appending. The default is `ForWriting`.

Create is an optional True/False value specifying whether a new file will be created if *filename* does not exist. The default is False.

Format is a tristate argument (one that can have three values) that determines the format of the file. `TriStateTrue` opens the file as Unicode, `TriStateFalse` (the default) opens the file as ASCII, and `TristateUse-Default` uses the system default format setting.

Unicode

Computers use numbers to represent the characters and punctuation marks in text data. There are two coding schemes for this: ACSII (or ANSI) and Unicode. ASCII uses one byte for each character, which permits only 256 different symbols to be represented. This is adequate for English but not for many other languages. Unicode uses 2 bytes per character, allowing for more than 65,000 different symbols. Which text file format you use will depend on the specific requirements of your project.

Another way to obtain a `TextStream` object is to create a `File` object that is associated with an existing file (you cannot use this method to create a new file). Then, use the `File` object's `OpenAsTextStream` method to create the `TextStream` object. Here's how to create a `File` object associated with the file *filename* (as before, assuming that fso is a `FileSystemObject`):

```
Dim f As Scripting.File
Set f = fso.GetFile(filename)
```

Once the `File` object exists you call the `OpenAsTextStream` method. The syntax is:

```
f.OpenAsTextStream(iomode, format)
```

The *IOMode* and *format* arguments are both optional, and are the same as described earlier in this chapter for the `CreateTextFile` and `OpenTextFile` methods. The code shown below illustrates how to create a `TextStream` object associated with the existing file "myfile.txt":

```
Dim fso As Scripting.FileSystemObject
Dim ts As Scripting.TextStream
Dim f As Scripting.File

Set fso = CreateObject("Scripting.FileSystemObject")
Set f = fso.GetFile("myfile.txt")
Set ts = f.OpenAsTextStream
```

Once you have a `TextStream` object associated with the text file—either a new or an existing file—then you are ready to start working with the file. Note that the `TextStream` object has a *current character position*, or *file pointer*, that indicates where the next read or write operation will take place. The `TextStream` object has properties and methods that you use to work with the file. The properties are described in Table 17.5, and the methods in Table 17.6. All of the `TextStream` object's properties are read-only.

Table 17.5	Properties of the `TextStream` object.
Property	**Description**
`AtEndOfLine`	True if the file pointer is at the end of a line; otherwise False. `AtEndOfLine` applies only to files that are open for reading, otherwise an error occurs.
`AtEndOfStream`	True if the file pointer is at the end of the file; otherwise False. `AtEndOf-Stream` applies only to files that are open for reading, otherwise an error occurs.
`Column`	Returns the column number of the file pointer. The first character on a line is at column 1.
`Line`	Returns the current line number of the file pointer.

Table 17.6	Methods of the `TextStream` object.
Method	**Description**
`Close`	Closes the file associated with the `TextStream` object. A file should always be closed when you are finished working with it.
`Read(n)`	Reads the next *n* characters from the file and returns the resulting string.
`ReadAll`	Reads the entire file and returns the resulting string.
`ReadLine`	Reads an entire line (up to, but not including, the newline character) from the file and returns the resulting string.
`Skip(n)`	Moves the file pointer forward by *n* characters.
`SkipLine`	Moves the file pointer to the beginning of the next line.
`Write(s)`	Writes the string *s* to the file without adding any extra or newline characters.
`WriteBlankLines(n)`	Writes *n* blank lines to the file.
`WriteLine(s)`	Writes the string *s* to the file followed by a newline character.

Some of these methods are applicable only when the file has been opened for reading or for writing. If you try to use a method that is inappropriate for the file's mode, an error will occur. To switch from writing to reading, or *vice versa*, you must close then re-open the file. Also, strangely enough, there does not seem to be a way to move the file pointer backward in a `TextStream` object. As far as I can tell, your only option is to close and then re-open the file, which resets the file pointer to the start of the file.

The procedure in Listing 17–3 shows how to write and read a text file using the object-oriented approach. A new file is created, overwriting any existing file of the same name. Lines of text are input from the user, and written to the file as they are entered. When the user signals he or she is done by entering a blank line, the file is closed. Then the file is re-opened, in For-Reading mode, and the lines of text read in and displayed one at a time until the end of the file is reached.

Listing 17–3   *Demonstrating object-oriented text file access.*

```
Public Sub FSODemo()

Dim fso As Scripting.FileSystemObject
Dim ts As Scripting.TextStream
Dim temp As String

Set fso = New Scripting.FileSystemObject
Set ts = fso.CreateTextFile("fso_demo.txt", True)
Do
    temp = InputBox("Enter text, a blank when done:")
    If temp = "" Then Exit Do
    ts.WriteLine temp
Loop While True
ts.Close

Set ts = fso.OpenTextFile("fso_demo.txt", ForReading)
Do Until ts.AtEndOfStream
    Debug.Print ts.ReadLine
Loop
ts.Close

End Sub
```

Traditional Text File Manipulation

If you want to use VBA's traditional file statements to work with text files, you will use the sequential file type that was described earlier in the chapter. The examples in this section assume that you have already opened a file in sequential mode, with the proper read or write access, as was explained earlier.

To write text to a sequential file, use the `Print #` statement. This statement does not delimit fields with commas or enclose strings in double quotes, but rather writes text to the file without any additions or changes, The syntax for this statement is:

```
Print #fn , list [,|;]
```

Fn is the number that was associated with the file when it was opened (in OUTPUT or APPEND mode).

List is an optional list of one or more string expressions to be written to the file. Multiple expressions in *list* should be separated by a comma or semicolon. If *list* is omitted, a blank line is written to the file.

The optional comma or semicolon at the end of the `Print #` statement determines the location of subsequent output to the file—in other words, the output of the next `Print #` statement that is executed:

- No comma or semicolon causes subsequent output to be placed on a new line.
- Semicolon causes subsequent output to be placed on the same line immediately following the previous output.
- Comma causes subsequent output to be placed on the same line at the next print zone (similar to a tab).

For the most part, you will use either a semicolon or nothing at the end of the `Print #` statement, as the usefulness of print zones is dubious. Thus, to output "Microsoft Office" to a file as a single line of text you could write this:

```
Print #fn, "Microsoft ";
Print #fn, "Office"
```

But to write these two words as two separate lines of text you would use this code:

```
Print #fn, "Microsoft "
Print #fn, "Office"
```

Using `vbCrLf`

VBA has the built-in constant, `vbCrLf`, which represents a carriage return/line feed character, sometimes called a newline character. You can control where lines break in a text file by inserting this character into your data at the desired locations. Thus, this code writes "Microsoft" and "Office" to the file on two separate lines:

```
Print #fn, "Microsoft" & vbCrLf & "Office"
```

To read text one line at a time from a sequential file, use the `Line Input #` statement. This statement reads an entire line of text from the file and assigns the text to a string variable. The syntax is:

```
Line Input #fn, var
```

Fn is the number assigned to the file when it was opened (for INPUT).
Var is the type `String` variable to receive the line of text.

When you execute `Line Input #` repeatedly, it reads lines of text from the file one after the other. To read an entire file, a line at a time, is simply a matter of opening the file and executing `Line Input #` repeatedly until the end of file is reached. The procedure in Listing 17–4 demonstrates traditional text file access. It does exactly the same things that were done in Listing 17–3 using the object-oriented text file methods.

| Listing 17–4 | *Demonstrating traditional text file access.* |

```
Public Sub TraditionalTextFileDemo()

Dim fn As Integer
Dim temp As String

fn = FreeFile
Open "tfa_demo.txt" For Output As #fn
Do
    temp = InputBox("Enter text, a blank when done:")
    If temp = "" Then Exit Do
    Print #fn, temp
Loop While True
Close #fn

fn = FreeFile
Open "tfa_demo.txt" For Input As #fn
Do
    Line Input #fn, temp
    Debug.Print temp
Loop Until EOF(fn)
Close #fn

End Sub
```

Selecting a File Access Method

VBA offers four different methods of accessing files: sequential, random, binary, and object oriented. This can be confusing—it's not always clear which type of file is best for a particular application. Here are some guidelines:

- For data that is organized as separate lines of text, use the object-oriented techniques (which are preferred) or a sequential file.
- To manipulate non-text files generated by other applications, use binary files.
- To store arrays of numbers, use binary files. You can also use sequential files for this type of storage, but binary files are preferred because they are faster and smaller.
- To store arrays of variable length strings, use sequential mode.
- To store arrays of fixed length strings, use either binary or sequential files. Again, binary mode has a size and speed advantage over sequential mode, although the difference is not as great as it is with numerical arrays.
- To store data that is organized in a record and field format, use either sequential or random mode. Random mode is faster but results in larger file size.

File Management

File management consists of tasks such as creating and deleting folders, moving and copying files, and getting information about the disk drives on a system. VBA offers two ways to perform file management tasks: the newer object-oriented techniques, and the traditional Basic statements and functions. Both methods work perfectly well, but I recommend that you use the object-oriented techniques in your own programs. This section is devoted mostly to covering the object-oriented file management techniques, and presents only a brief overview of the traditional methods so you can recognize them if you see them in someone else's code.

Object-Oriented File Management

The object-oriented file management techniques are based upon the FileSystemObject class (FSO). This is the same class as is used for object-oriented file access, as you saw earlier in this chapter. To review briefly, you must create an instance of this object as the first step in performing any file management tasks:

```
Dim fso As Scripting.FileSystemObject
Set fso = New Scripting.FileSystemObject
```

The FSO is the top object in the object-oriented file system hierarchy. It gives you access to all the drives (both local and network), folders, and files on the system. The other objects in the hierarchy represent the way the file system is organized:

- The `Drive` object corresponds to a single disk drive on the system.
- The `Folder` object corresponds to a single folder, or subdirectory, on a drive.
- The `File` object corresponds to a single file in a folder.

The organization of the FSO object hierarchy follows very closely the way the actual objects are organized on the system, and is also similar in some ways to the object hierarchies of the Office object models you learned about in Chapters 5 through 11. Here is a brief outline of how the FSO system works:

- Each drive on the system is represented by a `Drive` object. The `Drive` object's properties provide information about the drive. All of the system's `Drive` objects are contained in the `Drives` collection of the `FileSystemObject`.
- Each `Drive` object contains a `Folder` object that represents the top-level, or root, folder on the drive.
- Each `Folder` object contains a `Folders` collection that contains a `Folder` object for each subfolder within the folder.
- Each `Folder` object also contains a `Files` collection that contains a `File` object for each file in the folder.

FSO METHODS

The `FileSystemObject` itself has a set of methods that are useful in file management. Some of these methods duplicate the effect of other object methods, as you'll see when you read the rest of this chapter. For example, you can delete a file using either the FSO's `DeleteFile` method or the `File` object's `Delete` method. Table 17.7 lists the more important FSO object methods that are not duplicated elsewhere. You can obtain information about the full set of FSO methods in the VBA help system.

Table 17.7	Methods of the `FileSystemObject`.
Method	**Description**
`BuildPath(path, name)`	Returns a new path consisting of *path* with *name* appended.
`CreateFolder(foldername)`	Creates a new folder as specified in *foldername*. If the folder already exists, an error occurs.
`DriveExists(drivespec)`	Returns True if the specified drive exists. *Drivespec* is a drive letter or the name of a network drive.
`FileExists(filespec)`	Returns True if the specified file exists. *Filespec* is the filename, including relative or absolute path information if needed.
`FolderExists(folderspec)`	Returns True if the specified folder exists. *Folderspec* is the folder name, including relative or absolute path information if needed.
`GetAbsolutePathName(path)`	Returns a complete and unambiguous path specification corresponding to *path*.
`GetDrive(path)`	Returns a `Drive` object representing the drive of the specified path.
`GetFileName(pathspec)`	Returns the filename portion of the specified path, or an empty string if *pathspec* does not contain a filename.
`GetFolder(path)`	Returns a `Folder` object corresponding to the specified path.
`GetSpecialFolder(folderspec)`	Returns a `Folder` object corresponding to the specified special folder: `WindowsFolder` (the Windows folder), `SystemFolder` (the Windows system folder), or `TemporaryFolder` (the temporary folder).
`GetTempName`	Returns a string containing a temporary folder or filename that is guaranteed not to already be in use.

THE `Drive` OBJECT

The `FileSystemObject` has a `Drives` property (in fact, its only property) that is a reference to the `Drives` collection, which contains all of the `Drive` objects on the system. This includes all local drives as well as shared network drives. The `Drives` collection is a standard VBA collection, and uses the same collection syntax that you learned in previous chapters. The `Drive` object has properties that provide information about the physical drive. These properties are listed in Table 17.8. These properties are all read-only except where noted.

Table 17.8	Properties of the `Drive` object.
Property	**Description**
`AvailableSpace`	The amount of space available on the drive. In general, the same as the `FreeSpace` property but may differ on systems that support quotas.
`DriveLetter`	The drive letter associated with the drive. Returns a zero-length string for network drives that have not been mapped to a drive letter.
`DriveType`	A value indicating the type of drive. Possible values are 0 (unknown), 1 (removable), 2 (fixed), 3 (network), 4 (CD-ROM), and 5 (RAM disk).
`FileSystem`	The type of file system. Available return types include FAT, NTFS, and CDFS.
`FreeSpace`	The amount of space available to a user on the specified drive or network share. In general, the same as the `AvailableSpace` property but may differ on systems that support quotas.
`IsReady`	Returns True if the drive is ready, False if it is not ready. False is returned for removable media and CD-ROM drives if the media has not been inserted.
`Path`	The path of the drive. This consists of the drive letter followed by a colon.
`RootFolder`	Returns a `Folder` object representing the drive's root path.
`SerialNumber`	The unique serial number identifying a disk. Use this property to verify that a removable media drive contains the proper media.
`ShareName`	The share name assigned to a network drive. For non-network drives, this property returns a zero-length string.
`TotalSize`	The total capacity of the drive, in bytes.
`VolumeName`	The volume name of the drive. Write to this property to change a drive's volume name.

Listing 17–5 shows how easy it is to obtain information about a system's drives using the `Drives` collection. This code displays the drive letter, free space, and volume name of all the system's drives. If a removable media drive is not ready, a message to that effect is displayed.

Listing 17–5	*Displaying information about the system drives.*

```
Public Sub GetDriveInfo()

Dim fso As Scripting.FileSystemObject
Dim d As Scripting.Drive

Set fso = New Scripting.FileSystemObject
Debug.Print "Drive", "Free space", "Name"
```

```
For Each d In fso.Drives
    If d.IsReady Then
        Debug.Print d.Path, d.AvailableSpace, d.VolumeName
    Else
        Debug.Print d.Path & " is not ready."
    End If

Next d

End Sub
```

THE `Folder` OBJECT

Each folder on a drive is represented by a `Folder` object. The `Folder` object provides the VBA programmer with:

- Methods to copy, move, or delete the folder.
- Properties to obtain information about the folder.
- A `Files` collection containing a `File` object for each file in the folder.
- A `SubFolders` collection containing a `Folder` object for each sub-folder in the folder.

Your entry point to the folders on a given drive is the `RootFolder` property of the corresponding `Drive` object, which represents the root, or top-level, folder on that drive. From here you can "drill down" to locate any subfolder on the drive. You can also start at any subfolder and "move up" in the folder hierarchy, as needed. Table 17.9 describes the properties of the `Folder` object, and its methods are explained following the table.

Table 17.9	Properties of the `Folder` object.
Property	**Description**
DateCreated	Returns a type `Date` specifying the date and time the folder was created.
DateLastAccessed	Returns a type `Date` specifying the date and time the folder was last accessed.
DateLastModified	Returns a type `Date` specifying the date and time the folder was last modified.
Drive	Returns the drive letter of the drive where the folder resides.
Files	Returns a `Files` collection containing one `File` object for each file in the folder.
IsRootFolder	True if the folder is the root, otherwise False.
Name	Sets or returns the name of the folder.
ParentFolder	Returns a `Folder` object representing the folder's parent folder.

Table 17.9	Properties of the `Folder` object. (Continued)
Property	**Description**
`Path`	Returns the path of the folder, including the drive letter.
`ShortName`	Returns the folder's short name used by programs that require the old 8.3 naming convention.
`ShortPath`	Returns the folder's short path used by programs that require the old 8.3 naming convention.
`Size`	Returns the size, in bytes, of all files and subfolders contained in the folder.
`SubFolders`	Returns a `Folders` collection containing one `Folder` object for each subfolder in the folder.

The `Folder` object has three methods:

The Copy Method

The `Copy` method copies the folder and its contents to a new location. The syntax is:

```
Copy destination, overwrite
```

Destination is a `Folder` object representing the destination folder where the folder is to be copied to. *Overwrite* is an optional True/False value specifying whether existing files or folders should be overwritten. The default is True.

The Move Method

The `Move` method moves the folder and its contents from one location to another. The syntax is:

```
Move destination
```

Destination is a `Folder` object representing the destination folder where the folder is to be moved.

The Delete Method

The `Delete` method deletes a folder and its contents. The syntax is:

```
Delete force
```

Force is an optional True/False value specifying whether files or folders with the read-only attribute are to be deleted. The default setting is False.

Listing 17–6 demonstrates use of the Folder object. The procedure DisplayFolderNames is passed a Folder object as its one argument. It then displays the names of all the subfolders in that folder, in its subfolders, and so on. If, for example, you pass this procedure a drive's root folder, it will list all the subfolders on that drive. The code is deceptively simple, and makes use of a programming technique called *recursion* in which a procedure calls itself in order to perform a repetitive task. With minor modifications, this code could be used for other purposes, such as determining whether a folder of a specific name exists on a drive.

Listing 17–6	*Demonstrating folder access.*

```
Public Sub DisplayFolderNames(folder As Scripting.folder)

' Displays the names of all subfolders in the
' specified folder.

Dim f As Scripting.folder

For Each f In folder.SubFolders
    Debug.Print f.Path
    DisplayFolderNames f
Next f

End Sub
```

THE `File` OBJECT

The FSO model represents each file on a disk by a File object. The File object has methods and properties that permit you to get information about the file and to manipulate it. By *manipulate* I mean actions such as moving and copying the file, not reading or writing its data (which were covered earlier in the chapter). Before you can do anything with a file, however, you must get a reference to the corresponding File object. There are two ways to do this.

If you know the path and the name of the file, you can use the Get-File method to return a File object that is associated with that file. Assuming that fso is a reference to the FileSystemObject, the syntax is:

```
Dim f As Scripting.File
Set f = fso.GetFile(filename)
```

Filename is the name of the file, including path. If *filename* does not exist, an error occurs.

You can also obtain a `File` object from a folder's `Files` collection. This collection contains one `File` object for each file in the specified folder. You can look through the collection, and obtain references to one or more files of interest.

When you have obtained a `File` object associated with a particular file, you can then use the object's methods to manipulate the file, and use its properties to get information about the file. The `File` object's properties are listed in Table 17.10.

Table 17.10	Properties of the `File` object.
Property	**Description**
Attributes	Returns a value summarizing the file's attributes (see below for details).
DateCreated	Returns the date and time the file was created.
DateLastAccessed	Returns the date and time the file was last accessed.
DateLastModified	Returns the date and time the file was last modified.
Drive	Returns the drive letter of the drive where the file resides.
Name	Sets or returns the name of the file.
ParentFolder	Returns a `Folder` object representing the file's parent folder.
Path	Returns the full path of the file, including drive letter.
ShortName	Returns the short filename used by programs that require the old 8.3 naming convention.
ShortPath	Returns the short path used by programs that require the old 8.3 naming convention.
Size	Returns the size of the file, in bytes.
Type	Returns a string containing information about the type of file. For example, for files with the .DOC extension this property returns "Microsoft Word Document."

The `Attributes` property provides information about the file's attributes, such as whether it is read-only or a system file. Some file attributes can be changed in code as well. This property returns a single numerical value, which is a logical combination of the individual attribute values. The individual attributes, and whether they are read-only or read/write, are described in Table 17.11.

Table 17.11	Individual file attributes.	
Attribute	**Value**	**Description**
Normal	0	Normal file with no attributes set.
ReadOnly	1	The file is read-only. Read/write.
Hidden	2	The file is hidden. Read/write.
System	4	The file is a system file. Read/write.
Volume	8	The file is a disk drive volume label. Read-only.
Directory	16	The file is a folder. Read-only.
Archive	32	The file has changed since the last backup. Read/write.
Alias	64	The file is a link or shortcut. Read-only.
Compressed	128	The file is compressed. Read-only.

To extract individual attributes from the value of the `Attributes` property, you use VBA's logical operators. To determine if a specific attribute is set, use `And`. If `f` is a `File` object, then the following code determines if the file's `Hidden` attribute is set:

```
If f.Attributes And 2 Then
    ' Hidden attribute is set.
Else
    ' Hidden attribute is not set.
End If
```

This code checks to see if the file's `ReadOnly` attribute is set and, if it is, clears it:

```
If f.Attributes And 1 Then
    f.Attributes = f.Attributes - 1
End If
```

The `File` object has three methods for moving, copying, and deleting the corresponding file. They are described in Table 17.12. The `File` object's one other method, `OpenAsTextStream`, was described earlier in this chapter.

Table 17.12	Methods of the `File` object.
Method	**Description**
`Copy dest, overwrite`	Copies the file to `dest`. An existing file is overwritten only if the optional `overwrite` argument is True (the default).
`Move dest`	Moves the file to `dest`.
`Delete force`	Deletes the files. Read-only files are deleted only if the optional `force` argument is True. The default is False.

Traditional File Management

As has been mentioned previously, the traditional file management methods are rarely used any more as they have been replaced by the object-oriented techniques that were described in the previous section. You should have at least a basic familiarity with these program statements and functions, if only because you may see them in older code. The traditional file management techniques are described in Table 17.13.

Table 17.13	Traditional VBA file management statements.
Statement or Function	**Description**
`Kill filespec`	Deletes the specified file. `Filespec` can contain the wildcards * and ?.
`RmDir folderspec`	Deletes the specified folder.
`MkDir folderspec`	Creates the specified folder.
`ChDir path`	Makes the specified path current.
`ChDrive drive`	Makes the specified drive current.
`CurDir(drive)`	Returns the current path on the specified drive. If the `drive` argument is omitted, uses the current drive.
`Dir(template)`	Returns the name of a file that matches a template. `Template` can include drive and path information as well as the * and ? wildcards. If there is no matching file, returns an empty string. Call Dir the first time with the `template` argument to find the first matching files, then one or more additional times with no argument to find additional matching files, if any.
`Name old As new`	Renames the file or folder specified by `old` to `new`.
`FileAttr(fn, flag)`	Returns information about the open file `fn`. If `flag` = 1 then the return value specifies the file mode, as follows: 1 = INPUT, 2 = OUTPUT, 4 = RANDOM, 8 = APPEND, 32 = BINARY. If `flag` = 2 the return value is the file's operating system handle.

Summing Up

VBA provides a complete set of tools for file access, which refers to storing data in and reading data from files. For text data you are better off using the object-oriented file access methods based on the `FileSystemObject` class. For other types of data, you must use the traditional file access statements and the three supported file formats: random, sequential, and binary. File management—deleting, moving, and copying files and folders—is also best done using the `FileSystemObject` class. Regardless of the type of data you need to store or read, VBA has the tools you need.

Creating Custom Classes and Objects

You have seen throughout this book how the Office development environment makes heavy use of classes and objects. While the objects exposed by the various Office applications are indeed powerful and flexible, they cannot, of course, cover every possible development need. Hence, VBA offers you the ability to create your own classes. With the full power of the VBA language at your disposal, your custom classes can do just about anything you need them to. The classes you can create in VBA fall into two categories. A class module *is for classes that have properties and methods but do not present a visual interface to the user. A* user form *is for classes that have a visual interface. I will explain how to use class modules in this chapter. User forms are covered in Chapter 19.*

Why Create Classes?

Some readers may be wondering why they should go to the trouble of creating custom classes. It's true that there is nothing a class can do that could not also be done in "regular" VBA code without a class. The major advantage of classes comes in the areas of programming ease and reusability. Once you have created the class, you can use it in your program—and reuse it in other programs—much more easily than if you had implemented the same functionality outside of a class. This is called *encapsulation*, meaning that all the functionality related to a specific program task is contained within the class. Letting others use your code is a lot easier with classes too.

Do these advantages outweigh the extra work involved in creating a class? That's a difficult question to answer because as far as I can tell there *is* no extra work involved! Yes, creating a class is different from non-class programming, but it is not any harder. Once you get the hang of it, I think you'll agree with me.

Classes can be used for just about any programming need. Generally speaking, classes are created to hold data and to manipulate that data, and are designed to parallel real-world objects. For example, you could create a "Bank Account" class that replicates the functionality of a real bank account. It would contain the requisite data, such as account holder's name, account number, and current balance. It would perform the needed manipulations, such as recording deposits and withdrawals while automatically updating the balance, calculating monthly interest and service charges, and so on. Whenever you need a new account, simply create a new instance of the class and all of its functionality is instantly available.

Class Module Fundamentals

Each class that you create exists in its own class module. To add a new, empty class module to your VBA project, select Class Module from the Insert menu. When the class module is active, its properties will display in the Properties window. There are only two properties. Name is the name of the class, and your first action when creating a new class is to assign a Name property that describes the function of the class you are creating. The other class module property, Instancing, can be ignored for now.

Once your class has been named, you are ready to start adding the code that defines the class. For the most part, this consists of adding properties and methods to the class. A property stores data, and a method carries out an action. Most of this chapter will be devoted to showing you how to create properties and methods for your custom classes.

Classes and Objects

Remember that a class is a blueprint. To use a class, you must create an instance of it—in other words, an object. Once you have defined a class you can create as many instances as you need, and each of these objects is completely independent from the others. Creating instances of custom classes is done the same way as for Office's built-in classes, which you learned how to do in earlier chapters. I'll review the basics of object creation later in this chapter.

Once you create a class, it is available for use in the current project. Since code reusability is an important benefit of classes, you need to be able to use a class in projects other than the one it was created in. Here's how:

1. In the original project, make the class active.
2. Select File, Export File from the menu bar.
3. Select a path for the exported file. The default name is the class name followed by the .cls extension, and generally you should use this name.
4. Click Save.
5. Make the second project active—that is, the one you want to use the class in.
6. Select File, Import File from the menu bar.
7. Locate the file that you exported in steps 1 through 4.
8. Click Open. The class will now be available in the second project.

Note, however, that subsequent changes to the class do *not* automatically become available in all projects when it has been imported. If you modify the class code, you must re-export it and then import it again into all projects that use it.

When a class is part of a project, then its type becomes available throughout the project, and you can declare instances of it just as you do with Office's built-in classes. The class name will be available on VBA's automatic lists, as will its methods and properties.

Creating Class Properties

A class property requires two or three separate elements to be functional. These are:

- A variable in the class module where the value of the property is kept.
- A Property Get procedure that lets code outside the class retrieve the value of the property. Property Get procedures are functions that return a value.

- A `Property Let` procedure that lets code outside the class set the value of the property. If the property is an object reference, you'll use a `Property Set` procedure instead. The `Property Let` (or `Set`) procedure is optional, and can be omitted to create a read-only property.

Why do we need property procedures to create a property? It would be possible to declare a global variable in the class module, which would then be available outside the class without the need for special procedures. There are a number of excellent reasons why we do not use this method, but rely on property procedures instead. First, using global variables would not permit the definition of read-only properties. Also, by using property procedures it is possible to write code that is automatically executed every time the property is referenced. This code can perform a variety of useful tasks, most importantly the task of data validation—making sure that a property is not set to an invalid value.

To add a property to a class module, select Procedure from the Insert menu to display the Add Procedure dialog box, which is shown in Figure 18–1. Select the Property option, and enter the property name in the box. This is the name that will be used to access the property, so it should be a descriptive name. Then click OK.

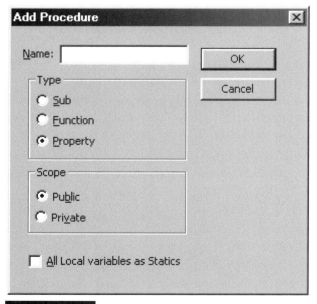

Figure 18–1   *The Add Procedure dialog box.*

VBA adds the skeletons of the two property procedures (`Let` and `Get`) to the class module, as shown in Listing 18–1 for a property named `Total`. You should note the following things:

- Both procedures have the same name—the name of the property.
- The `Property Get` procedure is a function with a return type of `Variant`.
- The `Property Let` procedure is passed one argument, also with a type of `Variant`.

Listing 18–1   *The empty property procedures created by Add Property dialog box.*

```
Public Property Get Total() As Variant

End Property

Public Property Let Total(ByVal vNewValue As Variant)

End Property
```

Once you have the outlines of the property procedures, here are the remaining steps required to fully implement the property:

1. Declare a `Private` module-level variable to hold the property value. The data type of this variable should be the same as the types of the property procedure's return value and argument (which can be changed from the default `Variant`).
2. If required by the type of data the property will hold, change the data type of the `Property Get` procedure's return value and the `Property Let` procedure's argument. These can be any VBA data type, including UDT's and enumerations. The only restriction is that they must both be the same type.
3. If the property is an object reference, change the `Property Let` procedure to a `Property Set` procedure (simply edit Let to Set).
4. Add code to the `Property Let` (or `Set`) procedure to transfer the argument value to the module-level property variable.
5. Add code to the `Property Get` procedure to assign the module-level property variable's value as the function's return value.

Listing 18–2 shows the final code after performing these steps for the `Total` property. In this example we assume that the data type `Double` is best suited for this property.

Listing 18–2	*Final implementation of the Total property.*

```
Private pTotal As Double

Public Property Get Total() As Double

    Total = pTotal

End Property

Public Property Let Total(ByVal vNewValue As Double)

    pTotal = vNewValue

End Property
```

To see how the property procedures work, assume that you have created an instance of the class named MyObject. To set the object's Total property you would write the following:

```
MyObject.Total = 999
```

When this code executes, the object's Property Let procedure is called with the value 999 as its argument. Code in that property procedure stores the value in the appropriate internal variable. Then, to retrieve the value of the property you would write this:

```
X = MyObject.Total
```

This causes the Property Get procedure to be called, and code in that procedure retrieves the property value from the internal variable and returns it to the calling program.

Naming Property Variables

There are no special rules for naming the internal class variables that are used to store property values. However, it is a good idea to use some naming convention to help identify these variables and distinguish them from other module-level variables. My approach is to use the same name as the property with the "p" prefix—p for "property."

Read-Only Properties

To create a read-only property, delete the Property Let procedure. In some cases, read-only properties do not use an internal class variable to hold their value because the property value is calculated each time the Property Get procedure is called. Suppose, for example, you created a class to hold string data, and the class has a read-only property named Length that returns the length of the string that is currently stored. If pValue is the internal variable where the string is stored, the Property Get procedure for the Length property might look like this:

```
Property Get Length() As Long

    Length = Len(pValue)

End Property
```

Variant Properties

A type Variant property can present a special programming challenge. If the property will hold only numeric and text data, then there is no problem. However, remember that a type Variant can also hold object references, so in theory a class could use a type Variant property to hold both object and non-object data. There are two things you must do in this case.

First, the property must have both Property Let and Property Set procedures. This is simple enough, as the proper one is called depending on whether an object reference or a regular data item is being assigned to the property. For a property named MyProp, for example, the class module would contain the following code:

```
Private pMyProp As Variant

Public Property Let MyProp(ByVal vNewValue As Variant)

    pMyProp = vNewValue

End Property

Public Property Set MyProp(ByVal vNewValue As Variant)

    Set pMyProp = vNewValue

End Property
```

What about the Property Get procedure? How do you know whether you need to use the Set keyword? The trick is to use the IsObject function, which is passed the name of a variable and returns True if the variable contains an object reference. Then, you can use Set, or not, as required. Here is the Property Get procedure for the MyProp property:

```
Public Property Get MyProp() As variant

    If IsObject(pMyProp) Then
        Set MyProp = pMyProp
    Else
        MyProp = pMyProp
    End If

End Property
```

Multiple Argument Properties

In most cases, you will use single value properties, as has been described above. However, there is also the option of creating multiple value properties, also called property arrays. To implement this, the `Property Get` procedure, which normally takes no arguments, will take one or more arguments. Also, the `Property Let` (or `Set`) procedure, which normally takes a single argument, will take two or more arguments—one more argument than the `Property Get` procedure. It is essential that the extra arguments in the two procedures match exactly in type and number, that they be declared with the `ByVal` keyword, and that the one regular argument of `Property Let` be at the end of the argument list. Here are property procedures (omitting the `End Property` statements) for a property that takes one extra type `Integer` argument:

```
Public Property Get SomeProperty(ByVal a As Integer) _
    As Variant

Public Property Let SomeProperty(ByVal a As Integer, _
    ByVal vNewValue As Variant)
```

These examples are for a property with three extra arguments, all type `Variant`:

```
Public Property Get SomeProperty(ByVal a, ByVal b, _
    ByVal c) As Variant

Public Property Let SomeProperty(ByVal a, ByVal b, _
    ByVal c, ByVal vNewValue As Variant)
```

While there are other uses for properties with extra arguments, the most common is to implement a property that is an array. The extra arguments are used to pass the array index that is being set or retrieved. The code in Listing 18–3 shows how to implement a property that is a one dimensional array.

Listing 18-3   *Implementing a property array.*

```
Private pArray(100)

Public Property Get Array(ByVal index As Integer) As Variant

    If index >= LBound(pArray) And Index <= UBound(pArray) Then
        Array = pArray(index)
    Else
        Array = Null
    End If

End Property

Public Property Let Array(ByVal index As Integer, _
    ByVal vNewValue As Variant)

    If index >= LBound(pArray) And Index <= UBound(pArray) Then
        pArray(index) = vNewValue
    End If

End Property
```

Saving Property Data

There will be times when you need to save the value of object properties between sessions. There are no special techniques for saving object properties—it is no different from saving the contents of regular VBA variables. You use the file access commands covered in Chapter 17 to save the data before terminating the program, then use them to read the data back in when the program runs again.

Data Validation with Property Procedures

One of the most common uses for property procedures is the validation of data. Often, an object property will be restricted in some way as to the data it should contain. A telephone number, for example, must be in the XXX-XXX-XXXX format, with each X representing a single digit. Likewise, a 5-digit ZIP code must be in the XXXXX format. By placing data validation code in the Property Let procedure you can make sure that invalid data is never accepted.

Listing 18-4 shows an example. This is the Property Let procedure for the ZipCode property, which stores the 5-digit zip code as part of an address. To permit the display of leading zeros, ZIP codes are typically stored as strings rather than as numbers. The code in the procedure checks the value passed as the `ZipCode` property, and displays a message if it is invalid. The variable `pZipCode` is used for internal storage of the property.

| **Listing 18–4** | *Validating ZIP code data.* |

```
Property Let ZipCode(ByVal vNewValue As String)

    Dim temp As String

    temp = "1" & vNewValue
    If Val(temp) >= 100000 And Val(temp) <= 199999 Then
        pZipCode = vNewValue
    Else
        MsgBox("Invalid ZIP code: " & vNewValue)
    End If

End Property
```

The validation code in this procedure works as follows. A proper ZIP code passed to the procedure will be a string consisting of 5 digits. If we put a "1" at the beginning of the string, we should have a string in the form 1XXXXX in which each X is a digit. Then, using the `Val` function to convert the string to a value, the result should be in the range 100000 (for the ZIP code 00000) to 199999 (for the ZIP code 99999). Any other values indicate that an invalid ZIP code was passed.

Classes and UDTs

UDTs, or user defined types, are useful for combining related data items into a single "package." They were covered in detail in Chapter 12. In many situations, a class can serve the same function as a UDT while providing additional capabilities. From the program's point of view, a class with properties looks pretty much the same as a UDT with members. However the class can offer the additional power of data validation and methods. Each time you think about using a UDT for data storage, consider using a class instead.

Creating Class Methods

A *method* is nothing more than a procedure inside a class module. You can have methods that return a value (function procedures), as well as methods that do not return a value (sub procedures). Everything you learned about procedures in Chapter 14 applies to methods as well, and you also use the same Insert, Procedure command and dialog box to create a method. Please refer to Chapter 14 if you need to brush up on the details.

Remember that to be available outside the class, a method must be public, which is the default. To make it available only within the class, to be called from other class methods, change the setting to `Private`.

You should note the similarity between function methods and `Property Get` procedures. Both return a value to the calling program, and in fact from the point of view of the programmer they are impossible to tell apart. For example, look at this code:

```
X = MyObject.Value
```

There is no way to tell whether `Value` is a property or a function, and in fact it does not matter. The point is that when it comes to returning data—particularly read-only data—from an object, you can use either a property procedure or a function.

Class Events

A class has two events associated with it, `Initialize` and `Terminate`. As the name suggests, the `Initialize` event occurs when the class is instantiated. You use this event to set the default values for object properties. For example, the following statement creates an instance of the MyClass class and fires its `Initialize` event procedure:

```
Dim obj As New MyClass
```

The `Terminate` event is fired just before the instance of the class is destroyed. You can put code in this event procedure to perform any necessary clean-up tasks or, when required, to save the object's data to a disk file. It is not at all uncommon, however, for the `Terminate` event procedure to remain unused.

A Class Demonstration

To demonstrate a simple class, and how it is used, I have created `BankAccount`, a class that encapsulates the basic functionality of a bank account. It has a read-only balance property that returns the current account balance. The balance can be changed only by making deposits and withdrawals, which is done by methods. Withdrawals are permitted only if the balance is sufficient to cover them. Listing 18–5 shows the code for the `BankAccount` class, and Listing 18–6 shows a procedure that demonstrates how you would make use of the class. I have omitted saving and retrieving data, but that is easily implemented using a random or binary file.

Listing 18–5   *The BankAccount class implements a basic bank account.*

```
Private pBalance As Currency
Private pOwnerName

Public Property Get Balance() As Currency

' Read-only Balance property.

    Balance = pBalance

End Property

Private Sub Class_Initialize()

' Initialize account balance to zero.

    pBalance = 0

End Sub

Public Property Get OwnerName() As Variant

    OwnerName = pOwnerName

End Property

Public Property Let OwnerName(ByVal vNewValue As Variant)

    pOwnerName = vNewValue

End Property

Public Sub MakeDeposit(amount As Currency)

' Adds a deposit to the account.

    pBalance = pBalance + amount

End Sub

Public Function MakeWithdrawal(amount As Currency) As Boolean

' Withdraws the specified amount from the account. If
' the balance is not sufficient to cover, the function
' returns False. Otherwise True is returned.

If amount <= pBalance Then
    pBalance = pBalance - amount
    MakeWithdrawal = True
```

```
Else
    MakeWithdrawal = False
End If

End Function
```

| Listing 18–6 | *Demonstrating the BankAccount class.* |

```
Public Sub TestBankAccount()

Dim accounts(2) As BankAccount

Set accounts(0) = New BankAccount
accounts(0).OwnerName = "George Smith"
Set accounts(1) = New BankAccount
accounts(1).OwnerName = "Alice Walker"
Set accounts(2) = New BankAccount
accounts(2).OwnerName = "Bill Gates"

accounts(0).MakeDeposit (12.5)
accounts(1).MakeDeposit (200.25)
accounts(2).MakeDeposit (20000000)

With accounts(1)
    If Not .MakeWithdrawal(1000) Then
        MsgBox ("Insufficient balance for " & .OwnerName)
    End If
End With

With accounts(2)
    If Not .MakeWithdrawal(100000) Then
        MsgBox ("Insufficient balance for ") & .OwnerName
    End If
End With

End Sub
```

Summing Up

In my experience, a lot of programmers don't realize the advantages of class modules right away. They understand how to use them, but don't really see their benefits until they have a bit of programming experience under their belts. The ability to encapsulate data and code in a class can have major advantages in many development scenarios, and is particularly valuable in large, complex projects. The better you understand class modules, the better you will be able to use them in your own work.

Creating User Forms

One of the most powerful tools available to the Office developer is the User Form. A User Form lets you create customized dialog boxes and windows that serve just about any imaginable program requirement. All of the elements that you see in Office's built-in dialog boxes are available for use on User Forms: text boxes for displaying and editing text, check boxes for selecting options, list boxes for displaying lists, and so on. In this chapter you will learn how to create User Forms and to use them in your Office applications.

Creating a User Form

Each User Form is represented by a `UserForm` object. All of the User Forms that are loaded as part of a project are contained in the `UserForms` collection. Each User Form has a set of properties that control various aspects of its appearance and behavior, such as color, size, and borders. All of the controls on a User Form are represented in the object's `Controls` collection. Each control has a unique name and its own set of properties. Each control as well as the User Form itself has a set of events that can be detected automatically, such as mouse clicks and key presses. A User Form can contain sub and function procedures, and can also be given custom properties by means of property procedures.

To add a User Form to a project, select UserForm from the Insert menu. The VBA editor creates a new, blank User Form and displays it on-screen for you to work with. This is shown in Figure 19–1.

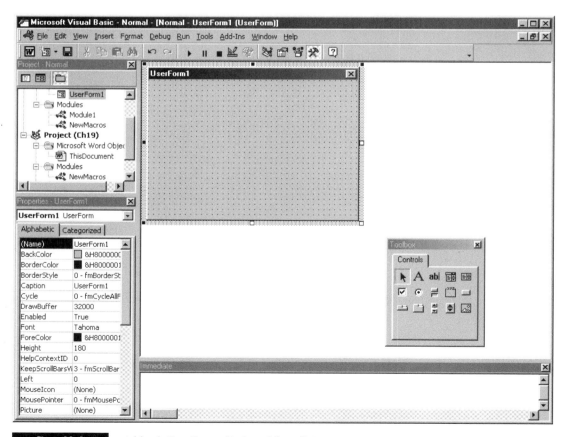

Figure 19–1   *A blank User Form displayed for editing.*

There are several elements on this screen you need to know:

- The empty dialog box in the center is the blank User Form. To change its size, point at one of the white handles (small boxes) on its edge and drag to the new size. The mouse pointer changes to a two-headed arrow when over a handle.
- The small window below and to the right of the User Form is the Toolbox, which contains icons for the various controls you can place on the User Form.
- The Properties window displays the properties for the current object. If the User Form is selected, it displays the User Form properties. If a control is selected, it displays the control properties. You can view the properties either alphabetically or by category by clicking one of the tabs at the top of the Property window.
- At the top of the Project window are two buttons. Click View Code or View Object to display either the User Form's code or its visual interface.

User Form Properties

You can see that a User Form has a large number of properties. Some properties can be set at design time or at runtime, using code. Other properties can be set only at design time, and are read-only when the application is running. If you select a property in the Properties window, then press F1, VBA Help will display detailed information about the property. Some of the more important properties are explained in Table 19.1.

Table 19.1   Important User Form properties.

Property	Description
Caption	The text displayed in the User Form's title bar.
Height	The height of the User Form, in points (1 point = 1/72 inch).
MousePointer	The appearance of the mouse pointer when over the User Form.
Name	The name that you will use in code to refer to the User Form.
Picture	Specifies a picture file to use as the background image on the User Form.
PictureAlignment	Specifies where a picture is displayed on the User Form.
PictureSizeMode	Specifies how the picture's size is modified to fit the User Form.
ShowModal	If True (the default), the User Form must be closed before other parts of the application continue executing. If False, the User Form can remain displayed while the user switches to another part of the application.

Table 19.1	Important User Form properties. (Continued)
Property	**Description**
SpecialEffect	Changes the appearance of the User Form.
StartUpPosition	Specifies where the User Form is displayed on-screen. If you select 0 - Manual, then the position is determined by the Left and Top properties.
Width	The width of the User Form, in points.
Zoom	Specifies the display size of the User Form's contents, as percent of normal.

Adding Controls to a User Form

A large part of creating a custom User Form is adding the appropriate controls to it. A blank User Form is not very useful! In the next section I'll explain some details of what controls are available, but for now let's see how you go about putting a control on a User Form.

The Toolbox contains one icon for each type of control. The one exception is the arrow icon, at the top left of the Toolbox, which you select when you want to work with controls already on the User Form. If you rest the mouse pointer over an icon, a tooltip will be displayed describing the associated control.

To add a control to the User Form, click the desired icon and then do one of the following:

- To add a default size control, click on the User Form at the location where you want the control's top left corner located.
- To add a custom size control, drag on the User Form.

WHAT CONTROLS ARE AVAILABLE?

The Toolbox contains 14 different controls that should meet just about any programming need. They are described briefly in Table 19.2, and you can use the VBA Help system to explore the details.

Table 19.2	The available controls for creating a User Form.

Control	Description
Label	Displays text that cannot be edited by the user.
TextBox	Displays text that the user can edit.
ListBox	Displays a list of items from which the user can select.
ComboBox	Combines the function of a TextBox and a ListBox.
CheckBox	Displays an option that can be turned on or off.
OptionButton	Similar to a CheckBox, but only one OptionButton in a group can be "on" at one time. To create a group of OptionButton controls, place a Frame control on the User Form first, then draw the OptionButton controls on the Frame.
ToggleButton	A button that can be either "up" or "down" permitting the user to select and deselect items.
Frame	Used to group other controls, such as OptionButtons.
CommandButton	Displays a button that is selected by the user to carry out some action.
TabStrip	Displays two or more tabs at the edge of the User Form, permitting the user to select from multiple "pages."
MultiPage	Does essentially the same thing as a TabStrip, but is easier to use.
ScrollBar	Displays a vertical or horizontal scroll bar on the User Form.
SpinButton	Increments and decrements numbers by clicking with the mouse.
Image	Displays an image.

Naming Controls

Every control, regardless of type, has the Name property that you use to refer to the control in code. When a control is first added to a User Form it is assigned a default name, but it is a good idea to change this to something more descriptive. I find it useful to prefix each control name with some indication of the type of control, which adds to your code's readability. For example, TextBox controls that are used for entering a person's name could be called txtFirst-Name and txtLastName. Likewise, OptionButton controls for selecting a color might be called optBlue, optRed, and so on.

One situation where the default control name is fine is when the control will not be referred to in code. This is often the situation with Label controls.

Working with Controls

After you have placed some controls on a User Form, you will usually need to modify them in some way: changing their size and position, changing property values, and so on. These techniques are covered in this section.

SELECTING CONTROLS

To work with a control, you must first select it (or several controls, as needed). Here's how:

- To select one control, click it.
- To select multiple controls, select the first one, then hold down the Shift key and click one or more additional controls.
- Another method of selecting multiple controls is to drag over them.

The selected control is indicated by having handles (small boxes) displayed on its corners and edges. When multiple controls are selected, they all have black handles except for the last one selected, which has white handles. To deselect a control or group of controls, click any other control. To select the User Form, click on the form outside of any control.

CONTROL PROPERTIES

Every control has a set of properties that determine its appearance and behavior. There is also a property that holds the control's data, whatever that data might be. For many controls it is the `Value` property that returns the control's data. The nature of the data, of course, depends on the specific control. Table 19.3 explains the data returned by the `Value` property for some controls.

Table 19.3	Data returned by the `Value` property.

Control	Value Property
OptionButton CheckBox ToggleButton	True if the option is turned on, False if it is turned off, Null if the option is indeterminate.
TextBox	The text in the box.
ScrollBar SpinButton	A numerical value indicating the scroll or spin position.
ComboBox Listbox	The value in the bound column of the current row.
CommandButton	Always False.

Some other properties you will use frequently, and which are shared by most or all controls, are listed here. Needless to say there are many other properties available for most controls, and you can obtain the details in online help.

Visible	Set to True to make the control visible, or to False to hide the control.
Enabled	Set to True to enable the control (the user can interact with it). Set to False to disable the control. It's still visible but displayed "grayed out" and the user cannot interact with it.
ControlTipText	The text that is displayed when the mouse pointer rests briefly over the control.
Font	References a Font object that controls the display of text in the control.
ForeColor	Specifies the control's foreground color.
BackColor	Specifies the control's background color.
Locked	Set to True to prevent the control from being edited or changed.
Tag	Used to store arbitrary information associated with the control. This information is not used by VBA in any way, but is solely for the programmer's convenience.

MOVING, RESIZING, ALIGNING, AND DELETING CONTROLS

Once you have selected a control, or a group of controls, you can change its position, its size, or get rid of it altogether.

- To move the selected control(s), point at it and drag to the new location. For some controls, such as MultiPage, you must point at the control's border to move it.
- To resize the selected control(s), point at one of its handles (the mouse pointer will change to a two-headed arrow) and drag to the new size.
- To delete the selected control, press Del.

For an attractive User Form layout, it is usually desirable to have the controls arranged so they align with each other. This can be accomplished in several ways. The User Form has a grid of dots on it, and VBA's default is for the edges of controls to always align with the grid. That is, when you place, move, or resize a control, its edges cannot be located between the dots. This simplifies the task of aligning controls and making them the same size as each other. You can modify the grid spacing, or turn it off altogether, as follows.

1. Select Tools, Options to display the Options dialog box.
2. Click the General tab (Figure 19–2).
3. To change the grid spacing, enter new values in the Width and Height boxes.
4. To turn the grid display on or off, click the Show Grid box.
5. To turn alignment on or off, click the Align Controls to Grid box.

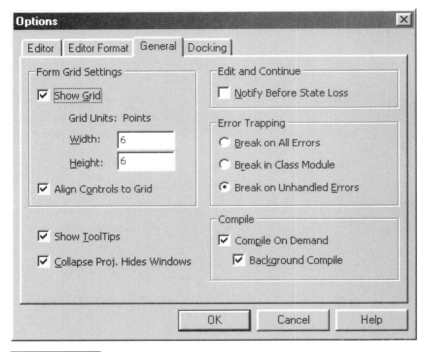

Figure 19–2   *You set grid options on the General tab of the Options dialog box.*

When alignment is turned off, you can move and resize controls smoothly, without any restrictions. Changing the grid alignment settings does not affect controls that are already on the User Form, only new controls.

You can also perform alignment tasks with the UserForm toolbar. To display this toolbar, select Toolbars from the View menu, then click UserForm. The UserForm toolbar is shown in Figure 19–3.

| Figure 19–3 | *The UserForm toolbar.* |

Some of the buttons on this toolbar may not be available, depending on whether one or more controls are selected on the User Form. The functions of the items on this toolbar, from right to left, are:

Bring to Front	When controls are overlapping, puts the selected control on top of other controls.
Send to Back	When controls are overlapping, puts the selected control beneath other controls.
Group	Combines multiple selected controls into a single unit.
Ungroup	Breaks a group back into its individual constituent controls.
Align	Select from the drop-down list to align controls with each other, or with the grid.
Center	Select from the drop-down list to center the control vertically or horizontally.
Make Width	Select from the drop-down list to make selected controls the same size.
Zoom	Select a zoom percentage to change the size of all controls on the User Form (not just selected controls).

Drop-Down Menus

If you right-click a control or the User Form, VBA will display a drop-down menu that contains available commands, including many of the alignment and sizing commands discussed here. Depending on your personal working style, you may prefer to use the drop-down menu instead of the User Form toolbar for some tasks.

SETTING CONTROL PROPERTIES

When a control is selected, its properties are displayed in the Properties window, with the property names in the left column and the current settings in the right column. To change a property, click it, then enter the new value in the right column. Some properties provide you with a drop-down list of settings to choose from. Others display a dialog box from which you make a selection. Sometimes you just enter the property value directly.

If multiple controls are selected, the Property window displays those properties that are common to both controls. For example, if you have selected a `TextBox` and a `Label`, the Property window will contain the `ForeColor` property (among others) as both controls have this property. However, the `Text` property will not be displayed as only the `TextBox` has it. In this situation, changing a shared property changes the property for all selected controls.

Note that control properties can also be set in code, at least in most cases. Depending on the specifics of your project, you may prefer to set properties in code, at runtime, rather than at design time.

USING THE TAB ORDER

When a User Form is displayed, the user can move the focus to a specific control by clicking on it. The focus can also be moved by pressing Tab or Shift+Tab, which moves the focus either forward or backward in the *tab order*. The tab order is determined by the `TabIndex` properties of the individual controls on the User Form. This property has a value of 0 to *n-1* where *n* is the number of controls on the form. By default, the `TabIndex` property is assigned starting at 0 with the first control placed on the User Form. To change the tab order, change the `TabIndex` properties of the controls on the User Form.

If you set a control's `TabStop` property to False, it will be bypassed when the user is tabbing. It still keeps its `TabIndex` property, however, and can be put back in the same location in the tab order by returning `TabStop` to True. Some controls, such as Label, have `TabStop` set to False by default, as the user will rarely, if ever, need to set the focus to them.

Another way to modify a User Form's tab order is to execute its `SetDefaultTabOrder` method, which must be done in code when the project is running. This method sets the tab order starting at the top left corner, then moving across the form and then down.

User Form Code and Event Procedures

A User Form can contain code as well as controls, and in fact, the code is an essential part of a User Form's functionality. A User Form can contain just about any VBA code, including:

- Module level declarations of variables, UDTs, and constants. Note that UDTs in a User Form must be declared as `Private`.
- Property procedures.
- Methods—in other words, sub and function procedures.
- Event procedures.

In general, it is best to think of a User Form as a class module with a user interface. It can have methods and properties, just like a class module, but it also has controls and the events associated with the controls. You learned about module-level declarations in Chapter 12, about methods in Chapter 14, and about property procedures in Chapter 18, so the only thing new to you is event procedures.

What events are available? Each object—the User Form as well as each control—has a set of events it can detect. Many events are common to most or all objects, while some are restricted to one or a few objects. I'll explain the most commonly used events, and you can refer to the VBA online help for details on other events and which events are available for specific objects. If you are designing the User Form and select a control, pressing F1 brings up VBA help for that control.

All event procedures are private, and they are all named the same way:

```
Private Sun ObjectName_EventName()

End Sub
```

ObjectName is the name (that is, the Name property) of the object, and *EventName* is the name of the event. Thus, for an OptionButton control named optWhatever, the name of the Click event procedure will be optWhatever_Click.

In the code window, when you are working with a User Form's code, there are two drop-down lists at the top. The list on the left lists all the objects that are part of the module, which means the User Form itself, all controls, as well as a (General) category that refers to module-level code, such as declarations as well as property procedures and general procedures. The list on the right contains all procedures for the object selected in the left list. For (General) this includes all existing general and property procedures. For an object it includes all available event procedures, whether or not you have added code to them. To edit code, or to add a new event procedure, simply select the object in the left list, then select the procedure in the right list.

The MultiPage and TabStrip Controls

Many event procedures have a slightly different syntax for the MultiPage and TabStrip controls than for other controls. This involves passing an *index* argument to the event procedure, with the argument identifying which page or tab on the control received the event.

Change

The Change event occurs when an object's setting is changed, specifically when its Value property changes. This event fires whether the change was initiated by the user or was caused by code. For example, clicking a Check-Box, editing text in a TextBox, or moving a ScrollBar all fire the Change event for the object.

Click

The Click event occurs when the user clicks the object with the mouse (using the left button). It also fires when a control's value is changed by the user via the keyboard. The latter case applies, for example, when the value of a CheckBox is changed by pressing the spacebar. When the user clicks an object, the MouseDown and MouseUp events occur before the Click event.

DblClick

The DblClick event occurs when an object is double-clicked. This event procedure is passed an argument Cancel of type MSForms.ReturnBoolean (essentially identical to the type Boolean you already are familiar with). If code in the event procedure sets Cancel to True, the control ignores the second click. This is useful with controls, such as the CheckBox, when clicking changes its value and a double-click would normally change the value twice, returning it to the original setting. By setting Cancel to True you can have a double-click change the value of the control (because only the first click is registered) while still firing the DblClick event:

```
Private Sub CheckBox1_DblClick(ByVal Cancel As MSForms.ReturnBoolean)

    ' Other code to handle the event.
    Cancel = True

End Sub
```

When an object is double-clicked, the MouseDown, MouseUp, and Click events occur first, before DblClick.

Enter, Exit

The Enter event occurs when the focus moves to a control from another control on the same form. The Exit event occurs when the focus leaves a control and moves to another control on the same form. These events actually occur before the focus moves. You can, for example use the Enter event to display information to the user about the control they are moving the focus to.

The Exit event is passed an argument named Cancel of type MSForms.ReturnBoolean. If this argument is left at its default value of False, the change of focus away from the control proceeds normally. Setting Cancel to True prevents the focus from moving away from the control.

KeyDown, KeyUp

These events occur when a key is pressed and released while a control has the focus. The syntax for the event procedures is as follows:

```
Private Sub object_KeyDown(ByVal KeyCode As MSForms.ReturnInteger, _
    ByVal Shift As fmShiftState)

Private Sub object_KeyUp(ByVal KeyCode As MSForms.ReturnInteger, _
    ByVal Shift As fmShiftState)
```

KeyCode is an integer that gives the key code of the key that was pressed. The key code is not the same as the ASCII value, as many keys do not correspond to characters. The code identifies only the key that was pressed; for example, the key code is the same for a letter key whether upper- or lowercase. You distinguish case based on the Shift argument. The Appendix lists constants and values for all of the key codes.

The *Shift* argument indicates whether the Shift, Alt, and/or Control keys were down at the time the key was pressed. Values are:

Constant	Value	Meaning
fmShiftMask	1	SHIFT was pressed
fmCtrlMask	2	CTRL was pressed
fmAltMask	4	ALT was pressed

If more than one key was pressed, the *Shift* argument is the sum of the values. For example, if both the Ctrl and Alt are down when a key is pressed, *Shift* will have the value 6. The following code detects if the user has pressed Shift+F5 while the control has the focus:

```
Private Sub TextBox1_KeyDown(ByVal KeyCode As MSForms.ReturnInteger, _
    ByVal Shift As Integer)

    If KeyCode = vbKey5 And Shift = fmShiftMask Then
        ' Code to execute goes here.
    End If

End Sub
```

When a user presses and releases a key that represents a character, the sequence of events is KeyDown, KeyPress, KeyUp.

KeyPress

The KeyPress event occurs when the user presses an ANSI key (a key that represents a printable ANSI character). The event procedure syntax is:

```
Private Sub object_KeyPress(ByVal KeyAscii As MSForms.ReturnInteger)
```

KeyANSI is the ANSI (ASCII) code of the key that was pressed. If code in the event procedure sets *KeyAscii* to 0, the keystroke is cancelled. This can be useful for restricting input to TextBox controls. The KeyPress event procedure in Listing 19–1 permits only the digits 0–9 to be entered (these characters have ASCII values 48–57).

Listing 19–1	*Restricting TextBox input to numbers.*

```
Private Sub TextBox1_KeyPress(ByVal KeyAscii As MSForms.ReturnInteger)

If KeyAscii < 48 Or KeyAscii > 57 Then
    KeyAscii = 0
End If

End Sub
```

A KeyPress event occurs when any of the following keys are pressed:

- Any printable keyboard character
- CTRL combined with a character from the standard alphabet
- CTRL combined with any special character
- BACKSPACE
- ESC

However, KeyPress does not occur for these keys:

- TAB
- ENTER
- An arrow key
- A keystroke that causes the focus to move

MouseDown, MouseUp, MouseMove

These events occur when the user presses or releases a mouse button while the pointer is over a control, or when the mouse pointer is moved while over a control. The syntax for these event procedures is as follows:

```
Private Sub object_MouseDown( ByVal Button As fmButton, _
   ByVal Shift As  fmShiftState, ByVal X As Single, ByVal Y As Single)

Private Sub object_MouseUp( ByVal Button As fmButton, _
   ByVal Shift As fmShiftState, ByVal X As Single, ByVal Y As Single)
```

```
Private Sub object_MouseMove( ByVal Button As fmButton, _
   ByVal Shift As fmShiftState, ByVal X As Single, ByVal Y As Single)
```

The *Button* argument identifies the mouse button that was pressed. If no button is pressed (MouseMove only) the value is 0. Possible values and associated constants are:

fmButtonLeft	1	The left button
fmButtonRight	2	The right button
fmButtonMiddle	4	The middle button

The *Shift* argument identifies which, if any, of the Shift, Ctrl, and Alt keys were pressed when the mouse was clicked. Possible values are:

Constant	**Value**	**Meaning**
fmShiftMask	1	SHIFT was pressed
fmCtrlMask	2	CTRL was pressed
fmAltMask	4	ALT was pressed

If more than one key was pressed, the *Shift* argument is the sum of the values.

The *X* and *Y* arguments give the location of the mouse pointer, in points, expressed as distance from the top left corner of the User Form.

Mouse-Related Events

When the user clicks or double-clicks an object, the mouse-related events occur in the following order:

1. MouseDown
2. MouseUp
3. Click
4. DblClick
5. MouseUp

If the mouse button is pressed while the pointer is over a control, that object *captures* the mouse. This means that all mouse events up to the final MouseUp are received by that object even if the pointer has been moved off the object before releasing the mouse button. However, the *X* and *Y* values passed to the MouseUp event procedure will accurately reflect the pointer position.

The MouseMove event is fired repeatedly while the mouse pointer moves over an object.

Displaying, Using, and Hiding User Forms

Once you have designed a User Form, how exactly do you go about displaying it, accessing its controls, and so on? You'll see the specifics in the demonstration to be presented later, but it will be helpful to outline the steps first.

1. Create an instance of the User Form:

```
Dim TheForm As New MyUserForm
```

2. If necessary, set initial values for form controls and properties:

```
TheForm.txtName.Value = "Enter name here"
```

3. Display the form using its Show method:

```
TheForm.Show
```

4. The user will now work with the form, entering data, and so on.

5. Close the form by executing its Hide method. This is usually done in the form code, in the event procedure for a Command Button:

```
Private Sub cmdOK_Click()

    Hide

End Sub
```

6. Retrieve data from the form's controls and properties, as needed:

```
Name = TheForm.txtName.Value
```

7. 7. If you will not be using the form again, destroy it (which also deletes any data stored in the form):

```
Set TheForm = Nothing
```

A User Form Demonstration

To end this chapter we will take a look at a User Form demonstration. This is a relatively simple form, but it makes use of almost all the important techniques that are required to get the most from User Forms. The form is intended to gather some information from the user: name, gender, and some favorite foods. Code in the form makes sure that the name and gender information was in fact entered. Following are instructions for creating the form, and for creating a procedure that uses the form and retrieves its data.

1. Use the Insert, User Form command to add a new User Form to your VBA project.

2. Change the User Form's Name property to "DemoForm" and its Caption property to "Demonstrating a User Form." Change the StartUpPosition property to 2-CenterScreen.

3. Add a Label control near the top left of the form. Change its Caption property to "Your name:".

4. Add a TextBox to the right of the label, and change its Name property to "txtName."

5. Draw a Frame underneath the TextBox. Change its Caption property to "Gender."

6. Draw two OptionButtons on the frame. Be sure to draw them right on the frame. You cannot, for example, draw them elsewhere on the form and move them onto the frame, or they will not be treated as a group. Change the Name and Caption properties of one of the OptionButton controls to "optMale" and "Male," and of the other to "optFemale" and "Female."

7. Add a Label to the form and change its Caption property to "Favorite foods:".

8. Add five CheckBox controls in a column under the Label control. Change their Caption and Name properties as follows:

Name	Caption
chkItalian	Italian
chkChinese	Chinese
chkFrench	French
chkMexican	Mexican
chkThai	Thai

9. Add a CommandButton to the form. Change its Caption property to "OK" and its Name property to "cmdOK."

10. Double-click the CommandButton to display code for its Click event procedure. Add the code shown in Listing 19–2.

Listing 19–2   *The Click procedure for the demonstration's CommandButton.*

```
Private Sub cmdOK_Click()

' Make sure something has been entered in the TextBox.
If txtName.Value = "" Then
    MsgBox ("You must enter a name.")
    Exit Sub
End If

' Make sure a gender has been selected.
If optMale.Value = False And optFemale.Value = False Then
    MsgBox ("Please indicate your gender.")
    Exit Sub
End If

' Now we can close the form.
Hide

End Sub
```

The User Form is complete, and should look something like Figure 19–4 (although the exact placement of the controls does not matter).

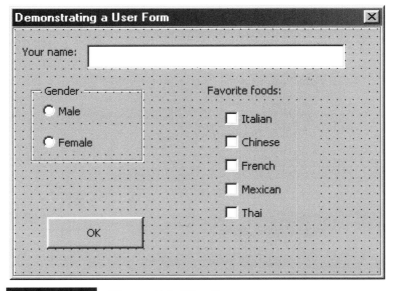

Figure 19–4   *The completed User Form.*

The next step is to write the code that will call the form. This code can be placed in a code module, and is shown in Listing 19–3.

| Listing 19-3 | *The procedure that calls the User Form.* |

```
Public Sub UserFormDemo()

Dim temp
Dim MyForm As New DemoForm

MyForm.Show

' Get the user's name.
Debug.Print "User's name: " & MyForm.txtName.Value

' Get the gender.
If MyForm.optMale.Value = True Then
    Debug.Print "Gender: male"
Else
    Debug.Print "Gender: female"
End If

' Get favorite food selections.
temp = "Favorite foods: "
If MyForm.chkItalian = True Then
    temp = temp & "Italian "
End If
If MyForm.chkChinese = True Then
    temp = temp & "Chinese "
End If
If MyForm.chkFrench = True Then
    temp = temp & "French "
End If
If MyForm.chkMexican = True Then
    temp = temp & "Mexican "
End If
If MyForm.chkThai = True Then
    temp = temp & "Thai "
End If

Debug.Print temp

End Sub
```

Summing Up

Despite the myriad screens and dialog boxes provided by the Office applications, sometimes you need something else. User Forms provide the developer with the ability to create completely customized forms and dialog boxes. Not only can a User Form present a visual interface to the user, but it can also contain code that responds to the user's actions, processes data, and interacts with other parts of the application. Because User Forms are created as a type of object, they also have the many advantages of the object-oriented approach to programming.

Other Office Development Tools

In the previous three sections you learned a lot about Office development, and by now you probably have a reasonably good command of the Office object model and the VBA programming language. There are some other programming topics that have not yet been covered, and because they do not all fall neatly into a single category, I have grouped them here. The first chapter in this section deals with a very important topic, the handling of runtime errors. Next, you will learn about debugging, deploying, and supporting your Office application. These two chapters should be required reading for any aspiring Office developer.

The third and fourth chapters in this section delve into some more advanced Office development technologies: the Windows API, the Windows Registry, and Office Web technologies. The techniques and tools you will learn about in these chapters will not be required in every Office project, but when you do need them they can be very valuable.

VBA Error
Handling

•••••••••••••••••••••

Believe it or not, this may be the most important chapter in the entire book. Errors are hardly a glamorous topic, but it is essential that a developer pay close attention to them in any application he or she writes. Runtime errors can be placed on the list, along with death and taxes, of things you cannot avoid. There may not be much you can do about death and taxes, but there definitely is a lot you can do about errors. Furthermore, there are situations in which errors can become tools you use in your project. This chapter explains ways to minimize the occurrence of errors in your projects, and how to deal with the inevitable errors that cannot be prevented.

Writing Solid Code

All developers strive to write solid code—or at least they should! Solid code is code that is as free as possible of errors, is free of bugs, is easy to understand, and is easy to maintain. The ability to write solid code does not come easily—it is the result of a lot of effort and experience. It is sort of like learning to play a musical instrument—you can learn the basics from a teacher, but it takes experience and practice to get really good at it! Writing solid code is not really any more difficult that writing "mushy" code, once you get in the habit of doing it. Now, when you are fairly new to programming, is the best time to start developing good habits. In this section I'll explain some of the most fundamental aspects of solid code—then you take it from here.

Require variable declaration. By including the `Option Explicit` statement at the start of each module you tell VBA that all variables in the program must be explicitly declared. This simple step is probably the most important part of writing solid code, as it prevents all of the pesky, hard-to-find errors and bugs that can occur with misspelled variable names. You can even do this automatically by turning on the Require Variable Declaration option in the Options dialog box.

Avoid use of Variants. The `Variant` data type is indeed flexible and very useful, but can sometimes be the cause of subtle bugs in your code. Use the `Variant` data type only when it is really necessary, and not just as a minor convenience.

Avoid the Object data type. The `Object` data type can hold a reference to any type of object, and this very flexibility can be the source of problems. Whenever possible, declare object variables as the specific type they will refer to, such as `Word.Application`. Use type `Object` only when really necessary.

Validate data. Do not make unwarranted assumptions about the data your program is working with. This includes data that is passed as arguments to procedures as well as data entered by the user. When there is any doubt, validate the data before using it.

Be consistent with variable declarations. I suggest placing all variable declarations at the start of the procedure, and limiting them to one per line. Also, type Variant variables should be explicitly declared as such rather than relying on the fact that Variant is VBA's default data type. Thus, this would be considered well written code:

```
Dim X As Variant
Dim Y As Integer
Dim Z As Double
```

This, on the other hand, would be considered poor style:

```
Dim X, Y As Integer, Z As Double
```

Do not place multiple statements on one line. You can place multiple VBA statements on one line by separating them with a colon, but you should not. They can be hard to spot.

Runtime Errors

As the name suggests, a runtime error is an error that occurs when an application is running. They are distinct from bugs, which are errors in program logic (dealing with bugs will be covered in Chapter 21). Often, the cause of a runtime error is something you have no control over. You cannot prevent the error, but your code can deal with it, or *handle* it, as programmers typically say. What happens if your code does not handle errors? Then VBA will use the default error handling mechanism which is to display a message identifying the error and then terminate the program. This is definitely a bad thing! When a program terminates unexpectedly there can be all sorts of negative consequences ranging from the serious problem of lost data to, at the very least, an annoyed user.

What kinds of errors am I talking about? Most are hardware related, such as trying to open a nonexistent file for reading, or trying to access a network share when it is not available. Others are user-related, such as a person pressing the wrong key or entering inappropriate data.

Dealing with errors is something that the programmer must keep in mind from the first stages of writing an application. Much of the code you have seen previously in this book lacked error handing, an intentional omission on my part as I did not want the error handling code to obscure the point that the code was trying to get across. Any well written program will have error handling code throughout, and the time to start putting that code in is right at the beginning—it is not something you should leave to the end!

There are really two aspects of dealing with errors, and both are equally important. The first is to avoid errors in the first place, and the second is to deal with those errors that cannot be avoided. Let's look at these in turn.

Preventing Errors from Happening

One of the most powerful weapons against errors is simply to follow good programming practices. These practices are equally effective against errors as they are against bugs, and they were covered in the section "Writing Solid Code" on page 374.

Another way to prevent errors from happening is to anticipate them and then take action to prevent them from happening. One example has to do with file operations, many of which will cause an error under the wrong circumstances, such as trying to access a file that does not exist or trying to write to a file that is read-only. Being aware of these possibilities, you can use

VBA's file commands to check first that the file does in fact exist, or that it does have read/write permission. If not, you can display a message to the user and bypass the code that would have caused an error.

Another example of avoiding errors has to do with data entry. You never know what silly things your users are going to type in, and such mistakes can be the cause of errors—as when the program is expecting a number and the user enters some letters. Rather than dealing with the resulting error when and if it happens, a better approach is to prevent the entry of inappropriate data in the first place. For example, the Text Box control's `KeyPress` method can be used to screen out all inappropriate keys, as you learned in Chapter 19. Or, you can use the `LostFocus` to make sure that a data entry field is not mistakenly left blank. VBA has plenty of tools that you can use to prevent inappropriate data entry.

You can prevent some but not all errors. The inevitable ones that remain must be handled, or *trapped*, as described in the next section.

Trapping Errors

At the most basic level, error trapping consists of telling VBA "if an error occurs, do such-and-such." Your code deals with the error, and not VBA's default error handling mechanism. All error handing is done at the procedure level, which means that each procedure that needs error handling must have its own error handling code. If a procedure does not handle its own errors, then any errors will be "passed up" to the procedure that called the procedure where the error occurred, to be handled there. With rare exceptions, your error handling code should not rely on this passing up of errors, but rather should handle errors in each and every procedure.

You enable error trapping with the statement:

```
On Error Goto label
```

Label is a program label identifying the location of the error handling code. In general, the On Error Goto statement is the first statement in a procedure, and the error handling code is placed at the end of the procedure. Thus, the structure of a procedure with error handling is as follows:

```
Public MySub()

' Data declarations here.

On Error Goto ErrorHandler

' Procedure code here.

Exit Sub
```

```
ErrorHandler:
' Error Handling code here.

End Sub
```

Note the use of the `Exit Sub` statement just before the error handler. This is necessary to prevent execution from entering the error handling code in the absence of an error. In a function, you would use the `Exit Function` statement instead, of course.

The error handling code itself has three tasks. One is to identify the nature of the error. The second is to take steps to deal with the error, which may involve displaying a message to the user. Finally, the error handling code must specify where program execution is to resume. We will look at these in turn.

Error Handling and Procedures

As I mentioned earlier, error handling is done at the procedure level in VBA. If a procedure does not have its own error handler (that is, no `On Error` statement), any errors that occur in that procedure are "passed up" to the code that called the procedure. For example, if procedure A calls procedure B, and procedure B does not have error handling, any errors occurring in procedure B will be passed up to procedure A and, if procedure A has error handing enabled, those errors will be handled by that code. In theory, you can use this to centralize error handling to some degree, by having one procedure that calls several other procedures to provide the error handling code for them all. In reality, this is rarely a good idea. The idea behind procedures, after all, is that they are separate and independent sections of code. If one procedure's error handling is located in another procedure, then the first procedure is no longer independent. It may seem like extra work, but I advise that you give each procedure its own error handling code, as required.

THE `Err` OBJECT

To obtain information about an error, you use the `Err` object. This is an intrinsic object with global scope, so you do not need to create an instance of it in your code. When an error occurs, VBA puts information about the error in the `Err` object's properties. Your error handling code can query those properties to identify the error. The properties are identified in Table 20.1.

Table 20.1	Properties of the `Err` object.
Property	**Description**
`Description`	Returns a string describing the error.
`HelpContext`	Contains the context identifier for online help related to the error.
`HelpFile`	Contains the full path to the help file containing information related to the error.
`LastDLLError`	If the error was generated by a call to a dynamic link library (DLL), this property contains the relevant system error code. Chapter 22 provides information on calling DLL's from your VBA code.
`Number`	Returns the number code representing the error. This is the `Err` object's default property.
`Source`	Contains the name of the object generating the error.

You use the `Number` property to identify specific errors. Since each error handler is in a procedure, and procedures are (or at least should be) devoted to performing a specific task, the possible errors will be limited. For example, in a procedure that reads data from a disk file you need to be on the lookout for file-related errors but not, say, division by zero or subscript out of range errors. You can find a list of the codes for VBA's trappable errors in the VBA online help system under the topic Trappable Errors. For example, the File Not Found error has the code 53, and the File Already Open error has the code 55. In a file-related procedure, the error handling code (or at least part of it) might look like this:

```
ErrorHandler:
    If Err = 53 Then
        MsgBox("The file cannot be found.")
    ElseIf Err = 55 Then
        MsgBox("The file is already open.")'
    End If
```

Note that you do not have to specify the `Number` property in your code as it is the default property of the `Err` object.

The information returned by the `Description` property is rather terse, but can be useful in some situations. For example, the following code displays a message with information about any error that occurs:

```
ErrorHandler:
    MsgBox("Error " & Err & "occurred: " & Err. Description)
```

You can use the `HelpFile` and `HelpContext` properties to permit the user to view the online Help information about an error. I find this to be of limited usefulness as the help information is usually more relevant to the developer than to the user. To make the help information available, pass the `HelpContext` and `HelpFile` information to the `MsgBox` function, which makes that information the default, which will be displayed if the user presses F1 when the message box is displayed. Here's an example:

```
ErrorHandler:
    temp = "An error has occurred. Number: " & Err
    temp = temp & " , Description: " Err.Description & vbCRLF
    temp = temp & "Press F1 to view Help information about this error."
    MsgBox(temp, , , "Error", Err.HelpFile, Err.HelpContext)
```

The `Source` property identifies the project component that generated the error. This property is useful primarily when the error is generated by an object used by your program. For example, if your VBA project is automating Excel, and an error occurs in Excel, then the `Err.Number` property will be set to Excel's error code and the `Err.Source` property will be set to `Excel.Application`. If the error occurs within a standard module in your project, `Source` will contain the project name. If the error occurs in a class module, `Source` will contain the project name followed by a period and the class name.

The `Err` object's `Clear` method clears all of the object's properties. You should execute `Clear` when you want to be sure that `Err` does not contain old information from a previous error. Note that `Clear` is implicitly called whenever any type of `Resume` statement is executed, when an `Exit Sub`, `Exit Function`, or `Exit Property` statement is executed, or when any `On Error` statement is executed.

HANDLING AN ERROR

There are no special tricks to handling an error. How an error is handled depends on the specifics of your program and the error that occurred. You must know the situation that can cause a specific error, as well as knowing what that error means to your program, and then write error handling code as appropriate.

Let's look at an example. Suppose your program expects to find a database file located on a network share. There are several things that can go wrong and cause an error:

- The file is not found (error 53).
- The path is not found (error 76).
- The device is unavailable (error 68).
- There is a path/file access error (error 75).

Depending on which error occurs, you may want to retry the operation, alert the user to contact the network administrator or department head, or take some other course of action. You also need to make sure the program "knows" that the file has not been loaded, so the user is not permitted to carry out any actions that depend on up-to-date data.

The bottom line is that there is no "tool" for handling errors. Rather, you need to be aware of the possible errors, what causes them, and—in the context of your program and the user's situation—what action needs to be taken.

RESUMING EXECUTION

Once you have handled an error, what happens with program execution? It is very rarely appropriate to let execution simply exit the procedure, which is what would happen by default as the error handling code is typically placed at the end of the procedure. You can control where execution resumes with the `Resume` statement. This statement comes in three varieties:

- `Resume` causes execution to resume with the statement that caused the error. Use `Resume` when you want to retry the operation that caused the error. This would be appropriate, for example, if the error was caused by having no diskette in a diskette drive; you can prompt the user to insert the diskette and then try again.
- `Resume Next` causes execution to resume with the statement following the one that caused the error. Use `Resume Next` when you do not want to retry the operation that caused the error, for example, if a file is not found.
- `Resume label` causes execution to resume with the statement identified by `label`. The location must be in the same procedure as the `Resume` statement. Use `Resume label` when neither `Resume` nor `Resume Next` is appropriate. You can resume at a location before or after the statement that caused the error.

On Error Resume Next

`On Error Resume Next` is a special variant of the `On Error` statement. You use this statement, instead of `On Error Goto`, when you want to defer error trapping. When an error occurs and `On Error Resume Next` is in effect, VBA makes note of the error but does not do anything about it—execution simply continues with the next statement. You are not ignoring the error, but simply deferring handling of it. `On Error Resume Next` is most useful when your program is accessing objects, such as automation objects, because all of the information you need to handle the error will not be available at the very instant the error occurs.

The way to use `On Error Resume Next` is as follows. When working with objects, identify the locations in code where an object-related error might occur—when trying to create an instance of an object, for example.

Immediately after a statement that might cause an error, test the `Err` object to see if an error has occurred and, if so, handle it. Here's some sample code showing the way this is done.

```
On Error Resume Next

' This line may cause an object error.
MyObj = GetObject("some object")
If Err.Number > 0 Then ' An error occurred.
    ' Test for and handle specific errors here.
    ' Use the Err object's Source property to
    ' Identify the object that caused the error.
    Err.Clear
End If
```

ADO Errors

ADO (ActiveX Data Objects) have their own error reporting system. Because an ADO operation can generate more than one error, the standard VBA error trapping mechanism is not sufficient, as the `Err` object is limited to providing information about the one most recent error. With ADO, error information is accumulated by the `Connection` object that represents the program's connection to the data source. The `Connection` object has an `Errors` collection that contains one `Error` object for each error that occurred during the most recent ADO operation. If an ADO error occurs you can use this collection to obtain information about the error(s) that occurred.

Some ADO operations do not require the existence of a `Connection` object. When there is no `Connection` object, you are limited to using the `Err` object to obtain error information.

Raising Errors

You can mimic the occurrence of a VBA error by using the `Raise` method of the `Err` object. When you execute this method VBA reacts exactly as if a "real" error had occurred, but the error number and other information are specified by you. The syntax for `Raise` is:

```
Err.Raise number, source, description, helpfile, helpcontext
```

Number is the only required argument, and specifies the number of the error. It can be any value in the range 0–65,535.

Source is an optional argument specifying the source of the error. If omitted, the programmatic ID of the current project is used.

Description is a string describing the error. If *description* is omitted, then *number* is compared with VBA's predefined errors and if it matches one, the corresponding description is used. Otherwise, *description* is left blank.

Helpfile and *helpcontext* specify the file and context for help information related to the error. If omitted, the name of the VBA helpfile is used for *helpfile* and the context associated with *number* (if one exists) is used for *helpcontext*.

You may have noticed that the arguments for the Raise method correspond exactly to the properties of the Err object, and that's exactly where the arguments are placed when Raise is called. However, if you omit one or more arguments from the call to Raise and the Err object has property values left over from an earlier error, then those old values will remain. For this reason it is a good idea to call Err.Clear before calling Err.Raise.

The Raise method is typically used in two contexts. One is when testing your error handling code—you can mimic the occurrence of various errors and verify that your error handlers are doing what they are supposed to. The other is in raising custom errors from class modules, which is covered next.

Class Module Errors

Class modules are not immune to runtime errors, but the way you handle them is a bit different from standard modules. Also, you can define custom errors that represent other object occurrences your application needs to react to.

In general, you do not want a class to handle its own errors directly. Instead, a class should report errors to the program that is using it, so that the program can handle the errors in a manner appropriate to the situation. This includes VBA's built in errors, as well as error situations that are specific to your class, such as an inappropriate value being passed as a method argument.

To define custom errors, it is necessary to associate a number with each error. Clearly, you cannot use a number that is already associated with a built-in error. In class modules, you can use any number starting with vbObjectError + 512 and ranging up to vbObjectError + 65536. The constant vbObjectError is available automatically in VBA. Numbers in this range are guaranteed to be available, not used in conjunction with any VBA errors.

In general, it is a good idea to define constants for error numbers and descriptions as well as for help filenames and contexts if these are used. At the module level you could declare some base constants as follows, to identify the error source and the base value for error numbers:

```
Private Const CLASS_ERROR_SOURCE As String = _
    "Class ClassName"
Private Const CLASS_ERROR_BASE As Long = vbObjectError + 512
```

Then you can define constants for specific custom errors that you may raise from the class:

```
Private Const CLASS_ERROR_INVALID_ARGUMENT_NUM As Long = _
    CLASS_ERROR_BASE + 1
Private Const CLASS_ERROR_INVALID_ARGUMENT_DESC As String = _
    "Invalid argument - string cannot be zero length."
Private Const CLASS_ERROR_TIMEOUT_NUM As Long = _
    CLASS_ERROR_BASE + 2
Private Const CLASS_ERROR_TIMEOUT_DESC As String = _
    "The operation timed out."
```

In the class module, raise your custom errors as needed. For example, this code fragment checks the argument passed to a method and raises the Invalid Argument error as needed.

```
Private Sub MySub(Name As String)

    If Len(Name) = 0 then
        Err.Raise Number := CLASS_ERROR_INVALID_ARGUMENT_NUM, _
            Description := CLASS_ERROR_INVALID_ARGUMENT_DESC, _
            Source := CLASS_ERROR_SOURCE
        Exit Sub
    End If

End Sub
```

Remember that errors raised with the Raise method are treated like any other errors as far as VBA's error trapping is concerned. This means that if you raise an error in a procedure in which error trapping is enabled, the error will be handled by that procedure's own error handing code, which will prevent the error from being passed up to the program that is using the object. To pass an error up from a class module procedure that has its own error trapping, call the Raise method again in the error handling code. This procedure passes all errors that occur in the procedure up to the calling program, including custom errors that are raised elsewhere in the procedure and VBA's built-in errors:

```
Private MySub()

On Error Goto ErrorHandler

' Procedure code here
```

```
Exit Sub

ErrorHandler:
    Err.Raise Number := Err.Number, _
        Description := Err.Description, _
        Source := Err.Source, _
        Helpfile := Err.Helpfile, _
        Helpcontext := Err.HelpContext

End Sub
```

Returning Errors from Functions

It is common programming practice to have functions return True if they executed without problem, and False if there was some irregularity. However, this makes it impossible, or at least difficult, to return any other information from the function. VBA's `Variant` data type comes to the rescue. One of this data type's abilities is to hold different types of data. Thus, a type `Variant` can hold a number that is just a number (to be specific, that is considered to be subtype `Numeric`) or it can hold a number that is subtype `vbError`. You use the `CVErr` function to convert a `Variant` to a subtype error, then use the `IsError` function to determine whether a `Variant` is subtype `vbError`. This technique permits a function to return any numeric value to the calling program, and have that value indicate an error by being the appropriate subtype. Note that using the subtype `vbError` does not invoke VBA's error trapping mechanism in any way.

Listing 25–1 shows an example. This is a function to calculate the square root of its argument. Since negative numbers do not have square roots, the function will obviously not work with a negative argument. To deal with the possibility of a negative argument, the function tests its argument and returns a subtype `vbError` as appropriate. The calling program can test the return value and take appropriate action. In this example the value 2001 as a return value is purely arbitrary. If there is more than one potential error condition, you can define your own error values to return and test.

Listing 20–1	*Using CVErr to return a user-defined error from a function.*

```
Public Function SquareRoot(value As Variant) As Variant

    If value < 0 Then
        SquareRoot = CVErr(2001)
    Else
        SquareRoot = value ^ 0.5
    End If
End Function
```

This is how a program could call this function and test the return value:

```
Dim x, y

x = InputBox("Enter number for square root:")
y = SquareRoot(x)

If IsError(y) Then
    MsgBox("Cannot take square root of a negative number.")
Else
    MsgBox("The square root of " & x & " is " & y)
End If
```

Testing Your Error Handling Code

Like any code, error handling code needs to be thoroughly tested before an application is ready for distribution. With regard to errors, most of the testing involves causing the errors to occur and seeing how the program responds. Some errors can be triggered directly, such as leaving a diskette drive door open. Others must be mimicked using the `Raise` method. Error testing is not fun but it is an important part of the development process. It is always wise to get some other people involved in the process, since you may not be able to think of all the possible error situations that might arise.

VBA has a few options that affect the way errors are handled inside the VBA development environment. You access these options by selecting Tools, Options and then clicking the General tab in the dialog box. This tab is shown in Figure 20–1. The settings control when the project enters break mode (break mode will be explained in detail in Chapter 21):

- Break on All Errors. Any error causes the project to enter break mode regardless of whether an error handler is active or whether the code is in a class module.
- Break in Class Module. Only errors that are unhandled and in class modules cause the project to enter break mode.
- Break on Unhandled Errors. Any unhandled error, regardless of the type of module it occurs in, causes the project to enter break mode.

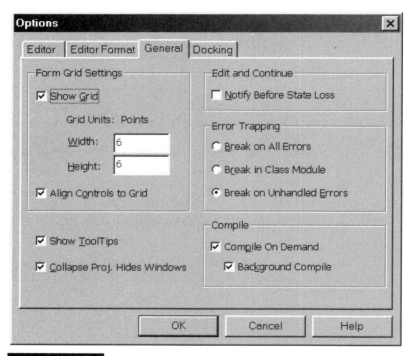

Figure 20-1 *Setting error trapping options in the VBA editor.*

Error Logging

Error logging—keeping a permanent record of errors that occur—can be a useful tool. During development an error log can sometimes help you track down and eliminate the factors that cause certain pesky errors. Even after an application has been distributed, an error log can help you diagnose those errors that crop up unexpectedly.

An error log typically consists of a disk file. Each time an error occurs, information about the error is written to the file, along with the time and date and any other relevant information. It is easiest to implement an error log as a class, then incorporate the class in the project as a global object. A `Write` method (or some similar name) would be called to save the current properties of the `Err` object to a file, appending new entries to the end so the log file maintains a day-to-day record of errors.

Dealing with Unanticipated Errors

No matter how carefully you plan, you cannot always anticipate every specific error that may crop up in a procedure. For this reason it's a good idea to include generic error handling code in all procedures, in addition to code to handle specific anticipated errors. By definition, an unanticipated error is not one you can handle in a specific manner, but you can at least provide a display of information about the error (and write it to a log file if one is being used).

When dealing with unanticipated errors it is very useful to know exactly where the error occurred—in other words, in which procedure. There is no way for VBA to provide this information automatically, but you can do it yourself fairly easily. In each procedure, declare a constant that holds the procedure name, as here:

```
Public Sub SomeProcedure()

Const PROC_NAME As String = "SomeProcedure"
Dim msg As String
...

End Sub
```

Then the generic error handling code would look like this:

```
ErrorHandler:
    ' Code to handle specific anticipated errors goes here.
    ' Execution reaches this point only when an unanticipated
    ' error has occurred.
    msg = "An unanticipated error has occurred. Please write "
    msg = msg & "down the following information:" & vbCrLf
    msg = msg & "Error number: " & Err & vbCrLf
    msg = msg & "Desription: " & Err.Description & vbCrLf
    msg = msg & "Source: " & Err.Source & vbCrLf
    msg = msg & "Location: " & PROC_NAME
    MsgBox(msg)
```

Summing Up

Even the cleverest, most careful programmer cannot prevent certain error conditions from cropping up when a program is executing. Diskettes not inserted, network outages, bad data entry, and misplaced files are just a few of the goof-ups that can, and probably will, occur. A well-written VBA program will take such potential errors into account and will trap them, so that when an error occurs there is no data loss and no program crash. Omit error handling from your programs at your own peril!

Debugging, Deploying, and Supporting Your Application

Writing the code for your Office application is only the first step in creating a finished custom solution. It is perhaps the biggest step, the one that will take the most time, but you cannot stop there. Once all of the program's features are complete, you then need to thoroughly debug and test the application, making sure that it performs as you intended and that unanticipated problems, or bugs, do not crop up. Once the application is thoroughly tested, it must be deployed, which is the process of getting it into the hands of your end users. Finally, most applications also require some maintenance, which consists of fine-tuning and other changes added at the users' request or in response to bugs and errors that slipped through your testing. These topics are covered in this chapter.

With bugs, as with errors, prevention is usually the best medicine. Some of the programming techniques that are effective in minimizing the occurrence of runtime errors can also help to prevent bugs. These were covered in the section "Writing Solid Code" on page 374.

Debugging Your Applications

A bug is a logical error in your code that prevents your program from operating correctly. Bugs are distinct from errors, which were covered in Chapter 20. Whereas an error can (if not trapped) prevent your program from running at all, a bug does not interfere with the program running but rather causes it to behave improperly. Calculations producing erroneous results is one example of a bug. Data being placed in the wrong field of a database table is another bug. E-mail being sent to the wrong recipients is yet another bug. Any program has hundreds of areas where bugs can appear, and while some bugs are impossible to miss, others can be subtle and hard to detect. Unlike errors, which are caught by VBA, bugs can be detected only by you or by other users of your program. Hence the need for thorough testing before deployment, particularly for programs that work with critical data. The time to find a bug is *not* after it has corrupted your client's main business database!

The `Debug.Print` Statement

A very useful tool for debugging programs is the `Debug.Print` statement. You have seen this statement used previously in this book. All it does is display the specified data in the Immediate window of the VBA editor. There are all sorts of uses for `Debug.Print` during program development and debugging, such as verifying the value of variables, seeing where program execution goes, and so on. The beauty of `Debug.Print` is that outside of the VBA environment, when your program is being used by the end user, the statement has no effect.

VBA cannot help you detect bugs—only testing can do that. VBA does, however, have some powerful tools to help you track down the causes of bugs, and to fix them. These tools fall into three main categories:

- **Breakpoints.** Temporarily suspending the program's execution at specified lines of code or when specified conditions are met.
- **Watches.** Examining the value of variables during program execution.
- **Controlling execution.** Executing a program one line at a time, and controlling the path execution takes.

Working with Breakpoints

When a VBA application is executing inside the VBA editor, you can temporarily pause program execution. This is called *break* mode. The usual way to enter break mode is to set a breakpoint, which specifies that the program should enter break mode either when a specified line of code is reached, or when a certain condition is met. While a program is in break mode, the next statement to be executed is highlighted in the editor window (if possible), and you can carry out various actions to help track down the cause of a bug. Then, you can continue execution normally, or terminate the program.

While you are in break mode, you can rest the mouse pointer over a variable name in your code and VBA will display a small window with the current value of the variable. You can also edit your code, with some limitations. The other tools described in this section are also available in break mode.

If you want to enter break mode when execution reaches a certain location in code, you need to set a breakpoint on that line. Move the editing cursor to the line and press F9. A line that has a breakpoint set is displayed in a different color and with a dot in the left margin. Execution will pause just before executing the line with the breakpoint. You can set breakpoints on as many lines as you want. Press F9 again to remove the breakpoint from a line. Press Ctrl+Shift+F9 to remove all breakpoints in a module.

You can also enter break mode based on the value of variables in your program. This technique is covered in the next section, "Using Watches."

Finally, you can enter break mode manually by clicking the Break button on the VBA toolbar. When you enter break mode manually, it is usually impossible to say exactly where in your code the program has paused. This is because manual break mode almost always catches the program while it is waiting for user input—in other words, waiting for an event to happen. In this case it is not possible to specify exactly which line of code is next, because the path of program execution usually depends on the input that is received—for example, which Command Button is clicked on a User Form. As a result, when you enter break mode manually, you will usually not see a line of code highlighted in the editor as the next line to be executed.

When you are finished working in break mode, press F5 to continue program execution. Other options for controlling program execution are covered in the section "Controlling Program Execution" on page 395.

Using Watches

During debugging you can use watch expressions to keep track of the data your program is working with. A watch can be any expression—variables, properties, objects, and so on. Many program bugs are the result of variables and properties taking on unexpected values, so the use of watches is an essential debugging tool.

VBA has two types of watches, so you can choose the one that's right for your needs. Regular watches are displayed in the Watches window, which can be displayed by selecting Watch Window from the View menu. You can have multiple watch expressions in the window, and VBA displays the value, type, and context (module) for each expression. The Watches window is shown in Figure 21–1.

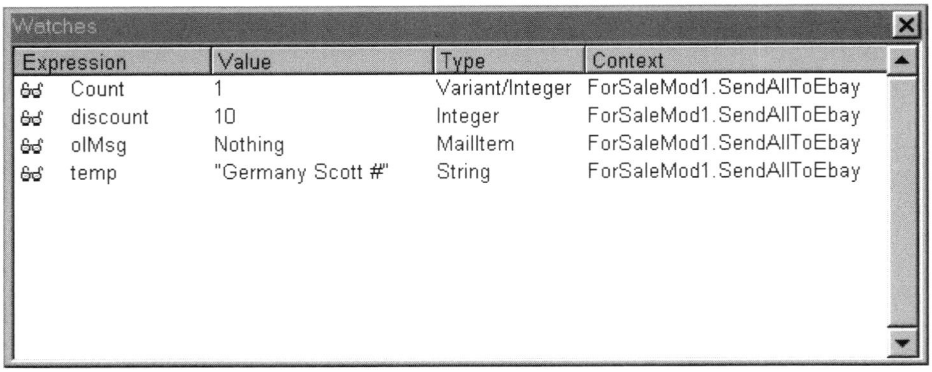

Expression	Value	Type	Context
Count	1	Variant/Integer	ForSaleMod1.SendAllToEbay
discount	10	Integer	ForSaleMod1.SendAllToEbay
olMsg	Nothing	MailItem	ForSaleMod1.SendAllToEbay
temp	"Germany Scott #"	String	ForSaleMod1.SendAllToEbay

Figure 21–1 *The Watches window displays information about program variables and properties.*

A watch expression can be a single variable or property, or it can be an expression made up of variables and any of VBA's operators and functions. Creating watch expressions can be useful when you are not interested in the exact value of variables but rather in the relationship between them. For example, you may want to keep track of whether the variable X is greater than the variable Y without regard to their actual values. The watch expression X >Y will do the job, displaying a result of either True or False depending on the data. Likewise, if you want to see if a string's length is less than 50, you would use the watch expression `Len(MyString)<50`. Follow these steps to add a watch to the Watches window:

1. Move the editing cursor to the section of code of interest—the procedure and module where the variables or properties are in scope.
2. Select Add Watch from the Debug menu. VBA displays the Add Watch dialog box (Figure 21–2).
3. Enter the desired watch expression in the Expression box.
4. Make sure the Watch Expression option is selected.
5. Click OK.

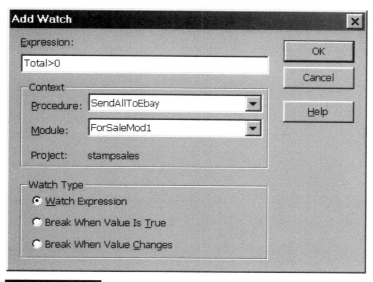

Figure 21-2   *You use the Add Watch dialog box to add a watch expression.*

When you have one or more watches set, each time the program enters break mode the display in the Watches window is updated. You can examine the values of your watch expressions and see if they tell you anything about the causes of a bug you are trying to solve. You can also edit a watch expression, or delete it from the window, by right-clicking it and selecting from the pop-up menu.

VBA's second type of watch is called a quick watch. In break mode, you can highlight, or select, an expression in your code, then select Quick Watch from the Debug menu. VBA displays a box containing the current value of the expression as well as its data type and context. Figure 21.3 shows a Quick Watch display.

Figure 21-3   *Displaying Quick Watch information about an expression.*

You can also coordinate watches with break mode, specifying that the program break either when a watch expression is True or when a watch expression changes value. This type of watch is added using the Add Watch dialog box (Figure 21–2), and is displayed in the Watches window as well. To add this kind of watch, type the expression in the Expression box of the Add Watch dialog box, then select either the Break When Value is True or Break When Value Changes option. You can see in the Watches window that the three types of watches—regular, break on true, and break when changes—display with different symbols in the left column. When a program breaks based on a watch expression, the expression is highlighted in the Watches window.

Watches and Scope

To be available for a watch, a variable or property must currently be in scope. Thus, if you are debugging code in one module, the private variables in a second module will not be available as they are out of scope. You can still have out of scope variables in a watch expression, but it will display as Out Of Context until it comes back into scope.

The Locals Window

Another useful way of keeping track of the values of program variables is the Locals window. To display this window, shown in Figure 21–4, select Locals Window from the View menu. You do not select what is contained in this window. Rather, the Locals window displays the values and types of all variables, properties, objects, and constants that are in scope at the time the program enters break mode.

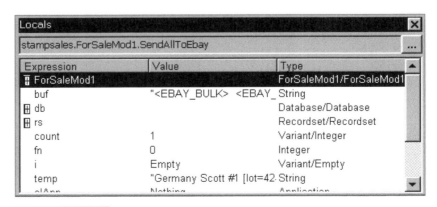

Figure 21–4 *The Locals window.*

Controlling Program Execution

Controlling the execution of your program is often a useful tool during debugging. You have already seen how you can pause execution, entering break mode based on code location or on the value of program variables. Once you are finished working in break mode, then what? You have several choices:

- **Continue (F5).** Continues execution normally.
- **Step Into (F8).** Executes the next statement then pauses in break mode. If the next statement is a procedure call, pauses at the first statement in the procedure.
- **Step Over (Shift+F8).** Executes the next statement then pauses in break mode. If the next statement is a procedure call, executes the entire procedure then pauses after exiting the procedure. This command has the same effect as Step Into if the next statement is not a procedure call.
- **Step Out (Ctrl+Shift+F8).** Executes to the end of the current procedure, then pauses in break mode.
- **Run to Cursor (Ctrl+F8).** Executes to the line of code containing the cursor, then pauses in break mode.

Note that the Step Into and Run to Cursor commands are available even when you are not in break mode. By starting the project with one of these commands, rather than the usual Run Sub/User Form command (or pressing F5), you can start the project and run it one line at a time, or up to the cursor.

Using the Call Stack

During debugging it is sometimes useful not only to know where execution is, but where it has been. The Call Stack provides a display of all active procedures—that is, all procedures that have not yet terminated. This list can get quite long, as in the structure of a typical Office application various procedures call each other all the time. Suppose you have a bug in a particular procedure that is caused by an inappropriate argument being passed to the procedure. If the procedure is called from various other procedures, you can use the Call Stack to determine which other procedure calls it when the bug occurs.

To display the Call Stack, select Call Stack from the View menu or press Ctrl+L. You must be in break mode to do this. Figure 21–5 shows the Call Stack. In this case we can see that execution is currently paused in procedure Test2 in the module NewMacros in the project named TemplateProject. We can also see that the procedure Test2 was called by the procedure Test1, which in turn was called by the procedure Test.

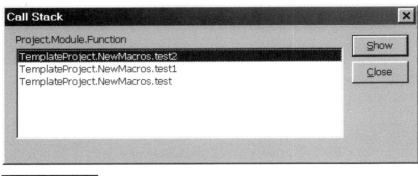

Figure 21-5 *The Call Stack displays a list of active procedures.*

Using the Immediate Window

You have already seen how you can use the `Debug.Print` statement to display information in the Immediate window. This window has other uses as well. When in break mode, the Immediate window has the same scope as the current procedure. You can change the value of a variable by simply typing the new value in the Immediate window. For example, if the current procedure has a variable Total, then by typing

```
Total = 100
```

in the Immediate window (on its own line) and pressing Enter you assign the new value to the variable. When you continue program execution you can see the effects of the new value.

Deploying Your Application

When it comes time to deploy your custom Office solution to your end users, you have numerous options. Which approach you will use depends on the details of your application and the scope of the deployment. You need to have a good understanding of the way Office applications and custom solutions work together in order to decide on the best method.

For example, your application may be contained in a Word template. In this case deployment can consist merely of distributing the template file to your end users, or perhaps making it available on a network share.

Sometimes such a simple distribution method is not applicable. In this case you can use the Package and Deployment Wizard to create a self-contained setup program that you can then distribute. End users will run this program to install the application, just like any other Windows program. You must have the Developer edition of Office, or Microsoft Visual Basic 6 or higher, to use the Package and Deployment Wizard.

When Not to Use the Package and Deployment Wizard

For templates and application-specific add-ins, the wizard is not the preferred method of distribution because it provides no way to install these types of applications to the specific folders that are reserved for them. On a Windows 95/98 system these folders are:

C:\Windows\Application Data\Microsoft\Templates
C:\Windows\Application Data\Microsoft\Addins

On Windows 95/98 systems with user profiles enabled, or on Windows NT, the folders are (where the main Windows folder is `WindowsFolder` and the user's name is `UserName`):

C:\WindowsFolder\Profiles\UserName\Application Data\Microsoft\Templates
C:\WindowsFolder\Profiles\UserName\Application Data\Microsoft\Addins

Strictly speaking, add-ins and templates do not have to be installed in these reserved folders, but there are advantages to doing so. I suggest that you not change the installation target unless you have a specific reason for doing so.

The wizard can perform a variety of tasks, but there are two specific tasks that you will be most concerned with:

- Package an application into a compressed distribution file. This file is used with a Setup.Exe program to install the application.
- Deploy the distribution file to a distribution site such as a Web server or a network share.

Using the wizard for the first task requires a number of steps, but the wizard automates most parts of the process. Here are the steps required:

1. Open the Office project that you want to distribute. Be sure any changes to the project have been saved.
2. Select Package and Deployment Wizard from the VBA AddIns menu. If it is not listed on the menu you will have to use the Addin Manager to load it.
3. On the opening Wizard screen, click the Package button. The wizard will take a few seconds to analyze your project.
4. The next screen appears only if you have created deployment packages previously. If you want to recreate a previous package, select the script name from the list. Otherwise, select (none).

5. On the next screen select Standard Setup Package. The other option, Dependency File, creates a file containing a list of all the runtime components your project requires. This can be useful at times but cannot be used for installation.

6. On the next screen you must select a folder for the setup files to be placed. You can select an existing folder or create a new one.

7. The next screen (Figure 21–6) displays a list of all the components that will be part of your distribution file, as determined by the wizard. You can click the Add button to include other files, such as Help files or a Read.Me that you want to accompany the installation. You can also delete files by unchecking them in this list, but you should do this only if you are sure the user already has the file(s) on his or her system.

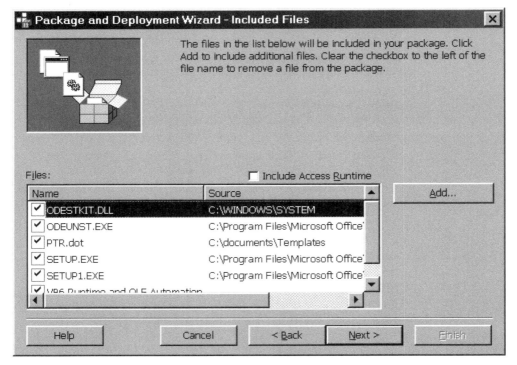

Figure 21–6 *Selecting components to include in your distribution.*

8. The next screen gives you the option of creating a single CAB file or multiple CAB files, each 1.44 MB or less. Use the latter option if you will be distributing the application on diskettes.

9. Next you must specify a title for the installation, which by default is the project name. You can optionally specify a command to run when the

installation is finished (such as starting a Web browser and directing it to a page related to the application).

10. You next can specify which items, if any, are added to the Windows Start menu by the installation. This screen is shown in Figure 21–7. By default, a single item that is a shortcut to your application is added, in its own subgroup within the Programs group. Your options are:

- Click New Group to create a new menu group.
- Click New Item to create a new menu item.
- Click Properties to change the properties of the current item.
- Click Remove to delete the current item or group from the menu.

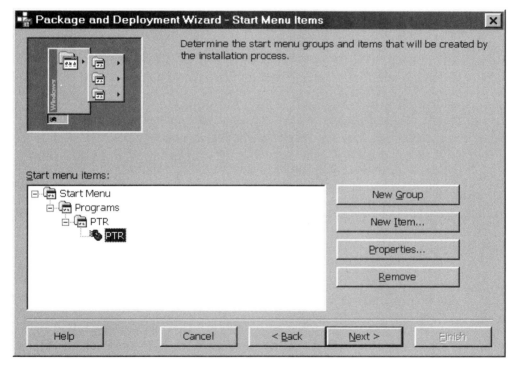

Figure 21–7   *Specifying Start Menu items to add as part of the installation.*

11. The next screen lets you specify the install locations for the application. In general, the default locations should be accepted unless you have a specific reason to select a different location.

12. On the next screen you can specify whether any of the package's files should be installed as shared files. A shared file can be used by more than one application.

13. The final screen lets you assign a script name to the package options you just specified. If you save a script, you can use it (in step 4) to load the package options used previously.

When you click the Finish button, the wizard creates the distribution files using the various options that you specified. The folder that you specified as the target will contain the following:

- Setup.exe. The setup program that must be run to install the application.
- Setup.lst. A text file containing setup information used by Setup.exe.
- *xxxx*.cab. A compressed file containing the setup components. *xxxx* is the name of your application.
- A folder named Support. Contains the setup components in uncompressed form.

To distribute your application, copy the files in the target folder (but not the Support folder) to the desired location—for example, a CD-ROM or a network folder. If you selected the multiple CABs option, put Setup.exe and Setup.lst and the first CAB file on the first diskette, and each other CAB file on additional diskettes.

You can also use the wizard to deploy your package. First you must have created the distribution package, as just described. Then, start the Package and Deployment Wizard and click the Deploy button. The wizard walks you through a few simple steps, including selecting a local or an Internet based deployment. At the end, the wizard copies the package files to the deployment location, and your end users can access it there.

Supporting an Application with Online Help

Most applications require some level of support once they are distributed. Some fairly simple projects may be support-free, but generally you can count on having to provide some assistance to the users, whether it be training, correcting bugs, or assisting with installation. Particularly with more complex solutions, you can reduce the amount of support required by providing online help as part of the application. A question that the user can answer by referring to the help file is one less question you'll have to answer in person!

Microsoft HTML Help

The latest generation in Windows help authoring is Microsoft HTML Help, which replaces the older format help system, WinHelp 4.0, for most uses. HTML help is designed to create Help for a wide variety of products, including multimedia titles, intranets, extranets, and of course, applications programs. HTML Help files are standard HTML files, and can be created using any HTML authoring tool including Microsoft Word and FrontPage, and the HTML editor that is part of the HTML Help Workshop. In this section I will explain what HTML Help is, what components it contains, and the fundamentals of using it. You can explore further on your own as your needs dictate.

In order to use HTML Help, a user must have certain components available on his or her system. These components are a part of the Office 2000 installation, Windows 98/2000, or any version of Microsoft Internet Explorer 4 and greater. You can see that it will be a rare user who does not have the required components. You might encounter this situation if you are distributing an Access runtime application on a computer that is running Windows 95 and does not have Office installed. In this case the easiest way to obtain the required Help viewing components is to install Internet Explorer version 4 or greater, or to include it in your distribution package.

The easiest way to work with HTML Help is to use the HTML Help Workshop, which can be downloaded for free from Microsoft at:

http://msdn.microsoft.com/workshop/author/htmlhelp/default.asp.

The Workshop is a Help authoring tool that lets you create Help project files, HTML topic files, index files, content files, and all the other elements that go into an HTML Help system. In addition to the HTML Help Workshop, the HTML Help system consists of the following elements:

- HTML Help ActiveX Control for adding Help navigation, secondary windows, and other features to an HTML Help file.
- HTML Help Java Applet, which provides the same functionality as the HTML Help ActiveX Control in a Java applet.
- HTML Help Image Editor for creating screenshots and working with images.
- HTML Help Authoring Guide, which contains instructions and reference information for HTML Help authoring.
- HTML Help Viewer, a program that displays and runs your Help system.
- A utility to convert old format Windows Help files to HTML help.
- A compression utility that packs all of the components of your finished Help system into a single file.

There are two types of Help systems you can create using HTML Help. The first is a compiled Help file that the user views using the HTML Help Viewer, which is shown in Figure 21–8. The left side of the viewer window is the Navigation Pane, which provides three ways for the user to find information: a table of contents, an index, and a search facility. The Help information itself is displayed in the topic pane on the right. Buttons at the top of the window let the user hide or display the navigation pane, move forward and backward among topics, and set options.

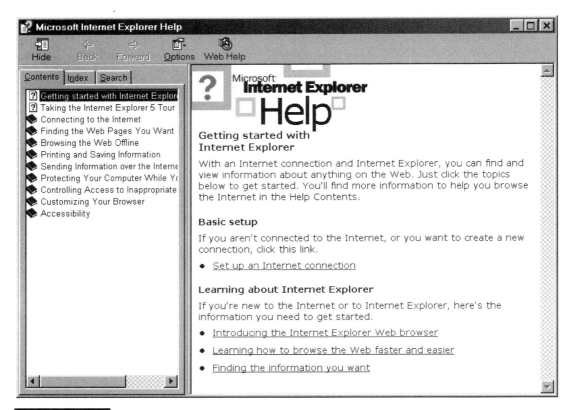

Figure 21–8 *Help displayed in the HTML Help Viewer.*

The second type of Help is Web-based, in which you are using the HTML Help authoring tools to create a Web site where your users can turn for information. By using the HTML Help ActiveX Control or the HTML Help Java Applet you can implement navigation and secondary window features so the Web site "acts" more like a traditional Help file.

There are two additional types of Help that HTML Help does not currently support for Office applications. One is context sensitive pop-up Help, which is used to display small pop-up windows describing user elements such as User Form controls and command bar controls. You must use WinHelp 4.0 to create this kind of Help. The other is Help that is displayed in response to querying the Office Assistant, which requires the Answer Wizard Software Development Kit to create the necessary files.

WinHelp 4.0

For many aspects of Help authoring, WinHelp 4.0 has been superseded by Microsoft HTML Help. However, you still must use WinHelp 4.0 to create pop-up context sensitive help for your custom Office applications. You can download the Microsoft Help Workshop, which lets you create WinHelp 4.0 help, at http://support.microsoft.com/download/support/mslfiles/.

Summing Up

An essential part of Office development is thoroughly debugging your applications. This can be difficult to do yourself—it is usually invaluable to put the program in the hands of some testers or end users and have them document problems that they encounter. Just like cars are tested on racetracks, you want your application to experience the worst conditions possible to make sure it can stand up to the abuse that your end users will dish out. Deploying the finished application, and supporting it with online help, are two more essential tasks of the Office developer.

Using the Windows API and Registry

•••••••••••••••••••••••

Despite the power of VBA and the Office object model, there may be times when they just don't provide the functionality that you need in your custom Office application. Fortunately, VBA is extensible, meaning that VBA code can call procedures in the Windows Application Programming Interface (API) and in other dynamic link libraries. The result is that your VBA program can do essentially anything that can be done in Windows. In addition, a VBA program can access the Windows registry, which is a centralized repository for all sorts of information about applications, users, and option settings. This chapter covers these techniques.

The Windows API

The Windows API is a large collection of procedures that is behind just about anything that Windows or any Windows program does. Screen windows, menus, dialog boxes, mouse control, keyboard input—you name it, and the API is behind it. The Windows operating system itself relies on the API, and any VBA application you create does so as well. For example, when you create a User Form, VBA is calling API procedures to display the window. Thus, many of the capabilities of the API are made available to you, indirectly, through the VBA language and development environment.

It is not practical to include all of the capabilities of the API in a high level programming language such as VBA. However, VBA can call the API procedures directly, which means that any API capabilities left out of the VBA language are still available to the developer. What are these capabilities? They are too numerous to list, but here are some examples:

- Access parts of the Windows registry not accessible with VBA statements.
- Manipulate the Windows clipboard.
- Obtain information about the operating system, such as the display resolution.
- Determine what other applications are running.

The API can and has been the subject of entire books, so there is no way I can present information on all of the various functions in the API. Rather my goal is to show you how to use the API and present a few specific examples of API functions that I find useful. You should refer to one of the available API books if you need more information.

Declaring API Procedures

Before a VBA program can call an API procedure, it must declare the procedure. The declaration provides VBA with information about the procedure—its name, its location, its arguments, and its return type (for functions). The basic structure of a Declare statement is as follows:

```
Public Declare Function FuncName Lib LibName Alias Alias _
    (ArgList) As ReturnType
```

FuncName is the name of the API procedure (essentially all API procedures are functions). Note that API function names are case sensitive.

LibName is the name of the DLL file where the procedure is located. You do not need to include the DLL extension or the path, as the API libraries are always kept in the \Windows\System folder.

Alias is an optional alias for the function, indicating the actual name of the procedure in the API when it is different from *FuncName*. An alias is useful when an API procedure name conflicts with another procedure name in your program. Also, some API procedure names begin with an underscore, which is not legal in VBA.

ArgList is a list of arguments, with data types, that is passed to the procedure. Almost all arguments are passed to API procedures by value, using the ByVal keyword.

ReturnType is the data type of the procedure's return value (for functions).

Here's an example of an actual API function declaration:

```
Public Declare Function GetTempFileName Lib "kernel32" _
    Alias "GetTempFileNameA" (ByVal lpszPath As String, _
    ByVal lpPrefixString As String, ByVal wUnique As Long, _
    ByVal lpTempFileName As String) As Long
```

This declaration tells us the following:

- The function is named GetTempFileNameA in the API.
- It will be referred to as GetTempFileName in the VBA program.
- It is located in the Kernel32 DLL.
- It takes four arguments, with data types as indicated.
- It returns a type Long.

The Declare statements must be at the module level. If they are in a standard module, and the Public keyword is used (as in the above example), then the API procedure can be called from anywhere in the project. If the Private keyword is used, then the procedure can be called only from within that module. In class modules only the Private keyword can be used with Declare.

Calling Procedures in Other DLLs

You are not limited to calling procedures in the Windows API DLLs. Any DLL is fair game, which provides you with the flexibility of creating DLLs in another language, such as C++, then using the procedures in your program. If a DLL has a type library, then setting a reference to the DLL in VBA means that you can call the library procedures without declaring them in your code. (The Windows API DLLs do not have a type library.)

The API Text Viewer

Entering the Declare statement for API procedures looks to be a tedious business, prone to errors. Fortunately, there is a handy tool that makes it relatively painless. The Developer edition of Office 2000 comes with the API Text Viewer utility, which lets you view the information in a file named Win32API.txt. This information includes declarations for all the API procedures, ready to be copied and pasted into your VBA code. This file also contains definitions of Windows constants and data types that you may want to use in your program.

The API Text Viewer is shown in Figure 22–1. When you first start the program and load Win32API.txt, you should use the command on the File menu to convert the file from text to Access database format. The information will be the same, but the database file loads and searches faster.

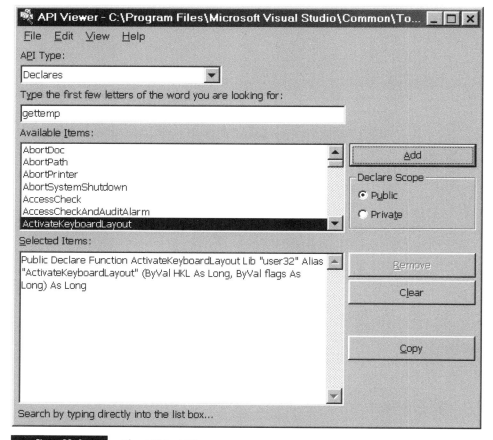

Figure 22–1 *The API text Viewer.*

Here's how to use the viewer:

1. Select the desired category in the API Type box: Declares, Constants, or Types.
2. If you have an idea of what you are looking for, type the first few letters in the box. Or, scroll through the list to find the desired item.

3. Highlight the item with the mouse, then select either `Public` or `Private` scope in the Declare Scope box.
4. Click Add to copy the item to the Selected Items Window.
5. Repeat steps 2 through 4 until you have all of the desired items.
6. Click the Copy button to copy all of the selected items to the clipboard.
7. Switch back to the VBA editor and paste the definitions into your code.

Calling API Procedures

Calling an API procedure is no different than calling a VBA procedure. As most API procedures are functions, you call them by placing the call on the right side of an assignment statement:

```
ReturnValue = SomeAPIProcedure()
```

If the library specified in the procedure's `Declare` statement is not found, then the call to the procedure will fail with error number 48 "Error in loading DLL." You should trap this error using VBA's error trapping to guard against the possibility that the DLL file has been moved (although this is not possible with the Windows API files).

Basic and C/C++ Data Types

Almost all DLLs, including the Windows API DLLs, are written in C or C++. The data types used in the languages are different from those use in VBA. However the procedure declarations in the API Text Viewer are written specifically for VBA so you do not have to worry about data type conversions. When you cannot use the API Text Viewer, use the guidelines shown in Table 22.1.

Table 22.1	Equivalent C/C++ and VBA data types.

C/C++ Data Type	VBA Data Equivalent	Description
BOOL	Boolean	True/False values
BYTE	Byte	8-bit unsigned integer
HANDLE	Long	Used to refer to Windows objects, such as screen windows
int	Integer	16-bit signed integer
long	Long	32-bit signed integer
LP	Long	Pointer (memory address)
LSZSTR	Long	Pointer to a string

Strings and API Procedures

One of the major differences between C/C++ and VBA is the way string data is handled. In C/C++ a string is treated simply as an array of characters. The name of the string variable is a pointer to the first character in the string—in other words, the memory address where that character is stored. The end of the string is indicated by the null character, which is represented in C/C++ as \0 and in VBA by the constant vbNullChar. This is different from VBA, in which there is no special character used to mark the end of a string; rather the string length is maintained separately.

This difference in string handling becomes important when using API procedures that return string information to the calling program. The API works differently than you might expect, and does not return the string as the procedure's return value. Rather, the string is returned in one of the API procedure's arguments (which is passed by reference, giving the code in the API procedure access to it), and the procedure's actual return value is something else, usually a number indicating the length of the returned string.

To use one of these API procedures, you need to pass it a string argument in which the data will be returned—and, most important, it must be a string that C/C++ can work with. This means that the string (1) must be long enough to hold any returned data, and (2) must be terminated with a null character. The usual technique is to create a string of the desired length that is completely filled with null characters. The API procedure will put data in this string starting at the beginning, and unused positions at the end will remain filled with null characters. It is then trivial to extract the useful data from the returned string.

To demonstrate, I will use the API function GetTempPath, which is used to get the path to the Windows temporary folder. The declaration of this procedure is:

```
Public Declare Function GetTempPath Lib "kernel32" _
    Alias "GetTempPathA" (ByVal nBufferLength As Long, _
    ByVal lpBuffer As String) As Long
```

The argument *lpBuffer* is the string where the temporary folder path will be placed, and *nBufferLength* is the length of this string. The return value is the number of characters written to *lpBuffer*. To use this API procedure, first create a string full of null characters. We use a length of 256, which is certainly more than sufficient, using the String$ function as follows:

```
TempPath = String$(256, vbNullChar)
```

Then, call the API procedure as shown here:

```
RetVal = GetTempPath(256, TempPath)
```

If the return value is greater than 0, we know a temporary path was found and returned in `TempPath`. The desired string can be extracted—that is, trailing null characters trimmed off—as follows:

```
If RetVal > 0 Then
    TempPath = Left(TempPath, Instr(1, TempPath, _
                    vbullChar), 1)
End If
```

You will see this technique demonstrated later in the chapter, in Listing 22–1. You need to fill a string with null characters only if the API procedure is using that argument to return information to the calling program. If the string argument is only being used to pass information to the API procedure, just use a regular VBA string variable.

Using Callbacks

Some of the API procedures require additional help from your program, and they get this help using a technique known as *callbacks*. A callback is a function in your VBA program that provides the extra help that the API procedure needs. You do not call this function directly; rather it is called by the API procedure. Here's how it works:

1. Your program calls the API procedure. One of the arguments to the procedure is the address of the callback function.
2. The API procedure calls the callback function when it is needed.
3. The callback function performs whatever tasks are required, then execution returns to the API procedure.
4. In some cases, steps 2 and 3 repeat multiple times.
5. The API procedure terminates and returns execution to the calling program.

Which API procedures require callbacks? Typically, it is those procedures that perform some repetitive task. One example is `SetTimer`, which requires a callback function that is called every time a specified time interval elapses. Code in the callback function can then, for example, update a clock display on a User Form. Another example is functions that enumerate through a collection of objects, such as `EnumWindows`, `EnumPrinters`, and `EnumFontFamilies`. The first of these functions, `EnumWindows`, for example, loops through all of the current windows and calls the callback function once for each one, passing information about the window to the callback function.

With callbacks, there are two things you must know. First, which API procedures use callbacks, and second, what is the signature (the arguments and return type) of the callback function? The first question can usually be answered based on the API procedure's declaration provided by the API Text Viewer. An argument to an API procedure that represents the address of a callback function can usually be identified by the argument name, which is of the form *lpXXXXFunc* in which the *XXXX* represents the name of the procedure. The argument type is always `Long`, which is how VBA represents addresses. For example, the declaration of the `SetTimer` API procedure is as follows:

```
Public Declare Function SetTimer Lib "user32" Alias "SetTimer" _
    (ByVal hWnd As Long, ByVal nIDEvent As Long, _
    ByVal uElapse As Long, ByVal lpTimerFunc As Long) As Long
```

You can see that the last argument, `lpTimerFunc`, represents the address of the callback function. When calling the API procedure, you obtain the address of the callback function by using the `AddressOf` operator followed by the name of the callback function. You'll see how this works in the example to be presented later in this chapter.

The second question, regarding the signature of the callback function, can be answered only by referring to an API reference, as this information is not provided in the API Text Viewer or in the Office online help. It is essential that the callback function you write have the exact same number and data type of arguments, and return type, as required by the API procedure. Also, if your reference material is intended for C/C++ programmers, you need to convert the C/C++ data types to the corresponding VBA data types, as detailed earlier in this chapter. The name of the callback function does not matter as long as it conforms to VBA's naming rules.

Let's take a look at an example of using a callback function. The API procedure `EnumWindows` can be used to loop through all of the top-level windows on the screen, and can be used to obtain information about the window or to perform some action with them. The declaration for this function is:

```
Declare Function EnumWindows lib "user32" ( _
    ByVal lpEnumFunc As Long, _
    ByVal lParam As Long) As Long
```

The first argument, `lpEnumFunc`, is the address of the callback function. The second argument, `lParam`, is a parameter that the API procedure passes to the callback function when it is called. This is often seen with API procedures that use a callback. The API procedure itself does not make use of `lParam`; rather it is a way for you to pass additional information to the callback as needed. Whether this information is needed, and what the information might be, will depend on exactly how your callback function operates.

The callback function used by `EnumWindows` has the following signature:

```
Function CallBackName(hWnd As Long, lParam As Long) As Long
```

The argument hWnd is a type Long specifying the handle of the screen window, and lParam is the parameter passed in the call to EnumWindows. The callback function's return value is also a type Long. As with most callback functions, the return value is used to tell the API procedure whether to continue or to terminate. A return value of True (non-zero) signals the API procedure to continue, while a return value of 0 (False) specifies that the API procedure should terminate and return control to the calling program.

Here's what will happen in our EnumWindows demonstration program.

1. The program will call EnumWindows, passing it the address of the callback function. Since there is no need to pass an additional parameter to the callback function, a dummy argument will be used for the second argument.
2. The API procedure will locate the first window on the screen. It will then call the callback function, passing the window's handle as an argument.
3. Code in the callback function will use the window handle to obtain information about the window (using another API procedure), and then display that information in the Immediate window.
4. The callback function will return True to the API procedure.
5. The API procedure will locate the next window on the screen, and the process will be repeated.
6. When all windows have been processed, the API procedure will return execution to the calling program.

Listing 22–1 presents the code to demonstrate the use of EnumWindows and a callback function. The code makes use of two other API procedures, GetWindowText, which is passed the handle of a window and returns its title text, and GetClassName, which returns the name of the class the window is associated with. Note that both of these procedures use the technique of returning string information in one of their arguments, as was covered earlier in this chapter. Figure 22–2 shows the program's output.

Listing 22–1   *Demonstrating the use of a callback function.*

```
Option Explicit

Declare Function GetWindowText Lib "user32" _
    Alias "GetWindowTextA" (ByVal hWnd As Long, _
    ByVal lpString As String, ByVal cch As Long) _
    As Long

Declare Function GetClassName Lib "user32" _
    Alias "GetClassNameA" (ByVal hWnd As Long, _
    ByVal lpClassName As String, _
    ByVal nMaxCount As Long) As Long
```

```
Declare Function EnumWindows Lib "user32" _
    (ByVal lpEnumFUnc As Long, _
    ByVal lParam As Long) As Long

Function EnumWindowsCallBack(ByVal hWnd As Long, _
    ByVal lParam As Long) As Long

' This is the callback function for the EnumWindows
' API procedure.

Dim s1 As String
Dim s2 As String
Dim s3 As String

' Fill the strings with null characters.
s1 = String$(255, vbNullChar)
s2 = String$(255, vbNullChar)

' Retrieve the window title.
GetWindowText hWnd, s1, 254
' retrieve the window class name.
GetClassName hWnd, s2, 254

' Trim trailing nulls off the strings.
s1 = Left(s1, InStr(1, s1, vbNullChar) - 1)
s2 = Left(s2, InStr(1, s2, vbNullChar) - 1)

' Display only if the window has a title.
If Len(s1) > 0 Then
    s3 = "Title: " & s1 & ". "
    s3 = s3 & "Class: " & s2
    Debug.Print s3
End If

EnumWindowsCallBack = 1

End Function

Public Sub ListWindows()

Dim retval As Long

retval = EnumWindows(AddressOf EnumWindowsCallBack, 0)

End Sub
```

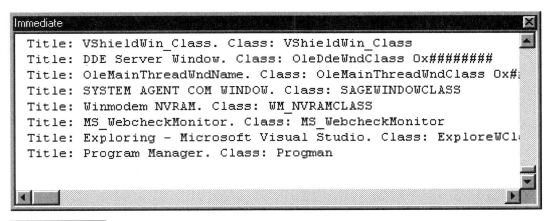

```
Immediate                                                                    ×
 Title: VShieldWin_Class. Class: VShieldWin_Class
 Title: DDE Server Window. Class: OleDdeWndClass 0x########
 Title: OleMainThreadWndName. Class: OleMainThreadWndClass 0x#:
 Title: SYSTEM AGENT COM WINDOW. Class: SAGEWINDOWCLASS
 Title: Winmodem NVRAM. Class: WM_NVRAMCLASS
 Title: MS_WebcheckMonitor. Class: MS_WebcheckMonitor
 Title: Exploring - Microsoft Visual Studio. Class: ExploreWCl:
 Title: Program Manager. Class: Progman
```

Figure 22–2   *The information displayed in the Immediate window by the EnumWindows example.*

The Windows Registry

The registry is one of most important but least understood aspects of Windows. Both Windows and various applications programs keep all sorts of information in the registry. Generally speaking, you do not want to mess around with the information in the registry unless you are sure you know what you are doing, as incorrect changes can have unexpected and serious effects on the operating system and your programs. However you can still use the registry to store information, and this can be particularly useful for saving program information between sessions. For example, if your custom application permits the user to select custom colors and fonts for screen display, you can save this information in the registry and automatically retrieve it each time the program starts.

The information in the registry is organized hierarchically. At the top of the hierarchy are six *root keys* that divide the registry information into broad categories:

    HKEY_CLASSES_ROOT
    HKEY_CURRENT_USER
    HKEY_LOCAL_MACHINE
    HKEY_USERS
    HKEY_CURRENT_CONFIG
    HKEY_DYN_DATA

Each root key contains subkeys that further divide the data, and each subkey contains keys and the associated data, called the key *value*. Thus, each piece of information, or value, in the registry is identified by its key, one or more subkeys, and the root key. Figure 22–3 shows some registry data displayed in the Windows Registry Editor. The left panel shows the hierarchy of keys and subkeys, and the right panel shows the data for the individual entries associated with the open subkey.

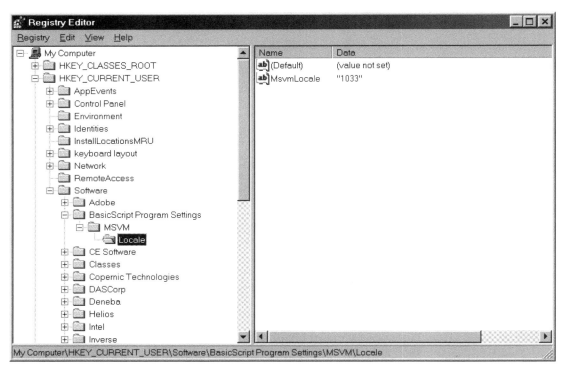

Figure 22–3   *Viewing the registry hierarchy in the Windows Registry Editor.*

Exploring the Registry

You can explore the registry by using a program called RegEdit (for Registry Editor). Select Run from the Start menu and enter RegEdit. You can examine the registry hierarchy, view keys and their values and, if desired, make changes. You can also make a backup copy of the registry by selecting Export from the Registry menu. Making a backup can be good insurance if you are going to make changes whose effects you are not sure of.

When programming in VBA you have two ways to access the registry. There are four VBA functions, which are easy to use but provide limited capabilities. Then there is a set of API functions that provide complete flexibility, but are more difficult to use (and also more dangerous!).

VBA Registry Functions

VBA has several functions and statements that let you retrieve and set registry values. The only limitation of these functions and statements is that they provide access only to one location in the registry: HKEY_CURRENT_USER\Software\VB and VBA Program Settings. For most applications this is all you need, but for complete access to the registry you need to use the API procedures, covered in the next section. The VBA statements and functions are listed in Table 22.2 and then explained in the following section.

Table 22.2	VBA registry statements and functions.
Function/Statement	**Description**
SaveSetting	Updates a key value or adds a new key
GetSetting	Retrieves a key value
GetAllSettings	Retrieves a list of all keys and their values
DeleteSetting	Deletes a subkey or a key

To update a key value, or to create a new key, use the SaveSetting statement. The syntax is:

```
SaveSetting appname, section, key, setting
```

All arguments are required. *Appname* is the name of the application to which the setting belongs. *Section* and *key* specify the subkey and key, respectively. *Setting* is the key value. If the specified key already exists, its value is updated. If not, the key is created. The following example sets a key for the program SalesReport:

```
SaveSetting "SalesReport", "Screen", "Position", "Centered"
```

The resulting registry entry would be as follows:

```
HKEY_CURRENT_USER\Software\VB and
   VBA Program Settings\SalesReport\Screen\Position
```

To retrieve a registry setting, use the `GetSetting` function. The syntax is:

```
GetSetting(appname, section, key, default)
```

The first three arguments are required and identify the application name, section, and key whose value you want to retrieve. The optional *default* argument specifies the value to return if the specified registry entry does not exist. The return value of the function is a string containing the registry value. If the entry does not exist, and no value is given for *default*, then the function returns an empty string.

To retrieve all keys and their values that are associated with a particular application and section, use the `GetAllSettings` function. The syntax is:

```
GetAllSettings(appname, section)
```

The return value is a type *Variant* containing a two-dimensional array that contains all the keys and the associated settings for the specified application and section.

To delete a registry entry, use the `DeleteSetting` statement. The syntax is:

```
DeleteSetting appname, section, key
```

The *appname* and *section* arguments are required, and specify the application and section. *Key* is optional and specifies the key to be deleted. If *key* is omitted, the entire section is deleted.

Here's an example of using the registry to save the screen location information for a User Form. The first time the User Form is displayed, it will be positioned at the top left of the screen. If the user moves it, then subsequently it will appear at the same position it was the last time it was closed.

To create this project, create a New User Form. Change its `StartUp-Position` property to 0-Manual and its `Name` property to RegTest. Place a single Command Button on the form and change its `Caption` property to close. Add code to the User Form's `Initialize` event procedure and the Command Button's `Click` event procedure as shown in Listing 22–2.

Listing 22–2   *Using the registry to save program display information.*

```
Private Sub CommandButton1_Click()

SaveSetting "RegTest", "Screen", "Top", Me.Top
SaveSetting "RegTest", "Screen", "Left", Me.Left
Hide

End Sub
```

```
Private Sub UserForm_Initialize()

Me.Top = GetSetting("RegTest", "Screen", "Top", 0)
Me.Left = GetSetting("RegTest", "Screen", "Left", 0)

End Sub
```

To test the User Form, create a procedure in a standard module containing the following two lines of code:

```
Dim uf As New RegTest
uf.Show
```

When you execute the procedure, the User Form will be displayed at the top left of the screen. Move the User Form to another location, then close it by clicking the button. When you run the procedure again you will see the User Form displays at the new position rather than at the top left of the screen.

API Registry Functions

For complete access to the registry you must use the API registry procedures. In my experience these procedures are rarely needed by the VBA programmer, and then only in unusual circumstances involving highly advanced programming tasks. You should treat these procedures as you would a loaded gun—they are potentially very dangerous! I cannot present complete information on using them, but Table 22.3 lists the registry API procedures with a brief explanation of what each one does.

Table 22.3　　The Windows API registry procedures.

API Registry Procedure	Description
RegCloseKey	Closes an open key
RegConnectRegistry	Opens a key on a remote system
RegCreateKey	Creates a new key
RegCreateKeyEx	Opens and existing key or creates a new key
RegDeleteKey	Deletes a key
RegDeleteValue	Deletes a key value but not the key itself
RegEnumKey	Enumerates the subkeys of a specified key
RegEnumKeysEx	Similar to RegEnumKeys but with more options

Table 22.3	The Windows API registry procedures. (Continued)
API Registry Procedure	**Description**
RegEnumValue	Returns the value(s) for a specified key
RegFlushKey	Makes sure that registry changes have been written to disk
RegGetKeySecurity	Returns a key's security information
RegLoadKey	Loads registry information from a disk file
RegNotifyChangeKeyValue	Notifies a program when a key value changes
RegOpenKey	Opens a key
RegOpenKeyEx	Same as RegOpenKey but with more options
RegQueryInfoKey	Returns information about a key
RegQueryValue	Returns a key value
RegQueryValueEx	Same as RegQueryValue but with more options
RegReplaceKey	Replaces information in the registry with data from a disk file
RegRestoreKey	Restores registry information from a disk file
RegSaveKey	Saves registry information to a disk file
RegSetKeySecurity	Sets security information for a key
RegSetValue	Sets a key value
RegSetVakueEx	Same as RegSetValue but with more options
RegUnloadKey	Closes a key on a remote system

Summing Up

Despite the incredible power of the VBA language, it cannot do everything. When the language falls short of your needs, you can call the Windows API directly to perform any task that the Windows operating system is capable of. The API is a complex subject, and you may not ever need it in your custom Office solutions, but it's nice to know it is available just in case. The Registry is another part of the Windows operating system that can be used to good advantage by Office developers. In particular, the ability to save and recall program settings can add an extra degree of sophistication and user friendliness to your programs.

Office Technologies for the Web

One of the most dramatic changes with Office 2000, compared with previous versions, is the tight integration of Web technologies with the Office applications. HTML, the language of the Web, is supported as a native file format, and many of the applications can use the Web for group-related tasks, such as collaborations and document revision. These are great from the end user's point of view, and in some situations can also make the developer's job a lot easier. As useful as the capability is to save any office document as an HTML page, it is limited by providing a static view of the data in the document. When browsing the document on the Web, users can view the data but cannot interact with it. This is OK for some applications, but can be very limiting for others. Can't we have a Web presentation with interactivity? With Office's specialized Web components, covered in this chapter, you can.

Web Components Overview

There are four Office Web components. Three of them display on-screen, in a Web browser, and let the user interact with data. The fourth works behind the scenes. They are:

- **PivotTable.** Permits users to work with data from a database table or a worksheet. The data can be sorted, grouped, filtered, or outlined as required.
- **Chart.** Displays charts, or graphs, of data. The data can originate in a database table, a worksheet, or a PivotTable.
- **Spreadsheet.** Provides a simple worksheet interface with recalculation and a function library.
- **DataSource.** Serves as a "behind the scenes" interface between a Web page (or controls on the page) and a data source.

The nomenclature on these controls—particularly the PivotTable and Chart controls—can be confusing. For the former, the actual name of the control is the PivotTable List control, but it is represented in the object model by the PivotTable object. For the latter, the Chart control actually represents Chart Workspace object, which itself provides a container for one or more charts. These details of object names are not all that important, but you need to be aware of them to avoid getting confused by the Office documentation.

Using the Web Components

All four of the Office Web components are ActiveX controls. Note that these components are not only for Web use, and can be used in settings other than the Web. For example, you can insert a PivotTable on an Excel spreadsheet for local use. To use them in your projects with early binding, and to view their properties and methods in the Object Browser, you must set a reference to the type library in your project (using the Tools, References command). The library is called Microsoft Office Web Components 9.0. If it is not listed in the References dialog box, you will have to browse for it; the relevant file is c:\Program Files\Microsoft office\Office\Msowc.dll.

There are some restrictions to using these components on the Web. Since they are viewed in a browser, the browser must be compatible with the ActiveX controls. At present this requires Microsoft Internet Explorer version 4.01 at the minimum, although version 5.0 is required for components on Access data access pages and also gives you improved functionality with the other components.

All of the Web components are programmable. Within an Office application they can be programmed using VBA. Outside of Office, on a Web page, they can be programmed using either of the Web scripting languages,

VBScript or JScript. Coverage of scripting languages is beyond the scope of this book. In brief, a scripting language lets you embed program commands in the HTML of a Web page, and the code is executed when the Web page is viewed in a compatible browser. VBScript is similar in many ways to VBA, while JScript is based on the Java language.

There are several options for using these components for interactivity on the Web from the various Office applications. These are discussed in the following sections.

Excel

You cannot publish an entire workbook to the Web with interactivity, but are limited to publishing part of the workbook—a single sheet, for example, or an individual chart or a `PivotTable`. Once the worksheet is ready, here are the required steps:

1. Select the sheet or object that you want to export to a Web page.
2. Select Save as Web Page from the File menu. Excel displays the Save As dialog box, as shown in Figure 23–1.

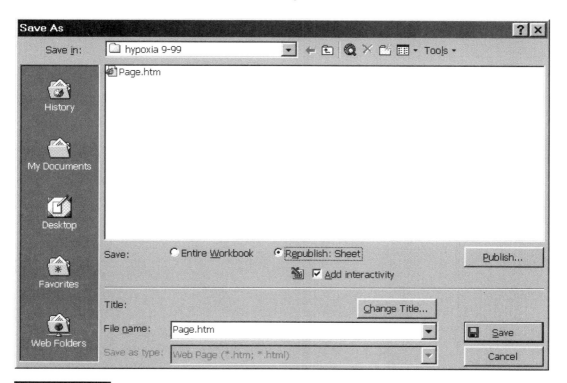

Figure 23–1   *You use the Save As dialog box to save part of a worksheet as a Web page.*

3. Turn off the Entire Workbook option, and turn on the adjacent option. The wording of this option will differ depending on what you selected in step 1. For example, if you selected a chart it will say Selection:chart. If the selection has been published previously, the option will say Republish.

4. Turn on the Add Interactivity option.

5. If desired, click the Title button to add a title to the published selection.

6. Click the Publish button to display the Publish as Web Page dialog box (Figure 23–2).

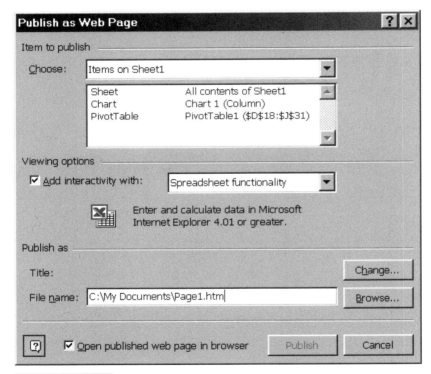

Figure 23–2   *Specifying details of Web page publishing in the Publish As Web Page dialog box.*

7. In the Item to Publish section of the dialog box, verify that the desired item is selected to be published.

8. Turn on the Add Interactivity With option and select the desired type of interactive component from the drop-down list.

9. In the Publish As section of the dialog box, specify a destination and name for the published file. If you are publishing directly to a remote site, enter the HTTP address here rather than a local file path.

10. Turn on the Open Published Web Page in Browser option if you want to view the page in a browser as soon as it is published.
11. Click the Publish button.

I'll present an example of publishing a Spreadsheet control to a Web page later in the chapter.

Access

When working with Access, you publish interactive components to the Web by means of data access pages. As you learned in Chapter 7, a data access page is, in fact, an HTML document, or Web page, that provides data access functionality over the Web. During design of a data access page, you can add a `Chart`, `PivotTable`, or `Spreadsheet` control to the page by selecting the corresponding tool in the toolbox and clicking on the page. Since a data access page is a Web page, there is no need for any special "publish as Web page" steps as there is in Excel. Please refer to Chapter 7 for more information on creating data access pages.

FrontPage

When designing a Web page in FrontPage, adding an Office Web component is no different than adding any other component. Place the cursor at the desired position on the page you are editing, then select Component from the Insert menu and select the desired component.

Other Web Page Editors

You can insert an Office Web component in a Web page using any Web page editor by including an `<OBJECT>` tag with the proper object Class Identifier (CLSID) for the object. Here are the programmatic identifiers for the Web components:

`Spreadsheet` object: CLSID:0002E510-0000-0000-C000-000000000046
`PivotTable` object: CLSID:0002E520-0000-0000-C000-000000000046
`ChartSpace`: CLSID:0002E500-0000-0000-C000-000000000046
`DataSource` object: CLSID:0002E530-0000-0000-C000-000000000046

This HTML tag, for example, inserts a `Spreadsheet` object in a Web page, assigning it the identifier `Spreadsheet1`:

```
<object id=Spreadsheet1 classid=CLSID:0002E510-0000-0000-
C000-000000000046 style="width:50%;height:375"></object>
```

Web Component Help

You'll find detailed Help information on the Office Web components in the Help file named Msowcvba.chm. This file is located in the C:\Program Files\Microsoft Office\Office\XXXX folder, where XXXX represents the language ID for your installation (1033 for US English).

Using the Spreadsheet Control

If you simply place a blank Spreadsheet control on a Web page, the person who views that Web page will have a small, empty spreadsheet to use—but this is not all that interesting. Rather you want to present a spreadsheet that already contains some data and/or formulas, making it useful for a specific application. You can start by creating the spreadsheet in Excel, then publishing it—data and formulas will be published as part of the spreadsheet. Or, you can use the Spreadsheet control's object model to manipulate cell contents programmatically.

One useful technique is to create a spreadsheet in which certain cells are designed for data entry, and other cells perform the desired calculations. Obviously, you do not want the user to be able to change the calculation formulas. You can achieve this by unlocking only those worksheet cells that you want the user to be able to change, then turning on worksheet protection. In Excel, here are the required steps:

1. Select the cell or range you want the user to be able to access.
2. Right-click the range and select Format Cells from the pop-up menu to display the Format Cells dialog box.
3. In the dialog box select the Protection tab.
4. Turn off the Locked option, then click OK.
5. Repeat steps 1 through 4 as needed for additional cells or ranges in the worksheet.
6. From the menus, select Tools, Protection, Protect Sheet.

When you publish the worksheet to a Web page, only the unlocked cells will be accessible to the user. It can be a good idea to format the locked and unlocked cells differently, such as a different background color, to make it clear which cells are available.

The Spreadsheet control's object model is very much like the object model for an Excel worksheet. In terms of manipulating cell contents and properties, you will often find that the code is identical in the two situations. You learned about the Excel object model in Chapter 6, and you should refer there for details.

Let's look at an example of creating a small calculator in Excel then publishing it to a Web page. The first steps involve creating the calculator in Excel:

1. Start a new worksheet and put the following text in the indicated cells:
   B3: Loan Calculator
   B5: Amount borrowed:
   B6: Annual interest rate:
   B7: Term (months):
   B9: Monthly payment:

2. Change cell B3 to a larger font.

3. Make column B wider so the labels in cells B5–B9 all fit in the column.

4. Put the following formula in cell C9:

   ```
   =-PMT(C6,C7,C5)
   ```

5. Format cell C6 as % with two decimal places.

6. Format cells C5 and C9 as currency, with no decimal places in C5, and two decimal places in C9.

7. Select the range A3–D10 and change its background color to gray.

8. Select the range C5–C7 and change its background color to white.

9. With the range C5–C7 still selected, select Format, Cells, and then on the Protection tab turn off the Locked option.

10. Select Tools, Protection, Protect Sheet, then in the dialog box that displays click OK.

Put some values in the input cells to test the calculation. As shown in Figure 23–3, a $10,000 loan at 6% for 36 months results in a monthly payment of $683.95.

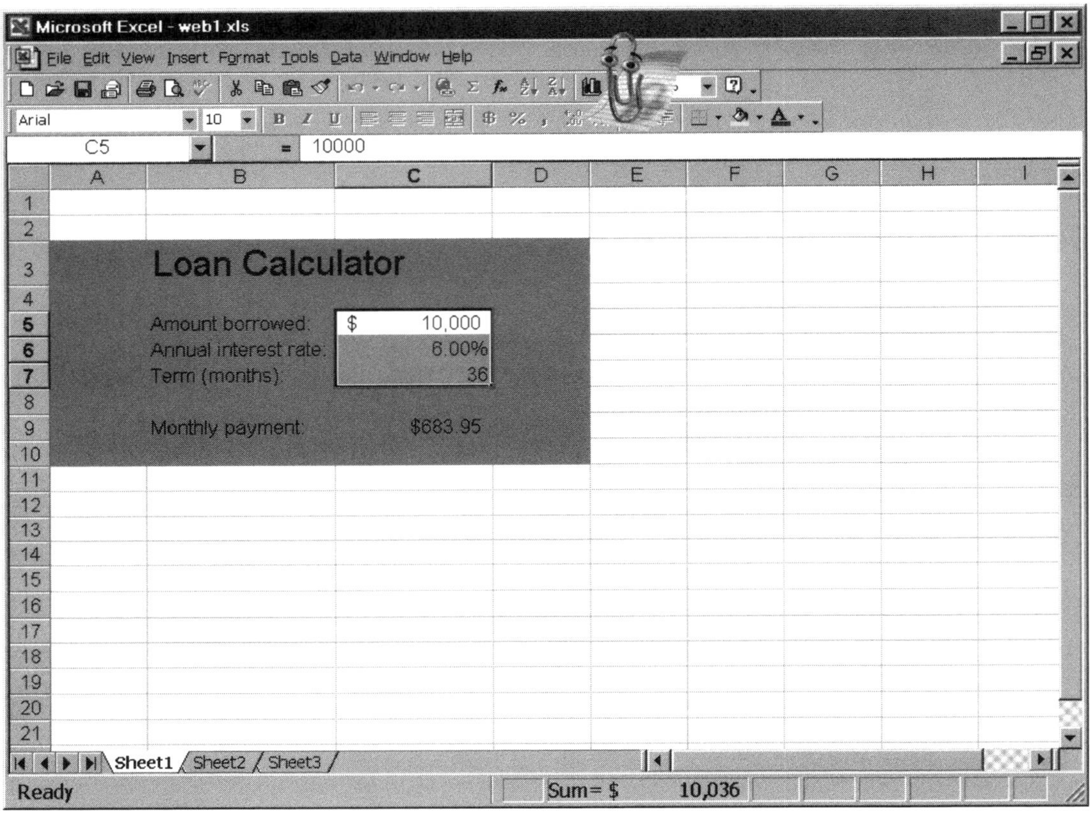

Figure 23-3   *The Excel worksheet to be published to a Web page.*

1. Select the range A3–D10.
2. Select Save As Web Page from the File menu.
3. In the Save As dialog box, select the Selection A3:D10 option and turn on the Add Interactivity option, then click Publish.
4. In the next dialog box, be sure that Spreadsheet Functionality is selected in the Viewing Options section. Enter the path for a local Web page, or the URL of a remote page, in the File Name box.
5. Click the Publish button.

The finished Web page is shown in Figure 23–4. You can see that the `Spreadsheet` control reproduces the loan calculator exactly, and when you try it out you'll see it works just like it did inside Excel.

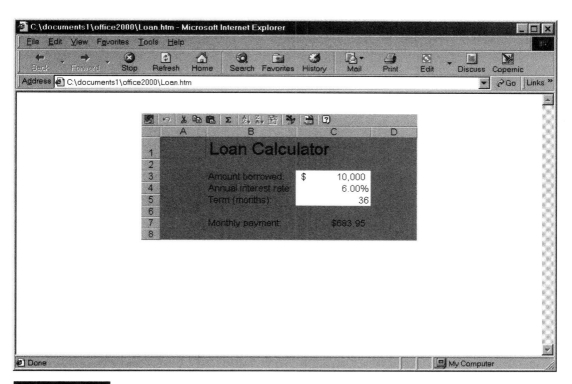

Figure 23–4
Running the loan calculator in the `Spreadsheet` *control in a Web page.*

Using the `PivotTable` Control

The `PivotTable` control is designed to analyze and summarize data. It is a dynamic control in that the user can control how the data is viewed. The data that is displayed by a `PivotTable` will usually come from an ADO data source or another of the Office Web components (such as the `DataSource` control). To get a feel for what the `PivotTable` can do, I recommend that you work with the control in an Excel spreadsheet and experiment with the different ways it can represent data.

The `PivotTable` object has two subsidiary objects, `PivotData` and `PivotView`. The `PivotData` object represents the data displayed in a `PivotTable List` control, while the `PivotView` object represents a specific view of that data. What the user actually sees is therefore a combination of the data and the view. Each of these objects has its own hierarchy of sub-objects that you can manipulate to determine exactly what is displayed.

The `PivotTable` control's `DataSource` property is used to specify the source of the data that the control will display. This can be an ADO data source created in code, as will be shown in the example program later in this section. It can also be a `Spreadsheet` control or a `DataSource` control displayed on the same page.

Listing 23–1 shows the HTML for a Web page that uses the `PivotTable` control to display data from the Northwinds database (which is a sample database installed with Office). This page includes VBScript code that initializes the `PivotTable` by connecting it to the database, using an ADO connection, and specifies the type of display. In this case the display is a simple list, but the user of the page can utilize the interactive features of the `PivotTable` to modify the view as needed. The resulting Web page is shown in Figure 23–5.

Listing 23–1	*HTML and VBScript code for a Web page that uses the* `PivotTable` *control.*

```
<HTML>
<HEAD>
<TITLE>PivotList Example</TITLE>
</HEAD>
<BODY>
<OBJECT classid=clsid:0002E520-0000-0000-C000-000000000046 id=PT1></
    OBJECT>
<SCRIPT language=vbscript>
<!--
Sub window_onLoad()
    InitializePivotTable
End Sub

Sub InitializePivotTable()

    DataBasePath = "c:\program files\microsoft office\office\samples\"
    DataBasePath = DataBasePath & "Northwind.mdb"

    Set adoConnection = CreateObject("ADODB.Connection")
    adoConnection.Provider = "Microsoft.Jet.OLEDB.4.0"
    adoConnection.Open DataBasePath

    ' Connection string.
    PT1.ConnectionString = adoConnection.ConnectionString

    ' Select all fields from the Products table.
    PT1.CommandText = "SELECT * FROM Products"

    Set view = PT1.ActiveView

    ' Put all result columns in the detail area.
    view.AutoLayout
```

```
' Specify PivotTable title.
view.Titlebar.Caption = "Northwind Company Product List"

' Hide the drop areas.
view.RowAxis.Label.Visible = False
view.ColumnAxis.Label.Visible = False

' Set maximum width and height of detail area.
view.DetailMaxHeight = 32000
view.DetailMaxWidth = 32000

' Turn off AutoFit and grouping.
PT1.AutoFit = False
PT1.Width = "100%"
PT1.Height = "65%"
PT1.AllowGrouping = False

End Sub
-->
</SCRIPT>
</BODY></HTML>
```

Using the Chart Control

The Chart control provides several styles of two-dimensional graphs. The source of the data for the chart can be one of several: a DataSource control, a Spreadsheet control, a PivotTable control, an ADO recordset created programmatically, or any other ActiveX control that supports data binding. Data can also be provided locally, in HTML code, for example.

If you create a chart in Excel or Access, you will usually use the Chart Wizard to create the chart and connect it to its data. When you then publish the chart to a Web page, the connection is already established. For example, in Excel you can create a chart that is based on data in the spreadsheet. When you use the Publish command, as described earlier in this chapter, specify that the page be published with Chart functionality. Both the chart and the spreadsheet containing the data will be published to the page, as a Chart and a Spreadsheet control, respectively.

In Access, you can create a chart that is linked to data in a table or query in the database, or to a PivotTable on the same data access page. In this case there is no Spreadsheet control but rather the chart is linked directly to the source of its data. If the data changes, the chart on the Web page will reflect the change as soon as the browser is refreshed.

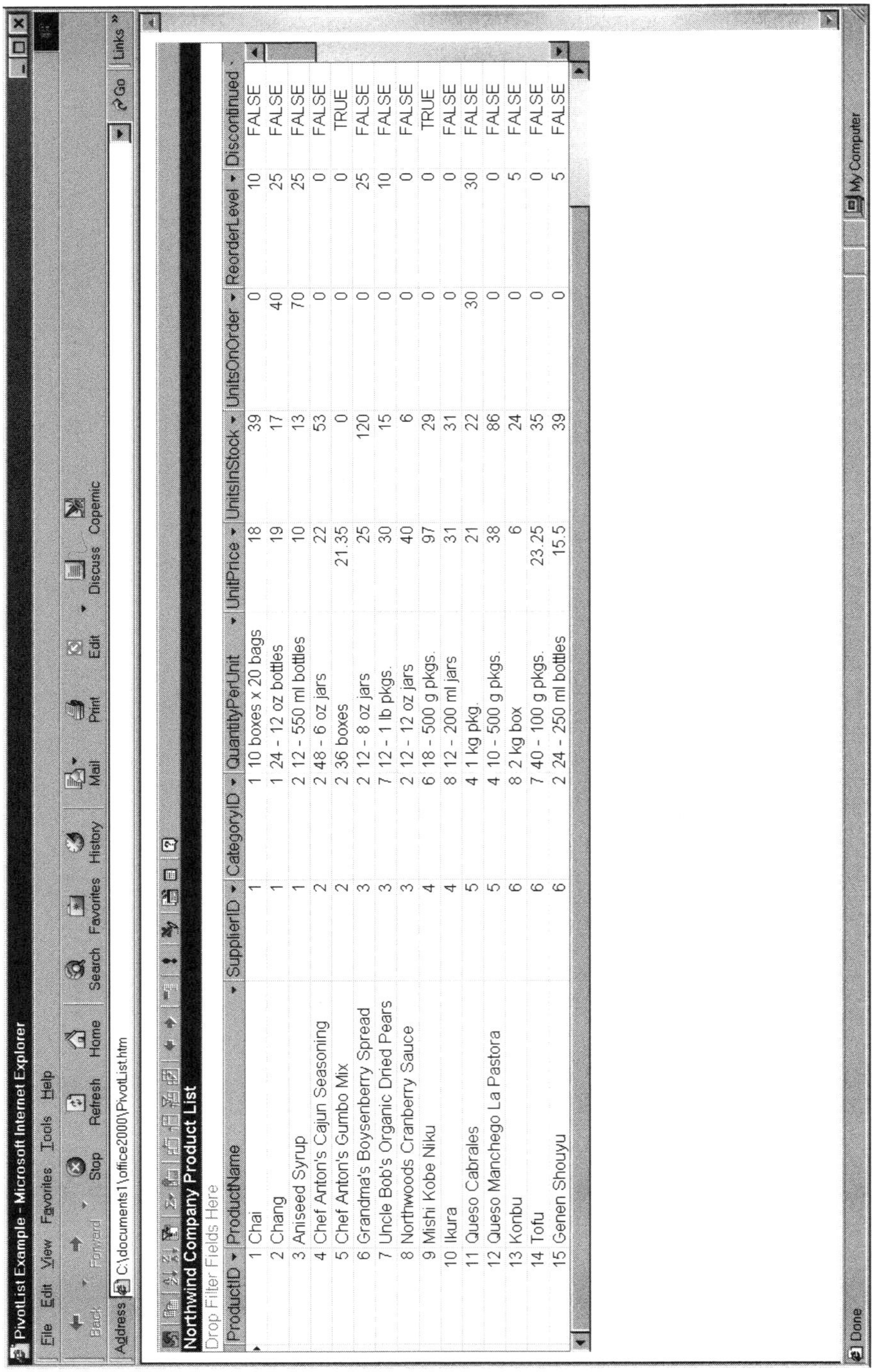

Figure 23–5   *Using the PivotTable control on a Web page.*

In the `Chart` object model, the `Chart` component is actually a `ChartSpace` object, which can contain one or more charts. The `Chart` control has a `WCCharts` collection, and you add a chart to it with the `Add` method, up to a maximum of 16 (although a single chart is most common). Each chart is represented by a `WCChart` object, which has a set of properties that determine the chart's appearance. For example, the `Type` property determines the type of chart (line, bar, etc.), and the `WCLegend` property references a `WCLegend` object that represents the chart's legend.

The data displayed on a chart is contained in data series, each represented by a `WCSeries` object. A chart can contain as many as 255 series. The `WCSeriesCollection` property references a collection containing all of the chart's `WCSeries` objects. Each `WCSeries` object has a set of properties that control how that series' data will be displayed. The `WCSeries` object also has the `SetData` method, which you use to specify the series data.

When working with charts there are many predefined constants that you can use in your code. These constants are made available to you in the `Constants` collection of the `Chart` object. Suppose you have a `Chart` object named `Chart1`. The following code creates a new chart and sets its type to a clustered column chart using one of the constants in this collection:

```
Set cht = Chart1.Charts.Add
Set c = Chart1.Constants
cht.Type = c.chChartTypeColumnClustered
```

In addition to having a `Chart` control linked to a spreadsheet or database table, you can provide it with data programmatically in your VBScript code. In a normal HTML page this would result in a static chart, but if you use Active Server Pages technology you could create a dynamic graph that updates each time it is viewed. Listing 23–2 shows the HTML and VBScript code for a Web page that incorporates a `Chart` control and fills it with data using code. Figure 23–6 shows the resulting Web page.

Listing 23–2   *HTML and VBScript code to display a chart on a Web page.*

```
<html>

<head>
<title>Chart Object Demo</title>
</head>

<body>

<h1>Latest Sales Data</h1>
<p>
<object classid="clsid:0002E500-0000-0000-C000-000000000046" id="CS1"
    width="720" height="480">
```

```
</object>
</p>
<SCRIPT language=vbscript>
<!--
sub window_OnLoad()
    InitChart
End Sub

Sub InitChart()

' Arrays for the data.
Dim Categories(6)
Dim Values(6)

' Load the data into the arrays.
Categories(0) = "Jan"
Categories(1) = "Feb"
Categories(2) = "Mar"
Categories(3) = "Apr"
Categories(4) = "May"
Categories(5) = "Jun"

Values(0) = 50345
Values(1) = 65788
Values(2) = 78445
Values(3) = 61440
Values(4) = 82347
Values(5) = 79022

' Create a new chart.
Set cht = CS1.Charts.Add

' Reference to the constants collections.
Set c = CS1.Constants

' Assign the category data.
cht.SetData c.chDimCategories, c.chDataLiteral, Categories

' Assign the value data.
cht.SeriesCollection(0).SetData c.chDimValues, c.chDataLiteral, Values

' Format the Y axis lavels as currency.
cht.Axes(c.chAxisPositionLeft).Numberformat = "$#"

End Sub

-->
</SCRIPT>
</body>

</html>
```

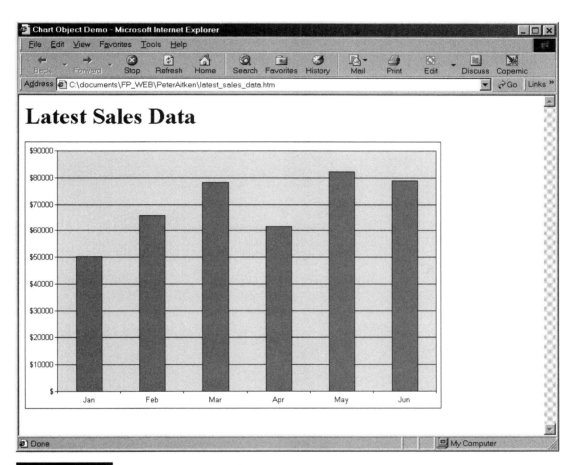

Figure 23–6   *The chart created by the HTML in Listing 23–2.*

Using the **DataSource** Control

The DataSource control does not display on the screen at all, but rather works behind the scenes to connect PivotTable and Chart controls to their underlying data. Data access pages also use this control. The DataSource control uses ADO technology, and can be bound to Microsoft Access, Microsoft SQL Server, and Oracle databases. In many development scenarios, such as creating an Access data access page, the DataSource control is added and configured automatically and you do not have to deal with it in code. When required, however, you can programmatically manipulate this control and then bind it to one or more other controls, such as a Chart control, to display the data.

The HTML and VBScript code shown in Listing 23–3 shows an example. This code makes use of the Northwind sample database that is installed along with Office. The code refers to a query in the database named Product Sales for 1994. A recordset is created that contains only those records from the query where the `ProductName` field is "Beverages." Then the categories and values from this recordset are assigned as the data series for the `Chart` control. The resulting chart is shown displayed in a browser in Figure 23–7.

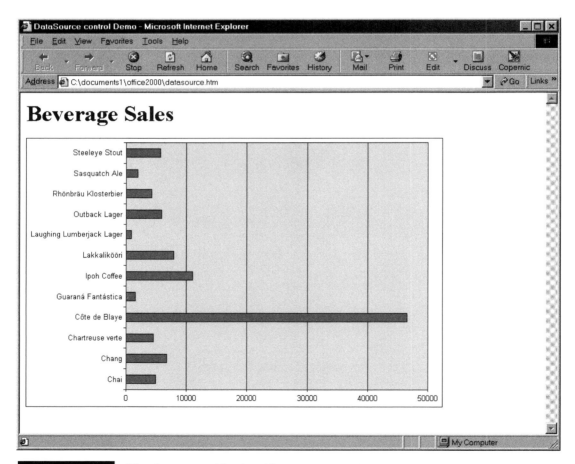

Figure 23–7   *The chart created by the HTML is Listing 23–3.*

| Listing 23–3 | *Using a DataSource control to bind a Chart control to a database table.* |

```html
<html>

<head>
<title>DataSource control Demo</title>
</head>

<body>

<h1>Beverage Sales</h1>
<p>
<object classid="clsid:0002E500-0000-0000-C000-000000000046" id="CS1"
    width="720" height="480">
</object>
<object classid="CLSID:0002E530-0000-0000-C000-000000000046"
    id="DS1"></object>
</p>
<SCRIPT language=vbscript>
<!--
sub window_OnLoad()
    InitChart
End Sub

Sub InitChart()

Dim adoCN
Dim sqlCMD
Dim dbName

dbName = "c:\program files\microsoft "
dbName = dbName & "office\office\samples\northwind.mdb"

' Connect to the database.
Set adoCN = CreateObject("ADODB.Connection")
adoCN.Provider="Microsoft.Jet.OLEDB.4.0"
adoCN.Open dbName

' Link the DataSource control to the database.
DS1.ConnectionString = adoCN.ConnectionString

' Construct the SQL command.
sqlCMD = "SELECT * FROM [Product Sales for 1994] WHERE "
sqlCMD = sqlCMD & "[CategoryName]='Beverages' ORDER BY [ProductName]"

' Create a recordset named "BeverageSales" based on the SQL command.
DS1.RecordSetDefs.AddNew sqlCMD, dscCommandText, "BeverageSales"

' Assign the Chart control's data source and member.
CS1.DataSource = DS1
```

```
CS1.DataMember = "BeverageSales"

' Add a chart and set its type.
Set ch = CS1.Charts.Add
Set c = CS1.Constants
ch.Type = c.chChartTypeBarClustered

' Assign the data series.
ch.SetData c.chDimCategories, 0, "ProductName"
ch.SeriesCollection(0).SetData c.chDimValues, 0, "ProductSales"

End Sub

-->
</SCRIPT>
</body>

</html>
```

Summing Up

Perhaps the greatest change in Office 2000, compared with previous editions, is the significantly expanded support for the Web. This support exists not only in the applications programs, but also in the development tools that are part of Office. With the four Web components covered in this chapter, your custom Office applications can provide an unprecedented level of Web interactivity. With the increasing importance of the Web in all aspects of business, government, and education, I think that these capabilities will be welcomed gladly by all Office developers.

Putting It All To Work

The development tools provided by Office are extensive and powerful. Combining the object models of the Office applications with the full-featured VBA language, you can accomplish just about any imaginable task relating to text, numbers, charts, e-mail, and the various other elements that make today's enterprises run. You have learned a lot of details in the previous sections, and there's no avoiding the fact that there are a lot of details to learn if you are going to be a successful Office developer.

It's also necessary, however, to see how all the parts work together. That's the purpose of this fifth and last section of the book. Here I will walk you through all the steps of developing three complete custom Office applications, starting with the conceptualization and planning stages all the way to testing and fine-tuning. It's impossible to cover all aspects of Office programming, but I have made an effort to cover what I consider the most important areas: e-mail, documents, spreadsheets, and data report generation. It goes without saying that your Office applications will be a lot different from these, but you will find many of the same techniques and principles in use.

Web Publishing of a Multi-Author Compound Document

One of the most common tasks that is performed by custom Office solutions involves the gathering of information from various sources and combining it into a finished form. There are endless variations on this theme, both in terms of the sources of the information and the design of the finished product. In this chapter we will create a custom application to deal with one such scenario, showing how Office's powerful capabilities can be put together to automate a time-consuming task.

The Scenario

Your firm requires that the company policy manual be updated regularly, and that it be available as a Web page on the company site. The policy manual is a joint effort, with different sections contributed by various individuals scattered throughout the company offices. In the past, the compilation was done manually. Each contributor would update their section, or subdocument, when and if needed, then e-mail the document to the person responsible for the compilation. This individual would manually edit the policy manual to include the modified section, then publish it to the Web page. This method was time consuming and prone to errors. Your assignment, as the company's Office programming guru, is to write a custom application that automates the process as much as possible.

The specifics of the task include the requirement that each section of the manual be updated at least once a month. Even if there are no changes to be made, this ensures that the person responsible for a specific section has not simply forgotten about it. The plan is for this custom application to be executed once a month.

Planning

The first step in planning any custom Office solution is to decide which of the Office applications will play the central role. In this scenario Word is the obvious choice. We will be combining multiple subdocuments, each created in Word, into a single master document, then publishing it as a Web page—all tasks best done by Word. Other Office applications will be used as well, but clearly Word will be central.

Early in the planning process it is advisable to sketch out the main steps the application will need to perform, and make at least a preliminary determination of how the task will be performed.

Step 1: Keeping the Required Information

When executing, the application will need the following information:

- The name and e-mail address of each person who is responsible for the various sections of the document.
- The path and file name of the individual Word documents that will be combined to make the final document.
- The path and file name where the resulting Web page is to be published.

This information could be hard-coded into the application's VBA code, but that would make it more difficult to modify if some of the information changes. Since it is a small amount of information, an Excel workbook will be an ideal place. The information can easily be accessed in VBA code, and can also be edited as needed without having to manipulate source code.

Step 2: Checking for Updates

In order to ensure that the various component documents are updated regularly, the application can check each subdocument's "Modified" property, which is one of the many document properties maintained automatically by Word. If this date is more than a month earlier, it will indicate that the document has not been updated as required. If this is the case, then the person responsible for that document will be sent an e-mail message reminding him or her of the need to perform the update. The subdocument, even though possibly out of date, will still be incorporated in the final document.

Step 3: Assembling and Publishing the Document

These steps are easily done with Word commands. The Insert, File command inserts a disk file into the current document, and the File, Save As Web Page command saves the current document as a Web page.

Step 4: Possible Errors and Bugs

The operations of this application are primarily disk-based, so the possible errors will mostly be disk and file related. Let's look at the potential errors:

- The Excel file containing the information is not found. In this case there is no possible remedy, so the application will abort with a message to the user.
- The information in the Excel file is incorrect or arranged improperly. There are so many ways that the information in the spreadsheet could be wrong that it is not feasible to trap every possible error. A better approach is to design the Excel file so that the possibility of incorrect information is minimized or, when possible, eliminated. We can, however, trap the error that would occur if there is no information at all at the specified location in the Excel file.
- An individual subdocument file cannot be found in the specified location. If this occurs, the application will be terminated and a message displayed to the user.
- Unspecified network problems. Errors caused by network problems are always a possibility for any custom application that reads or writes files over a network. In this case there is not anything that can be done other than to display a message identifying the error, and terminate the application.

The Excel Spreadsheet

The Excel spreadsheet will hold the information required by the application, as detailed previously. We want to design the spreadsheet to prevent or minimize the chance of incorrect data entry. It also needs to allow for the possibility that the number of sections in the policy manual, and hence the number of subdocuments, will change. The first requirement can be met by including detailed instructions in the spreadsheet, and by locking all cells except those where data should be entered. The second requirement can be met by keeping the data as an open-ended list with one entry per section, in the order the sections are to appear in the final document. The application can start at the top of the list and work its way down until it finds a blank row.

I will not explain all of the details of creating the final spreadsheet, which is shown in Figure 24–1. Most of it is fairly simple. The worksheet has protection turned on, and the gray cells are locked to prevent inadvertent changes. As designed there is a maximum of 10 subdocuments for the policy manual, but this limit could be easily extended as needed. Note that cell C10 marks the start of the table where the subdocument information is kept.

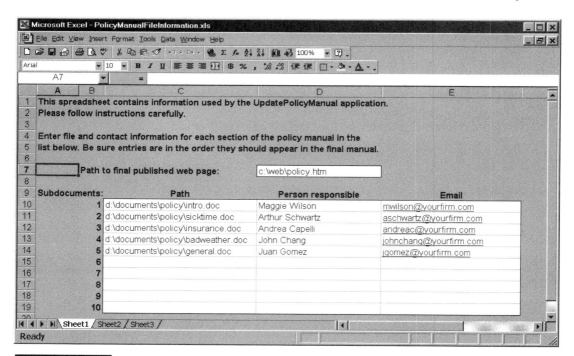

Figure 24–1   *The spreadsheet where the application information is kept.*

Writing Pseudocode

Pseudocode refers to creating an outline of the steps your program will perform, in the order they will be performed, using regular English descriptions of the actions to be performed. Some developers like to do this with pencil and paper. Others prefer to use the VBA editor, creating the pseudocode as comments, then going back and filling in the real code later. Here is the first draft of the pseudocode for our application.

1. Open spreadsheet file that contains subdocument information and read information into the program.
2. Create a new, blank Word document.
3. Start with the first subdocument.
4. Verify that it exists.
5. Determine if it has been updated in the past 30 days. If yes, go to step 7.
6. Send an e-mail to the subdocument's author reminding him or her to update the subdocument.
7. Insert the subdocument into the main document.
8. Go to the next subdocument, then return to step 4.
9. Save the main document as a Web page.

Now that the broad outline of the project is in place, we can start working on the specifics.

The SubDocument Object

The subdocuments that this application will work with are obvious candidates for being represented by objects. Each subdocument will have information associated with it, such as its path, and also will have actions to be carried out, such as checking for a recent update. A good place to start the coding for any project is to design the classes that will represent the data, or entities, that the program will work with. What will our SubDocument class need?

- A property named Path, which holds the path and filename of the subdocument. This will be a read/write property.
- A property named Author, which holds the name of the document author. This too will be read/write.
- A property named AuthorEmail for the author's e-mail address—again a read/write property.
- A method named Exists that returns True only if the subdocument exists.
- A method named VerifyUpdate that checks the subdocument's last modified date and sends an e-mail to the author if it needs updating.

We may think of more requirements later, but this is enough to start writing code. Since we will be working with files, the Scripting Runtime must be referenced in the project. Also, since the `FileSystemObject` will be required in more than one procedure, it will be more efficient to set a global reference to it, which means an instance will have to be created only once. The code for the `SubDocument` class is shown in Listing 24–1. Note that comments have been used at the start of the file to provide some information about the class.

Listing 24–1   *Code in the SubDocument class module.*

```
' Class SubDocument
' Requires: Nothing
' Used by: UpdatePolicyManual

' Author: Peter G. Aitken
' Date: November 11, 1999


'**********************************************

Option Explicit

' Properties.
Private pPath As String
Private pAuthor As String
Private pAuthorEmail As String

' The global reference to the FileSystemObject.
Private fso As Scripting.FileSystemObject

Public Property Get Path() As String

    Path = pPath

End Property

Public Property Let Path(ByVal vNewValue As String)

    pPath = vNewValue

End Property

Public Property Get Author() As String

    Author = pAuthor

End Property

Public Property Let Author(ByVal vNewValue As String)
```

```
        pAuthor = vNewValue

End Property

Public Property Get AuthorEmail() As String

        AuthorEmail = pAuthorEmail

End Property

Public Property Let AuthorEmail(ByVal vNewValue As String)

        pAuthorEmail = vNewValue

End Property

Public Function Exists() As Boolean

' Returns True if the file specified in the Path property
' exists. Returns False otherwise, or if the pPath
' has not been set.

If Len(pPath) > 0 Then
    Exists = fso.FileExists(pPath)
Else
    Exists = False
End If

End Function

Public Function VerifyUpdate(Days As Long) As Boolean

' Returns True if the subdocument has been modified in the
' past Days days, False otherwise or if the file does not
' exist.

Dim f As Scripting.File

If Exists() Then
    Set f = fso.GetFile(pPath)
    If Now - f.DateLastModified > Days Then
        VerifyUpdate = False
    Else
        VerifyUpdate = True
    End If
Else
    VerifyUpdate = False
End If

End Function
```

```
Private Sub Class_Initialize()

' Create the FileSystemObject object.
Set fso = New Scripting.FileSystemObject

End Sub

Private Sub Class_Terminate()

' Destroy the FileSystemObject
Set fso = Nothing

End Sub
```

The Main Application

Once we have the SubDocument class to take care of storing the data for each subdocument, we can turn our attention to the remainder of the project. The tasks required have all been covered in earlier chapters: opening an Excel workbook and reading information from specific cells, creating a new Word document, inserting files into the document, and so on. The code for the remainder of the application is presented in Listing 24–2. I have commented the code so you can follow along, but for the most part I think this code will all be familiar to you.

Listing 24–2   *Code for the UpdatePolicyManual application.*

```
' Module UpdatePolicyManual.
' Execute: Procedure UpdatePolicyManual
' Run in: Word
' Requires: Class module SubDocument

' Author: Peter G. Aitken
' Date: November 11, 1999

' Summary: Using information in the Excel worksheet
' PolicyManualFileInformation.xls, assembles the
' company policy manual and publishes it to the Web directory.

'****************************************************************

' Information about the Excel file where
' the subdoc information is kept.
Const SUBDOC_INFO_FILE = "PolicyManualFileInformation.xls"
Const SUBDOC_INFO_PATH = "c:\documents1\office2000\"
```

```
' The cell in the Excel spreadsheet where the data starts.
Const START_ROW = 10
Const START_COL = 3

' The cell in the Excel spreadsheet where the publish path is located.
Const PUBLISH_PATH_ROW = 7
Const PUBLISH_PATH_COL = 4

' Days allowed to pass since subdoc update.
Const DAYS_SINCE_UPDATE = 30

' Global variable for publish to path.
Private gPublishPath As String

Public Sub UpdatePolicyManual()

' A dynamic array to hold the subdocument info.
Dim SubDocs() As SubDocument

Dim msg As String
Dim Errormsg As String
Dim i As Integer
Dim SubDocsNeedingUpdating As Integer
Dim SubdocNotFound As Boolean
Dim wdDoc As Word.Document

Const PROC_NAME = "UpdatePolicyManual"

On Error GoTo ErrorHandler

SubdocNotFound = False
SubDocsNeedingUpdating = 0

' Get the subdocument information.
If GetSubdocInfo(SubDocs()) = 0 Then
    msg = "Error getting data from information file." & vbCrLf
    msg = "The application will terminate."
    MsgBox (msg)
    Exit Sub
End If

msg = ""

' Now make sure each of the subdocuments exists.
For i = 1 To UBound(SubDocs)
    If Not SubDocs(i).Exists Then
        SubdocNotFound = True
        msg = msg & vbCrLf & "      " & SubDocs(i).Path
    End If
Next i
```

```
' If any subdocs were not found, display a message and terminate.

If SubdocNotFound Then
    msg = "These subdocument(s) were not found:" & msg
    msg = msg & vbCrLf & "The application will terminate."
    MsgBox (msg)
    Exit Sub
End If

msg = ""

' Now check for updated subdocs.
For i = 1 To UBound(SubDocs)
    If Not SubDocs(i).VerifyUpdate(DAYS_SINCE_UPDATE) Then
        SubDocsNeedingUpdating = SubDocsNeedingUpdating + 1
        msg = msg & vbCrLf & "     " & SubDocs(i).Path
        SendReminder SubDocs(i)
    End If
Next i

If SubDocsNeedingUpdating > 0 Then
    msg = "These subdocuments require updating:" & msg & vbCrLf
    msg = msg & "Reminders have been sent to the authors." & vbCrLf
    msg = msg & "The policy manual will include the outdated version."
    MsgBox (msg)
End If

' Once we reach here we are ready to compile and
' publish the policy manual.

' Create a new document based on the normal template.
Set wdDoc = New Word.Document
wdDoc.Activate

' Insert each subdocument.
For i = 1 To UBound(SubDocs)
    Selection.InsertFile FileName:=SubDocs(i).Path, _
        Range:="", ConfirmConversions:=False, Link:=False, _
        Attachment:=False
Next i

'Publish it then close it.
ActiveDocument.SaveAs FileName:=gPublishPath,
    FileFormat:=wdFormatHTML, _
    Password:="", AddToRecentFiles:=True

ActiveDocument.Close

MsgBox ("The policy manual was published successfully.")
```

```
Exit Sub

ErrorHandler:
    Errormsg = "An unanticipated error has occurred. Please write "
    Errormsg = Errormsg & "down the following information:" & vbCrLf
    Errormsg = Errormsg & "Error number: " & Err & vbCrLf
    Errormsg = Errormsg & "Desription: " & Err.Description & vbCrLf
    Errormsg = Errormsg & "Source: " & Err.Source & vbCrLf
    Errormsg = Errormsg & "Location: " & PROC_NAME
    MsgBox (Errormsg)
    Exit Sub

End Sub

Private Function GetSubdocInfo(s() As SubDocument) As Integer

' Loads the array s() with info about the subdocuments.
' Returns the total number of subdocuments.

Dim count As Integer
Dim xlApp As New Excel.Application
Dim wb As Excel.Workbook
Dim r As Excel.Range
Dim row As Integer
Dim col As Integer
Dim buf As String

On Error Resume Next

Set wb = xlApp.Workbooks.Open(SUBDOC_INFO_PATH _
    & SUBDOC_INFO_FILE)
' An error will occur if there is a problem
' opening the workbook.
If Err.Number > 0 Then
    GetSubdocInfo = 0
    Exit Sub
End If

count = 0
row = START_ROW
col = START_COL

Do While True
    buf = wb.Sheets("Sheet1").Cells(row, col).Value
    If Len(buf) = 0 Then Exit Do
    count = count + 1
    ReDim Preserve s(count)
    Set s(count) = New SubDocument
    s(count).Path = buf
    s(count).Author = wb.Sheets("Sheet1").Cells _
        (row, col + 1).Value
```

```
        s(count).AuthorEmail = wb.Sheets("Sheet1").Cells _
            (row, col + 2).Value
    row = row + 1
Loop

' Now get the publish path.
gPublishPath = wb.Sheets("Sheet1").Cells _
    (PUBLISH_PATH_ROW, PUBLISH_PATH_COL).Value
Debug.Print gPublishPath
wb.Close
Set xlApp = Nothing
GetSubdocInfo = count

End Function

Private Sub SendReminder(s As SubDocument)

' Send a reminder to the author of the specified subdocument
' that the document needs updating.

Dim olApp As New Outlook.Application
Dim olMsg As Outlook.MailItem
Dim msg As String

msg = "Dear " & s.Author & vbCrLf & vbCrLf
msg = msg & "The section of the policy manual you are responsible for "
msg = msg & "in file " & s.Path & " has not been updated in the past "
msg = msg & DAYS_SINCE_UPDATE & " days. Can you please see to this "
msg = msg & "at your earliest convenience? Thank you."

Set olMsg = olApp.CreateItem(olMailItem)
olMsg.Subject = "Document needs updating"
olMsg.To = s.AuthorEmail
olMsg.Body = msg
olMsg.Send

End Sub
```

When executed, the program will perform its actions and, if everything is successful, display a message at the end. If it runs into a problem, informational messages are displayed to the user. Anticipated errors are trapped, and unanticipated errors are handled by a generic error handling routine.

Summing Up

The application developed in this chapter is an excellent example of how Office applications can work together to create custom solutions. By combining the capabilities of Excel, Word, and Outlook we have almost completely automated a previously time consuming and tedious task. The time spent developing the project will be repaid quickly in increased efficiency and reduced errors. This is, after all, what Office development is all about!

Numeric Processing and Graphing

Numbers, numbers everywhere! Sometimes it seems that modern organizations run on numbers, and that trying to make sense of all this data is a hopeless task. We all know that summarizing numeric data in charts can be a powerful tool, but sometimes the very task of creating those charts occupies more time than managers and supervisors are able to spend. Fortunately, Office automation can ride to the rescue again. By using VBA to automate the numeric and charting capabilities of Office applications, graphical summaries of important data can be provided on an instant and automatic basis. The project developed in this chapter shows one example of how this can be done.

The Scenario

You are hired to write a program for a company that sells a variety of computer-related products, including hardware and software. As sales are made, they are automatically posted to a central database where they are organized in a table that contains date, category (hardware or software), and amount fields for each sale. This table is shown in Figure 25–1. The database name is ProductSales and the table name is DailySales.

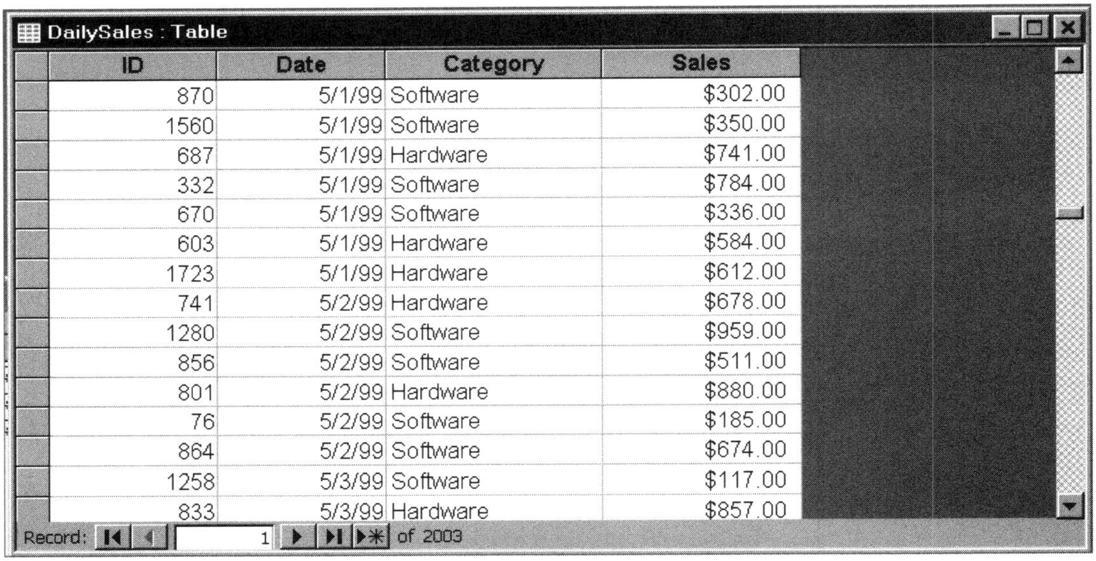

ID	Date	Category	Sales
870	5/1/99	Software	$302.00
1560	5/1/99	Software	$350.00
687	5/1/99	Hardware	$741.00
332	5/1/99	Software	$784.00
670	5/1/99	Software	$336.00
603	5/1/99	Hardware	$584.00
1723	5/1/99	Hardware	$612.00
741	5/2/99	Hardware	$678.00
1280	5/2/99	Software	$959.00
856	5/2/99	Software	$511.00
801	5/2/99	Hardware	$880.00
76	5/2/99	Software	$185.00
864	5/2/99	Software	$674.00
1258	5/3/99	Software	$117.00
833	5/3/99	Hardware	$857.00

Record: 1 of 2003

Figure 25–1 *The data table that serves as the data source.*

The firm's sales manager wants to be able to view recent sales figures, as both numbers and a chart, and needs to be sure that the data is always up-to-date. In addition, she wants the data and charts to be in Excel, and not an Access report. The three views of data that are desired are as follows:

- Monthly sales by category over the past 12 months.
- Weekly sales by category over the past three months.
- Sales by category by the day of the week, averaged over the past six months.

Planning

One of the main planning steps is rendered unnecessary by the fact that your client requires the application to run in Excel. Since the source data exists in an Access database, that decision is also made for you. There are two general approaches we can take to this project:

- Write VBA code that runs in Excel. The code would start with a blank workbook, and would perform the steps necessary to open the database table, extract the required data, then create the numerical tables and the charts from scratch.
- Create a "dummy" workbook that contains the necessary tables and charts, but with no data (or only fake data). Then write VBA code that runs in Excel, with the code serving to extract the required data from the database table and plug it into the proper locations in the workbook.

How can you choose between these two ways of approaching the project? The only real answer to this question is "experience." Once you have worked with Excel and VBA for a while, you will realize that the second approach is easier. Creating tables and charts is always easier when you are working directly in Excel, as compared with doing it with VBA code. This is particularly true when you would like to use special formatting to make the workbook as attractive and easy to read as possible.

Creating the Workbook

The workbook for the application will have three worksheets, one for each of the data views that are required. Let's start with the "monthly sales by category" worksheet. For the data we will need a block of cells two wide (for the two categories) and 12 high (for the 12 months). We will also want labels to identify the data (although some of these labels will be replaced later). Finally, some attractive formatting will make the worksheet easier to view. My final result is shown in Figure 25–2, but you can design the table any way you want. The only thing you should do that is not obvious in the figure is to format the data cells as currency with no decimal places.

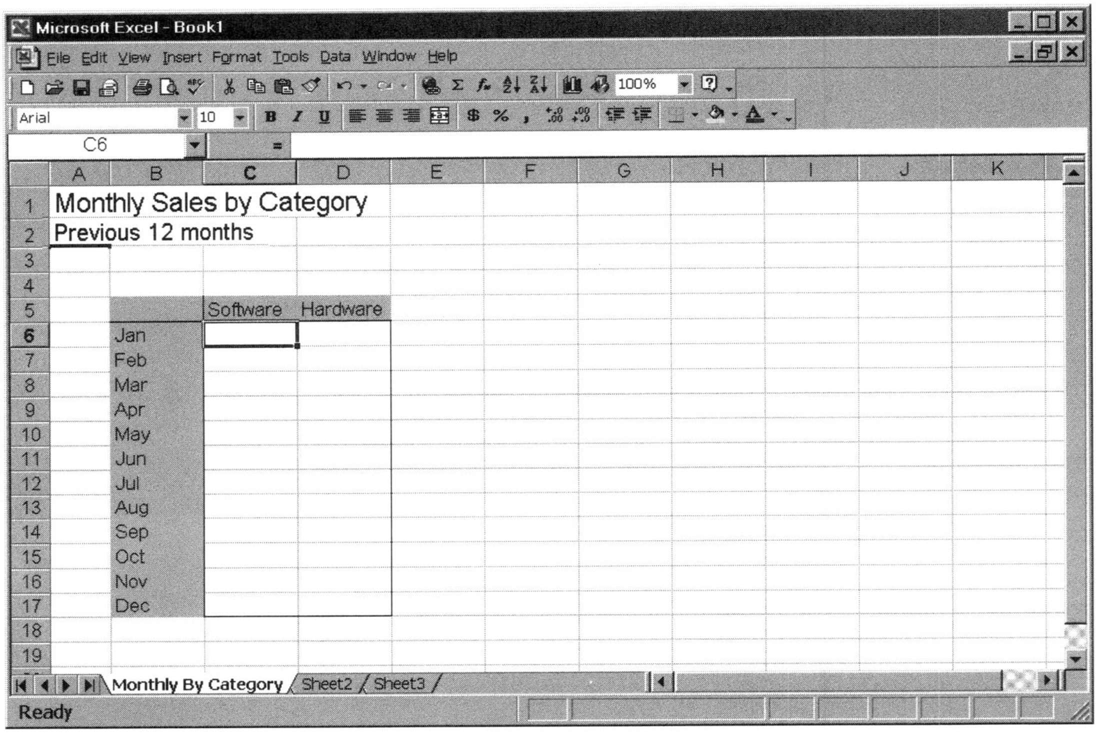

Figure 25–2   *The preliminary worksheet for the fist view of the data.*

The next step is to create a chart. For this you should put some fake data in the cells, which will make the resulting chart a lot easier to work with in terms of formatting and such. I decided to use a column chart, but you can use another chart style if desired. Again, the formatting of the chart is up to you, and all that is really required is that the chart display the data in the range of the data table—in this case, B5:D17. My finished worksheet is shown in Figure 25–3.

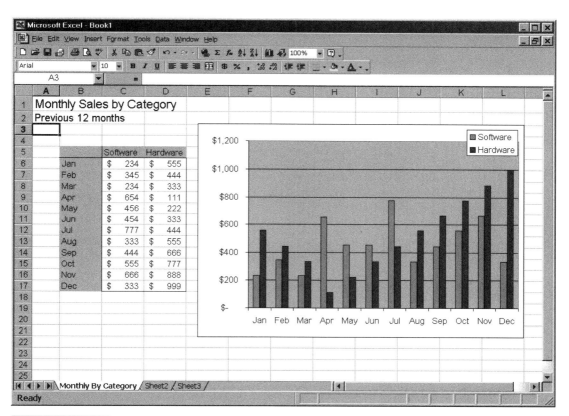

Figure 25–3 *The completed worksheet for the Monthly by Category view of the data.*

The other two workbooks, for the other two data views, are created in much the same way. You can use an arrangement and formatting that suit your tastes, but the idea is the same: create a table for the data and a chart that refers to that table. When we later fill in the table with data from the data source, the charts will automatically update as needed. (See Figures 25–4 and 25–5.)

Once the workbook is ready, we can turn our attention to the code.

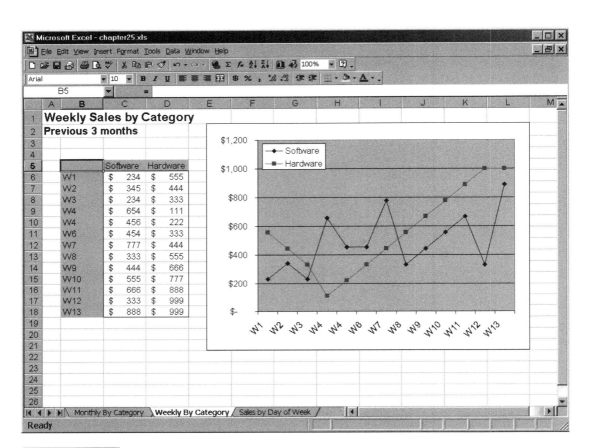

Figure 25–4 *The final worksheet for the Weekly By Category data display.*

Planning the Code

The first step in planning the VBA code is to decide how it will access the data source. There is no need to automate the Access application, as it will be more efficient to use ADO data access directly. We are interested in records going back three months for one data view, six months for another, and 12 months for the third. We could create a recordset containing all records from the DailySales table going back 12 months, then extract the six month and three month subsets using VBA code. However, why not use the power of ADO to simply create three separate recordsets—one for 12 months worth of data, one for six months, and one for three months? This will simplify the VBA code required by the project. This means, of course, that the project will require a reference to the Microsoft ActiveX Data Object Library.

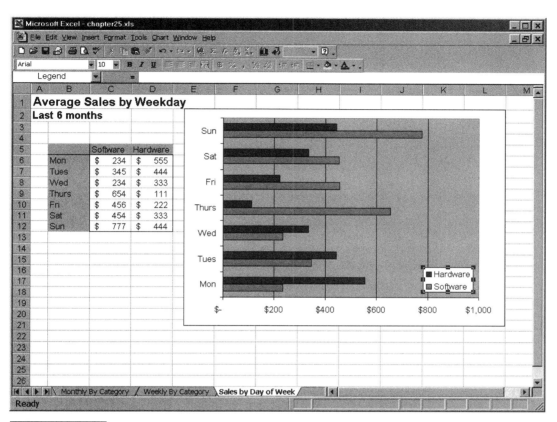

Figure 25–5   *The final worksheet for the Sales by Day of Week display.*

The approach I decided on for this application is to create a single global reference to the database, as an `ADO Connection` object. Then there will be three separate procedures, each dealing with one of the three worksheets. Code in each procedure will create its own recordset, containing just those records it needs to work with.

Potential Errors and Bugs

There are relatively few opportunities for errors and bugs in this project. There is no direct interaction with the user, which removes one main source of these problems. Other than accessing the database, there is no file manipulation, another source of potential errors. Since Excel will have to be open for the application to run at all, automation errors should not be a problem. The one possible problem we will have to trap is an error accessing the database. As you learned in Chapter 20, errors generated when accessing objects should be trapped using the `On Error Resume Next` statement, which is what we will do.

The Main Procedure

For this application, execution will start in a main procedure that will then call the various other procedures, which will extract data from the database and insert it into the three individual worksheets. The job of this main procedure is only to open a connection to the database file, call the other procedures, then destroy the database connection and exit. For lack of imagination I called this procedure main, and its code is shown in Listing 25–1 (which also includes the project's module-level code). Note that this procedure and all the project's other code should be placed in the ThisWorkbook module of the Excel workbook that we created earlier in the chapter.

Automatic Macro Execution

To have a macro procedure such as the one in this project execute automatically, put a call to it in the workbook's Workbook_Open event procedure as shown here:

```
Private Sub Workbook_Open()

    Call main

End Sub
```

Listing 25–1 *The main procedure for the custom application.*

```
Option Explicit

' Path to the sales database.
Const DB_PATH = "C:\documents1\office2000\productsales.mdb"

Private adoCN As ADODB.Connection

Private Sub main()
' Execution starts here.

Dim msg As String

On Error Resume Next

' Open the database.
Set adoCN = New ADODB.Connection
With adoCN
    .Provider = "Microsoft.Jet.OLEDB.4.0"
```

```
      .Open DB_PATH
End With

If Err > 0 Then
    msg = "There has been an error opening the database:" & vbCrLf
    msg = msg & "Error number: " & Err.Number & vbCrLf
    msg = msg & "Description: " & Err.Description & vbCrLf
    msg = msg & "Source: " & Err.Source & vbCrLf
    MsgBox msg
    Exit Sub
End If

Call DoWorksheet1
Call DoWorksheet2
Call DoWorksheet3

' Execution ends here.
adoCN.Close
Set adoCN = Nothing

End Sub
```

The Secondary Procedures

The plan is to write one secondary procedure to handle each of the three worksheets. Let's start with the worksheet that will display monthly sales, by category, for the past 12 months. By "past 12 months" I mean the 12 most recent completed months. Thus, if the worksheet is opened sometime during March of 2000 it will display data for the months March 1999 through February 2000.

The procedure will have to calculate 24 totals: the two categories Software and Hardware for each of the 12 months. An ideal way to store this data is in a 12 × 2 element array. By increasing the array size to 12 × 3 we will have an extra element for each month's index.

The first task of the procedure is to determine the starting and ending dates of the records that should be retrieved from the database table. You can see how useful VBA's various date-related functions are in this regard. Once the starting and ending dates have been determined it is an easy matter to construct an SQL command that will extract the associated records from the database. The records are organized in an ADO recordset. Once the recordset has been populated with records, it's a fairly simple matter to go through all the records and add the value in each record's Sales field to the appropriate total in the data array. Finally, using the Excel VBA techniques that you learned about in Chapter 6, the code puts the month names and totals into the appropriate cells in the worksheet. Listing 25–2 presents the code for this procedure. The code is well commented, and you should be able to figure out how it works.

Listing 25–2   *This procedure updates the data in the Monthly By Category worksheet.*

```
Public Sub DoWorksheet1()

' This procedure retrieves the data and calculates
' subtotals for the "Monthly By Category" worksheet,
' then plugs the data into the appropriate cells.

' Location in worksheet where data begins.
Const START_ROW = 6
Const START_COL = 2

Dim adoRS As New ADODB.Recordset
Dim CutOffDateStart As Date
Dim CutOffDateEnd As Date
Dim sqlStr As String
Dim msg As String
Dim FirstMonth As Integer
Dim i As Integer
Dim month As Integer
Dim ws As Excel.Worksheet
Dim Data(2, 11)

' Data(1,x) and Data(2,x) hold totals for the
' software and hardware categories, respectively,
' for month x. Month 0 is 12 months ago, and month
' 11 is the most recent completed month. Date(0,x)
' holds the numerical representation (1-12) of the
' specific month.

On Error Resume Next

' Get a date referring to one year ago.
CutOffDateStart = DateAdd("yyyy", -1, Date)

' Now back up to the beginning of that month.
CutOffDateStart = CutOffDateStart - _
    DatePart("d", CutOffDateStart) + 1

' Get the last day of the previous month.
CutOffDateEnd = Date - DatePart("d", Date)

' Get all records within the specified date range.
sqlStr = "Select * From DailySales Where Date > #" _
    & CutOffDateStart & "# and Date < #" & _
    CutOffDateEnd & "#"

' The ADO connection adoCN is a global variable that
' is defined elsewhere.
adoRS.Open Source:=sqlStr, _
```

```
        ActiveConnection:=adoCN, _
        LockType:=adLockOptimistic

If Err > 0 Then
    msg = "There has been an error accessing the database:" & vbCrLf
    msg = msg & "Error number: " & Err.Number & vbCrLf
    msg = msg & "Description: " & Err.Description & vbCrLf
    msg = msg & "Source: " & Err.Source & vbCrLf
    MsgBox msg
    Exit Sub
End If

' Determine first month, which is the
' same as the current month one year ago.
FirstMonth = DatePart("m", Date)

' Fill in the array with month numbers.
For i = 0 To 11
    Data(0, i) = FirstMonth
    FirstMonth = FirstMonth + 1
    If FirstMonth = 13 Then FirstMonth = 1
Next i

Do While Not adoRS.EOF
    ' Get the month number of the current record.
    month = DatePart("m", adoRS!Date)
    ' Loop through the array looking for the element
    ' With the matching month number.
    For i = 0 To 11
        If Data(0, i) = month Then
            If adoRS!Category = "Hardware" Then
                Data(1, i) = Data(1, i) + adoRS!Sales
            Else
                Data(2, i) = Data(2, i) + adoRS!Sales
            End If
        End If
    Next i
    adoRS.MoveNext
Loop

' Now the data are in the array. We can
' Put it in the proper worksheet cells.

' Make the first worksheet active.
Set ws = Worksheets("Monthly By Category")

' Plug in the data.
For i = 0 To 11
    ' Month name for this entry.
    ws.Cells(START_ROW + i, START_COL).Value = MonthName(Data(0, i), _
        True)
```

```
    ' Data for the two categories.
    ws.Cells(START_ROW + i, START_COL + 1).Value = Data(2, i)
    ws.Cells(START_ROW + i, START_COL + 2).Value = Data(1, i)
Next i

' Destroy objects.
adoRS.Close
Set adoRS = Nothing

End Sub
```

When developing this project I was aware that the code in the three procedures (one for each worksheet) would have a lot of similarities. Each procedure's code would have to extract a subset of records from the database table, then go through those records, calculate the required summary data, then put the data in the appropriate worksheet cells. I knew that my task as a developer would be simplified if I completed and tested one procedure first, then adapted its code to the other two procedures.

The code for the procedure DoWorksheet2, which calculates the data for the Weekly By Category chart, is shown in Listing 25–3. This code is a bit simpler than the previous procedure because there is no need to deal with month names. Also, since weeks—unlike months—all contain the same number of days, it is a simpler matter to decide which week a given record's data belongs in. However, you can clearly see the similarity between the two procedures, and using the code from the first procedure as the basis for the second procedure saved me a lot of time.

Listing 25–3   *This procedure updates the data in the Weekly By Category worksheet.*

```
Public Sub DoWorksheet2()

' This procedure retrieves the data and calculates
' subtotals for the "Weekly By Category" worksheet,
' then plugs the data into the appropriate cells.
' Weeks are assumed to run Sun-Sat, the VBA default.

' Location in worksheet where data begins.
Const START_ROW = 6
Const START_COL = 2

Dim adoRS As New ADODB.Recordset
Dim CutOffDateStart As Date
Dim CutOffDateEnd As Date
Dim sqlStr As String
Dim msg As String
```

```
Dim week As Integer
Dim ws As Excel.Worksheet
Dim Data(2, 12)

' Data(1,x) and Data(2,x) hold totals for the
' software and hardware categories, respectively,
' for week x. Week 0 is 13 weeks ago, and week
' 12 is the most recent completed week. Date(0,x)
' is not used.

On Error Resume Next

' Get a date referring to the previous Sunday,
' the end of the most recent week. Start with
' yesterday and work backwards.
CutOffDateEnd = Date - 1

Do While DatePart("d", CutOffDateEnd) <> 1
    CutOffDateEnd = CutOffDateEnd - 1
Loop

' The start date is 90 days (13 weeks minus 1 day)
' in the past.

CutOffDateStart = CutOffDateEnd - 90

' Get all records within the specified date range.
sqlStr = "Select * From DailySales Where Date > #" _
    & CutOffDateStart & "# and Date < #" & _
    CutOffDateEnd & "#"

' The ADO connection adoCN is a global variable that
' is defined elsewhere.
adoRS.Open Source:=sqlStr, _
    ActiveConnection:=adoCN, _
    LockType:=adLockOptimistic

If Err > 0 Then
    msg = "There has been an error accessing the database:" & vbCrLf
    msg = msg & "Error number: " & Err.Number & vbCrLf
    msg = msg & "Description: " & Err.Description & vbCrLf
    msg = msg & "Source: " & Err.Source & vbCrLf
    MsgBox msg
    Exit Sub
End If

' By subtracting the start date from a given record's date,
' then dividing by 7 and discarding the fractional part,
' we get the array index where the record's data is to
' be added.
```

```
Do While Not adoRS.EOF
    week = (adoRS!Date - CutOffDateStart) \ 7
    If adoRS!Category = "Hardware" Then
        Data(1, week) = Data(1, week) + adoRS!Sales
    Else
        Data(2, week) = Data(2, week) + adoRS!Sales
    End If
    adoRS.MoveNext
Loop

' Now the data are in the array. We can
' put it in the proper worksheet cells.

' Make the first worksheet active.
Set ws = Worksheets("Weekly By Category")

' Plug in the data.
For i = 0 To 12
    ' Data for the two categories.
    ws.Cells(START_ROW + i, START_COL + 1).Value = Data(2, i)
    ws.Cells(START_ROW + i, START_COL + 2).Value = Data(1, i)
Next i

' Destroy objects.
adoRS.Close
Set adoRS = Nothing

End Sub
```

The final procedure we need to write will calculate the average sale for each day of the week, over the past six months. For simplicity's sake we will define the past six months as being the most recent 26 weeks, or 182 days, starting with yesterday. By taking this approach we know there are the same number of each weekday in the data sample, making the calculation of the averages easy. Again, using the already tested code from one of the other procedures makes the development task go quicker. The code for the procedure DoWorksheet3 is presented in Listing 25–4.

Listing 25–4   *This procedure calculates the data for the Sales by Day of Week worksheet.*

```
Public Sub DoWorksheet3()

' This procedure retrieves the data and calculates
' subtotals for the "Sales by Day of Week" worksheet,
' then plugs the data into the appropriate cells.
```

```
' Data from the past 13 weeks are used.

' Location in worksheet where data begins.
Const START_ROW = 6
Const START_COL = 2

Dim adoRS As New ADODB.Recordset
Dim CutOffDateStart As Date
Dim CutOffDateEnd As Date
Dim sqlStr As String
Dim msg As String
Dim i As Integer
Dim weekday As Integer
Dim ws As Excel.Worksheet
Dim Data(2, 6)

' Data(1,x) and Data(2,x) hold totals for the
' software and hardware categories, respectively,
' for weekday x. Weekday 0 is Monday, and so on.

On Error Resume Next

' Get a date referring to yesterday.
CutOffDateEnd = Date - 1

' The start date is 181 days (26 weeks minus
' 1 day) in the past.

CutOffDateStart = CutOffDateEnd - 181

' Get all records within the specified date range.
sqlStr = "Select * From DailySales Where Date > #" _
    & CutOffDateStart & "# and Date < #" & _
    CutOffDateEnd & "#"

' The ADO connection adoCN is a global variable that
' is defined elsewhere.
adoRS.Open Source:=sqlStr, _
    ActiveConnection:=adoCN, _
    LockType:=adLockOptimistic

If Err > 0 Then
    msg = "There has been an error accessing the database:" & vbCrLf
    msg = msg & "Error number: " & Err.Number & vbCrLf
    msg = msg & "Description: " & Err.Description & vbCrLf
    msg = msg & "Source: " & Err.Source & vbCrLf
    MsgBox msg
    Exit Sub
End If
```

```
Do While Not adoRS.EOF
    ' Get day of week with Monday as day 1.
    ' Subtract 1 to mesh with array indices.
    weekday = DatePart("w", adoRS!Date, vbMonday) - 1
    If adoRS!Category = "Hardware" Then
        Data(1, weekday) = Data(1, weekday) + adoRS!Sales
    Else
        Data(2, weekday) = Data(2, weekday) + adoRS!Sales
    End If
    adoRS.MoveNext
Loop

' Divide to get averages.

For i = 0 To 6
    Data(1, i) = Data(1, i) / 26
    Data(2, i) = Data(2, i) / 26
Next i

' Now the data are in the array. We can
' put it in the proper worksheet cells.

' Make the first worksheet active.
Set ws = Worksheets("Sales by Day of Week")

' Plug in the data.
For i = 0 To 6
    ' Data for the two categories.
    ws.Cells(START_ROW + i, START_COL + 1).Value = Data(2, i)
    ws.Cells(START_ROW + i, START_COL + 2).Value = Data(1, i)
Next i

' Destroy objects.
adoRS.Close
Set adoRS = Nothing

End Sub
```

This project may look like a lot of code, but it really did not take all that long to complete. The fact that there were three procedures, each performing similar tasks, made it possible to reuse code from one procedure, with minor modifications, in the other two procedures. The final product is just what the client ordered: a graphical representation, in an Excel spreadsheet, summarizing company sales data in three different ways.

Summing Up

Today's businesses rely on accurate data to make decisions that affect productivity. However, having the data may not be enough—the data needs to be in a form that can easily be understood. This is most often a chart of some kind, and Office's many chart making capabilities are well suited to almost any task. By automatically retrieving the latest data from a database table, and displaying it as charts in three different ways, the application developed in this chapter will help the client make the necessary decisions. It should be noted that Office provides other methods by which essentially the same result could be obtained. That's a mark of the flexibility of the Office development environment.

Custom Report Generation

In the previous chapter you saw how Office can be automated to cre-ate graphical representations of data. There is another commonly used method for summarizing data: the database report. Rather than charts, a report typically uses lists, tables, subtotals, and summaries to extract meaningful information from raw data. In this chapter we will look at a technique that is not used all that often by Office devel-opers, but which can be extremely powerful when circumstances call for it. An Access report is a very flexible way to present dynamic data, and in most cases you will use the Access report designer to create any reports that are part of your custom solution. At times, however, you may need to generate a report "on-the-fly," so to speak. In other words, a report is created when needed, based on the user's needs and desires at the moment. Clearly, the report designer cannot be used for this—the report must be generated dynamically in code. By using VBA and Access methods and objects, you have almost complete flexibility when it comes to dynamic report generation.

Before you even think about programming reports generation, you should be familiar with Access reports as created with the report designer. It is essential that you understand the structure of an Access report and the various components it can contain before you try to duplicate them in code. It is not possible for me to cover every detail of Access reports in this chapter, but I can show you the fundamentals of how to write code to create a report. If you understand Access reports, you fill find it straightforward to extend these techniques to all aspects of report creation.

The Scenario

Because the generation of custom reports can become rather complex, this chapter's demonstration will stay rather simple to better illustrate the basic principles involved. The custom report to be generated consists of a summary list of records from the database table DailySales. More details are presented later in the chapter. First, however, we need to look at some of the tools of custom report generation.

Report Generation Basics

Each report in Access is represented by a Report object. All open reports are contained in the Reports collection. Most Office collections have an Add method, which is used to create a new member and add it to the collection. However, Access reports do not work this way. Instead you use the Create-Report method to create a report. The syntax is:

```
CreateReport(database, reporttemplate)
```

Both arguments are optional. Reporttemplate is the name of the report that you want to use as the template for the new report. Database is the name of the database that contains the template. In this case the database specified must be open as a library database. If the template is in the current database, the database argument can be omitted. If both arguments are omitted, a default blank report is created. When created, the new report is in design mode and is minimized. The following code creates a new, blank report and restores its window for editing:

```
Dim rpt As Report
Set rpt = CreateReport
DoCmd.Restore
```

In our situation, however, opening the new report for editing by the user is rarely appropriate. Rather we would want to save the report for later use, or display or print it immediately (or perhaps a combination of these actions). For these tasks you use Access's DoCmd object (which you learned about is Chapter 7). To create a report then save it, use code like this:

```
Dim rpt As Report
Set rpt = CreateReport
' Code to design report goes here.
DoCmd.Close , , acSaveYes
```

Reports are saved under their default names, which have the form Report1, Report2, etc. This code creates a report then prints it:

```
Dim rpt As Report
Set rpt = CreateReport
' Code to design report goes here.
DoCmd.OpenReport rpt.Name
```

To create a report and then preview it on the screen, pass an argument to the `OpenReport` method as follows:

```
Dim rpt As Report
Set rpt = CreateReport
' Code to design report goes here.
DoCmd.OpenReport rpt.Name, acViewPreview
```

Structure of a Report

All Access reports are broken up into sections. One of the most important parts of designing a report is understanding what these sections are, and how they work. The five most important sections are:

- **Detail.** This section contains the actual data of the report—the individual records and fields that the report is designed to display. The detail section is displayed on every page of the report.
- **Header.** The Header section appears at the top of the first page of the report. It is typically used for information such as the report title and date.
- **Footer.** The Footer section appears at the end of the report. It is used to display summary information, such as totals and averages, that apply to the entire report.
- **Page Header.** The Page Header section appears at the top of every page of the report; on the first page it is below the header section. This section can be used to display labels identifying columns of data in the Detail section.
- **Page Footer.** The Page Footer section appears at the bottom of every page in the report. It can be used to display page numbers and subtotals for each page.

You can see how these sections are laid out in the Access report designer. Figure 26–1 shows a blank report in the designer with the five sections displayed. When using the designer, you would add report components to the various sections of the report as needed. To create a report in code, you will write code that adds components to the report's various sections, as we will see soon.

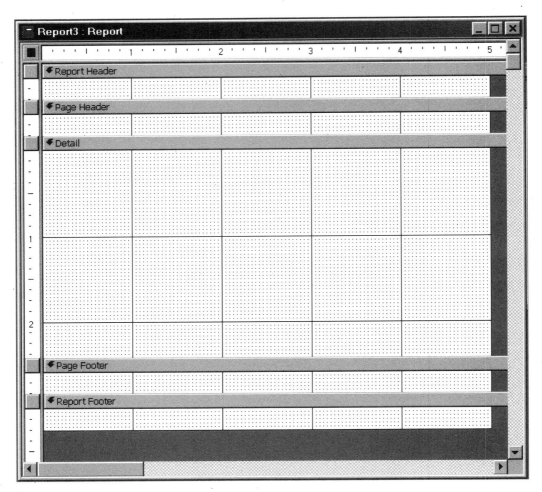

Figure 26-1 *The report designer displays the report's five main sections.*

A report also gives you the option of adding group sections, which are used to group report data based on information in the database. An Access report can have as many as nine grouping levels, and each grouping level can have its own header and footer.

Adding Report Elements

Once you have created a blank report as described above, the main task of designing it consists of adding controls to the various report sections. This is done with the `CreateReportControl` method:

```
CreateReportControl(reportname, controltype, _
    section, parent, columnname, left, top, width, height)
```

Reportname is a required argument specifying the name of the report to add the control to.

Controltype is a required argument specifying the type of control to add. Possible values are described in Table 26.1.

Section is an optional argument specifying the section of the report to which the control is to be added. Constants specifying the sections are listed in Table 26.2. If this argument is omitted, the control is placed in the detail section of the report.

Parent is an optional argument identifying the parent control when you are adding an attached control. For example, if you want to add a Label control attached to an existing Text Box control, specify the name of the Text Box control in this argument. For Check Box, Option Button, and Toggle Button controls, use this argument to specify the Option Group (if any) that the control is to be part of.

Columnname is an optional argument specifying the data column to which the control is to be bound, for data bound controls. For non-data bound controls, omit this argument or use it to specify the control's value.

Left and *top* are optional arguments that specify the position of the control with respect to the report section it is in. The units are twips. If omitted, the control is placed at coordinates 0, 0.

Height and *width* are optional arguments specifying the dimensions of the control, in twips. If omitted the control will have its default size.

Here are some examples. This code adds a Label control to the Page Footer section of the report referenced by `rpt`, at coordinates 100, 100. The label displays the text in the variable `TextForLabel`, in a bold font, and is set to size itself automatically to fit the text it contains.

```
Dim lb As Access.Label
Set lb = CreateReportControl(rpt.Name, acLabel, _
    acPageFooter, , _
    TextForLabel, 100, 100)
lb.FontBold = True
lb.SizeToFit
```

| Table 26.1 | Constants for the `CreateReportControl` method's `controltype` argument. |

Constant	Control Type
acLabel	Label
acRectangle	Rectangle
acLine	Line
acImage	Image
acCommandButton	Command button
acOptionButton	Option button
acCheckBox	Check box
acOptionGroup	Option group
acBoundObjectFrame	Bound object frame
acTextBox	Text box
acListBox	List box
acComboBox	Combo box
acSubform	Subform
acObjectFrame	Unbound object frame
acPage	Page
acPageBreak	Page break
acCustomControl	ActiveX control
acToggleButton	Toggle button
acTabCtl	Tab control

| Table 26.2 | Constants for the `CreateReportControl` method's *section* argument. |

Constant	Report Section
acDetail	Detail section
acHeader	Form or report header
acFooter	Form or report footer
acPageHeader	Page header
acPageFooter	Page footer
acGroupLevel1Header	Group-level 1 header
acGroupLevel1Footer	Group-level 1 footer
acGroupLevel2Header	Group-level 2 header
acGroupLevel2Footer	Group-level 2 footer

The following code adds a default size Text Box to the Detail section of the same report. The control is bound to the data field referenced by fld, and is left-aligned.

```
Dim tb As Access.TextBox
Set tb = CreateReportControl(rpt.Name, acTextBox, acDetail, , _
    fld.Name, 0, 1500,)
tb.TextAlign = 1
```

Clearly, designing a report in code is a complex business. You need to be familiar with all of the report controls that are available, and how to use them. For example, most reports use various methods to summarize data, for example, by displaying sums or averages of numbers that are part of the report. This requires understanding Access's formulas and how to put them into Text Box and other controls. You'll see an example of how this is done in the demonstration program.

A Demonstration

To demonstrate the technique of generating a report in code, I will use the database table DailySales which is shown in Figure 26–2.

ID	Date	Category	Sales	SalesPerson
1	1/2/99	Hardware	$234.65	Oscar Perez
2	1/4/99	Software	$123.40	Oscar Perez
3	11/15/99	Hardware	$25.55	Mary Smith
4	9/16/99	Software	$580.00	Nelson Chang
5	8/1/99	Hardware	$360.00	Nelson Chang
6	4/22/99	Software	$798.00	Nelson Chang
7	1/7/99	Hardware	$785.00	Mary Smith
8	10/26/99	Software	$738.00	Oscar Perez
9	1/18/99	Hardware	$473.00	Oscar Perez
10	11/12/99	Software	$812.00	Arthur Williams
11	5/18/99	Hardware	$966.00	Bill Walczak
12	11/16/99	Software	$150.00	Oscar Perez
13	12/14/99	Hardware	$427.00	Bill Walczak
14	7/12/99	Software	$791.00	Oscar Perez

Record: 1 of 2342

Figure 26–2 *The DailySales table.*

The goal is to create a fairly simple report that displays the database table records in a nicely formatted manner, with page numbers on each page. Listing 26–1 shows the procedure to create and display the report, and Figure 26–3 shows the first page of the finished report. The code is fully commented, so you should be able to understand its workings.

| Listing 26–1 | *Creating a custom report from the DailySales table.* |

```
Public Sub CreateCustomReport()

Dim rpt As Report
Dim adoRS As ADODB.Recordset
Dim tb As Access.TextBox
Dim lb As Access.Label
Dim fld As ADODB.Field
Dim LeftPos As Long
Dim TopPos As Long
Dim buf As String

LeftPos = 0
TopPos = 100

' Create a new report.
Set rpt = CreateReport

' Set the report data source.
rpt.RecordSource = "DailySales"

' Create a recordset based on the data source.
Set adoRS = New ADODB.Recordset
adoRS.Open "Select * From DailySales", CurrentProject.Connection, _
    adOpenForwardOnly

' Add the page header labels.
For Each fld In adoRS.Fields
    Set lb = CreateReportControl(rpt.Name, acLabel, acPageHeader, , _
        fld.Name, LeftPos, TopPos)
    lb.FontBold = True
    lb.SizeToFit
    LeftPos = LeftPos + 1400
Next fld

LeftPos = 0

' Add text boxes to the detail section for each of the fields.
For Each fld In adoRS.Fields
    Set tb = CreateReportControl(rpt.Name, acTextBox, acDetail, , _
        fld.Name, LeftPos, TopPos)
```

```
    tb.TextAlign = 1
    LeftPos = LeftPos + 1400
Next fld

' Add a page number to the footer.
buf = "=" & Chr$(34) & "Page " & Chr$(34) & " & [Page] &" & _
    Chr$(34) & " of " & Chr$(34) & " & [Pages]"
Set tb = CreateReportControl(rpt.Name, acTextBox, acPageFooter, , _
    buf, 5500, 100)

' Make the detail section slightly higher than one data row.
rpt.Section(acDetail).Height = tb.Height * 1.5

' Set the report caption.
rpt.Caption = "Report from Daily Sales"

' Display the report in preview mode.
DoCmd.OpenReport rpt.Name, acViewPreview

End Sub
```

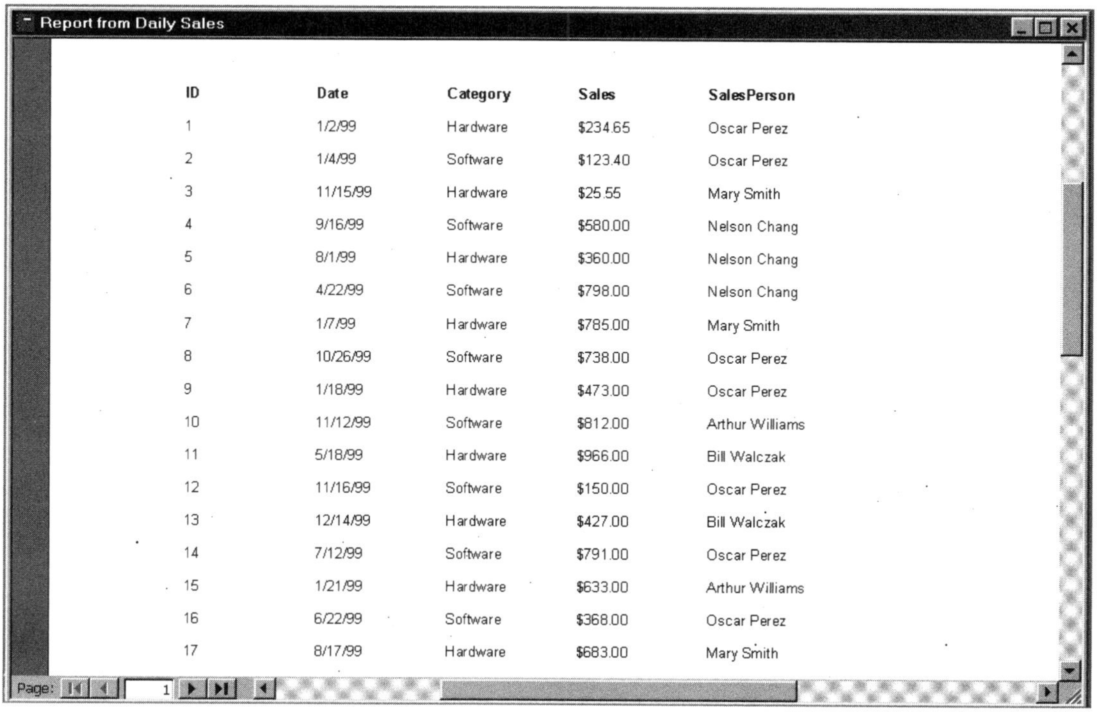

Report from Daily Sales

ID	Date	Category	Sales	SalesPerson
1	1/2/99	Hardware	$234.65	Oscar Perez
2	1/4/99	Software	$123.40	Oscar Perez
3	11/15/99	Hardware	$25.55	Mary Smith
4	9/16/99	Software	$580.00	Nelson Chang
5	8/1/99	Hardware	$360.00	Nelson Chang
6	4/22/99	Software	$798.00	Nelson Chang
7	1/7/99	Hardware	$785.00	Mary Smith
8	10/26/99	Software	$738.00	Oscar Perez
9	1/18/99	Hardware	$473.00	Oscar Perez
10	11/12/99	Software	$812.00	Arthur Williams
11	5/18/99	Hardware	$966.00	Bill Walczak
12	11/16/99	Software	$150.00	Oscar Perez
13	12/14/99	Hardware	$427.00	Bill Walczak
14	7/12/99	Software	$791.00	Oscar Perez
15	1/21/99	Hardware	$633.00	Arthur Williams
16	6/22/99	Software	$368.00	Oscar Perez
17	8/17/99	Hardware	$683.00	Mary Smith

Page: 1

Figure 26–3 *The report created by the code in Listing 26–1.*

Admittedly, this is a very simple report, but the important thing is that it shows you the basic techniques of generating reports using VBA code. It would be a simple matter to make the report more sophisticated, adding titles, for example, as well as summary fields. Once you understand how Access reports are constructed, you can create almost any kind of report as needed.

Summing Up

The generation of custom Access reports on-the-fly, as demonstrated in this chapter, is a fairly advanced Office programming technique, but one that has great power. One possibility is to create the report differently based on the data that is in the report—one type of report formatting for an upward sales trend, another for a downward trend, for instance. Another powerful use of this technique is to let users "design" their own reports. You can present a series of dialog boxes asking the user what he or she wants to see in the report, then generate the report according to the user's desires. This can involve some complicated programming, but the results—particularly in terms of a satisfied client—are often worth it.

KeyCode Constants and Values

These constants can be used when programming the KeyDown and KeyUp event procedures for controls.

Constant	Value	Description
vbKeyBack	&H8	BACKSPACE key
vbKeyTab	&H9	TAB key
vbKeyClear	&HC	CLEAR key
vbKeyReturn	&HD	ENTER key
vbKeyShift	&H10	SHIFT key
vbKeyControl	&H11	CTRL key
vbKeyMenu	&H12	MENU key
vbKeyPause	&H13	PAUSE key
vbKeyCapital	&H14	CAPS LOCK key
vbKeyEscape	&H1B	ESC key
vbKeySpace	&H20	SPACEBAR key
vbKeyPageUp	&H21	PAGE UP key
vbKeyPageDown	&H22	PAGE DOWN key

Constant	Value	Description
vbKeyEnd	&H23	END key
vbKeyHome	&H24	HOME key
vbKeyLeft	&H25	LEFT ARROW key
vbKeyUp	&H26	UP ARROW key
vbKeyRight	&H27	RIGHT ARROW key
vbKeyDown	&H28	DOWN ARROW key
vbKeySelect	&H29	SELECT key
vbKeyPrint	&H2A	PRINT SCREEN key
vbKeyExecute	&H2B	EXECUTE key
vbKeySnapshot	&H2C	SNAPSHOT key
vbKeyInsert	&H2D	INS key
vbKeyDelete	&H2E	DEL key
vbKeyHelp	&H2F	HELP key
vbKeyNumlock	&H90	NUM LOCK key

Constant	Value	Description
vbKeyA	65	A key
vbKeyB	66	B key
vbKeyC	67	C key
vbKeyD	68	D key
vbKeyE	69	E key
vbKeyF	70	F key
vbKeyG	71	G key
vbKeyH	72	H key
vbKeyI	73	I key
vbKeyJ	74	J key
vbKeyK	75	K key
vbKeyL	76	L key
vbKeyM	77	M key

Constant	Value	Description
vbKeyN	78	N key
vbKeyO	79	O key
vbKeyP	80	P key
vbKeyQ	81	Q key
vbKeyR	82	R key
vbKeyS	83	S key
vbKeyT	84	T key
vbKeyU	85	U key
vbKeyV	86	V key
vbKeyW	87	W key
vbKeyX	88	X key
vbKeyY	89	Y key
vbKeyZ	90	Z key

Constant	Value	Description
vbKey0	48	0 key
vbKey1	49	1 key
vbKey2	50	2 key
vbKey3	51	3 key
vbKey4	52	4 key
vbKey5	53	5 key
vbKey6	54	6 key
vbKey7	55	7 key
vbKey8	56	8 key
vbKey9	57	9 key

Keys on the Numeric Keypad

Constant	Value	Description
vbKeyNumpad0	&H60	0 key
vbKeyNumpad1	&H61	1 key
vbKeyNumpad2	&H62	2 key
vbKeyNumpad3	&H63	3 key
vbKeyNumpad4	&H64	4 key
vbKeyNumpad5	&H65	5 key
vbKeyNumpad6	&H66	6 key
vbKeyNumpad7	&H67	7 key
vbKeyNumpad8	&H68	8 key
vbKeyNumpad9	&H69	9 key
vbKeyMultiply	&H6A	Multiplication Sign (*) key
vbKeyAdd	&H6B	Plus Sign (+) key
vbKeySeparator	&H6C	Enter (keypad) key
vbKeySubtract	&H6D	Minus Sign (-) key
vbKeyDecimal	&H6E	Decimal Point (.) key
vbKeyDivide	&H6F	Division Sign (/) key

Function Keys

Constant	Value	Description
vbKeyF1	&H70	F1 key
vbKeyF2	&H71	F2 key
vbKeyF3	&H72	F3 key
vbKeyF4	&H73	F4 key
vbKeyF5	&H74	F5 key
vbKeyF6	&H75	F6 key
vbKeyF7	&H76	F7 key

Constant	Value	Description
vbKeyF8	&H77	F8 key
vbKeyF9	&H78	F9 key
vbKeyF10	&H79	F10 key
vbKeyF11	&H7A	F11 key
vbKeyF12	&H7B	F12 key
vbKeyF13	&H7C	F13 key
vbKeyF14	&H7D	F14 key
vbKeyF15	&H7E	F15 key
vbKeyF16	&H7F	F16 key

INDEX

Symbols